Letters
from New-York

Letters
from New-York

Lydia Maria Child

Edited by Bruce Mills

THE UNIVERSITY OF

GEORGIA PRESS

Athens & London

© 1998 by the University of Georgia Press
Athens, Georgia 30602
All rights reserved
Designed by Betty Palmer McDaniel
Set in 10 on 12 Minion by G & S Typesetters, Inc.
Printed and bound by Maple-Vail Book Group
The paper in this book meets the guidelines for
permanence and durability of the Committee on
Production Guidelines for Book Longevity of the
Council on Library Resources.
Printed in the United States of America
02 01 00 99 98   C   5 4 3 2 1
02 01 00 99 98   P   5 4 3 2 1

Library of Congress Cataloging in Publication Data
Child, Lydia Maria Francis, 1802–1880.
Letters from New-York / Lydia Maria Child ; edited by Bruce Mills.
p.   cm.
Includes bibliographical references (p.   ).
ISBN 0-8203-2038-2 (alk. paper).
ISBN 0-8203-2077-3 (pbk. : alk. paper)
1. New York (N.Y.)—Description and travel.   2. New York (N.Y.)—
Social life and customs.   I. Mills, Bruce, 1958–   .   II. Title.
F128.44.C533   1998
974.7′1—dc21   98-19480
CIP

British Library Cataloging in Publication Data available

Contents

Acknowledgments

I would like to thank the many people who have made important contributions to the editing of this book. At various stages in the editorial process, I have been assisted by Jessica Walsh, Shasta Osborne, Brent Luchies, Antonie Boessenkool, Katie Ivester, Jennifer Mrozowski, and Erik Olsen, Kalamazoo College students whose insights into Child's letters, advice regarding annotation, and diligence in attending to the preparation of the manuscript have significantly enhanced the work. The brevity of this acknowledgment can only begin to suggest the spirit of comradery that enriched the collaboration.

To secretaries Sandy Caldwell and Donna Lakin who helped type the manuscript, I owe an immeasurable debt. To Laura Behling and Amy Milligan, I wish to offer thanks for the diligent proofreading of the manuscript. To Kalamazoo College librarians Maria Klitch, Russell Cooper, Paul Smithson, and especially Carol Smith, I have incurred the debt of hours spent tracking down obscure references and texts and the general goodwill and interest that becomes sustaining over the long trek toward publication. To Gail Griffin and the Women's Studies Program at Kalamazoo College, thanks for supporting the cost of Xeroxing the seemingly endless pages of microfilm. To Western Michigan University reference librarian David Isaacson, I owe thanks for his so generously allowing me special access to volumes of the *National Anti-Slavery Standard*. I also want to credit the Division of Rare and Manuscript Collections, Cornell University Library, for permitting me to print excerpts from Lydia Maria Child's manuscripts. Finally, I wish to thank the University of Georgia Press for their support and advice, especially Karen Orchard, Cisley Owen, Jennifer Manley Rogers, copyeditor Kim Cretors, and the two reviewers of the manuscript.

To Mary Holtapp, I offer my heartfelt thanks for the endless evenings of shared proofreading during the trying days of our early parenthood. The book we pass on to Sarah, Jacob, and ensuing generations teaches much about the nature of this democratic experiment and the ongoing struggle to formulate the artistic vision to make it work.

Introduction

> I am not aware that any of these whirling eddies have, at any time, made me swerve one hair's breadth from the course I had marked out for myself. This was not because I thought myself so much wiser than others; but because I knew, by experience, that he who turns from the light of his *own* judgment, and the convictions of his *own* conscience, has neither rudder or pilot in the storm.—"Farewell," 190

In her "Farewell" to readers of the *National Anti-Slavery Standard* on 4 May 1843, Lydia Maria Child voiced the philosophy that guided her through two turbulent years of editorship. While her metaphor reduces this turbulence to whirling eddies, she and the nation as a whole steered through waters that did more than circle calmly against the banks of literary and social life. For Child, her words veil some profoundly unsettling events: an estrangement from her husband David Lee Child and from the Garrisonian abolitionists who had placed her at the helm of the *Standard*. And, for the nation, the enthusiasm of the early 1840s—an optimism that generated a policy of manifest destiny and spawned utopian endeavors satirized by Hawthorne in "Earth's Holocaust" (1844) and *The Blithedale Romance* (1852)—seems to be the euphoria of having escaped an apocalypse rather than that of having initiated a new millennium. Memories of the mob violence in Boston, Philadelphia, and New York (often sparked by conflict between proslavery and antislavery forces) in the mid-1830s and the economic collapse of 1837 lingered beneath the rhetoric of Western opportunity and utopian communitarianism. Initially written for the *Standard* and later collected in a volume that would see eleven editions, *Letters from New-York* writes large the cultural struggle to accommodate, in real and imaginative terms, the diverse peoples and perspectives unsettling one representative hub of national life. Evolving from extensive reflection on abolitionist and Transcendentalist principles and revealing an astute understanding of popular narratives on race and gender, Child's rendering of New York life survives as one of the period's telling attempts to mediate enduring cultural tensions through an inclusive literary and social vision.

Born 1802 in Medford, Massachusetts, the youngest of her parents' five surviving children (three daughters and two sons), Child achieved a prominence that embodied the mythic tale of American success drawn so vividly in such texts as Benjamin Franklin's *Autobiography* and J. Hector St. Jean de Crèvecoeur's "What Is An American?" According to both writers, democratic social and political conditions promised ample reward for those of talent and industry. Her parents Susannah Rand and Convers Francis Sr. had themselves endured the hardship of the Revolutionary War: the Rands had been forced from their home during the Battle of Bunker Hill and the Francis family had been compelled to solicit food from neighbors during their father's service in the colonial army. As a baker, Convers would endure an apprenticeship to a harsh master, purchase the business of his former employee, and become known in the Boston area for his baked goods. Not surprisingly, then, young Lydia imbibed the values of frugality and industry strongly inculcated through family lore and the direct example of her parents.

The relative prosperity of the Francis household, however, belied a childhood that proved antithetical to imaginative pursuits. Prompted by the death of brother Convers Jr. in 1863, Child briefly reminisced upon this aspect of her childhood. Describing her parents as "hard-working people, who had had small opportunity for culture," she admits that "there was, at that time, nothing like literary influences in the family, or its surroundings" (*Selected Letters* 425). Growing up, she experienced the limited opportunities for an extended formal education common to many artisan families in general and to women in particular. Still, as the youngest in the family, Lydia benefited from her father's growing financial success and thus, with the exception of Harvard educated Convers, apparently fared better than her older siblings, attending a dame school for two years (from ages five to seven) before graduating into the town grammar school. For a year beginning in 1814, she attended Miss Swan's Female Academy that, if consistent with the fashion of such women's schools, included a curriculum of French as well as the "feminine" arts of music, drawing, and sewing. As the sibling closest in age and temperament, however, Convers provided the most significant guidance, a fact that Child herself affirmed at the time of his death: "I owe my own literary tendencies entirely to his early influence. When I came from school, I always hurried to his bed-room, and threw myself down among his pile of books. As I devoured everything that came in my way, I, of course, read much that was beyond my childish comprehension. I was constantly calling upon him to explain: 'Convers, what does Shakespeare mean by this? What does Milton mean by that?'" (*SL* 426). In fact, while accurately representing the importance of her brother's contribution to her self-education during her adolescence, Child's earliest surviving letter reveals a more independent intellectual temperament. "I perceive," she wrote him when just fifteen, "that I never shall convert you to my opinions concerning Milton's treatment of our sex" (*SL* 2). In questioning Convers's literary assumptions, Child challenged more than a brother's attitudes toward "sacred" texts and authors. In debating a student who attended Harvard (beginning in 1811) and who was eventually ordained a Unitarian minister, she displays a willingness to differ from "authoritative" attitudes and thus, even in this playful exchange, demonstrates a defining quality in her career as a literary reformer.

Just as Convers's intellectual presence proved critical to Child's formative years, so too did her move to join newly married sister Mary Preston in Norridgewock, Maine, during the summer of 1814. In May of the previous year, Susannah Francis had died from tuberculosis, and, as the youngest child in the home was now lacking any womanly guidance, the decision to remove to the "frontier" town ushered Child from the uncongenial environment of her father's home to a landscape profoundly important to her literary imagination. While in Norridgewock, Child visited the Penobscot Indians near the Kennebec River and absorbed the atmosphere of a region still considered to be the edge of the wilderness. Moreover, as she matured, she continued to carry on correspondence with Convers, read voraciously, and learn the household skills that formed the heart of her domestic manuals. In 1820, she moved to Gardiner, Maine, to teach school, where she remained until returning to Massachusetts in late summer of 1821 to live with Convers, now minister of the First Church in Watertown.

The romantic influences of the Maine years and the stimulating environment of her brother's household contributed to literary ambitions remarkable for a young woman in a period when authorship was considered a masculine calling. Given such attitudes, the circumstances surrounding the publication of Child's first work could only be considered extraordinary. Inspired by John Gorham Palfrey's call for a national literature in the *North American Review,* the twenty-two year old Lydia Francis composed *Hobomok* (1824) in just six weeks. The historical novel sets the plot in the colonial period during the time of King Philip's uprising, celebrates the grandeur of the wilderness, and, importantly, follows the travails of the newly arrived Mary Conant, a young woman attracted to the beauty of the landscape and oppressed by a strict Calvinist father. Prominent figures in the Boston literary community eventually championed the novel, though, ironically, the prestigious *Review* first described the tale's amalgamation of a "high born and delicate" Puritan woman and an "Indian chief" as "not only unnatural, but revolting . . . to every feeling of delicacy in man or woman" (263). Child soon followed the book with *The Rebels, or Boston before the Revolution* (1825), an historical novel dedicated to Harvard professor and early patron George Ticknor. (Apparently, Ticknor had intervened on the young author's behalf after her bold appeal for his support following the *Review* article: "You may ask, what do you wish, or expect me to do? I answer, your influence in the literary and fashionable world is very great, and a few words timely spoken by you would effect more than my utmost exertions" [SL 4].) Not surprisingly, Child's letter to her sister Mary in the beginning of 1827 voices the elation of early literary success: "The rich and fashionable people, who I thought would consign me to oblivion as soon as I left Boston, and the first novelty had worn off,—continue as attentive as if I were their equal" (SL 8). Having met a youthful Ralph Waldo Emerson during her residence with Convers and carrying on personal and professional correspondence with such major writers as Catherine Maria Sedgwick, Lydia Huntley Sigourney, and a precocious adolescent, Margaret Fuller, Child steadily secured the reputation that guaranteed her rare status as a respected woman author.

She would continue to justify this standing when she turned her attention more fully to that sphere carved out for women of the republic. Her children's magazine *Juvenile Miscellany* (1826–34), domestic manual, *The Frugal Housewife* (1829), advice volume on child rearing, *The Mother's Book* (1831), biographies of famous women published in the early 1830s, and *The History of the Condition of Women, in Various Ages and Nations* (1835) marked a period of exceptional creativity and productivity. While Child herself had also modestly acknowledged to her sister that "children's books are more profitable than any others, and that I am American enough to prefer money to fame" (SL 8), her record betrays an unmistakable drive to gain critical respect. In *The First Woman in the Republic* (1994), Carolyn L. Karcher demonstrates that Child's fiction and nonfiction represented an astute accommodation of literary forms to the specific circumstances of American life and thus offered a profoundly influential body of literature to generations of readers. Extensive evidence from the period supports recent assessment affirming Child's influence and wide appeal. *The History of the Condition of Women,* for instance, contributed to the work of Sarah Grimké, Margaret Fuller, and Elizabeth Cady Stanton. In 1829, two years before he thrust himself on the national scene with the publication of the *Liberator,* William Lloyd Garrison was already proclaiming Child "the first woman in the republic" (Karcher 173), an appraisal echoed four years later when *North American Review* contributor Grenville Mellen asserted that "[f]ew female writers, if any, have done more or better things for our literature, in its lighter or graver departments" (139).

For Child and many of her contemporaries, however, broad appeal was frequently purchased at the cost of conscience. With her marriage to lawyer and reformer David Lee Child in 1828 and her introduction to Garrison not long after his praise, Child herself began to discern how popular renderings of national life neglected—as writers from Frederick Douglass to Toni Morrison have so powerfully sketched—the stories inscribed in hieroglyphic marks on the feet and backs of slaves. With the publication of *An Appeal in Favor of That Class of Americans Called Africans* (1833), Child dramatically announced a shift from her more equivocal gradualist position of the late 1820s to an immediate abolitionist stance. This extensively researched argument for immediate emancipation altered the story of Child's own life. From the mid- to late 1830s, she saw her currency within the literary marketplace fall sharply. With the help of Ticknor, she had become only the second woman to be granted access to the library resources of the prestigious Boston Athenaeum—only to have the privilege later rescinded. In 1834, she also ended her editorship of the lucrative *Juvenile Miscellany* when parents started dropping subscriptions. And, behind these more conspicuous signs of displeasure, Child suffered the subtle social censure of Boston's elite. Clearly, in offering narratives inclusive of both Native Americans and "that class of Americans called Africans," she discovered that living and writing American success stories become more problematic once one envisions new terms and endings.

During the years just prior to her editorship of the *National Anti-Slavery Standard,* Child and her husband—who had burdened the marriage with debts incurred during his editorship of the Whig publication *Massachusetts Journal* (1826–32) and court costs associated with libel convictions—were caught in the widening eddy of inadequate resources and unpromising reform ventures. In 1838, Maria and David Child relocated to Northampton, Massachusetts, to raise sugar beets, hoping that the enterprise would prove successful enough to initiate a challenge to the market monopolized by the slave-produced sugar of the South. Exhausted by the domestic labor that accompanied the endeavor and oppressed by her own precarious financial condition, Child grew despondent. In April 1839, she wrote of her "sinking heart" to friends Ellis Gray Loring, Boston abolitionist and lawyer, and his wife, Louisa, voicing a desire to turn her back on Northampton and describing her effort to see if she "cannot get some sort of editing, or compiling, or writing, or coloring maps" (*SL* 113) from Samuel Griswold Goodrich, publisher of a literary gift annual. The financial and personal difficulties of this period would eventually lead to a painful estrangement from her husband during the 1840s.

Magnifying this private turmoil was the American Anti-Slavery Society's own emerging factionalism. While in Northampton, Maria and David Child witnessed a growing divisiveness over two central questions: Should women have a public role in the movement and should the society refine its Garrisonian stance that slavery was a moral not a political issue? Concern over women's place in the movement had begun, in part, because of the popularity of Angelina and Sarah Grimké's lectures on slavery based upon their own experiences in the South. Abolitionist ministers, especially those who presided over more conservative congregations, felt such actions transgressed proper spheres of influence and undermined efforts to win over an already unsympathetic audience. In addition to the "Woman Question"—as the period termed it—a number of tried and true abolitionists were beginning to reconsider the effectiveness of "moral means" to address a problem intricately connected to legal and political processes. In the late 1830s and early 1840s, conscience proved as persuasive in leading reformers to politics as in initially convincing them to join Garrison and his moral crusade.

Eventually these pressures led to the formation of the New Organization, an orthodox faction that centered its work in New York and usurped control of the American Anti-Slavery Society newspaper, *The Emancipator*. Garrisonian abolitionists established the *National Anti-Slavery Standard* in 1840 to respond to the schism.

By the time Lydia Maria Child took up the editorship of the *National Anti-Slavery Standard* and began signing her initials to the unique essays "Letters from New-York," she had left an imprint on almost every department of the national literature. The journalistic essays collected in *Letters* marked a return rather than an entrance to the literary world. And, significantly, her decision to accept editorship of the *Standard* transported the well-known abolitionist and author to the very heart of controversy—and, appropriately, to the urban emblem of the shifting economic, political, and social forces that threatened a nation still largely rooted in agrarian values. As editor, Child chose to abandon the inflammatory rhetoric and excessively sectarian spirit of a number of ultra-abolitionists, reserving more space for the poetic and less for the polemic. In a time of such turmoil, *Letters from New-York* attempts to cultivate a way of addressing unsettling political and moral issues without turning away from an inner or spiritual light; it strives to identify enduring principles in the confusion of external threats.

   That she named her epistles "Letters from New-York" in the *Standard* and kept the title for the collected essays seems especially appropriate given her personal and professional circumstances. Child was a New Englander whose career was deeply rooted in Boston reform and literary sensibility. In fact, even while she might have challenged certain beliefs and values of her readers, her early Boston years as the author of *Hobomok*, editor of the *Juvenile Miscellany*, and compiler of popular biographies intimately involved her in the region's intellectual and social life. To a large degree, then, she imagined an audience who shared the same place, at one point confessing to Ellis Gray Loring that she had originally envisioned him as the reader when composing the letters. In her mind, her letters in part were sent "from" New York to an audience unfamiliar with the city. Given the division between Boston and New York abolitionists, the title hints at the difficulty of both attempting to heal severed relationships and needing to picture a sympathetic readership.

   Perhaps of even more significance, however, the title signals a kind of transience and thus underscores the psychological circumstances confronting those who found themselves "from" New York. While she did not arrive on board a ship nor experience the culture shock of transatlantic resettlement, Child still came as a visitor, a voyeur, as one of the tens of thousands flooding the area during the decade. U.S. Census Reports reveal that, from 1830 to 1850, the total number of residents in Manhattan, Bronx, Brooklyn, Queens, and Staten Island grew from 242, 278 to 696,115 (figures cited in *The Encyclopedia of New York City* [1995]).

Such statistics suggest that even long-time residents must have found the emerging metropolis to be an unfamiliar place; old boundaries and alliances disappeared and new ones arose at a breathtaking pace.

In such a context, the popularity of Child's letters is not surprising. The descriptions of New York can be read as a kind of travel narrative defining—even discovering at times—the fluid borders of a disorienting new place. Her literal and figurative travels were essential to her own sense of order. Only through this outward movement—to the Crosby Street Synagogue, to the deplorable conditions of Five Points, to the engineering miracle of Croton waterworks, to the Washington Temperance Society parade—and back could she process the flux and diversity not to be accommodated in a static worldview. In her willingness to travel widely, Child provides current readers with an invaluable portrayal of people, traditions, and events that have fallen outside of and perhaps are only recently being configured into a record of the national imagination: the preaching of African American Methodist minister Julia Pell, the unique conceptions of what defines the self arising from animal magnetism and phrenology, the performance of Native Americans at Barnum's American Museum. These and other columns not only supplement the sparse and sometimes understudied record of private lives but also contribute significantly toward reconstructing how the dynamic interplay of such lives shaped an urban and even national identity.

Mediating the tensions inherent in describing such a diverse landscape contributed to the voice and form of the letters themselves. For Child, stepping out into the unsettling realities of urban life and then returning to the writing table to face the inner conflict of "editing" such flux fostered a narrative perspective that opened doors rather than closed them. Not unlike Walt Whitman who also worked as a journalist in New York during the decade, Child discovered that her outward glance resulted in and sometimes demanded a sensibility tempered not with an urbane and dismissive cynicism but an embracing innocence.

Consistently, Child begins her letters by introducing readers to a person, place, or an event that, to many of her northern white readers, describes an unfamiliar and at times disorienting feature of nineteenth-century New York. While obligated as any journalist to offer a detailed account of an unfamiliar topic, she still strays enough from this need to invest observations with her own personal reflections on the subject. Significantly, in this hybrid of "objective" journalism and "subjective" editorial, Child persistently poses as the innocent and youthful reporter. (Readers, for instance, are often surprised to know that Child turned forty during her tenure at the *Standard*.) Such a stance certainly reflected the genuine wonder and surprise at various New York realities. In addition, however, it offered a strategy that not only enabled her to generate copy under the stress of burdensome weekly deadlines but also provided a way of aligning readers more positively toward the unfamiliar. In other words, the epistles—though certainly not rigidly formulaic—depend upon this narrative perspective to ease the psychological threat inherent to a period of profound change.

New to the place or unfamiliar with the tradition, Child negotiates this dynamic between description and reflection by often providing the outlines of the scene (e.g., the physical description of the place or person) or context (e.g., historical, biographical, social). Clearly, however, the letters demonstrate an unwillingness to remain purely descriptive, for they consistently betray the desire for resolution or closure in their return from a venturing out to real and imaginative landscapes. Time and again, Child comes "home" to underscore principles that offer stability after exhilarating and sometimes unsettling shifts of perspective.

Not surprisingly, generations of readers have seen *Letters* as Child's best work. Such a judgment can be linked in part to the use of a form that enabled a more inclusive and intimate voice. Quite simply, in writing essays that rooted her in the concrete and immediate historical realities of New York life yet that allowed for reflection upon the spiritual implications of such realities, Child found a voice and form that harmonized her reform and literary passions. Prior to the early 1840s, Child had written in a range of genres, including historical novels, biographies, short sketches or tales, and abolitionist treatise and tracts. Yet, at this juncture in her career, such genres did not fit her own personal and professional needs. The demands of editing a weekly newspaper, for instance, would certainly not easily accommodate the scope of a lengthy historical novel. Moreover, a distinctive feature of Child's novels was the way they deflected antebellum attitudes and debates concerning race, religion, and gender into distant settings. In her third novel *Philothea* (1836), the decade's growing interest in a transcendentalist sensibility and emerging debate over the slavery question find expression in the republic of ancient Athens. And, significantly, in her previous record of antislavery writings, Child sought a less strident utterance of Garrisonian principles in part by providing unadorned facts, believing that such a straightforward recording of cruelties practiced under slavery and verifiable accounts of the effects of enslavement upon moral and intellectual development would inevitably convert readers to the cause. But, by the early 1840s, her experiences within the literary world and abolitionist reform led to the realization that previous genres and sectarian antislavery efforts did not reach an important set of readers nor allow her the voice necessary to consider more fully the spiritual meanings of urban life. It is not surprising that, after her stint as editor, she continued to write her "letters" for the *Boston Courier,* letters that would eventually be collected in *Letters from New York, Second Series* (1845). Moreover, she also devoted time to writing in another evolving form; between January 1845 and February 1849, Child published twenty-six stories and sketches in the *Columbian Lady's and Gentleman's Magazine* and the *Union Magazine of Literature and Art.* While returning more directly to the abolitionist cause in the 1850s and 1860s with numerous pamphlets and her "antiprejudice" novel *A Romance of the Republic* (1867), her decade in New York was a period of Child's most artistically rich writings. In both the journalistic essays and short fiction, she found the narrative poetic that, for many readers, best captured the dynamic of democratic life.

Further insight into Child's purpose for creating "Letters from New-York" and the perspective that shaped the form of the columns can also be found in her editorial "Farewell" to the *Standard*. "The New-York Letters," she writes, "were inserted upon something of the same principle that the famous Timothy Dexter sent a stock of Bibles to the West Indies, with warming pans, to be used for sugar ladles and strainers. No purchaser was allowed to have a pan, unless he would buy a Bible also" (190). In this way, Child suggests, she drew people to the abolitionist cause with the "garland of imagination and taste" (190). Clearly, through the letters, she hoped that spiritual laws might enter into the material affairs of readers' lives. The domestic metaphor suggests that, without the leavening of transformative stories and metaphors, abolitionist cant promised little fullness and thus less potential to promote lasting private and public change.

To look at the paper itself is to understand the leavening intent of her "Letters." Not uncommon to many newspapers of the period, the *Standard* consisted of four pages of six fine-print columns. The first and second pages most often introduced readers to recent (or recently acquired) news of interest to reformers: reports of regional antislavery conventions, letters from correspondents, and updates concerning legislative and political affairs most often pertaining to the slavery question. Readers perusing the first two pages of Child's 19 August 1841 edition—the issue containing "Letter from New-York.—No. 1"—would find "Abolitionist Missionary," "Letters from Jamaica," "The Horrors of the Slave Trade," "Negroes and Indians," and "Law and Lynching." Inserted throughout the paper, however, were articles of interest to more than the abolitionist: a description of "The Mammoth Cave" in Kentucky and "Anecdote of a Sleep Walker," an item that would appeal to the antebellum audience's growing fascination with dreams and the unconscious. Child's letter is located in the transition from the leading stories of the first two pages to the literary offerings on the back page, from the arena of public affairs to the intimate space of the reading room. While seemingly lost in the clutter of random columns, Child's letters most often "centered" the paper.

In lifting the letters from the *Standard* pages and revising them for the volume *Letters from New-York* (1843), Child further demonstrates her profound concern over the sectarian spirit threatening the voice of conscience or the Transcendentalist "God within," a voice often veiled by the material realities of city life and the incessant bickering within antislavery reform. The opening letter sketches the worldly discord that threatens citizens of the nineteenth century: "You ask what is now my opinion of this great Babylon; . . . Nor do you forget my first impression of the city, when we arrived at early dawn, amid fog and drizzling rain, the expiring lamps adding their smoke to the impure air, and close beside us a boat called the 'Fairy Queen,' laden with dead hogs." The opening lament soon turns into a litany of discord: the juxtaposition of a "blind negro beggar" opposite the mansion of a slave trader, the cool calculations of Mammon on Wall Street ("extracting a penny from war, pestilence, and famine"), the cries of street children selling "hot corn!"

Child follows these sobering reminders of the chaos of city life, however, with a clear pronouncement that her primary aim in the letters lies not in describing material (or finite facts) but in discerning spiritual truth. "But now," she writes, "I have lost the power of looking merely on the surface. Every thing seems to me to come from the Infinite, to be filled with the Infinite, to be tending toward the Infinite." She continues: "Do I see crowds of men hastening to extinguish a fire? I see not merely uncouth garbs, and fantastic flickering lights of lurid hue, like a tramping troop of gnomes,—but straightway my mind is filled with thoughts about mutual helpfulness, human sympathy, the common bond of brotherhood, and the mysteriously deep foundations on which society rests; or rather, on which it now reels and totters." Time after time, Child records events or realities that threaten a larger harmony and demand a more acute attention to permanent or eternal values (i.e., the Infinite). In Letter XIII, she sees in the collage of advertisements on Division Street the mercenary sensibility of antebellum American culture. Caught in the visual discord of 'Change (economic exchange), the letter asserts, individuals can be divided from their better self. Is not the effect of such consumerism—a term perhaps more appropriate to our time but synonymous with Child's lament concerning overemphasis upon the Practical—as deadening to the soul as selling slaves? It is a question that Thoreau would ask in his own exploration of economic captivity in *Walden*.

Perhaps even more poignant in *Letters from New-York* are the omnipresent voices and images of the city's displaced and impoverished: the four-year-old newspaper boy "screaming street cries" (Letter XIV), "a tall, gaunt-looking woman leading a ragged girl, of five or six years old" from door to door selling matches (Letter XXVIII), the "street-walkers" at the Blackwell's Island penitentiary (XXIX). Unlike some New England contemporaries with whom she shared a Transcendentalist sensibility, however, these examples suggest that Child did not have the same horizon; her crowded landscape, furrowed with streets and buildings and peopled with immigrants, offered a more immediate reminder of larger social forces. While conscious of the higher truth, then, Child's "letters" did not forsake the facts of lived experience. The epistles seem to answer Carlyle's injunction—expressed to Emerson regarding the Transcendentalist journal the *Dial*—that the writings should come down from their "perilous altitudes": "Surely I could wish you *returned* into your own poor nineteenth century, its follies and maladies, its blind or half-blind but gigantic toilings, its laughter and its tears, and trying to evolve in some measure the hidden Godlike that lies in *it;*—that seems to me the kind of feat for literary men" (*Correspondence of Emerson and Carlyle* 328–29).

This incessant exegesis of the spiritual good behind the fragmented and fragmenting realities of city life remained one of Child's main interpretive impulses in many of the separate letters and in the first volume as a whole. Though her abolitionist work tempered her mystical sympathies, *Letters from New-York* (later known as the *First Series*) and the *Second Series* clearly can be placed beside Emerson's *Essays: First and Second Series* (1841, 1844) and Fuller's *Woman in the Nineteenth Century* (1845) as a revealing expression of Transcendentalist thought. (In fact, her connection with the social and literary reform movement of the 1830s is an intimate one; her brother Convers Francis was one of the attendees at Bronson Alcott's Symposium Club, the initial gathering of Transcendentalists in September 1836.) Her admission that she had "lost the power of looking merely on the surface" and that "[e]very thing seems to me to come from the Infinite" resonates with Emerson's definition of the Idealist in "The Transcendentalist": "The idealist, in speaking of events, sees them as spirits. He does not deny the sensuous fact: by no means; but he will not see that alone. He does not deny the presence of this table, this chair, and the walls of this room, but he looks at these things as the reverse side of the tapestry, as the *other end,* each being a sequel or completion of a spiritual fact which nearly concerns him" (193). Thus, the turbulent effects of material realities—such as Child's concluding letter on the chaotic ritual of the May first moving day in New York—in and of themselves can be disheartening. "And I, who have almost as strong a love of localities as poor puss," Child laments in this closing letter, "turn away from the windows, with a suppressed anathema on the nineteenth century, with its perpetual changes." Yet, demonstrating the power of the imagination, Child can contain the threat through the poetic eye: "That people should move so *often* in this city, is generally a matter of their own volition. Aspirations after the infinite, lead them to perpetual change, in the restless hope of finding something better and better still."

Such Transcendentalist musings reflect neither Pollyannish simplicity nor sentimental optimism. Rather, Child's eventual assertion that "[m]an is moving to his highest destiny through manifold revolutions of spirit" and that "the outward must change with the inward" marks a faith tempered by both a contemplation of the inherent violence of American racism and of the redemptive power of religious and domestic metaphor. Writing Convers seven years earlier (27 July 1834), she had articulated a "rationale" for focusing—both in content and style—upon affections in urging individual change. "I believe there can be no real religion where reason does not perform her high and very important office, but here again comes the important point, reason cannot do her perfect work unless the affections are pure" (*Letters of Lydia Maria Child,* 14). Understanding early in her career the powerful emblems arising from domestic space and motherhood (a power tapped by Harriet Beecher Stowe in *Uncle Tom's Cabin* [1852] and Harriet Jacobs in *Incidents in the Life of a Slave Girl* [1861], a book that Child edited and supported financially), she astutely saw that Transcendentalist views and literary method further enhanced the ability to move readers.

A fuller understanding of the intended influence of her "garland of the imagination" emerges through an examination of the way Child deleted, combined, and reorganized letters in the shift from the *National Anti-Slavery Standard* to *Letters from New-York*. Of the fifty-eight letters originally composed for the *Standard* from 19 August 1841 to 4 May 1843, forty-eight were retained in some form in *Letters*. A close look at the published collection reveals that she repeatedly combined entire letters or sections of separate letters or articles. Some of these changes indicate her attempt to place like with like, joining discourses on similar subjects to create greater coherence. For instance, she combines in Letter XXXIII ("The Catholic Church. Puseyism. Worship of Irish Labourers. Anecdotes of the Irish") reflections on Catholicism and the Irish that had occurred in three distinct places in the *Standard*. In fact, though dating the letter 8 December 1842 and opening by noting that she "went, last Sunday, to the Catholic Cathedral," she actually describes a visit that took place in November 1841 (*Standard*, "Letters from New-York.—No. 11.," 25 November 1841). To arrive at the final form, she joins this narration with thoughts on Puseyism (*Standard* 14 July 1842) and a brief excerpt on "moral truth" (*Standard*, "Letters from New-York.—No. 46.," 5 January 1843). In the combining of letters, Child seems guided by the desire to eliminate repetitious subject matter rather than by peripheral restrictions such as space limitations. Significantly, though still constrained by the original form and sequence of the letters, she clearly makes choices that reveal the effort to create more than a collection of disparate essays.

To an extent, some changes also reflect the influence of close friend Ellis Gray Loring. Starting with a letter dated 21 February 1843, Child sought his advice concerning what letters might be best kept or omitted. After asking Loring to send a story that she had written for his daughter, Child articulates some concerns about what might be appropriate for the book: "I am hesitating whether or not to print [the story] in the volume of my N. York Letters, to give a little novelty and variety to it. Would you? I shall not print *all* the letters; only the best ones. Would you omit the last two about Women's Rights, or not? I think it best to omit them. Would you publish the one about the execution of Colt, and against Capital Punishment?" (*SL* 188). In reply, Loring had evidently encouraged Child to include the entirety of the "New York Letters" and offered to review them on their trek toward publication, thus prompting her response in a letter written 6 March: "I do not agree with you about inserting all of them. Some are of a merely temporary and transient interest, and a few more merely written to fill up. The doubts

I had about the letter on Colt's execution was that it describes a scene of local and temporary interest, and painful without. As for the letter on Women's Rights, they did not seem to me to amount to much" (*Collected Correspondence* 16/463). Significantly, Child acknowledges and accepts her friend's offer "of overlooking" the letters and invites him to pay specific attention to the "quotations or mottoes." On 21 March, she was able to forward a "portion of the N. York Letters" which had been prepared for the press and urged Loring to "[a]lter, amend, strike out, or add, as you please" (*CC* 17/470). Just more than a month later, Child wrote a final letter concerning his work with the manuscript:

> You need not make so many apologies about your criticisms. I am too thankful to you for doing the tiresome business, to expect you to take off your hat and make a bow, whenever you point out a fault, or suggest an alteration. My early education, as you know, was very superficial, and I have in general been in a position extremely unfavorable to a patient remedying of this defect.
>
> I shall follow nearly all your suggestions exactly; but my attachment is rather strong to the "thee and thou." Moreover, if I am to *copy* anybody, why should I not copy Carlyle as well as Dr. Channing? For in this instance, there is certainly no grammatical incorrectness. I did not *think* of Carlyle when I "*thoued* it," though I doubtless caught it unconsciously from my great admiration of his writings. I see you have put marks of quotation to the phrase "the eye of Wordsworth, and the mouth of Moliere." If it be a quotation, I am not aware of it. (*CC* 17/484)

Her friend's suggestions for the first eleven letters of the published collection still survive among the Loring papers housed in Schlesinger Library at Radcliffe College and, for the most part, reveal relatively minor copyediting changes. It appears, however, that he did recommend a way to combine portions of *Standard* "Letters from New-York.—No. 22" depicting a Washingtonian Temperance Society parade with the discussion of the reform organization first described at greater length in the second letter. Because all of his suggestions do not appear in the surviving annotations to his *Standard* clippings of the letters, the final impact of his involvement cannot be fully traced. Clearly, however, Child's correspondence and the existing changes suggest that Loring primarily served the role of copyeditor, a role that proved invaluable in timely shepherding the book to print.

Of particular interest in the transition from abolitionist newspaper to book is Child's decision to omit some of her epistles addressing antislavery issues. While in the end Child includes the letters on Women's Rights (combining them to form Letter XXXIV) and Colt and capital punishment (Letter XXXI), she does leave out material that addresses issues and events more directly related to the slavery question and thus, apparently in her mind, matter that seemed more relevant to an abolitionist newspaper: letters on the *Amistad* captives (No. 12, 2 December 1841), an ex-slave woman (No. 14, 16 December 1841), and the British abolitionist George Thompson (No. 33, 18 August 1842). (These letters and the others omitted from *Letters from New-York* are included in the Appendix.)

While such telling deletions signal efforts to meet a broader readership on its own terms, Child does deal with slavery throughout the volume. Rather than confront her audience so directly, however, she invites her readers to draw their own conclusions from the facts and thus to come to abolitionist principles without feeling coerced. In short, she employed a method that she had characterized to fellow reformer Caroline Weston in March 1839: "I often attack bigotry with 'a troop of horse shod with felt'; that is, I try to *enter* the wedge of general principles, letting inferences unfold themselves very gradually" (*SL* 109). Her interview with the Florida slave trader Z. Kinsley (Letter XXIII) demonstrates this strategy. Anticipating the equivocating slaveholder St. Clair in *Uncle Tom's Cabin*, Kinsley condemns himself through his own self-serving distortion of public opinion. Having shown a restraint readers might not associate with an abolitionist, Child canters forth a central reform principle: "How shall we fulfil this sacred trust, which each holds for the good of all? Not by calculating consequences; not by balancing evils; but by reverent obedience to our own highest convictions of individual duty."

If her deletions in part accommodate readers' reluctance to embrace certain reform issues and ideals, Child's combining and rearranging of letters on women's rights, the electric, and Indians urge her audience to entertain more "ultraist" views concerning the spiritual and the feminine. Thus, while Child first considered eliminating her most overt and incisive reflections on the "Women's Question," she still revised one of her most striking sequences of letters to magnify the transformative power of the feminine principle, a principle that for Child seems to manifest its power in the inexplicable magnetic and electric forces linked with animal magnetism. Perhaps nowhere does this perspective become clearer than in two central revisions. First, Child inserted a more thoroughly developed letter on the spiritual essence of "electricity" between writings on women's rights (Letter XXXIV) and "the Indians" (Letter XXXVI). While the initial version of the letter focusing upon the electric (no. 53) had been relatively brief and had followed by two weeks Child's discussion of "the Indians," the revised Letter XXXV embodies a telling expansion of the reflections through a compilation of no. 36 (22 September 1842) and no. 53 (16 March 1843) from the *Standard*. Second, she revised Letter XXXVI to include consideration of phrenology, craniometry (the study of facial angle), and cultural and racial differences. Clearly, these changes reflect Child's efforts to address—in psychological and philosophical terms— her own era's conflicts concerning gender and race.

Significant in its assertion that "the present position of women in society is the result of physical force" and in its critique of Emerson's failure to see women as "souls" in his address "Being and Seeming," Letter XXXIV begins to define more clearly the "feminine ideal" and the potential for a higher harmony between men and women. "That the feminine ideal," she writes, "approaches much nearer to the gospel standard, than the prevalent idea of manhood, is shown by the universal tendency to represent the Saviour and his most beloved disciple with mild, meek expression, and feminine beauty. None speak of the bravery, the might, or the intellect of Jesus; but the devil is always imagined as a being of acute intellect, political cunning, and the fiercest courage. These universal and instinctive tendencies of the human mind reveal much." While Child's notions of what constitutes "universal" tendencies certainly strike a disharmonious chord with current conceptualizations of gender, her effort to delineate the features of this higher ideal embodies an attempt to assert the central role of the feminine in understanding and even mediating psychological and social discord.

More than simply expressing a commonplace cognizance of gender differences, Child's revisions subtly communicate her evolving belief that the feminine ideal manifests the presence of a physical agent or energy woven into the very substance of life. By inserting her expanded reflections on electric or magnetic forces between the letters that directly deal with gender and race, she offers a revealing attempt to negotiate those divisions that profoundly threatened her culture. In the feminine, she finds the most dramatic demonstration of these forces and thus the physical energy that seems necessary for spiritual reform. "What *is* this invisible, all-pervading essence," she asks, "which thus has power to put man into communication with all?" To Child, the inexplicable incidents related to mesmerism and clairvoyance suggested the presence of "animal magnetism," a substance connecting all organisms. The implications of these embryonic investigations into the unconscious were not lost on Child: "Is there a universal medium by which all things of spirit act on the soul, as matter on the body by means of electricity? And is that medium the WILL whether of angels or of men?" Wary that some answers to these questions might lead to ridicule, Child nonetheless refuses to dismiss these psychological insights, insights that suggest the means to enact profound individual and social reforms: "I believe the most remarkable of these accounts [of foresight] give but a faint idea of the perfection to which man's moral and physical instincts might attain, if his life were obedient and true."

And what might nurture this obedient and true life? Suggestive answers to this question arise from a brief look at Margaret Fuller's *Woman in the Nineteenth Century* (1845), a feminist treatise first published in the *Dial* in 1843 as "The Great Lawsuit. Man versus Men. Woman versus Women." It would appear that, as revealed in their conception of the feminine principle, Fuller as well as Child believed that woman was the most powerful embodiment and "conductor" of the electric and thus the conduit for greater harmony between the inward and outward, the material and spiritual. In *Woman in the Nineteenth Century*, Fuller quotes an article in the *New York Pathfinder* on "Femality" that sees "the feminine nature as a harmonizer of the vehement elements" and that forcibly asserts "the lyrical, the inspiring, and inspired apprehensiveness of her being" (*Woman* 309). Interestingly, in the revision from "The Great Lawsuit" to *Woman*, Fuller added lines that even further underscore the importance of the electric: "This view being identical with what I have before attempted to indicate, as to her superior susceptibility to magnetic or electric influence, I will now try to express myself more fully." She then continues with the ideas that had been previously published: "The especial genius of woman I believe to be electrical in movement, intuitive in function, spiritual in tendency. She excels not so easily in classification, or re-creation, as in an instinctive seizure of causes, and a simple breathing out of what she receives that has the singleness of life, rather than the selecting and energizing of art" (309). Woman, then, is not simply a passive harmonizer; her powers, if allowed to flow freely, promise significant social reforms. It is essential to underscore, however, that both Fuller and Child did not see the feminine as solely that which resided in woman. According to Fuller, "[m]ale and female represent the two sides of the great radical dualism. But, in fact, they are perpetually passing into one another. Fluid hardens to solid, solid rushes to fluid. There is no wholly masculine man, no purely feminine woman" (310). In other words, the feminine principle characterizes an active power that cannot entirely be understood in terms of biological sex.

Given the fact that Fuller and Child had reestablished their friendship during their time in New York in the 1840s, that they had the opportunity in their work to address such similar issues as prostitution and women's rights (Fuller was a journalist for Horace Greeley's *New York Tribune*), and that Child had read *Woman in the Nineteenth Century* in manuscript form and praised it in February 1845 reviews for Boston and New York newspapers, it is not surprising that some resonance exists between Fuller's and Child's views. Both shaped their "art" with similar assumptions. For Fuller, the "Muse is the unimpeded clearness of the intuitive powers which a perfectly truthful adherence to every admonition of the higher instincts would bring to a finely organized human being" (310). For Child, this unimpeded clearness might be seen in the remarkable accounts associated with the electric, accounts that again give the "faint idea" of moral and physical perfection.

If Child's letter on the "electric" offers an idea as to the transformative power inherent in the feminine principle, then her ensuing reflections upon "The Indians" at Barnum's American Museum further illuminate the potential of this magnetic presence. In the *Standard* account of the Indians ("Letter from New-York.—No. 52," 2 March 1843), Child focused on the spectacle of the event. She goes as an observer and, while she offers some broader philosophical judgments, she remains for the most part in this journalistic rather than editorial (and metaphysical) mode. In the revised letter, however, she incorporates her earlier discussion of "The Different Races of Men" from the *Standard* (5 January 1842), an article that in part focused on recent studies regarding facial and cranial angles.

This antebellum manifestation of scientific racism seemed the material evidence for Caucasian supremacy, for, coupled with phrenological "evidence" that centered moral and intellectual propensities in the forehead, the higher facial angle appeared to indicate a more advanced moral and intellectual state.

In hearing an abolitionist apparently leave unchallenged those "facts" of racial difference that seem so obviously informed by racist assumptions (as Stephen Jay Gould has more recently demonstrated in *The Mismeasure of Man* [1981]), modern readers inevitably experience some confusion. While problematic in its acceptance of the authority of this information, her letter still resists the popular predilection to center views on race in what her time asserted to be the empirical evidence of an inherent racial hierarchy. Instead, she speculates that the differences in physical appearance and seeming racial characteristics indicate the complex interplay of outward influences. Significantly, these influences again seem to signal the primacy of the feminine upon human development, for the Caucasian race demonstrated—to use Fuller's terms concerning women—"a superior susceptibility to magnetic or electrical influences." "That [the Caucasian race] started, *first* in the race," Child writes, "might have been owing to a finer and more susceptible nervous organization, originating in climate perhaps, but serving to bring the physical organization into more harmonious relation with the laws of spiritual reception."

While trying to diminish the constraints of what seemed fact, Child distinguished herself from many of her contemporaries. Clearly, however, her own amalgamation of views on the feminine, the electric or magnetic, and race still betrays the troubling hierarchies that she sought to question. The "congress of ages, each with a glory on its brow" gives little agency to Native Americans and African Americans in the centuries of evolution. Thus, we are left to puzzle through the contradictions inherent in Child's more disturbing assertions:

> You ask, perhaps, what becomes of my theory, that races and individuals are the product of ages, if the influences of half a life produce the same effects on the Caucasian and the Indian? I answer, that white children brought up among Indians, though they strongly imbibe the habits of the race, are generally prone to be the geniuses and prophets of their tribe. The organization of nerve and brain has been changed by a more harmonious relation between the animal and the spiritual; and this comparative harmony has been produced by the influences of Judea, and Greece, and Rome, and the age of chivalry; though of all these things the young man never heard.

At the same time she argues that "[c]limate has had its effect too on the religious ideas of nations" and that "we are all, in some degree, the creatures of outward circumstance," she implicitly accepts the idea that biblical tradition and Greek and Roman literature and philosophy represent the prerequisite influence for this "harmonious relation between the animal and the spiritual." In effect, her notions of the feminine and of beauty drawn from imaginative forms of Western tradition create the terms and the criterion with which to judge the "animalism" of the "Indian" and other "barbarous" civilizations. Child's reflections, then, still exist as an unsettling legacy to a contemporary audience, especially for those readers who see themselves as linked by heritage, race, or culture to those who might have looked back at Child from Barnum's stage, from the Irish tenements at Five Points, from the Crosby Street Synagogue, or from Julia Pell's congregation. Perhaps, we could apply to Child Margaret Fuller's critique of her own attempt to articulate a different vision of human relations: "some fair effigies that once stood for symbols of human destiny have been broken; those I still have with me, show defects in this broad light" (*Woman* 348).

In her reflections upon women's rights, the electric, and Indians in Letters XXXIV–XXXVI, then, Child expanded, revised, and reordered the essays in order to connect the feminine principle and its spiritual dimension to central questions of her day. Though Child offers uneasy resolutions in the face of these difficult questions, a central belief remains less equivocal and problematic; in a city and a country marked by profound differences, she asserts, harmony exists in the paradoxical truth that we might be "the treble and bass of the same harmonious tune" (Letter XXXIV) and that "we are all unequal, yet equal" (Letter XXXV).

The publication history of *Letters* offers another lesson in the period's sometimes uneasy acceptance of a writer associated with abolitionist reform. While the book emerged in response to appeals for a collected volume of essays, appeals voiced in the *New York Tribune, Graham's Magazine,* and by the publishers of the *Democratic Review,* its actual publication history reveals that publishers still feared response from conservative readers. Originally calling for a collection of the letters, the Langley brothers, publishers of the *Democratic Review,* showed interest in the manuscript yet urged Child to eliminate material that might still offend southern readers. She subsequently dismissed a possible relationship with the firm. Desiring a broader audience, Child also rejected offers from abolitionist Oliver Johnson, indicating in an 11 April 1843 letter to Loring that she was "exceedingly anxious to get well-established in business connexions [in New York], and make publishers and printers *desirous* to be in connection with me" (*CC* 17/481). In the end, Child printed *Letters* at her own expense, and, much to the surprise of both Child and the firm that printed the book, Charles S. Francis (New York) and James Munroe (Boston), the volume sold out its first printing of fifteen hundred copies in just four months. It would go through eleven editions within seven years.

In the end, *Letters from New-York* began to win back the readership and literary currency lost with the publication of *An Appeal in Favor of That Class of Americans Called Africans.* Not surprisingly, Child embraced the opportunity to reenter the literary world. Exhausted by fellow abolitionists' intrusions into her editorial efforts and energized by readers' genuine enthusiasm for her book, she quit the editorship of the *Standard* and, in letters written the year following her exit from the newspaper, frequently asserted the reasons for her new direction. To Loring on 16 May 1844, Child described the suffocating effects of attempts to coerce her to support a more extremist stance and editorial tone: "I bore and forebore, and tried to do my best, until this ultraist pressure, on all sides, almost drove me mad. It no longer depended on my will. Such a night-mare was on me, that I *could* not write, either one thing or another" (*SL* 207). The letter ends with the hopeful assertion that her "prospects are very good" and that she has "a good deal of profitable work on [her] hands . . ." (*SL* 208). To Francis Shaw, she announced her intent to "devote the remainder of [her] life to the attainment of literary excellence" (*SL* 209). Her twenty-six stories and sketches in the *Columbian* and *Union* magazines evinced this devotion.

Contemporary reviews of *Letters* consistently voice the praise that led to its popular success. In an October 1843 review in the *Knickerbocker,* the critic, quoting Child's prefatory apologia that the book was "deeply tinged with romance and mysticism," finds that the "pages exhibit a far greater amount of *truth,* undeniable, and of deep import to society at large, and to our own metropolitan community especially" (372). In the Transcendentalist *Dial,* Margaret Fuller confirms such sentiments, calling the book "a contribution to *American* literature, recording in a generous spirit, and with lively truth, the pulsations in one great center of the national existence" and noting that the "writer never loses sight of the hopes and needs of all men, while she faithfully winnows grain for herself from the chaff of every day, and grows in love and trust, in proportion with her growth in knowledge" (*Dial* 407). When reviewers offer negative assessments, they most often focus on what Fuller termed her generous spirit, a spirit some reviewers saw as overly sentimental and undiscriminating. The *Knickerbocker,* for instance, views her "ultra-sentimentalities" not as "*intellectually* feminine" but "as defects in the generally natural and fresh style of our gifted author" (374). Not surprisingly, the more strident condemnations hint of profound discomfort with Child's reform sensibility and Transcendentalist perspective and style. In her inclusiveness and sympathetic spirit, Donald Mitchell of the *American Review* discerns an inability to discriminate acutely between mercy and justice and to check taste in favor of judgment (62). Did it ever occur to Child, Mitchell asks, "that our nature does not need to be choked before it is full of depravity and rottenness;— that man is not sweet and pure, but rather the opposite, by nature . . . ?" (62).

Certainly, Child must have felt the tempting force of Mitchell's Calvinist vision. For more than a decade, she had experienced the profoundly unsettling realities of personal and professional rejection and, in her tireless abolitionist work, witnessed the sometimes inexpressible inhumanity of slavery. Her intimate identification with readers, her Transcendentalist belief in the divinity of the individual, and her desire for inclusiveness, however, manifest a social and literary vision

tenaciously faithful to the possibilities of the human spirit. Given the disconcert-
ing but vital social forces exemplified in New York, Child faced the challenge of
any artist attempting to embody such a vision: the need to craft the sometimes
contradictory dynamic of present conditions into a meaningful form. Equivocal
though some of Child's ideas might be to us, such a conflation of abolitionist reform, Transcendentalist sensibility, and feminine perspective captures in emblematic ways the paradoxical "resolutions" that ensued from representative, though
deeply disruptive, national realities. Determining the influence and relevance of
Child's *Letters from New-York* to the larger patterns in American life and myth remains the ongoing task of succeeding generations engaged in their own dialogue
with enduring cultural realities.

Works Cited

Carlyle, Thomas, and Ralph Waldo Emerson. *The Correspondence of Emerson and Carlyle.*
    Ed. Joseph Slater. New York: Columbia UP, 1964.
Child, Lydia Maria. *The Collected Correspondence of Lydia Maria Child, 1817–1880.* Ed. Pa-
    tricia G. Holland and Milton Meltzer. Millwood, NY: Kraus Microform, 1980.
———. "Farewell." *National Anti-Slavery Standard* 4 May 1843: 190–91.
———. *Letters of Lydia Maria Child, with a Biographical Introduction by John G. Whittier
    and an Appendix by Wendell Phillips.* Boston: Houghton, 1882.
———. *Lydia Maria Child: Selected Letters, 1817–1880.* Ed. Milton Meltzer, Patricia G.
    Holland, and Francine Krasno. Amherst: U of Massachusetts P, 1982.
Emerson, Ralph Waldo. "The Transcendentalist." In *Selections from Ralph Waldo Emerson.*
    Ed. Stephen E. Whicher. Boston: Houghton Mifflin, 1957.
[Fuller, Margaret.] Review of *Letters from New-York. Dial* 4 (January 1844): 407.
———. *Woman in the Nineteenth Century.* In *The Essential Margaret Fuller.* Ed. Jeffrey
    Steele. New Brunswick, NJ: Rutgers UP, 1992.
Jackson, Kenneth T., ed. *The Encyclopedia of New York City.* New Haven, CT: Yale UP, 1995.
Karcher, Carolyn L. *The First Woman in the Republic: A Cultural Biography of Lydia Maria
    Child.* Durham, NC: Duke UP, 1994.
[Mellen, Grenville.] "Works of Mrs. Child." Review of *The Biographies of Madame de Staël
    and Madame Roland, The Biographies of Lady Russell and Madame Guyon, Good Wives,*
    and *The Coronal. North American Review* 37 (July 1833): 138–64.
[Mitchell, Donald G.] Review of *Letters from New-York. The American Review: A Whig
    Journal of Politics, Literature, Art and Science* 1 (January 1845): 60–74.
Review of *Hobomok. North American Review* 19 (July 1824): 262–63.
Review of *Letters from New-York. Knickerbocker* 22 (October 1843): 372–74.

A Note
on the Text

Child first published the essays entitled "Letters from New-York" in the *National Anti-Slavery Standard* beginning 19 August 1841 and running through 4 May 1843. Later revised and collected in a single volume and made available to the public in late August 1843, this first edition of *Letters from New-York* (the only edition to hyphenate New York on its title page) sold out its initial run of fifteen hundred copies in less than four months. Having produced the book at her own expense, Child informed printers Munroe & Co. of the status of sales on 20 December 1843 and queried them concerning their interest in coming out with another edition (*CC* 18/524). To meet demands for the book, publishers C. S. Francis (New York) and J. H. Francis (Boston) reset the text. On 27 February 1844, Child wrote bookseller J. Miller McKim of Philadelphia that the second edition was ready for sale. Finally, Child's letter to a friend on 12 November 1844 indicates that *Letters from New York* was stereotyped and thus typeset for a third and final time. With this third edition (dated 1845), the book would remain unchanged through the eleventh edition (1850).

In 1845, the same publishers issued Child's companion volume, *Letters from New York, Second Series,* a collection of additional "Letters from New-York" that, with the exception of a few pieces originally included in the *National Anti-Slavery Standard,* were written for the *Boston Courier* from the end of 1843 through 1844. The preface to this volume reflects that, while following a similar form, Child saw the first book as distinct from the second series of essays: "I do not call this volume Letters from New York, on account of the unexpected popularity of the first volume, or because I consider it altogether appropriate; but I can think of no better name, under which to arrange the articles so miscellaneous and incongruous in their character." With this first edition of the *Second Series,* the initial book sometimes came to be referred to as the first series—though at no time did the publishers append this name to any title page of its numerous editions.

While Child added a preface to the second edition of *Letters from New York,* textual changes incurred after the first edition—the addition and deletion of commas, the standardization of certain spellings, the typesetting of poetry, the use of single rather than double quotation marks—reflect compositors', not author's, hands. Having charted changes from the *Standard* version of the letters to the first edition and having reviewed revisions from the first through the third editions, I can only conclude that Child remained distant from the publication process after making alterations for the first volume. In short, substantive changes occur in Child's preparation of the newspaper letters for the first edition and not between first and second or second and third editions. I only located two exceptions to this pattern. First, in the letter on the Croton waterworks (Letter XXX), the first and second editions of *Letters* note that "the great jet of water" in Harlem "rises a hundred feet into the air"; the third edition cites the distance as 118 feet. Second, describing the city tradition of moving on the first of May in the first edition (Letter XL), Child wrote: "The object of this regulation is to have the Directory for the year arranged with accuracy. For, as theologians, and some reformers, can perceive no higher mission for human souls than to arrange themselves rank and file in sectarian platoons, so the civil authorities do not apprehend that a citizen has any more important object for living, just at this season, than to have his name set in a well-ordered Directory." In the second and third editions, the text reads differently: "This regulation, handed down from old Dutch times, proves very convenient in arranging the Directory with promptness and accuracy; and as theologians, and some reformers, can perceive no higher mission for human souls, than to arrange themselves rank and file in sectarian platoons, so perhaps the civil authorities may imagine there is nothing more important to a citizen than to have his name set in a well-ordered Directory."

Arguably, then, the evidence provided by examination of the first three editions suggests that the first edition more clearly reflects Child's immediate involvement with the manuscript. Moreover, in the considerable wealth of Child's correspondence, she at no point indicates a turning back to the book after the first edition to make even minor changes. Given these facts, I have chosen the first edition as the text that best represents Child's own substantive and stylistic intentions for *Letters from New-York.* In reproducing the first edition, I retain spelling and punctuation of the period. The changes in this new text are limited to the silent emendation of errors attributable to the earlier typesetting of the manuscript, verified when possible through comparison to the *Standard* letters.

The current volume also includes letters from the *National Anti-Slavery Standard* that Child chose to omit in *Letters from New-York [First Series].* Intriguing in their own right, these letters also offer students of the period insight into Child's conception of what would be acceptable for a readership less sympathetic to the abolitionist cause and other reforms. Except for the correction of obvious typographical errors, the omission of dashes peculiar to newspaper typesetting, and the addition of two words (in brackets) that were omitted from the original text, these letters appear as they did in the *Standard*.

Finally, the annotation of *Letters* provided significant challenges. Because the individual essays were initially part of the *Standard* and, of course, written during a period distant from our own, they include allusions to particular events and people that an antebellum audience might have more readily known but that remain unknown to modern readers. Moreover, it was not unusual for nineteenth-century authors to allude to or cite works without acknowledgment of the source. To give greater clarity and context to the text, I have provided information about various public figures, cultural realities, and historical events. I have chosen, however, not to annotate the source of the more than one hundred unattributed quotations and the nearly seventy passages associated with particular writers. In my mind, recovering all the sources for the poetic, fictional, and nonfictional passages would have been virtually impossible, especially given the obscurity of many of the references and the uncertainty as to whether or not Child composed some of the poetry herself. What could have been recovered would have inevitably resulted in an incomplete and seemingly arbitrary acknowledgement of various passages. I found it more useful and potentially more informative to offer a full annotation of the substantive changes made between the *Standard* letters and their counterparts in the current volume and indicate when such changes may have been suggested by the copyediting advice of Ellis Gray Loring. These revisions consistently underscore the particularities of Child's imagination and the aesthetic tastes of her audience. Moreover, in revealing her attempt to negotiate the tensions between readers' beliefs and values and her own, we can trace larger cultural patterns, patterns that underscore the difficulty of addressing reforms associated with economic, gender, and racial inequities. In short, such changes offer some insights into what mattered most to Child, to her readers, and even to the culture as a whole.

New York Jan 1?

Dear Friend,

Letters
from New-York

To John Hopper

These pages are so deeply tinged with romance and mysticism,
that they might seem an unfit offering to one who has the crowning merit
of the nineteenth century—that of being a cautious and energetic "business man."
But in a city of strangers you have been to me as a brother;
most of the scenes mentioned in these Letters we have visited together;
and I know that the young lawyer, busily making his way in a crowded world,
has not driven from his mind a love for nature and poetry, or closed his heart
against a most genial sympathy for the whole family of man.
Therefore, this volume is inscribed to you, with grateful friendship, by

THE AUTHOR

Index

Letters from New-York

Letter I[1]
August 19, 1841

You ask what is now my opinion of this great Babylon; and playfully remind me of former philippics, and a long string of vituperative alliterations, such as magnificence and mud, finery and filth, diamonds and dirt, bullion and brass-tape, &c. &c.[2] Nor do you forget my first impression of the city, when we arrived at early dawn, amid fog and drizzling rain, the expiring lamps adding their smoke to the impure air, and close beside us a boat called the "Fairy Queen," laden with dead hogs.

Well, Babylon remains the same as then. The din of crowded life, and the eager chase for gain, still run through its streets, like the perpetual murmur of a hive. Wealth dozes on French couches, thrice piled, and canopied with damask, while Poverty camps on the dirty pavement, or sleeps off its wretchedness in the watch-house. There, amid the splendour of Broadway,[3] sits the blind negro beggar, with horny hand and tattered garments, while opposite to him stands the stately mansion of the slave trader, still plying his bloody trade, and laughing to scorn the cobweb laws, through which the strong can break so easily.

In Wall-street,[4] and elsewhere, Mammon, as usual, coolly calculates his chance of extracting a penny from war, pestilence, and famine; and Commerce, with her loaded drays, and jaded skeletons of horses, is busy as ever "fulfilling the World's contract with the Devil." The noisy discord of the street-cries gives the ear no rest; and the weak voice of weary childhood often makes the heart ache for the poor little wanderer, prolonging his task far into the hours of night. Sometimes, the harsh sounds are pleasantly varied by some feminine voice, proclaiming in musi-

cal cadence, "Hot corn! hot corn!" with the poetic addition of "Lily white corn!
Buy my lily white corn!"[5] When this sweet, wandering voice salutes my ear, my
heart replies—

> 'Tis a glancing gleam o' the gift of song—
> And the soul that speaks hath suffered wrong.

There *was* a time when all these things would have passed by me, like the flitting figures of the magic lantern, or the changing scenery of a theatre, sufficient
for the amusement of an hour. But now, I have lost the power of looking merely
on the surface. Every thing seems to me to come from the Infinite, to be filled
with the Infinite, to be tending toward the Infinite. Do I see crowds of men hastening to extinguish a fire? I see not merely uncouth garbs, and fantastic, flickering lights, of lurid hue, like a tramping troop of gnomes,—but straightway my
mind is filled with thoughts about mutual helpfulness, human sympathy, the
common bond of brotherhood, and the mysteriously deep foundations on which
society rests; or rather, on which it now reels and totters.

But I am cutting the lines deep, when I meant only to give you an airy, unfinished sketch. I will answer your question, by saying that, though New-York remains the same, I like it better. This is partly because I am like the Lady's Delight,
ever prone to take root, and look up with a smile, in whatever soil you place it; and
partly because bloated disease, and black gutters, and pigs uglier than their ugly
kind, no longer constitute the foreground in my picture of New-York. I have become more familiar with the pretty parks, dotted about here and there; with the
shaded alcoves of the various public gardens; with blooming nooks, and "sunny
spots of greenery." I am fast inclining to the belief, that the Battery rivals our
beautiful Boston Common.[6] The fine old trees are indeed wanting; but the newly-
planted groves offer the light, flexile gracefulness of youth, to compete with their
matured majesty of age. In extent, and variety of surface, this noble promenade
is greatly inferior to ours; but there is,

> "The sea, the sea, the open sea;
> The fresh, the bright, the ever free!"[7]

Most fitting symbol of the Infinite, this trackless pathway of a world! heaving
and stretching to meet the sky it never reaches—like the eager, unsatisfied aspirations of the human soul. The most beautiful landscape is imperfect without this
feature. In the eloquent language of Lamartine,[8] "The sea is to the scenes of nature what the eye is to a fine countenance; it illuminates them, it imparts to them
that radiant physiognomy, which makes them live, speak, enchant, and fascinate
the attention of those who contemplate them."

If you deem me heretical in preferring the Battery to the Common, consecrated
by so many pleasant associations of my youth, I know you will forgive me, if you
will go there in the silence of midnight, to meet the breeze on your cheek, like the

kiss of a friend; to hear the continual plashing of the sea, like the cool sound of oriental fountains; to see the moon look lovingly on the sea-nymphs, and throw down wealth of jewels on their shining hair; to look on the ships in their dim and distant beauty, each containing within itself, a little world of human thought, and human passion. Or go, when "night, with her thousand eyes, looks down into the heart, making it also great"—when she floats above us, dark and solemn, and scarcely sees her image in the black mirror of the ocean. The city lamps surround you, like a shining belt of descended constellations, fit for the zone of Urania; while the pure bright stars peep through the dancing foliage, and speak to the soul of thoughtful shepherds on the ancient plains of Chaldea.[9] And there, like mimic Fancy, playing fantastic freaks in the very presence of heavenly Imagination, stands Castle Garden [10]—with its gay perspective of coloured lamps, like a fairy grotto, where imprisoned fire-spirits send up sparkling wreaths, or rockets laden with glittering ear-drops, caught by the floating sea-nymphs, as they fall.

But if you would see the Battery in *all* its glory, look at it when, through the misty mantle of retreating dawn, is seen the golden light of the rising sun! Look at the horizon, where earth, sea, and sky, kiss each other, in robes of reflected glory! The ships stretch their sails to the coming breeze, and glide majestically along—fit and graceful emblems of the Past; steered by Necessity; the Will constrained by outward Force. Quick as a flash, the steamboat passes them by—its rapidly revolving wheel made golden by the sunlight, and dropping diamonds to the laughing Nereids, profusely as pearls from Prince Esterhazy's embroidered coat.[11] In that steamer, see you not an appropriate type of the busy, powerful, self-conscious Present? Of man's Will conquering outward Force; and thus making the elements his servants?

From this southern extremity of the city, anciently called "The Wall of the Half-Moon," you may, if you like, pass along the Bowery to Bloomingdale, on the north. What a combination of flowery sounds to take captive the imagination! It is a pleasant road, much used for fashionable drives; but the lovely names scarcely keep the promise they give the ear; especially to one accustomed to the beautiful environs of Boston.[12]

During your ramble, you may meet wandering musicians. Perhaps a poor Tyrolese with his street-organ, or a Scotch lad, with shrill bag-pipe, decorated with tartan ribbons. Let them who will, despise their humble calling. Small skill, indeed, is needed to grind forth that machinery of sounds; but my heart salutes them with its benison, in common with all things that cheer this weary world. I have little sympathy with the severe morality that drove these tuneful idlers from the streets of Boston. They are to the drudging city, what Spring birds are to the country. The world has passed from its youthful, Troubadour Age, into the thinking, toiling Age of Reform. This we may not regret, because it needs must be. But welcome, most welcome, all that brings back reminiscences of its childhood, in the cheering voice of poetry and song!

Therefore blame me not, if I turn wearily aside from the dusty road of reforming duty, to gather flowers in sheltered nooks, or play with gems in hidden
grottoes. The Practical has striven hard to suffocate the Ideal within me;[13] but it
is immortal, and cannot die. It needs but a glance of Beauty from earth or sky,
and it starts into blooming life, like the aloe touched by fairy wand.

Letter II [1]
August 26, 1841

You think my praises of the Battery exaggerated; perhaps they are so; but there
are three points on which I am crazy—music, moonlight, and the sea. There are
other points, greatly differing from these, on which most American juries would
be prone to convict me of insanity. You know a New-York lawyer defined insanity to be "a differing in opinion from the mass of mankind." By this rule, I am as
mad as a March hare; though, as Andrew Fairservice[2] said, "Why a hare should
be more mad in March than at Michaelmas, is more than I ken."

I admit that Boston, in her extensive and airy Common, possesses a blessing
unrivalled by any other city; but I am not the less disposed to be thankful for the
circumscribed, but well-shaded limits of the Washington Parade Ground, and
Union Park, with its nicely trimmed circle of hedge, its well-rolled gravel walks,
and its velvet greensward, shaven as smooth as a Quaker beau. The exact order of
its arrangement would be offensive in the country; and even here, the eye of taste
would prefer variations, and undulation of outline; but trimness seems more in
place in a city, than amid the graceful confusion of nature; and neatness has a
charm in New-York, by reason of its exceeding rarity. St. John's Park, though not
without pretensions to beauty, never strikes my eye agreeably, because it is shut
up from the people; the key being kept by a few genteel families in the vicinity.
You know I am an enemy to monopolies; wishing all Heaven's good gifts to man
to be as free as the wind, and as universal as the sunshine.[3]

I like the various small gardens in New-York, with their shaded alcoves of
lattice-work, where one can eat an ice-cream, shaded from the sun. You have none
such in Boston; and they would probably be objected to, as open to the vulgar
and the vicious. I do not walk through the world with such fear of soiling my garments. Let science, literature, music, flowers, all things that tend to cultivate the
intellect, or humanize the heart, be open to "Tom, Dick, and Harry;" and thus, in
process of time, they will become Mr. Thomas, Richard, and Henry. In all these
things, the refined should think of what they can *impart*, not of what they can
receive.

As for the vicious, they excite in me more of compassion than of dislike. The
Great Searcher of Hearts alone knows whether I should not have been as they are,
with the same neglected childhood, the same vicious examples, the same overpowering temptation of misery and want. If they will but pay to virtue the out-

ward homage of decorum, God forbid that I should wish to exclude them from the healthful breeze, and the shaded promenade. Wretched enough are they in their utter degradation; nor is society so guiltless of their ruin, as to justify any of its members in unpitying scorn.

And this reminds me that in this vast emporium of poverty and crime, there are, *morally* speaking, some flowery nooks, and "sunny spots of greenery." I used to say, I knew not where were the ten righteous men to save the city; but I have found them now. Since then, The Washington Temperance Society has been organized, and active in good works.[4] Apart from the physical purity, the triumph of soul over sense, implied in abstinence from stimulating liquors, these societies have peculiarly interested me, because they are based on the Law of Love. The Pure is inlaid in the Holy, like a pearl set in fine gold. Here is no "fifteen-gallon-law," no attendance upon the lobbies of legislatures, none of the bustle or manoeuvres of political party; measures as useless in the moral world, as machines to force water above its level are in the physical world. Serenely above all these, stands this new Genius of Temperance; her trust in Heaven, her hold on the human heart. To the fallen and the perishing she throws a silken cord, and gently draws him within the golden circle of human brotherhood. She has learned that persuasion is mightier than coercion, that the voice of encouragement finds an echo in the heart deeper, far deeper, than the thunder of reproof.[5]

The blessing of the perishing, and of the merciful God, who cares for them, will rest upon the Washington Temperance Society. A short time since, one of its members found an old acquaintance lying asleep in a dirty alley, scarcely covered with filthy rags, pinned and tied together. Being waked, the poor fellow exclaimed, in piteous tones, "Oh don't take me to the Police Office—Please don't take me there." "Oh, no," replied the missionary of mercy; "you shall have shoes to your feet, and a decent coat on your back, and be a Man again! We have better work for you to do, than to lie in prison. You will be a Temperance preacher, yet."

He was comfortably clothed, kindly encouraged, and employment procured for him at the printing office of the Washington Society. He now works steadily all day, and preaches temperance in the evening. Every week I hear of similar instances. Are not these men enough to save a city? This Society is one among several powerful agencies now at work, to teach society that it *makes its own criminals,* and then, at prodigious loss of time, money, and morals, punishes its own work.

The other day, I stood by the wayside while a Washingtonian procession, two miles long, passed by. All classes and trades were represented, with appropriate music and banners. Troops of boys carried little wells and pumps; and on many of the banners were flowing fountains and running brooks. One represented a wife kneeling in gratitude for a husband restored to her and himself; on another, a group of children were joyfully embracing the knees of a reformed father. Fire companies were there with badges and engines; and military companies, with gaudy colours and tinsel trappings. Toward the close, came two barouches, containing the men who first started a Temperance Society on the Washingtonian plan. These six individuals were a carpenter, a coach-maker, a tailor, a blacksmith, a wheelwright, and a silver-plater. They held their meetings in a carpenter's shop, in Baltimore, before any other person took an active part in the reform. My heart paid them reverence, as they passed. It was a beautiful pageant, and but one thing was wanting to make it complete; there should have been carts drawn by garlanded oxen, filled with women and little children, bearing a banner, on which was inscribed, WE ARE HAPPY NOW! I missed the women and the children; for without something to represent the genial influence of domestic life, the circle of joy and hope is ever incomplete.

But the absent ones were present to my mind; and the pressure of many thoughts brought tears to my eyes. I seemed to see John the Baptist[6] preparing a pathway through the wilderness for the coming of the Holiest; for like unto his is this mission of temperance. Clean senses are fitting vessels for pure affections and lofty thoughts.

Within the outward form I saw, as usual, spiritual significance. As the bodies of men were becoming weaned from stimulating drinks, so were their souls beginning to approach those pure fountains of living water, which refresh and strengthen, but never intoxicate. The music, too, was revealed to me in fullness of meaning. Much of it was of a military character, and cheered onward to combat and to victory. Everything about war I loathe and detest, except its music. My heart leaps at the trumpet-call, and marches with the drum. Because I cannot ever hate it, I know that it is the utterance of something good, perverted to a ministry of sin. It is the voice of resistance to evil, of combat with the false; therefore the brave soul springs forward at the warlike tone, for in it is heard a call to its appointed mission. Whoso does not see that genuine life is a battle and a march, has poorly read his origin and his destiny. Let the trumpet sound, and the drums roll! Glory to resistance! for through its agency men become angels. The instinct awakened by martial music is noble and true; and therefore its voice will not pass away; but it will cease to represent war with carnal weapons, and remain a type of that spiritual combat, whereby the soul is purified. It is right noble to fight with wickedness and wrong; the mistake is in supposing that spiritual evil can be overcome by physical means.[7]

Would that Force were banished to the unholy region, whence it came, and that men would learn to trust more fully in the law of kindness. I think of this, every time I pass a dozing old woman, who, from time immemorial, has sat behind a fruit stall at the corner of St. Paul's church.[8] Half the time she is asleep, and the wonder is that any fruit remains upon her board; but in this wicked city very many of the boys deposit a cent, as they take an apple; *for they have not the heart to wrong one who trusts them.*

A sea-captain of my acquaintance, lately returned from China, told me that the Americans and English were much more trusted by the natives, than their own countrymen; that the fact of belonging to those nations was generally considered good security in a bargain. I expressed surprise at this; not supposing the Yankees, or their ancestors, were peculiarly distinguished for generosity in trade. He replied, that they were more so in China, than at home; because, in the absence of adequate laws, and legal penalties, they had acquired the habit of *trusting in each others' honour and honesty;* and this formed a bond so sacred, that few were willing to break it. I saw deep significance in the fact.

Speaking of St. Paul's church, near the Astor House,[9] reminds me of the fault so often found by foreigners with our light grey stone as a material for Gothic edifices. Though this church is not Gothic, I now understand why such buildings contrast disadvantageously with the dark coloured cathedrals of Europe. St. Paul's has lately been covered with a cement of dark, reddish-brown sand. Some complain that it looks "like gingerbread;" but for myself, I greatly like the depth of colour. Its steeple now stands relieved against the sky, with a sombre grandeur, which would be in admirable keeping with the massive proportions of Gothic architecture. Grey and slate colour appropriately belong to lighter styles of building; applied to the Gothic, they become like tragic *thoughts* uttered in mirthful *tones.*

The disagreeables of New-York, I deliberately mean to keep out of sight, when I write to you. By contemplating beauty, the character becomes beautiful; and in this wearisome world, I deem it a duty to speak genial words, and wear cheerful looks.

Yet, for once, I will depart from this rule, to speak of the dog-killers. Twelve or fifteen hundred of these animals have been killed this summer; in the hottest of the weather at the rate of three hundred a day. The safety of the city doubtless requires their expulsion; but the *manner* of it strikes me as exceedingly cruel and demoralizing. The poor creatures are knocked down on the pavement, and beat to death. Sometimes they are horribly maimed, and run howling and limping away. The company of dog-killers themselves are a frightful sight, with their bloody clubs, and spattered garments. I always run from the window when I hear them; for they remind me of the Reign of Terror.[10] Whether such brutal scenes do not prepare the minds of the young to take part in bloody riots and revolutions is a serious question.

You promised to take my letters as they happened to come—fanciful, gay, or serious. I am in autumnal mood to-day, therefore forgive the sobriety of my strain.

Letter III [1]

September 2, 1841

Oh, these damp, sultry days of August! how oppressive they are to mind and body! The sun staring at you from bright red walls, like the shining face of a heated cook. Strange to say they are *painted* red, blocked off with white compartments, as numerous as Protestant sects, and as unlovely in their narrowness. What an expenditure for ugliness and discomfort to the eye! To paint bricks their own color, resembles the great outlay of time and money in theological schools, to enable dismal, arbitrary souls to give an approved image of themselves in their ideas of Deity.

After all, the God *within* us is the God we really believe in, whatever we may have learned in catechisms or creeds.[2]

Hence to some, the divine image presents itself habitually as a dark, solemn shadow, saddening the gladsomeness of earth, like thunder-clouds reflected on the fair mirror of the sea. To others, the religious sentiment is to the soul what Spring is in the seasons, flowers to the eye, and music to the ear.[3] In the greatest proportion of minds these sentiments are mixed, and therefore two images are reflected, one to be worshipped with love, the other with fear.

Hence, in Catholic countries, you meet at one corner of the road frightfully painted hell-fires, into which poor struggling human souls are sinking; and at another, the sweet Madonna, with her eye of pity and her lip of love. Whenever God appears to the eye of faith as terrible in power, and stern in vengeance, the soul craves some form of mediation, and satisfies its want. As the reprobate college-boy trusts to a mother's persuasive love to intercede for him with an angry father, so does the Catholic, terrified with visions of torment, look up trustingly to the "Blessed mother, Virgin mild."

Not lightly, or scornfully, would I speak of any such manifestations of faith, childish as they may appear to the eye of reason. The Jewish dispensation was announced in thunder and lightning; the Christian, by a chorus of love from angel voices. The dark shadow of the one has fearfully thrown itself across the mild radiance of the other. Those old superstitious times could not well do otherwise than mix their dim theology with the new-born glorious hope. Well may we rejoice that they could not transmit the blessed Idea completely veiled in gloom.[4] Since the Past *will* overlap upon the Present, and therefore Christianity *must* slowly evolve itself from Judaism, let us at least be thankful that,

> "From the same grim turret fell
> The *shadow* and the *song*."[5]

Whence came all this digression? It has as little to do with New-York, as a seraph has to do with Banks and Markets. Yet in good truth, it all came from a painted brick wall staring in at my chamber window. What a strange thing is the mind! How marvellously is the infinite embodied in the smallest fragment of the finite!

It was ungrateful in me to complain of those walls, for I am more blest in my prospect than most inhabitants of cities; even without allowing for the fact that more than most others, I always see much *within* a landscape—"a light and a revealing," every where.

Opposite to me is a little, little, patch of garden, trimly kept, and neatly white-washed. In the absence of rippling brooks and blooming laurel, I am thankful for its marigolds and poppies, |

> ——————"side by side,
> And at each end a hollyhock,
> With an edge of London Pride."

And then between me and the sectarian brick wall, there are, moreover, two beautiful young trees. An Ailanthus twisting its arms lovingly within its smaller sister Catalpa. One might almost imagine them two lovely nymphs suddenly transformed to trees in the midst of a graceful, twining dance. I should be half re-luctant to cut a cluster of the beautiful crimson seed-vessels, lest I should wound the finger of some Hamadryad,[6]

> "Those simple crown-twisters,
> Who of one favorite tree in some sweet spot,
> Make home and leave it not."

But I must quit this strain; or you will say the fair, floating Grecian shadow casts itself too obviously over *my* Christianity. Perchance, you will even call me "tran-scendental;" that being a word of most elastic signification, used to denote every thing that has no name in particular, and that does not especially relate to pigs and poultry.

Have patience with me, and I will come straight back from the Ilissus[7] to New-York——thus.

You too, would worship two little trees and a sunflower, if you had gone with me to the neighbourhood of the Five Points[8] the other day. Morally and physi-cally, the breathing air was like an open tomb. How souls or bodies could live there, I could not imagine. If you want to see something worse than Hogarth's Gin Lane,[9] go there in a warm afternoon, when the poor wretches have come to what they call home, and are not yet driven within doors, by darkness and con-stables. There you will see nearly every form of human misery, every sign of hu-man degradation. The leer of the licentious, the dull sensualism of the drunkard, the sly glance of the thief— oh, it made my heart ache for many a day. I regretted the errand of kindness that drew me there; for it stunned my senses with the amount of evil, and fell upon the strong hopefulness of my character, like a stroke of the palsy. What a place to ask one's self, "Will the millenium ever come!"

And there were multitudes of children— of little *girls*. Where were their guard-ian angels? God be praised, the wilfully committed sin alone shuts out their influ-ence; and therefore into the young child's soul they may always enter.

Mournfully, I looked upon these young creatures, as I said within myself, "And *this* is the education society gives her children—the morality of myrmidons,[10] the charity of constables!" Yet in the far-off Future I saw a gleam. For these too Christ has died. For these was the chorus sung over the hills of Judea; and the heavenly music will yet find an echo deep in their hearts.

It is said a spacious pond of sweet, soft water once occupied the place where Five Points stands. It might have furnished half the city with the purifying element; but it was filled up at incredible expense—a million loads of earth being thrown in, before perceivable progress was made. Now, they have to supply the city with water from a distance, by the prodigious expense of the Croton Water Works.[11]

This is a good illustration of the policy of society towards crime. Thus does it choke up nature, and then seek to protect itself from the result, by the incalculable expense of bolts, bars, the gallows, watch-houses, police courts, constables, and "Egyptian tombs," as they call one of the principal prisons here. If viewed only as a *blunder,* Satan might well laugh at the short-sightedness of the world, all the while toiling to build the edifice it thinks it is demolishing. Destroying violence by violence, cunning by cunning, is Sisyphus' work, and must be so to the end. Never shall we bring the angels among us, by "setting one devil up to knock another devil down;" as the old woman said, in homely but expressive phrase.[12]

Letter IV [1]
September 9, 1841

New-York enjoys a great privilege, in facility and cheapness of communication with many beautiful places in the vicinity. For six cents one can exchange the hot and dusty city, for Staten Island, Jersey, or Hoboken; three cents will convey you to Brooklyn, and twelve and a half cents pays for a most beautiful sail of ten miles, to Fort Lee. In addition to the charm of rural beauty, all these places are bathed by deep waters.[2]

The Indians named the most beautiful lake of New England Win-ne-pe-sauk-ey, (by corruption, Winnepiseogee,)[3] which means, the Smile of the Great Spirit. I always think of this name, so expressively poetic, whenever I see sunbeams or moonbeams glancing on the waves.

Because this feature is wanting in the landscape, I think our beautiful Massachusetts Brookline,[4]—with its graceful, feathery elms, its majestic old oaks, its innumerable hidden nooks of greenery, and Jamaica pond, that lovely, lucid mirror of the water nymphs,—is scarcely equal to Hoboken. I saw it for the first time in the early verdure of spring, and under the mild light of a declining sun. A small open glade, with natural groves in the rear, and the broad river at its foot, bears the imposing name of Elysian Fields.[5] The scene is one where a poet's disembodied spirit might be well content to wander; but, alas, the city intrudes her vices into this beautiful sanctuary of nature. There stands a public house, with its bar room, and bowling alley, a place of resort for the idle and the profligate; kept within the bounds of decorum, however, by the constant presence of respectable visiters.

Near this house, I found two tents of Indians. These children of the forest, like the monks of olden time, always had a fine eye for the picturesque. Wherever you find a ruined monastery, or the remains of an Indian encampment, you may be sure you have discovered the loveliest site in all the surrounding landscape.

A fat little pappoose, round as a tub, with eyes like black beads, attracted my attention by the comical awkwardness of its tumbling movements. I entered into conversation with the parents, and found they belonged to the remnant of the Penobscot tribe. This, as Scott says, was "picking up a dropped stitch" in the adventures of my life.

"Ah," said I, "I once ate supper with your tribe in a hemlock forest, on the shores of the Kennebec. Is the old chief, Capt. Neptune, yet alive?"

They almost clapped their hands with delight, to find one who remembered Capt. Neptune. I inquired for Etalexis, his nephew, and this was to them another familiar word, which it gave them joy to hear.

Long forgotten scenes were restored to memory, and the images of early youth stood distinctly before me.[6] I seemed to see old Neptune and his handsome nephew, a tall, athletic youth, of most graceful proportions. I always used to think of Etalexis, when I read of Benjamin West's exclamation, the first time he saw the Apollo Belvidere: "My God! how like a young Mohawk warrior!"[7]

But for years I had not thought of the majestic young Indian, until the meeting in Hoboken again brought him to my mind. I seemed to see him as I saw him last—the very dandy of his tribe—with a broad band of shining brass about his hat, a circle of silver on his breast, tied with scarlet ribbons, and a long belt of curiously-wrought wampum hanging to his feet. His uncle stood quietly by, puffing his pipe, undisturbed by the consciousness of wearing a crushed hat and a dirty blanket. With girlish curiosity, I raised the heavy tassels of the wampum belt, and said playfully to the old man, "Why don't *you* wear such an one as this!"

"What for *me* wear ribbons and beads?" he replied: "Me no want to catch 'em *squaw*."

He spoke in the slow, imperturbable tone of his race; but there was a satirical twinkle in his small black eye, as if he had sufficiently learned the tricks of civilization to enjoy mightily any jokes upon women.

We purchased a basket in the Elysian Fields, as a memento of these ghosts of the Past: preferring an unfinished one of pure white willow, unprofaned by daubs of red and yellow.

Last week I again saw Hoboken in the full glory of moonlight. Seen thus, it is beautiful beyond imagining. The dark, thickly shaded groves, where flickering shadows play fantastic gambols with the moonlight; the water peeping here and there through the foliage, like the laughing face of a friend; the high, steep banks, wooded down to the margin of the river; the deep loneliness, interrupted only by the Katy-dids; all conspired to produce an impression of solemn beauty.

If you follow this path for about three miles from the landing-place, you arrive at Weehawken; celebrated as the place where Hamilton fought his fatal duel with Burr, and where his son likewise fell in a duel the year preceding.[8] The place is difficult of access; but hundreds of men and women have there engraven their names on a rock nearly as hard as adamant. A monument to Hamilton was here erected at considerable expense; but it became the scene of such frequent duels, that the gentlemen who raised it caused it to be broken into fragments; it is still, however, frequented for the same bad purpose. What a lesson to distinguished men to be careful of the moral influence they exert! I probably admire Hamilton with less enthusiasm than those who fully sympathize with his conservative tendencies; but I find so much to reverence in the character of this early friend of Washington, that I can never sufficiently regret the silly cowardice which led him into so fatal an error. Yet would I speak of it gently, as Pierpont[9] does in his political poem:

> "Wert thou spotless in thy exit? Nay:
> Nor spotless is the monarch of the day.
> Still but *one* cloud shall o'er thy fame be cast—
> And that shall shade no action, but thy *last.*"

A fine statue of Hamilton was wrought by Ball Hughes, which, like all resemblances of him, forcibly reminded one of William Pitt.[10] It was placed in the Exchange, in Wall street, and was crushed into atoms by the falling in of the roof, at the great fire of 1835.[11] The artist stood gazing on the scene with listless despair; and when this favourite production of his genius, on which he had bestowed the labour of two long years, fell beneath the ruins, he sobbed and wept like a child.

The little spot at Weehawken, which led to this digression about Hamilton, is one of the last places which should be desecrated by the evil passions of man. It is as lovely as a nook of Paradise, before Satan entered its gardens. Where the steep, well wooded bank descends to the broad, bright Hudson, half way down is a level glade of verdant grass, completely embowered in foliage. The sparkling water peeps between the twining boughs, like light through the rich tracery of Gothic windows; and the cheerful twittering of birds alone mingles with the measured cadence of the plashing waves. Here Hamilton fought his duel, just as the sun was rising:

> "Clouds slumbering at his feet, and the clear blue
> Of Summer's sky in beauty bending o'er him—
> The city bright below; and far away,
> Sparkling in golden light, his own romantic bay."

> "Tall spire, and glittering roof, and battlement,
> And banners floating in the sunny air,

And white sails o'er the calm blue waters bent,
Green isle and circling shore, all blended there,
In wild reality."

We descended, to return to the steamboat, by an open path on the river's edge. The high bank, among whose silent groves we had been walking, now rose above our heads in precipitous masses of rugged stone, here and there broken into recesses, which, in the evening light, looked like darksome caverns. Trees bent over the very edge of the summit, and their unearthed roots twisted among the rocks like huge serpents. On the other side lay the broad Hudson in the moonlight, its waves rippling up to the shore with a cool, refreshing sound.

All else was still — still — so fearfully still, that one might almost count the beatings of the heart. That my heart *did* beat, I acknowledge; for here was the supposed scene of the Mary Rogers' tragedy;[12] and though the recollection of *her* gave me no uneasiness, I could not forget that quiet lovely path we were treading was near to the city, with its thousand hells, and frightfully easy of access.

We spoke of the murdered girl, as we passed the beautiful promontory near the Sybil's cave, where her body was found, lying half in and half out of the water. A few steps further on, we encountered the first human beings we had met during the whole of our long ramble — two young women, singing with a somewhat sad constraint, as if to keep their courage up.

I had visited the Sybil's cave in the day time; and should have entered its dark mouth by the moonlight, had not the aforesaid remembrances of the city haunted me like evil spirits.

We Americans, you know, are so fond of classic names that we call a village Athens, if it has but three houses, painted red to blush for their own ugliness. Whence this cave derives its imposing title I cannot tell. It is in fact rather a pretty little place, cut out of soft stone, in rude imitation of a Gothic interior. A rock in the centre, scooped out like a baptismal font, contains a spring of cool, sweet water. The entire labour of cutting out this cave was performed by one poor Scotchman, with chisel and hammer. He worked upon it an entire year; and probably could not have completed it in less than six months, had he given every day of his time. He expected to derive considerable profit by selling draughts from the spring, and keeping a small fruit stand near it. But alas, for the vanity of human expectations! a few weeks after he completed his laborious task, he was driven off the grounds, it is said, unrequited by the proprietor.

A little before nine, we returned to the city. There was a strong breeze, and the boat bounded over the waves, producing that delightful sensation of elasticity and vigour which one feels when riding a free and fiery steed. The moon, obscured by fleecy clouds, shone with a saddened glory; rockets rose from Castle Garden, and dropped their blazing jewels on the billowy bosom of the bay; the lamps of the city gleamed in the distance; and with painful pity for the houseless street-wanderer, I gratefully remembered that one of those distant lights illuminated a home, where true and honest hearts were ever ready to bid me welcome.

Letter V [1]
September 16, 1841

Since I wrote last, I have again visited Hoboken to see a band of Scotchmen in the old Highland costume.[2] They belong to a Benevolent Society for the relief of indigent countrymen; and it is their custom to meet annually in Gaelic dress, to run, leap, hurl stones, and join in other Highland exercises—in fond remembrance of

> "The land of rock and glen,
> Of strath, and lake, and mountain,
> And more————— of gifted men."

There were but thirty or forty in number, and a very small proportion of them fine specimens of manhood. There was one young man, however, who was no bad sample of a brave young chief in the olden time; with athletic frame, frank countenance, bold bearing, and the bright, eager eye of one familiar with rugged hills and the mountain breeze. Before I was told, my eye singled him out, as most likely to bear away the prizes in the games. There was mettle in him, that in another age and in another clime, would have enabled him to stand beside brave old Torquil of the Oak, and give the cheerful response, *"Bas air son Eachin."* (Death for Hector.)[3]

But that age has passed, blessed be God; and he was nothing more than a handsome, vigorous Scotch emigrant, skilful in Highland games.

The dresses in general, like the wardrobe of a theatre, needed the effect of distance to dazzle the imagination; though two or three of them were really elegant. Green or black velvet, with glittering buttons, was fitted close to the arms and waist; beneath which fell the tartan kilt in ample folds; from the left shoulder flowed a long mantle of bright-coloured plaid, chosen according to the varieties of individual taste, not as distinguishing marks of ancestral clans. Their shaggy pouches, call *sporrans,* were of plush or fur. From the knee to the ankle, there was no other covering than the Highland buskin of crimson plaid. One or two had dirks with sheaths and hilts beautifully embossed in silver, and ornamented with large crystals from Cairngorm; St. Andrew and the thistle, exquisitely wrought on the blades of polished steel.[4]

These were exceptions; for, as I have said, the corps in general had a theatrical appearance; nor can I say they bore their standards, or unsheathed their claymores, with a grace quite sufficient to excite my imagination. Two boys, of eight or ten years old, who carried the tassels of the central banner, in complete High-

land costume, pleased me more than all the others; for children receive gracefulness from nature, and learn awkwardness of men.

But though there were many accompaniments to render the scene common-
place and vulgar, yet it was not without pleasurable excitement, slightly tinged
with romance, that I followed them along the steep banks of Hoboken, and
caught glimpses of them between the tangled foliage of the trees, or the sinuosities of rocks, almost as rugged as their own mountain-passes. Banners and
mantles, which might not have borne too close inspection, looked graceful as
they floated so far beneath me; and the sound of the bagpipes struck less harshly
on my ear, than when the musicians stood at my side. But even softened by distance, I thought the shrill wailing of this instrument appropriate only to Clan
Chattan, whose Chief was called *Mohr ar chat,* or the Great Cat.

As a phantom of the Past, this little pageant interested me extremely. I thought
of the hatred of those fierce old clans, whose "blood refused to mix, even if poured
into the same vessel." They were in the State what sects are in the Church—
narrow, selfish, and vindictive.

The State had dissolved *her* clans, and the Church is fast following the good example; though there are still sectaries casting their shadows on the sunshine of
God's earth, who, if they were to meet on the Devil's Bridge, as did the two old
feudal chieftains of Scotland, would, like them, choose death rather than humble
prostration for the safe foot-path of an enemy.

Clans have forgotten old quarrels, and not only mingled together, but with a
hostile nation. National pride and national glory is but a more extended clanship,
destined to be merged in universal love for the human race. Then farewell to
citadels and navies, tariffs and diplomatists; for the prosperity of *each* will be the
prosperity of *all.*

In religion, too, the spirit of extended, as well as of narrow clanship will cease.
Not only will Christianity forget its minor subdivisions, but it will *itself* cease to
be sectarian. That only will be a genuine "World's Convention," when Christians,
with reverent tenderness for the religious sentiment in every form, are willing
that Mohammedans or Pagans should unite with them in every good work, without abstaining from ceremonies which to them are sacred.

"The Turks," says Lamartine, "always manifest respect for what other men ven-
erate and adore. Wherever a Mussulman sees the image of God in the opinion of
his fellow-creatures, he bows down and he respects; persuaded that the *intention*
sanctifies the *form.*"

This sentiment of reverence, so universal among Mohammedans, and so divine in its character, might well lead Pierpont to ask, when standing in the burying-ground of Constantinople,

> ————————————"If all that host,
> Whose turbaned marbles o'er them nod
> Were doomed, when giving up the ghost,

To die as those who have no God?
No, no, my God! They worshipped THEE;
Then let not doubts my spirit darken,
That Thou, who always hearest me,
To these, thy children too, didst hearken."

The world, regenerated and made free, will at last bid a glad farewell to clans
and sects! Would that their graves were dug and their requiems sung; and nothing but their standards and costumes left, as curious historical records of the benighted Past.

Letter VI [1]
September 23, 1841

I lately visited the Jewish Synagogue in Crosby-street, to witness the Festival of
the New Year, which was observed for two days, by religious exercises and a general suspension of worldly business. The Jewish year, you are aware, begins in
September; and they commemorate it in obedience to the following text of Scripture: "In the first day of the seventh month ye shall have a Sabbath, a memorial
of blowing of trumpets, a holy convocation. Ye shall do no servile work therein." [2]
It was the first time I ever entered any place of worship where Christ was not
professedly believed in. Strange vicissitudes of circumstance, over which I had no
control, have brought me into intimate relation with almost every form of Christian faith, and thereby given me the power of looking candidly at religious opinions from almost any point of view.[3] But beyond the pale of the great sect of
Christianity I had never gone; though far back in my early years, I remember an
intense desire to be enough acquainted with some intelligent and sincere Mohammedan, to enable me to look at the Koran [4] through *his* spectacles.
The women were seated separately, in the upper part of the house. One of the
masters of Israel came, and somewhat gruffly ordered me, and the young lady
who accompanied me, to retire from the front seats of the synagogue. It was un-
courteous; for we were very respectful and still, and not in the least disposed to
intrude upon the daughters of Jacob. However, my sense of justice was rather
gratified at being treated contemptuously as a Gentile and "a Nazarene;" for I remembered the contumely with which *they* had been treated throughout Christendom, and I imagined how they must feel, on entering a place of Christian worship, to hear us sing,

"With hearts as hard as stubborn Jews,
That unbelieving race."

The effect produced on my mind, by witnessing the ceremonies of the Jewish
Synagogue, was strange and bewildering; spectral and flitting; with a sort of vanishing resemblance to reality; the magic lantern of the Past.

Veneration and Ideality, you know, would have made me wholly a poet, had not the inconvenient size of Conscientiousness forced me into reforms;[5] between the two, I look upon the Future with active hope, and upon the Past with loving reverence. My mind was, therefore, not only unfettered by narrow prejudice, but solemnly impressed with recollections of those ancient times when the Divine Voice was heard amid the thunders of Sinai, and the Holy Presence shook the mercy-seat between the cherubim. I had, moreover, ever cherished a tenderness for

> "Israel's wandering race, that go
> Unblest through every land;
> Whose blood hath stained the polar snow
> And quenched the desert sand:
> Judea's homeless hearts, that turn
> From all earth's shrines to thee,
> With their lone faith for ages borne
> In sleepless memory."

Thus prepared, the scene would have strongly excited my imagination and my feelings, had there not been a heterogeneous jumbling of the Present with the Past. There was the Ark[6] containing the Sacred Law, written on scrolls of vellum, and rolled, as in the time of Moses; but between the Ark and the congregation, instead of the "brazen laver," wherein those who entered into the tabernacle were commanded to wash, was a common bowl and ewer of English delf, ugly enough for the chamber of a country tavern. All the male members of the congregation, even the little boys, while they were within the synagogue, wore fringed silk mantles, bordered with blue stripes; for Moses was commanded to "Speak unto the children of Israel, and bid them that they make them fringes in the borders of their garments, throughout their generations, and that they put upon the fringe of their borders a ribbon of blue;"—but then these mantles were worn over modern broadcloth coats, and fashionable pantaloons with straps. The Priest indeed approached more nearly to the gracefulness of oriental costume; for he wore a full black silk robe, like those worn by the Episcopal clergy; but the large white silk shawl which shaded his forehead, and fell over his shoulders, was drawn over a common black hat! Ever and anon, probably in parts of the ceremony deemed peculiarly sacred, he drew the shawl entirely over his face, as he stooped forward and laid his forehead on the book before him. I suppose this was done because Moses, till he had done speaking with the congregation, put a veil upon his face. But through the whole, priest and people kept on their hats. My spirit was vexed with this incongruity. I had turned away from the turmoil of the Present, to gaze quietly for a while on the grandeur of the Past; and the representatives of the Past walked before me, not in the graceful oriental turban, but the useful European hat! It broke the illusion completely.

The ceremonies altogether impressed me with less solemnity than those of the

Catholic Church; and gave me the idea of far less faith and earnestness in those engaged therein. However, some allowance must be made for this: first, because the common bond of faith in Christ was wanting between us; and secondly, because all the services were performed in Hebrew, of which I understood not one syllable. To see mouths opened to chant forth a series of unintelligible sounds, has the same kind of fantastic unreality about it, that there is in witnessing a multitude dancing, when you hear no music. But after making all these allowances, I could not escape the conclusion that the ceremonies were shuffled through in a cold, mechanical style. The priest often took up his watch, which lay before him; and assuredly this chanting of prayers "by Shrewsbury clock"[7] is not favourable to solemnity.

The chanting was unmusical, consisting of monotonous ups and downs of the voice, which, when the whole congregation joined in it, sounded like the continuous roar of the sea.

The trumpet, which was blown by a Rabbi, with a shawl drawn over his hat and face, was of the ancient shape, somewhat resembling a cow's horn. It did not send forth a spirit-stirring peal; but the sound groaned and struggled through it—not at all reminding one of the days when

> "There rose the choral hymn of praise,
> And trump and timbrel answered keen,
> And Zion's daughters poured their lays,
> With priest and warrior's voice between."

I observed, in the English translation on one side of an open prayer book, these words: "When the trumpet shall blow on the holy mountain, let all the earth hear! Let them which are scattered in Assyria, and perishing in Egypt, gather themselves together in the Holy City." I looked around upon the congregation, and I felt that Judea no longer awoke at the sound of the trumpet!

The ark, on a raised platform, was merely a kind of semicircular closet, with revolving doors. It was surmounted by a tablet, bearing a Hebrew inscription in gilded letters. The doors were closed and opened at different times, with much ceremony; sometimes, a man stood silently before them, with a shawl drawn over his hat and face. When opened, they revealed festoons of white silk damask, suspended over the sacred rolls of the Pentateuch;[8] each roll enveloped in figured satin, and surmounted by ornaments with silver bells. According to the words of Moses, "Thou shalt put into the ark the testimony which I shall give thee." Two of these rolls were brought out, opened by the priest, turned round toward all the congregation, and after portions of them had been chanted for nearly two hours, were again wrapped in satin, and carried slowly back to the ark, in procession, the people chanting the Psalms of David, and the little bells tinkling as they moved.

While they were chanting an earnest prayer for the coming of the Promised One, who was to restore the scattered tribes, I turned over the leaves, and by a singular coincidence my eye rested on these words: "Abraham said, see ye not the splendid light now shining on Mount Moriah? And they answered, *nothing but caverns do we see.*" I thought of Jesus, and the whole pageant became more spectral than ever; so strangely vague and shadowy, that I felt as if under the influence of magic.

The significant sentence reminded me of a German friend, who shared his sleeping apartment with another gentleman, and both were in the habit of walking very early in the morning. One night, his companion rose much earlier than he intended; and perceiving his mistake, placed a lighted lamp in the chimney corner, that its glare might not disturb the sleeper, leaned his back against the fire-place, and began to read. Sometime after, the German rose, left him reading, and walked forth into the morning twilight. When he returned, the sun was shining high up in the heavens; but his companion, unconscious of the change, was still reading by lamp-light in the chimney corner. And this the Jews are now doing, as well as a very large proportion of Christians.

Ten days from the Feast of Trumpets, comes the Feast of the Atonement. Five days after, the Feast of Tabernacles is observed for seven days. Booths of evergreen are erected in the synagogue, according to the injunction, "Ye shall dwell in booths seven days; all that are Israelites born shall dwell in booths. And ye shall take the boughs of goodly trees, branches of palm trees, and the boughs of thick trees, and willows of the brook; and ye shall rejoice before the Lord your God seven days."

Last week, a new synagogue was consecrated in Attorney-street; making, I believe, five Jewish Synagogues in this city, comprising in all about ten thousand of this ancient people. The congregation of the new synagogue are German emigrants, driven from Bavaria, the Duchy of Baden, &c., by oppressive laws.[9] One of these laws forbade Jews to marry; and among the emigrants were many betrothed couples, who married as soon as they landed on our shores; trusting their future support to the God of Jacob. If not as "rich as Jews," they are now most of them doing well in the world; and one of the first proofs they gave of prosperity, was the erection of a place of worship.

The oldest congregation of Jews in New-York, were called *Shewith Israel.*[10] The Dutch governors would not allow them to build a place of worship; but after the English conquered the colony, they erected a small wooden synagogue, in Mill-street, near which a creek ran up from the East River, where the Jewish women performed their ablutions. In the course of improvement this was sold; and they erected the handsome stone building in Crosby-street, which I visited. It is not particularly striking or magnificent, either in its exterior or interior; nor would it be in good keeping, for a people gone into captivity to have garments like those of Aaron,[11] "for glory and for beauty;" or an "ark overlaid with pure gold, within and without, and a crown of gold to it round about."

There is something deeply impressive in this remnant of a scattered people, coming down to us in continuous links through the long vista of recorded time; preserving themselves carefully unmixed by intermarriage with people of other nations and other faith, and keeping up the ceremonial forms of Abraham, Isaac, and Jacob, through all the manifold changes of revolving generations. Moreover, our religions are connected, though separated; they are shadow and substance, type and fulfilment. To the Jews only, with all their blindness and waywardness, was given the idea of one God, spiritual and invisible; and, therefore, among them only could such a one as Jesus have appeared. To us they have been the medium of glorious truths; and if the murky shadow of their Old dispensation rests too heavily on the mild beauty of the New, it is because the Present can never quite unmoor itself from the Past; and well for the world's safety that it is so.

Quakers were mixed with the congregation of Jews; thus oddly brought together, were the representatives of the extreme of conservatism, and the extreme of innovation!

I was disappointed to see so large a proportion of this peculiar people fair-skinned and blue-eyed. As no one who marries a Gentile is allowed to remain in their synagogues, one would naturally expect to see a decided predominance of the dark eyes, jetty locks, and olive complexions of Palestine. But the Jews furnish incontrovertible evidence that colour is the effect of climate. In the mountains of Bavaria they are light-haired and fair-skinned: in Italy and Spain they are dark: in Hindostan swarthy. The *Black* Jews of Hindostan are said to have been originally African and Hindoo slaves, who received their freedom as soon as they became converted to Judaism, and had fulfilled the rites prescribed by the ceremonial law; for the Jews, unlike Christians, deem it unlawful to hold any one of their own religious faith in slavery. In another respect they put us to shame; for they held a Jubilee of Freedom once in fifty years, and on that occasion emancipated all, even of their heathen slaves.

Whether the Black Jews, now a pretty large class in Hindostan, intermarry with other Jews we are not informed. Moses, their great lawgiver, married an Ethiopian. Miriam and Aaron were shocked at it, as they would have been at any intermarriage with the heathen tribes, of whatever colour. Whether the Ethiopian woman had adopted the faith of Israel is not mentioned; but we are told that the anger of the Lord was kindled against Aaron and his sister for their conduct on this occasion.

The anniversary meetings of the New-York Hebrew Benevolent Society present a singular combination. There meet together pilgrims from the Holy Land, merchants from the Pacific Ocean and the East Indies, exiles from the banks of the Vistula, the Danube, and the Dneiper,[12] bankers from Vienna and Paris, and dwellers on the shores of the Hudson and the Susquehannah. Suspended in their dining hall, between the American and English flags, may be seen the Banner of Judah, with Hebrew inscriptions in golden letters. How this stirs the sea of memory! That national banner has not been unfurled for eighteen hundred years. The last time it floated to the breeze was over the walls of Jerusalem, besieged by Titus Vespasianus.[13] Then, *our* stars and stripes were not foreseen, even in dim shadow, by the vision of a prophet; and here they are intertwined together over this congress of nations!

In New-York, as elsewhere, the vending of "old clo'" is a prominent occupation among the Jews; a fact in which those who look for spiritual correspondences can perceive significance; though singularly enough Sartor Resartus makes no allusion to it, in his "Philosophy of Clothes."[14] When I hear Christian ministers apologizing for slavery by the example of Abraham, defending war, because the Lord commanded Samuel to hew Agag in pieces, and sustaining capital punishment by the retaliatory code of Moses, it seems to me it would be most appropriate to have Jewish criers at the doors of our theological schools, proclaiming at the top of their lungs, "Old Clothes! Old Clothes! Old Clothes all the way from Judea!"[15]

The proverbial worldliness of the Jews, their unpoetic avocations, their modern costume, and mechanical mode of perpetuating ancient forms, cannot divest them of a sacred and even romantic interest.[16] The religious idea transmitted by this remarkable people, has given them a more abiding and extended influence on the world's history, than Greece attained by her classic beauty, or Rome by her triumphant arms. Mohammedanism and Christianity, the two forms of theology which include nearly all the civilized world, both grew from the stock planted by Abraham's children. On them lingers the long-reflected light of prophecy; and we, as well as they, are watching for its fulfilment. And verily, all things seem tending toward it. Through all their wanderings, they have followed the direction of Moses, to be *lenders* and not *borrowers.* The sovereigns of Europe and Asia, and the republics of America, are their debtors, to an immense amount. The Rothschilds[17] are Jews; and they have wealth enough to purchase all Palestine if they choose; a large part of Jerusalem is in fact mortgaged to them. The oppressions of the Turkish government, and the incursions of hostile tribes, have hitherto rendered Syria an unsafe residence; but the Sultan has erected it into an independent power, and issued orders throughout his empire, that the Jews shall be as perfectly protected in their religious and civil rights, as any other class of his subjects; moreover, the present controversy between European nations and the East seems likely to result in placing Syria under the protection of Christian nations. It is reported that Prince Metternich, Premier of Austria, has determined, if possible, to constitute a Christian kingdom out of Palestine, of which Jerusalem is to be the seat of government. The Russian Jews, who number about 2,000,000, have been reduced to the most abject condition by contempt and tyranny; but there, too, government is now commencing a movement in their favour, without requiring them to renounce their faith. As long ago as 1817 important privileges were conferred by law on those Jews who consented to embrace Christianity. Land was gratuitously bestowed upon them, where they settled, under the name of The Society of Israelitish Christians.[18]

These signs of the times cannot, of course, escape the observation, or elude the active zeal, of Christians of the present day. England has established many missions for the conversion of the Jews. The Presbyterian Church of Scotland have lately addressed a letter of sympathy and expostulation to the scattered children of Israel, which has been printed in a great variety of Oriental and Occidental languages. In Upper Canada, a Society of Jews converted to Christianity have been organized to facilitate the return of the wandering tribes to the Holy Land.

The Rev. Solomon Michael Alexander,[19] a learned Rabbi, of the tribe of Judah, has been proselyted to Christianity, and sent to Palestine by the Church of England; being consecrated the first Bishop of Jerusalem.

Moreover the spirit of schism appears among them. A numerous and influential body in England have seceded, under the name of Reformed Jews.[20] They denounce the Talmud as a mass of absurdities, and adhere exclusively to the authority of Moses; whereas, orthodox Jews consider the rabbinical writings of equal authority with the Pentateuch. They have sent a Hebrew circular to the Jews of this country, warning them against the seceders. A General Convention is likewise proposed, to enable them to draw closer the bonds of union.[21]

What a busy, restless age is this in which we are cast! What a difficult task for Israel to walk through its midst, with mantles untouched by the Gentiles.

> "And hath she wandered thus in vain,
> A pilgrim of the past?
> No! long deferred her hope hath been,
> But it shall come at last;
> For in her wastes a voice I hear,
> As from some prophet's urn,
> It bids the nations build not there,
> For Jacob shall return."

Letter VII [1]
Sept. 30, 1841

A few days since, I crossed the East River to Brooklyn, on Long Island; named by the Dutch, Breuck-len, or the Broken-land. Brooklyn Heights, famous in Revolutionary history, command a magnificent view of the city of New-York, the neighbouring islands, and harbour; and being at least a hundred feet above the river, and open to the sea, they are never unvisited by a refreshing and invigorating breeze. A few years ago, these salubrious heights might have been purchased by the city at a very low price, and converted into a promenade of beauty unrivalled throughout the world; but speculators have now laid hands upon them, and they are digging them away to make room for stores, with convenient landings from the river. In this process, they not unfrequently turn out the bones of soldiers, buried there during the battles and skirmishes of the Revolution.[2]

We turned aside to look in upon the small, neat burying-ground of the Methodist church, where lie the bones of that remarkable young man, the Rev. John Summerfield.[3] In the course of so short a life, few have been able to impress themselves so deeply and vividly on the memory of a thousand hearts, as this eloquent disciple of Christ. None who heard the fervid outpourings of his gifted soul could ever forget him. His grave is marked by a horizontal marble slab, on which is inscribed a long, well written epitaph. The commencement of it is the most striking:

> Rev. John Summerfield. Born in England; born again in Ireland. By the first, a child of genius; by the second, a child of God. Called to preach at 19; died at 27.

Dwellings were around this little burying-ground, separated by no fences, their thresholds divided from the graves only by a narrow foot-path. I was anxious to know what might be the effect on the spiritual character of children, accustomed to look out continually upon these marble slabs to play among the grassy mounds, and perchance to "take their little porringer, and eat their supper there."

About two miles from the ferry, we came to the marshy village of Gowannus,[4] and crossed the mill-pond where nearly a whole regiment of young Marylanders were cut off, retreating before the British, at the unfortunate battle of Long Island. A farm near by furnishes a painful illustration of the unwholesome excitement attendant upon speculation. Here dwelt an honest, ignorant, peaceful old man, who inherited from his father a farm of little value. Its produce was, however, enough to supply his moderate wants; and he took great pleasure in a small, neatly kept flower garden, from which he was ever ready to gather a bouquet for travellers. Thus quietly lived the old-fashioned farmer and his family, and thus they might have gone home to their fathers, had not a band of speculators foreseen that the rapidly increasing city would soon take in Brooklyn, and stretch itself across the marshes of Gowannus. Full of these visions, they called upon the old man, and offered him $70,000 for a farm which had, originally, been bought almost for a song. $10,000, in silver and gold, were placed on the table before him; he looked at them, fingered them over, seemed bewildered, and agreed to give a decisive answer on the morrow. The next morning found him a raving maniac! And thus he now roams about, recklessly tearing up the flowers he once loved so dearly, and keeping his family in continual terror.

On the high ground, back of this marsh, is Greenwood Cemetery, the object of our pilgrimage. The site is chosen with admirable taste. The grounds, beautifully diversified with hill and valley, are nearly covered with a noble old forest, from which it takes its cheerful name of the Green Wood.

The area of two hundred acres comprises a greater variety of undulating surface than Mount Auburn, and I think excels it in natural beauty.[5] From embowered glades and deeply shaded dells, you rise in some places twenty feet, and in others more than two hundred, above the sea. Mount Washington, the highest and most remarkable of these elevations, is two hundred and sixteen feet high. The scenery here is of picturesque and resplendent beauty;—comprising an admirable view of New-York; the shores of North and East river, sprinkled with villages; Staten Island, that lovely gem of the waters; the entire harbor, white with the sails of a hundred ships; and the margin of the Atlantic, stretching from Sandy Hook beyond the Rockaway Pavilion. A magnificent monument to Washington is to be erected here.

Thence we rambled along, through innumerable sinuosities, until we came to a quiet little lake, which bears the pretty name of Sylvan Water. Fish abound here, undisturbed; and shrubs in their wild, natural state, bend over the margin to dip their feet and wash their faces.

> "Here come the little gentle birds,
> Without a fear of ill,
> Down to the murmuring water's edge,
> And freely drink their fill."

As a gun is never allowed to enter the premises, the playful squirrels, at will, "drop down from the leafy tree," and the air of spring is redolent with woodland melody.

An hour's wandering brought us round to the same place again; for here, as at Mount Auburn, it is exceedingly easy for the traveller to lose his way in labyrinthian mazes.

> "The wandering paths that wind and creep,
> Now o'er the mountain's rugged brow,
> And now where sylvan waters sleep
> In quiet beauty, far below,
> Those paths which many a lengthened mile
> Diverge, then meet, then part once more,
> Like those which erst in Creta's isle,
> Were trod by fabled Minotaur."

Except the beautiful adaptation of the roads and paths to the undulating nature of the ground, Art has yet done but little for Greenwood. It is said the Company that purchased it for a cemetery, will have the good taste to leave the grounds as nearly as possible in a state of nature. But as funds are increased by the sale of burying lots, the entire precincts will be enclosed within terrace-walls, a handsome gate-way and chapel will be erected, and a variety of public monuments. The few private monuments now there, are mostly of Egyptian model, with nothing remarkable in their appearance.

On this spot was fought the bloody battle of Long Island.

> "Each wood, each hill, each glen,
> Lives in the record of those days
> Which 'tried the souls of men.'
> This fairy scene, so quiet now,
> Where murmuring winds breathe soft and low,
> And bright birds carol sweet,
> Once heard the ringing clash of steel,
> The shout, the shriek, the volley'd peal,
> The rush of flying feet!"

When the plan was first suggested, of finding some quiet, sequestered place, for a portion of the innumerable dead of this great city, many were very urgent to have it called The Necropolis, meaning The City of the Dead; but Cemetery was more wisely chosen; for the old Greeks signified thereby The Place of Sleep. We still need a word of *Christian* significance, implying, "They are not here; they have risen." I should love to see this cheerful motto over the gate-way.

The increase of beautiful burial-grounds, like Mount Auburn and Greenwood, is a good sign. Blessed be all agencies that bring our thoughts into pleasant companionship with those who have "ended their pilgrimage and begun their life." Banished for ever be the sable garments, the funeral pall, the dismal, unshaded ground. If we *must* attend to a change of garments, while our hearts are full of sorrow, let us wear sky-blue, like the Turks, to remind us of heaven. The horror and the gloom, with which we surround death, indicates too surely our want of living faith in the soul's immortality. Deeply and seriously impressed we must needs be, whenever called to contemplate the mysterious close of "our hood-winked march from we know not whence, to we know not whither;" but terror and gloom ill become the disciples of Him, who asked with such cheerful significance, "Why seek ye the Living among the Dead?"

I rejoice greatly to observe that these ideas are gaining ground in the community. Individuals of all sects, and in many cases entire churches, are abjuring the custom of wearing mourning; and Protestant christendom is fast converting its dismal, barricaded burial grounds into open, flowery walks. The Catholics have always done so. I know not whether the intercession of Saints, and long continued masses for the dead, bring their imaginations into more frequent and nearer communion with the departed; but for some reason or other, they keep more bright than we do the link between those who are living here, and those who live beyond.[6] Hence, their tombs are constantly supplied with garlands by the hand of affection; and the innocent babe lying uncoffined on its bier in the open church, with fragrant flowers in its little hand, and the mellow light from painted windows resting on its sweet uncovered face. Great is the power of Faith!

Letter VIII [1]
October 7, 1841

Among the many objects of interest in this great city, a stranger cannot overlook its shipping; especially as New-York lays claim to superiority over other cities of the Union, in the construction of vessels, which are remarked for beauty of model, elegance of finish, and gracefulness of sparring.[2]

I have often anathematized the spirit of Trade, which reigns triumphant, not only on 'Change,[3] but in our halls of legislation, and even in our churches. Thought is sold under the hammer, and sentiment, in its holiest forms, stands labelled for the market. Love is offered to the highest bidder, and sixpences are given to purchase religion for starving souls.

In view of these things, I sometimes ask whether the age of Commerce is better than the age of War? Whether our "merchant princes" are a great advance upon feudal chieftains? Whether it is better for the many to be prostrated by force, or devoured by cunning? To the imagination, those bloody old barons seem the nobler of the two; for it is more manly to hunt a lion, than to entrap a fox. But Reason acknowledges that merchandize, with all its cunning and its fraud, *is* a step forward in the slow march of human improvement; and Hope announces, in prophetic tones, that Commerce will yet fulfil its highest mission, and encircle the world in a golden band of brotherhood.

You will not think this millennium is nigh, when I tell you that the most graceful, fairy-like vessel in these waters was a slaver! She floated like a sea-nymph, and cut the waves like an arrow. I mean the Baltimore clipper, called the Catharine; taken by British cruisers, and brought here, with all her detestable appurtenances of chains and padlocks, to be adjudged by the United States' Court, condemned, and sold. For what purpose she is now used, I know not; but no doubt this city is secretly much involved in the slave-trade.[4]

At the Navy Yard, Brooklyn, I saw the ship of war Independence, which carried out Mr. Dallas and his family, when he went ambassador to Russia.[5] On their arrival at Cronstadt,[6] they observed a barge, containing sixteen of the emperor's state officers, put off from a steam boat near by, and row towards them. They came on board, leaving behind them the bargemen, and a tall, fine-looking man at the helm. While the officers were in the cabin partaking refreshments and exchanging courtesies, the helmsman leaped on board, and made himself "hail fellow, well met" with the sailors, accepting cuds of tobacco, and asking various questions. When the officers returned on deck, and he had resumed his place, one of the sailors said to his comrade, with a knowing look, "I tell you what, Tom, that 'ere chap's more than we take him for. He's a *land*-lubber, I can tell you. Old Neptune never had the dipping of him."

An officer of the Independence overheard these remarks, and whispered to Commodore Nicholson that he shrewdly suspected the tall, plainly-dressed helmsman, was the Emperor Nicholas,[7] in disguise; for he was said to be fond of playing such pranks. A royal salute, forty-two guns, was immediately ordered. The helmsman was observed to count the guns; and after twenty-one (the common salute) had been fired, he took off his cap and bowed. The Russian steamer instantly ran up the imperial flag; all the forts, and every ship in the harbor, commenced a tremendous cannonading; rending the air, as when from "crag to crag leaps the live thunder."

In courteous acknowledgment of his discovered disguise, the officers of the Independence were invited to make the palace their home, during their stay at St. Petersburg, and the Emperor's carriages, horses, and aids, were at their service; a compliment never before paid to a vessel of any nation.

Yet was similar honour conferred on an uncouth country boy from New England! The following is the substance of the story, as told by Mr. Dallas, at a public dinner given him in Philadelphia, on his return from Russia, in 1838.

One day a lad, apparently about nineteen, presented himself before our ambassador at St. Petersburg. He was a pure specimen of the genus Yankee; with sleeves too short for his bony arms, trowsers half way up to his knees, and hands playing with coppers and ten-penny nails in his pocket. He introduced himself by saying "I've just come out here to trade, with a few Yankee notions, and I want to get sight of the Emperor."

"Why do you wish to see *him?*"

"I've brought him a present, all the way from Ameriky. I respect him considerable, and I want to get at him, to give it to him with my own hands."

Mr. Dallas smiled, as he answered, "It is such a common thing, my lad, to make crowned heads a present, expecting something handsome in return, that I'm afraid the Emperor will consider this only a Yankee trick. What have you brought?"

"An acorn."

"An acorn! what under the sun induced you to bring the Emperor of Russia an acorn?"

"Why, jest before I sailed, mother and I went on to Washington to see about a pension; and when we was there, we thought we'd jest step over to Mount Vernon. I picked up this acorn there; and I thought to myself I'd bring it to the Emperor. Thinks, says I, he must have heard a considerable deal about our General Washington, and I expect he must admire our institutions. So now you see I've brought it, and I want to get at him."

"My lad, it's not an easy matter for a stranger to approach the Emperor; and I am afraid he will take no notice of your present. You had better keep it."

"I tell you I want to have a talk with him. I expect I can tell him a thing or two about Ameriky. I guess he'd like mighty well to hear about our rail-roads, and our free schools, and what a big swell our steamers cut. And when he hears how well our people are getting on, may be it will put him up to doing something. The long and the short on't is, I shan't be easy till I get a talk with the Emperor; and I should like to see his wife and children. I want to see how such folks bring up a family."

"Well, sir, since you are so determined upon it, I will do what I can for you; but you must expect to be disappointed. Though it will be rather an unusual proceeding, I would advise you to call on the vice-chancellor, and state your wishes; he may possibly assist you."

"Well, that's all I want of you. I will call again, and let you know how I get on."

In two or three days, he again appeared, and said, "Well, I've seen the Emperor, and had a talk with him. He's a real gentleman, I can tell you. When I give him the acorn, he said he should set a great store by it; that there was no character in ancient or modern history he admired so much as he did our Washington. He said he'd plant it in his palace garden with his own hand; and he did do it—for I see him with my own eyes. He wanted to ask me so much about our schools and rail-roads, and one thing or another, that he invited me to come again, and see his daughters: for he said his wife could speak better English than he could. So I went again, yesterday; and she's a fine, knowing woman, I tell you; and his daughters are nice gals."

"What did the Empress say to you?"

"Oh, she asked me a sight o' questions. Don't you think, she thought we had no servants in Ameriky! I told her poor folks did their own work, but rich folks had plenty of servants. 'But then you don't *call* 'em servants,' said she; 'you call 'em help.' I guess, ma'am, you've been reading Mrs. Trollope?[8] says I. We had that ere book aboard our ship. The Emperor clapped his hands, and laughed as if he'd kill himself. 'You're right, sir,' said he, 'you're right. We sent for an English copy, and she's been reading it this very morning!' Then I told him all I knew about our country, and he was mightily pleased. He wanted to know how long I expected to stay in these parts. I told him I'd sold all the notions I brought over, and I guessed I should go back in the same ship. I bid 'em good-bye, all round, and went about my business. Ain't I had a glorious time? I expect you didn't calculate to see me run such a rig?"

"No, indeed, I did not, my lad. You may well consider yourself lucky; for it's a very uncommon thing for crowned heads to treat a stranger with so much distinction."

A few days after, he called again, and said, "I guess I shall stay here a spell longer, I'm treated so well. T'other day a grand officer come to my room, and told me the Emperor had sent him to show me all the curiosities; and I dressed myself, and he took me with him, in a mighty fine carriage, with four horses; and I've been to the theatre and the museum; and I expect I've seen about all there is to be seen in St. Petersburg. What do you think of that, Mr. Dallas?"

It seemed so incredible that a poor, ungainly Yankee lad should be thus loaded with attention, that the ambassador scarcely knew what to think or say.

In a short time, his strange visiter re-appeared. "Well," said he, "I made up my mind to go home; so I went to thank the Emperor, and bid him good-bye. I thought I couldn't do no less, he'd been so civil. Says he, 'Is there anything else you'd like to see before you go back to Ameriky?' I told him I *should* like to get a peep at Moscow; for I'd heard considerable about their setting fire to the Krem-lin, and I'd read a deal about General Bonaparte;⁹ but it would cost a sight o' money to go there, and I wanted to carry my earnings to mother. So I bid him good-bye, and come off. Now what do you guess he did, next morning? I vow, he sent the same man, in regimentals, to carry me to Moscow in one of his own carriages, and bring me back again, when I've seen all I want to see! And we're going to-morrow morning, Mr. Dallas. What do you think now?"

And sure enough, the next morning the Yankee boy passed the ambassador's house in a splendid coach and four, waving his handkerchief, and shouting "Good-bye! Good-bye!"

Mr. Dallas afterward learned from the Emperor that all the particulars related by this adventurous youth were strictly true. He again heard from him at Moscow, waited upon by the public officers, and treated with as much attention as is usually bestowed on ambassadors.

The last tidings of him reported that he was travelling in Circassia, and writing a Journal, which he intended to publish.

Now, who but a Yankee could have done all that?

While speaking of the Emperor, I must not forget the magnificent steam frigate Kamschatka, built here to his order. Her model, drafted by Captain Von Shantz, of the Russian navy, is extremely beautiful. She sits on the water as gracefully as a swan; and it is said her speed is not equalled by any sea-steamer on the Atlantic or Pacific, the Black sea, the Indian, or the Baltic. It is supposed she could easily make the passage from here to England in ten days. The elegance of her rigging, and her neat, nimble wheels have been particularly admired. These wheels are constructed on a new plan; and though apparently slight, have great strength and power. Her engines are of six hundred horse power, and her tonnage about two thousand.

All the metal about her is American. In machinery and construction she carries two hundred thousand pounds of copper, fifty thousand of wrought iron, and three hundred thousand of cast iron. Two hundred and fifty men were eight months employed in building her. Her cabins are said to be magnificent. Two drawing-rooms are fitted up in princely style for the imperial family; the woodwork of these consists of mahogany, bird's-eye maple, rose-wood, and satinwood. Her hull is entirely black; the bows and stern surmounted with a large double-headed gilt eagle, and a crown. The machinery, made by Messrs. Dunham & Co. of this city, is said to be of the most superb workmanship ever produced in this country. She is considered a remarkably cheap vessel of the kind, as

she costs *only* four hundred thousand dollars. She was built under the superin-
tendence of Mr. Scott, who goes in her to Russia, as chief engineer. She sailed for
Cronstadt last week, being escorted out of the harbour by a large party of ladies
and gentlemen. Among these was Mr. Rhoades, of New-York, the Naval Con-
structor. You probably recollect that he built a large gun-ship for the Turkish Sultan; who was so much delighted when he saw the noble vessel launched right roy-
ally upon the waves, that he jumped and capered, and threw his arms about the
ship-builder's neck, and gave him a golden box, set with splendid jewels. Henry
Eckford, too, one of the most remarkable of marine architects, was of New-York.
He built the Kensington for the Greeks, and died prematurely while in the employ of Mahmoud. It is singular, is it not, that foreign powers send to this young
country, when they most want ingenious machinery, or skilful workmanship?
But I will quit this strain, lest I fall into our national sin of boasting.

I cannot bid you farewell without mentioning the French frigate Belle Poule,
commanded by the Prince de Joinville, son of Louis Philippe.[10] She is an interesting object seen from the Battery, with her tri-colour flying; for one seems to
see the rich sarcophagus, with its magnificent pall of black velvet, sprinkled with
silver stars, in which she conveyed the remains of Napoleon from St. Helena to
Paris. Every day, masses were said, and requiems sung on board, for the soul of
the great departed. Do not quarrel with the phrase. In its highest significance it is
ill applied to any warrior; but, nevertheless, in the strong will, successfully en-
forced, there is ever an element of greatness.

The same unrivalled band that attended the imperial remains, are now on
board, and sometimes refresh our citizens with most enchanting music. They are
twenty-six in number, paid from the Prince's own purse.

Sabbath before last, a youth of fourteen, much beloved, died on board, far from
home and kindred. It was an impressive sight to see the coffin of the young
stranger passing through our streets, covered with the tri-coloured flag, suspended upon ropes, after the manner of marine burials in Europe, and borne by
his mourning comrades.

The Prince's private state-room contains a bronze copy of the Joan of Arc,
which was exquisitely sculptured by his sister, Marie, who had great genius for
the fine arts, and was richly endowed with intellect. In the same room are minia-
tures of his royal parents, by the celebrated Madame de Mirbel,[11] and some very
spirited sketches by his own hand. It is worthy of remark, that the only royal family eminently distinguished for private virtues, combined with a high degree of
intellectual cultivation, were not *educated* to be princes; and that their father had
acquired wisdom and strength in the school of severe adversity.

The keeper of Castle Garden, when he saw me watching the barge that came
from the Belle Poule, repeated, at least half a dozen times, that I should not know
the Prince from any other man, if I were to see him. I was amused to hear him
thus betray the state of his own mind, though he failed to enlighten mine.

I love to linger about the Battery at sunset; to see the flags all drop down suddenly from the mast-head in honour of the retreating king of day; and to hear in the stillness of evening, some far-off song upon the waters, or the deep, solemn sound, "All's well!" echoed from one to another of those numerous ships, all lying there so hushed and motionless. A thousand thoughts crowd upon my mind, as I silently gaze on their twinkling lights, and shadowy rigging, dimly relieved against the sky. I think of the human hearts imprisoned there; of the poor sailor's toil and suffering; of his repressed affections, and benighted mind; and in that one idea of life spent without a home, I find condensed all that my nature most shudders at. I think, too, of the poor fugitive slave, hunted out by mercenary agents, chained on ship-board, and perchance looking up, desolate and heartbroken, to the same stars on which I fix my free and happy gaze. Alas, how fearfully solemn must their light be to *him,* in his hopeless sorrow, and superstitious ignorance.[12]

Letter IX [1]
October 14, 1841

Last week we went to Ravenswood, to visit Grant Thorburn's famous garden. We left the city by Hell-gate, a name not altogether inappropriate for an entrance to New-York.[2] The waters, though somewhat troubled and peevish, were more composed than I had expected. This was owing to the high tide; and it reminded me of Washington Irving's description:[3] "Hell-gate is as pacific at low water as any other stream; as the tide rises, it begins to fret; at half tide it rages and roars, as if bellowing for more water; but when the tide is full, it relapses again into quiet, and for a time seems to sleep almost as soundly as an alderman after dinner. It may be compared to an inveterate drinker, who is a peaceful fellow enough when he has no liquor at all, or when he is skin-full; but when half-seas over, plays the very devil." One of the steam-ferry boats that crosses this turbulent passage, is appropriately called the Pluto.[4] It is odd that men should have confounded together the deities that preside over Riches and over Hell, and that the god of Commerce should likewise be the god of Lies. Perhaps the ancients had sarcastic significance in this.

The garden at Ravenswood is well worth seeing. An admirable green-house, full of choice plants; extensive and varied walks, neatly kept; and nearly three thousand dahlias in full bloom—the choicest specimens, with every variety of shade and hue; and a catalogue of great names, from Lord Wellington, to Kate Nickleby and Grace Darling.[5] I never saw any floral exhibition more superb. They stood facing each other in regal groups, as if the court beauties of a coronation ball had been suddenly changed into blossoms by an enchanter's wand. The location of the garden is beautiful; in some places opening upon pretty rural scenes of wood and pasture, and fronting on the broad blue river, where, ever and anon, may be seen, through the intervening foliage, some little boat, or sloop, with snowy sail, gliding gracefully along in silence and sunlight.

Grant Thorburn, you know, of course; that little "spunk o' geni, in a rickety tabernacle," on whose history Galt built his Lawrie Todd.[6] The story derived small aid from fiction; the first volume being almost literally Grant Thorburn's history, as he tells it himself. To be sure, he never pushed into the wilderness, to lay out "Judiville," or any other new town. Though Ravenswood has grown up around him, and the tasteful name is of his own choosing, he never could have endured many of the hardships of a pioneer; for the village lies on the East River, a little south of Hallet's Cove, not more than five miles from the city. The name came from the Bride of Lammermoor; for though a strict adherent of Scotland's kirk, he is a great admirer of Sir Walter's romances. The pleasant old gentleman returned in the boat with us, and was highly communicative; for, in the first place, he loves to talk of himself and his adventures, with the innocent and inoffensive egotism of a little child; and in the next place, he favours Boston ladies, having a pleased recollection of the great attention paid him there. He told us he was born near St. Leonard's Crags, and in his boyhood was accustomed to pass Jeannie Dean's cottage frequently. His grandfather was alive and stirring at the time of the Porteous mob, and he had heard him recount the leading incidents in the heart of Mid Lothian a thousand times. I was charmed to hear him recite, in the pure Scotch accent, Jeannie's eloquent and pathetic appeal to the Queen. Speaking of Scott's fidelity to the national character, I asked him if he had not often met with a Dandie Dinmont; he replied, "Yes, and with Dumbiedikes, too; but much oftener with a 'douce Davie Deans.'"[7]

Lawrie Todd is very true to the life; yet it is slightly embellished with fictitious garniture, like a veritable portrait in masquerade dress. The old gentleman's love of matter of fact led him to publish a biographical sketch of himself; which, so far as it goes, is almost in the identical language used by Galt: both being in fact the very words in which he has been long accustomed to repeat his story. Another motive for giving an unadorned account of himself in his little book, probably was the very natural and not unpleasing propensity of an old man, to trace step by step the adventures and efforts whereby he fashioned such a flowery fortune from the barren sands.

The handsome country-seats of himself and son, standing side by side in the midst of this spacious and beautiful garden; urns supported by Cupids, (which they say in Yankee land should be called cupidities;) and oriental glimpses here and there, of some verdant mount among the winding walks, surmounted by the tufted Sago Palm, or spreading Cactus; all this contrasted oddly enough with his own account of himself, as a diminutive Scotch lad with "brief legs and shuffling feet," squatted down on the deck of the emigrant ship, which brought him here, poor and friendless, in 1794. He thus describes himself, helping the colored cook to prepare dinner, when they first drew near the wharves of New-York: "I sat down with Cato, as he was called, square on the deck, his feet against my feet, with a wooden bowl of potatoes between our legs, and began to scrape off the skins. While thus employed, a boat came alongside with several visiters. One inquired for a farmer's servant, wishing to engage one; another for a housemaid; and a third, thanks be and praise! asked if there was a nail-maker on board. My greedy ear snapped the word, and looking up, I answered, 'I am one.' 'You!' replied he, looking down as if I was a fairy; 'You! can you make nails?' 'I'll wager a sixpence,' (all I had) was my answer, 'that I'll make more nails in one day than any man in America.' This reply, the manner of it, and the figure of the bragger, set all present into a roar of laughter."

A curious sample of Scotch thrift was shown when he first opened a little shop, without capital to buy stock. Brick-bats, covered with ironmonger's paper, with a knife or fork tied on the outside, were ranged on the shelves like an imposing array of new cutlery; and a dozen snuff boxes, or shaving boxes, made a great show, fastened on round junks of wood.

"But although it must be allowed that this was a clever and innocent artifice," says Lawrie Todd, "yet, like other dealers in the devices of cunning, I had not been circumspect at all points; for by mistake, I happened to tie a round shaving box on a brick subterfuge, which a sly, pawky old Scotchman, who sometimes stepped in for a crack, observed.

"Ay, mon," says he, "but ye hae unco' queer things here. Wha ever saw a four corner't shaving box?"—Whereupon we had a hearty good laugh. "Od," he resumed, "but ye're an auld farrant chappy, and no doot but ye'll do weel in this country, where pawkrie[8] is no' an ill nest-egg to begin with."

There is, however, no "pawkrie" about his flowers and garden-seeds; they are genuine, and the best of their kind; as their celebrity throughout the country abundantly testifies.

I begged of the gardener a single sprig of acacia, whose light, feathery, yellow foliage looked like a pet plaything of the breezes; and which for the first time enabled me to understand clearly Moore's[9] poetic description of the Desert, where "The Acacia waves her yellow hair."

I likewise took with me a geranium leaf, as a memento of the rose-geranium which Grant Thorburn accidentally bought in the day of small beginnings, and which proved the nucleus of his present floral fame, and blooming fortune. The gardener likewise presented us with a bouquet of dahlias, magnificent enough for the hand-screen of a Sultana; but this politeness I think we owed to certain beautiful young ladies who accompanied us.

Altogether, it was a charming excursion; and I came away pleased with the garden and its environs, and pleased with the old gentleman, whose dwarf-like figure disappointed me agreeably; for, from his own description, I was prepared to find him ungainly and mis-shapen. I no longer deem it so very marvelous that his Rebecca [10] should have preferred the poor, canny little Scotchman to her rich New-York lover.

As I never deserved to be called "Mrs. *Leo* Hunter," [11] you will, perhaps, be surprised at the degree of interest I express in this man, whose claims to distinction are merely the having amassed wealth by his own industry and shrewdness, and having his adventures told by Galt's facetious pen. The accumulation of dollars and cents, I grant is a form of power the least attractive of any to the imagination; but yet, as an indication of ability of some sort, it *is* attractive to a degree; and moreover there is something in mere success which interests us—because it is a stimulus which the human mind spontaneously seeks, and without which it cannot long retain its energies. Added to this, there is a roseate gleam of romance, resting on the shrewd Scotchman's life. First, there is a sober sentiment, a quaint, homely pathos, in his account of his first love, which wraps the memory of his patient, quiet Rebecca in a sacred veil of tender reverence. Secondly, he is a sort of High Priest of Flora; and though not precisely such an one as would have been chosen to tend the shrine of her Roman Temple, yet this will give him a poetic claim upon my interest, so long as the absorbing love of beauty renders a Flower-Merchant more attractive to my fancy than a dealer in grain.

Were I not afraid of wearying your patience with descriptions of scenery, I would talk of the steamboat passage from Ravenswood; for indeed it is very beautiful. But I forbear all allusion to the gliding boats, the vernal forests, falling in love with their own shadows in the river, and the cozy cottages, peeping out from the foliage with their pleasant, friendly faces. I have placed the lovely landscape in the halls of memory, where I can look upon it whenever my soul needs the bounteous refreshings of nature. I congratulate myself for having added this picture to my gallery, as a blessing for the weary months that are coming upon us; for Summer has waved her last farewell, as she passed away over the summit of the sunlit hills, and I can already spy the waving white locks of old Winter, as he comes hobbling up, before the gale, on the other side. I could forgive him the ague-fit he bestows on poor Summer, as she hurries by; but the plague of it is, he will stand gossiping with Spring's green fairy, till every tooth chatters in her sweet little head.

Now, of a truth, my friend, I have been meaning to write sober sense; but what is written, is written. As the boy said of his whistling, "it did itself." I would gladly have shown more practical good sense, and talked wisely on "the spirit of the age," "progress of the species," and the like; but I believe, in my soul, fairies keep carnival all the year round in my poor brain; for even when I first wake, I find a magic ring of tinted mushrooms, to show where their midnight dance has been. But I did not bore you with scenery, and you should give me credit for that; we who live cooped up in cities, are so apt to forget that any body but ourselves ever sees blue sky enough for a suit of bed curtains, or butter-cups and greensward sufficient for a flowered coverlet. "Don't crow till you're out of the wood," though;

for the aforesaid picture hangs in the hall, and I may yet draw aside the curtain and give you a peep, if you are very curious. *Real* pictures, like everything else real, cannot be bought with cash. Old Mammon buys nothing but shadows. My gallery beats that of the Duke of Devonshire;[12] for it is filled with originals by the oldest masters, and not a copy among them all; and, better still, the sheriff cannot seize them, let him do his worst; others may prove property in the same, but they lie safely beyond the reach of trover or replevin.

As we passed Blackwell's Island,[13] I looked with thoughtful sadness on the handsome stone edifice erected there for a Lunatic Asylum. On another part of the island is a Penitentiary; likewise a noble building, though chilling the heart with its barred doors and grated windows. The morally and the intellectually insane—should they not both be treated with great tenderness? It is a question for serious thought; and phrenology,[14] with all its absurd quackery on its back, will yet aid mankind in giving the fitting answer. There has at least been kindness evinced in the location chosen; for if free breezes, beautiful expanse of water, quiet, rural scenery, and "the blue sky that bends o'er all," can "minister to the mind diseased," then surely these forlorn outcasts of society may here find God's best physicians for their shattered nerves.

Another object which interested me exceedingly was the Long-Island Farm School,[15] for foundlings, and orphans. Six or eight hundred children are here carefully tended by a matron and her assistants, until they are old enough to go out to service or trades. Their extensive play-ground runs along the shore; a place of as sweet natural influences as could well be desired. I thought of the squalid little wretches I had seen at Five Points, whose greatest misfortune was that they were not orphans. I thought of the crowd of sickly infants in Boston almshouse—the innocent victims of hereditary vice. And my heart ached, that it could see no end to all this misery, though it *heard* it, in the far-off voice of prophesy.

Letter X[1]
October 21, 1841

In a great metropolis like this, nothing is more observable than the infinite varieties of character. Almost without effort, one may happen to find himself, in the course of a few days, beside the Catholic kneeling before the Cross, the Mohammedan bowing to the East, the Jew veiled before the ark of the testimony, the Baptist walking into the water, the Quaker keeping his head covered in the presence of dignitaries and solemnities of all sorts, and the Mormon quoting from the Golden Book[2] which he has never seen.

More, perhaps, than any other city, except Paris or New Orleans, this is a place of rapid fluctuation, and never-ceasing change. A large portion of the population are like mute actors, who tramp across the stage in pantomime or pageant, and are seen no more. The enterprising, the curious, the reckless, and the criminal, flock hither from all quarters of the world, as to a common centre, whence they can diverge at pleasure. Where men are little known, they are imperfectly restrained; therefore, great numbers here live with somewhat of that wild license which prevails in times of pestilence. Life is a reckless game, and death is a business transaction. Warehouses of ready-made coffins, stand beside warehouses of ready-made clothing, and the shroud is sold with spangled opera-dresses. Nay, you may chance to see exposed at sheriffs' sales, in public squares, piles of coffins, like nests of boxes, one within another, with a hole bored in the topmost lid to sustain the red flag of the auctioneer, who stands by, describing their conveniences and merits, with all the exaggerating eloquence of his tricky trade.

There is something impressive, even to painfulness, in this dense crowding of human existence, this mercantile familiarity with death. It has sometimes forced upon me, for a few moments, an appalling night-mare sensation of vanishing identity; as if I were but an unknown, unnoticed, and unseparated drop in the great ocean of human existence; as if the uncomfortable old theory were true, and we were but portions of a Great Mundane Soul, to which we ultimately return, to be swallowed up in its infinity. But such ideas I expel at once, like phantasms of evil, which indeed they are. Unprofitable to all, they have a peculiarly bewildering and oppressive power over a mind constituted like my own; so prone to eager questioning of the infinite, and curious search into the invisible. I find it wiser to forbear inflating this balloon of thought, lest it roll me away through unlimited space, until I become like the absent man, who put his clothes in bed, and hung himself over the chair; or like his twin-brother, who laid his candle on the pillow and blew himself out.

You will, at least, my dear friend, give these letters the credit of being utterly unpremeditated; for Flibbertigibbet[3] himself never moved with more unexpected and incoherent variety. I have wandered almost as far from my starting point, as Saturn's ring is from Mercury; but I will return to the varieties in New-York. Among them I often meet a tall Scotsman, with sandy hair and high cheekbones—a regular Sawney,[4] with tartan plaid and bag-pipe. And where do you guess he most frequently plies his poetic trade? Why, in the slaughter-houses! of which a hundred or more send forth their polluted breath into the atmosphere of this swarming city hive! There, if you are curious to witness incongruities, you may almost any day see grunting pigs or bleating lambs, with throats cut to the tune of Highland Mary, or Bonny Doon, or Lochaber No More.

Among those who have flitted across my path, in this thoroughfare of nations, few have interested me more strongly than an old sea-captain, who needed only Sir Walter's education, his wild excursions through solitary dells and rugged mountain-passes, and his familiarity with legendary lore, to make him, too, a poet and a romancer. Untutored as he was, a rough son of the ocean, he had combined in his character the rarest elements of fun and pathos; side by side, they glanced through his conversation, in a manner almost Shakspearean. They shone, likewise, in his weather-beaten countenance; for he had "the eye of Wordsworth and the mouth of Molière."[5]

One of his numerous stories particularly impressed my imagination, and remains there like a cabinet picture, by Claude.[6] He said he was once on board a steamboat, full of poor foreigners, going up the Mississippi to some place of destination in the yet unsettled wilderness. The room, where these poor emigrants were huddled together, was miserable enough. In one corner, two dissipated-looking fellows were squatted on the floor, playing All-fours with dirty cards; in another, lay a victim of intemperance, senseless, with a bottle in his hand; in another, a young Englishman, dying of consumption—kindly tended by a venerable Swiss emigrant, with his helpful wife, and artless daughter. The Englishman was an intelligent, well-informed young man, who, being unable to marry the object of his choice, with any chance of comfortable support in his own country, had come to prepare a home for his beloved in the Eldorado of the West.[7] A neglected cold brought on lung fever, which left him in a rapid decline; but still, full of hope, he was pushing on for the township where he had planned for himself a domestic paradise. He was now among strangers, and felt that death was nigh. The Swiss emigrant treated him with that thoughtful, zealous tenderness, which springs from genial hearts deeply imbued with the religious sentiment. One wish of his soul they could not gratify, by reason of their ignorance. Being too weak to hold a pen, he earnestly desired to dictate to some one else a letter to his mother and his betrothed. This, Captain T. readily consented to do; and promised, so far as in him lay, to carry into effect any arrangements he might wish to make.

Soon after this melancholy duty was fulfilled, the young sufferer departed. When the steamboat arrived at its final destination, the kind-hearted Captain T. made the best arrangements he could for a decent burial. There was no chaplain on board; and, unused as he was to the performance of religious ceremonies, he himself read the funeral service from a book of Common Prayer, found in the young stranger's trunk. The body was tenderly placed on a board, and carried out, face upwards, into the silent solitude of the primeval forest. The sun, verging to the west, cast oblique glances through the foliage, and played on the pale face in flickering light and shadow. Even the most dissipated of the emigrants were sobered by a scene so touching and so solemn, and all followed reverently in procession. Having dug the grave, they laid him carefully within, and replaced the sods above him; then, sadly and thoughtfully, they returned slowly to the boat.

Subdued to tender melancholy by the scene he had witnessed, and the unusual service he had performed, Captain T. avoided company, and wandered off alone into the woods. Unquiet questionings, and far-reaching thoughts of God and immortality, lifted his soul towards the Eternal; and heedless of his footsteps, he lost his way in the windings of the forest. A widely devious and circuitous route brought him within sound of human voices. It was a gushing melody, taking its rest in sweetest cadences. With pleased surprise, he followed it, and came, suddenly and unexpectedly, in view of the new-made grave. The kindly Swiss matron, and her innocent daughter, had woven a large and beautiful Cross, from the broad leaves of the papaw tree, and twined it with the pure white blossoms of the trailing convolvulus. They had placed it reverently at the head of the stranger's grave, and kneeling before it, chanted their evening hymn to the Virgin. A glowing twilight shed its rosy flush on the consecrated symbol, and the modest, friendly faces of those humble worshippers. Thus beautifully they paid *their* tribute of respect to the unknown one, of another faith, and a foreign clime, who had left home and kindred, to die among strangers in the wilderness.

How would the holy gracefulness of this scene have melted the heart of his mother and his beloved!

I had many more things to say to you; but I will leave them unsaid. I leave you alone with this sweet picture, that your memory may consecrate it as mine had done.

Letter XI [1]
December 9, 1841

A friend passing by the Methodist church in Elizabeth street, heard such loud and earnest noises issuing therefrom, that he stepped in to ascertain the cause.[2] A coloured woman was preaching to a full audience, and in a manner so remarkable that his attention was at once rivetted. The account he gave excited my curiosity, and I sought an interview with the woman, whom I ascertained to be Julia Pell, of Philadelphia.[3] I learned from her that her father was one of the innumerable tribe of fugitives from slavery, assisted by that indefatigable friend of the oppressed, Isaac T. Hopper.[4] This was quite a pleasant surprise to the benevolent old gentleman, for he was not aware that any of Zeek's descendants were living; and it was highly interesting to him to find one of them in the person of this female Whitfield.[5] Julia never knew her father by the name of Zeek; for that was his appellation in slavery, and she had known him only as a freeman. Zeek, it seems, had been "sold running," as the term is; that is, a purchaser had given a very small part of his original value, taking the risk of not catching him. In Philadelphia, a coloured man, named Samuel Johnson, heard a gentleman making inquiries concerning a slave called Zeek, whom he had "bought running." "I know him very well," said Samuel; "as well as I do myself; he's a good-for-nothing chap; and you'll be better without him than with him." "Do you think so?" "Yes, if you gave what you say for him; it was a bite—that's all. He's a lazy, good-for-nothing dog; and you'd better sell your right in him the first chance you get." After some further talk, Samuel acknowledged that Zeek was his brother. The gentleman advised him to buy him; but Samuel protested that he was such a lazy, vicious dog, that he wanted nothing to do with him. The gentleman began to have so bad an opinion of his bargain, that he offered to sell the fugitive for sixty dollars. Samuel, with great apparent indifference, accepted the terms, and the necessary papers were drawn. Isaac T. Hopper was in the room during the whole transaction; and the coloured man requested him to examine the papers to see that all was right. Being assured that everything was in due form, he inquired, "And is Zeek now free?" "Yes, entirely free." "Suppose I was Zeek, and that was the man that bought me; couldn't he take me?" "Not any more than he could take me," said Isaac. As soon as Samuel received this assurance, he made a low bow to the gentleman, and, with additional fun in a face always roguish, said, "Your servant, sir; I am Zeek!" The roguishness characteristic of her father is reflected in some degree in Julia's intelligent face; but imagination, uncultivated, yet highly poetic, is her leading characteristic.

Some have the idea that our destiny is prophesied in early presentiments: thus, Hannah More,[6] when a little child, used to play, "Go up to London and see the bishops"—an object for which she afterwards sacrificed a large portion of her own moral independence and freedom of thought. In Julia Pell's case, "coming events cast their shadows before." I asked her when she thought she first "experienced religion." She replied, "When I was a little girl, father and mother used to go away to meeting on Sundays, and leave me and my brothers at home all day. So, I thought I'd hold class-meetings as the Methodists did. The children all round in the neighborhood used to come to hear me preach. The neighbours complained that we made such a noise, shouting and singing; and every Monday father gave us a whipping. At last, he said to mother, 'I'm tired of beating these poor children every week, to satisfy our neighbours. I'll send for my sister to come, and she will stay at home on Sundays, and keep them out of mischief.' So my aunt was brought to take care of us; and the next Sunday, when the children came thronging to hear me preach, they were greatly disappointed indeed to hear me say, in a mournful way, 'We can't have any more meetings now; because aunt's come, and she won't let us.' When my aunt heard this, she seemed to pity me and the children; and she said if we would get through before the folks came home, we might hold a meeting; for she should like to see for herself what it was we did, that made such a fuss among the neighbours. Then we had a grand meeting. My aunt's heart was taken hold of that very day; and when we all began to sing, 'Come to the Saviour, poor sinner, come!' she cried, and I cried; and when we had done crying, the whole of us broke out singing 'Come to the Saviour.' That very instant I felt my heart leap up, as if a great load had been taken right off of it! That was the beginning of my getting religion; and for many years after that, I saw all the time a blue smoke rising before my eyes—the whole time a blue smoke, rising, rising." As she spoke, she imitated the ascent of smoke, by a graceful, undulating motion of her hand.

"What do you suppose was the meaning of the blue smoke?" said I.

"I don't know, indeed, ma'am; but I always supposed it was my sins rising before me, from the bottomless pit."

She told me that when her mother died, some years after, she called her to her bed-side, and said, "Julia, the work of grace is only begun in you. You haven't got religion yet. When you can freely forgive all your enemies, and love to do them good, then you may know that the true work is completed within you." I thought the wisest schools of theology could not have established a better test.

I asked Julia, if she had ever tried to learn to read. She replied, "Yes, ma'am, I tried once; because I thought it would be such a convenience, if I could read the Bible for myself. I made good progress, and in a short time could spell B-a-k-e-r, as well as anybody. But it dragged my mind *down*. It dragged it *down*. When I tried to think, every thing scattered away like smoke, and I could do nothing but spell. Once I got up in an evening meeting to speak; and when I wanted to say, 'Behold the days come,' I began 'B-a—.' I was dreadfully ashamed, and concluded I'd give up trying to learn to read."

These, and several other particulars I learned of Julia, at the house of Isaac T. Hopper. When about to leave us, she said she felt moved to pray. Accordingly, we all remained in silence, while she poured forth a brief, but very impressive prayer for her venerable host; of whom she spoke as "that good old man, whom thou, O Lord, hast raised up to do such a blessed work for my down-trodden people."

Julia's quiet, dignified, and even lady-like deportment in the parlour, did not seem at all in keeping with what I had been told of her in the pulpit, with a voice like a sailor at mast-head, and muscular action like Garrick in Mad Tom.[7] On the Sunday following, I went to hear her for myself; and in good truth, I consider the event as an era in my life never to be forgotten. Such an odd jumbling together of all sorts of things in Scripture, such wild fancies, beautiful, sublime, or grotesque, such vehemence of gesture, such dramatic attitudes, I never before heard and witnessed. I verily thought she would have leaped over the pulpit; and if she had, I was almost prepared to have seen her poise herself on unseen wings, above the wondering congregation.

I know not whether her dress was of her own choosing; but it was tastefully appropriate. A black silk gown, with plain, white cuffs; a white muslin kerchief, folded neatly over the breast, and crossed by a broad black scarf, like that which bishops wear over the surplice.

She began with great moderation, gradually rising in her tones, until she arrived at the shouting pitch, common with Methodists. This she sustained for an incredible time, without taking breath, and with a huskiness of effort, that produced a painful sympathy in my own lungs. Imagine the following, thus uttered; that is, spoken without punctuation. "Silence in Heaven! The Lord said to Gabriel, bid all the angels keep silence. Go up into the third heavens, and tell the archangels to hush their golden harps. Let the mountains be filled with silence.

Let the sea stop its roaring, and the earth be still. What's the matter now? Why, man has sinned, and who shall save him? Let there be silence, while God makes search for a Messiah. Go down to the earth; make haste, Gabriel, and inquire if any there are worthy; and Gabriel returned and said, No, not one. Go search among the angels, Gabriel, and inquire if any there are worthy; make haste, Gabriel; and Gabriel returned and said, No, not one.[8] But don't be discouraged. Don't be discouraged, fellow sinners. God arose in his majesty, and he pointed to his own right hand, and said to Gabriel, Behold the Lion of the tribe of Judah; he alone is worthy. He shall redeem my people."

You will observe it was purely her own idea, that silence reigned on earth and in heaven, while search was made for a Messiah. It was a beautifully poetic conception, not unworthy of Milton.

Her description of the resurrection and the day of judgment, must have been terrific to most of her audience, and was highly exciting even to me, whose religious sympathies could never be roused by fear. Her figure looked strangely fantastic, and even supernatural, as she loomed up above the pulpit, to represent the spirits rising from their graves. So powerful was her rude eloquence, that it continually impressed me with grandeur, and once only excited a smile; that was when she described a saint striving to rise, "buried perhaps twenty feet deep, with three or four sinners atop of him."

This reminded me of a verse in Dr. Nettleton's Village Hymns:[9]

> "Oh how the resurrection light,
> Will *clarify* believers' sight,
> How joyful will the saints arise,
> And *rub the dust* from off their eyes."

With a power of imagination singularly strong and vivid, she described the resurrection of a young girl, who had died a sinner. Her body came from the grave, and her soul from the pit, where it had been tormented for many years. "The guilty spirit came up with the flames all around it—rolling—rolling—rolling." She suited the action to the word, as Siddons[10] herself might have done. Then she described the body wailing and shrieking, "O Lord! must I take that ghost again? Must I be tormented with that burning ghost for ever?"

Luckily for the excited feelings of her audience, she changed the scene, and brought before us the gospel ship, laden with saints, and bound for the heavenly shore. The majestic motion of a vessel on the heaving sea, and the fluttering of its pennon in the breeze, was imitated with wild gracefulness by the motion of her hands. "It touched the strand. Oh! it was a pretty morning! and at the first tap of Heaven's bell, the angels came crowding round, to bid them welcome. There you and I shall meet, my beloved fellow-travellers. Farewell—Farewell—I have it in my temporal feelings that I shall never set foot in this New-York again. Farewell on earth, but I shall meet you there," pointing reverently upward. "May we all be aboard that blessed ship." Shouts throughout the audience, "We will! We will!" Stirred by such responses, Julia broke out with redoubled fervour, "Farewell—farewell. Let the world say what they will of me, I shall surely meet you in Heaven's broad bay. Hell clutched me, but it hadn't energy enough to hold me. Farewell on earth. I shall meet you in the morning." Again and again she tossed her arms abroad, and uttered her wild "farewell;" responded to by the loud farewell of a whole congregation, like the shouts of an excited populace. Her last words were the poetic phrase, "*I shall meet you in the morning!*"

Her audience were wrought up to the highest pitch of enthusiasm I ever witnessed. "That's God's truth!" "Glory!" "Amen!" "Hallelujah!" resounded throughout the crowded house. Emotion vented itself in murmuring, stamping, shouting, singing, and wailing. It was like the uproar of a sea lashed by the winds.

You know that religion has always come to me in stillness; and that the machinery of theological excitement has ever been as powerless over my soul, as would be the exorcisms of a wizard. You are likewise aware of my tendency to *generalize;* to look at truth as *universal,* not merely in its particular relations; to observe human nature as a *whole,* and not in fragments. This propensity, greatly strengthened by the education of circumstances, has taught me to look calmly on all forms of religious opinion—not with the indifference, or the scorn, of unbelief; but with a friendly wish to discover everywhere the great central ideas common to all religious souls, though often re-appearing in the strangest disguises, and lisping or jabbering in the most untranslatable tones.

Yet combined as my religious character is, of quiet mysticism, and the coolest rationality, will you believe me, I could scarcely refrain from shouting Hurra for that heaven-bound ship; and the tears rolled down my cheeks, as that dusky priestess of eloquence reiterated her wild and solemn farewell.

If she gained such power over my spirit, there is no cause to marvel at the tremendous excitement throughout an audience so ignorant, and so keenly susceptible to outward impressions. I knew not how the high-wrought enthusiasm would be let down in safety. The shouts died away, and returned in shrill fragments of echoes, like the trembling vibrations of a harp, swept with a strong hand, to the powerful music of a war-song. Had I remembered a lively Methodist tune, as well as I recollected the words, I should have broke forth:

> "The gospel ship is sailing by!
> The Ark of safety now is nigh,
> Come, sinners, unto Jesus fly,
> Improve the day of grace.
> Oh, there'll be glory, hallelujah,
> When we all arrive at home!"

The same instinct that guided me, impelled the audience to seek rest in music, for their panting spirits and quivering nerves. All joined spontaneously in singing an old familiar tune, more quiet than the bounding, billowy tones of my favourite Gospel Ship. Blessings on music! Like a gurgling brook to feverish lips are sweet sounds to the heated and weary soul.

Everybody round me could sing; and the tones were soft and melodious. The gift of song is universal with Africans; and the fact is a prophetic one. Sculpture blossomed into its fullest perfection in a Physical Age, on which dawned the intellectual; Painting blossomed in an Intellectual Age, warmed by the rising sun of moral sentiment; and now Music goes forward to its culmination in the coming Spiritual Age. Now is the time that Ethiopia begins "to stretch forth her hands." Her soul, so long silenced, will yet utter itself in music's highest harmony.[11]

When the audience paused, Mr. Matthews, their pastor, rose to address them. He is a religious-minded man, to whose good influence Julia owes, under God, her present state of mind.[12] She always calls him "father," and speaks of him with the most affectionate and grateful reverence. At one period of her life, it seems that she was led astray by temptations, which peculiarly infest the path of coloured women in large cities; but ever since her "conversion to God," she has been strictly exemplary in her walk and conversation. In her own expressive language, "Hell clutched her, but hadn't energy enough to hold her." The missteps of her youth are now eagerly recalled by those who love to stir polluted waters; and they are brought forward as reasons why she ought not to be allowed to preach. I was surprised to learn that to this prejudice was added another, against women's preaching. This seemed a strange idea for Methodists, some of whose brightest ornaments have been women preachers. As far back as Adam Clarke's time,[13] his objections were met by the answer, "If an *Ass* reproved Balaam, and a *barn-door fowl* reproved Peter, why shouldn't a *woman* reprove sin?"

This classification with donkeys and fowls is certainly not very complimentary. The first comparison I heard most wittily replied to, by a coloured woman who had once been a slave. "Maybe a speaking woman *is* like an Ass," said she; "but I can tell you one thing—the Ass saw the angel, when Balaam didn't."[14]

Father Matthews, after apologizing for various misquotations of Scripture, on the ground of Julia's inability to read, added: "But the Lord has evidently called this woman to a great work. He has made her mighty to the salvation of many souls, as a cloud of witnesses can testify. Some say she ought not to preach, because she is a woman. But I say, 'Let the Lord send by whom he *will* send.' Let everybody that has a message, deliver it—whether man or woman, white or coloured! Some say women mustn't preach, because they were first in the transgression; but it seems to me hard that if they helped us *into* sin, they shouldn't be suffered to help us *out*. I say, 'Let the Lord send by whom he *will* send;' and my pulpit shall be always open."

Thus did the good man instil a free principle into those uneducated minds, like gleams of light through chinks in a prison-wall. Who can foretell its manifold and ever-increasing results in the history of that long-crippled race? Verily

great is the Advent of a true Idea, made manifest to men; and great are the miracles it works—making the blind to see, and the lame to walk.

Letter XII [1]
January 1, 1842

I wish you a Happy New-Year. A year of brave conflict with evil, within and without—a year of sinless victories. Would that some fairy, whose word fulfils itself
in fate, would wish *me* such a year! Yet scarcely are the words written, when I fall
to pitying myself, in view of the active images they have conjured up; and my soul
turns, with wistful gaze, towards the green pastures and still waters of spiritual
quietude, and poetic ease. Yet were the aforesaid fairy standing before me, ready
to grant whatsoever I might ask, I think I should have strength enough to choose
a year of conflict for the good of my race; but it should be warfare without poi-
soned arrows, and fought on the broad tableland of high mountains, never descending into the narrow by-paths of personal controversy, or chasing its foe
through the crooked lanes of policy. In all ages of the world, Truth has suffered
much at the hands of her disciples, because they have been ever tempted to use
the weapons her antagonists have chosen. Let us learn wisdom by the Past. The
warnings that sigh through experience, and the hope that smiles through prophecy, both have power to strengthen us.

   The Past and the Future! how vast is the sound, how infinite the significance!
Hast thou well considered of the fact, that all the Past is reproduced in thee, and
all the Future prophesied? Had not Pharaoh's daughter saved the Hebrew babe,
and brought him up in all the learning of the Egyptians; had not Plato's soul uttered itself in harmony with the great choral hymn of the universe; had not Judean
shepherds listened in the deep stillness of moonlight, on the mountains, to angels chanting forth the primal notes whence all music flows—Worship, Peace,
and Love; had any one of these been silent, wouldst *thou* have been what thou art?
Nay, thou wouldst have been altogether another; unable even to comprehend thy
present self. Had Christianity remained in dens and caves, instead of clothing itself in outward symbols of grandeur and of beauty; had cathedrals never risen in
towered state,

> "And over hill and dell
> Gone sounding with a royal voice
> The stately minster bell;"

had William the Norman never divided Saxon lands by force, and then united his
new piratical state in solemn marriage with the Church; had Luther never thrown
his inkstand at the Devil, and hit him hard; had Bishop Laud never driven here-
tics, by fire and faggot, to the rocky shores of New England; had William Penn

taken off his hat to the Duke of York—would thy present self have been known to thyself, couldst thou have seen its features in a mirror?[2]

Nay, verily. Thou art made up of all that has preceded thee; and thus was thy being predestined. And because it is thus in the inward spirit, it is so in the outward world. Our very shawls bear ornaments found in Egyptian catacombs, and our sofas rest on the mysterious Sphinx; Caryatides, which upheld the roof of Diana's ancient temple, stand with the same quiet and graceful majesty, to sustain the lighter burden of our candelabras and lamps; and the water of modern wells flows into vases, whose beautiful forms were dug from the lava of long-buried Herculaneum.[3]

Truth is immortal. No fragment of it ever dies. From time to time, the body dies off it; but it rises in a more perfect form, leaving its grave-clothes behind it, to be, perchance, worshipped as living things, by those who love to watch among the tombs. Every line of beauty is the expression of a thought, and shares the immortality of its origin; hence the beautiful acanthus leaf is transferred from Corinthian capitals to Parisian scarfs and English calicoes.

It is said that the bow of a violin drawn across the edge of a glass covered with sand, leaves notes of music written on the sand. Thus do the vibrations of the Present leave its tune engraven on the soul; and in the lapse of time, we call those written notes the language of the Past. Thus art thou the child of the Past, and the father of the Future. Thou standest on the Present, "like the sea-bird on a rock in mid ocean, with the immensity of waters behind him, ready to plunge into the immensity of waters before him."

Art thou a Reformer? Beware of the dangers of thy position. Let not the din of the noisy Present drown the music of the Past. Be assured there is no tone comes to thee from the far-off ocean of olden time, which is not a chord in the eternal anthem of the universe; else had it been drowned in the roaring waves, long before it came to thee.

Reform as thou wilt; for the Present and the Future have need of this; but let no rude scorn breathe on the Past. Lay thy head lovingly in her lap, and let the glance of her eye pass into thine; for she has been to thee a mother.

> "I can scorn nothing which a nation's heart
> Hath held for ages holy: for the heart
> Is alike holy in its strength and weakness;
> It ought not to be jested with nor scorned.
> All things to me are sacred that have been.
> And though earth like a river streaked with blood,
> Which tells a long and silent tale of death,
> May blush her history and hide her eyes,
> The Past is sacred—it is God's, not ours;
> Let her and us do better if we can."

At no season does the thoughtful soul so much realize that it ever stands "between two infinities"—never does it so distinctly recognise the presence of vast ideas, that look before and after, as when the Old Year turns away its familiar face, and goes off to join its veiled sisterhood beyond the flood. It is true that *every* day ends a year, and that which precedes our birth-day does, in an especial manner, end *our* year; yet is there somewhat peculiarly impressive in that epoch, which whole nations recognise as a foot-print of departing time.

The season itself has a wailing voice. The very sky in spring-time laughingly says, "How do you do?" but in winter it looks a mute farewell. "The year is dying away," says Goethe,[4] "like the sound of bells. The wind passes over the stubble, and finds nothing to move. Only the red berries of that slender tree seem as if they would fain remind us of something cheerful; and the measured beat of the thresher's flail calls up the thought that *in the dry and fallen ear lies so much of nourishment and life.*"

Thus Hope springs ever from the bosom of sadness. A welcome to the New-Year mingles with our fond farewell to the old. Hail to the Present, with all the work that it brings! Its restlessness, if looked at aright, becomes a golden prophecy. We will not *read* its prose, and count our stops, as schools have taught; but the heart shall *chant* it; and tones shall change the words to music, that shall write itself on all coming time.

New-York welcomes the new year, in much the same style that she does every thing else. She is not prone, as the Quakers say, "to get into the stillness," to express any of her emotions. Such a hubbub as was kept up on the night of the 31st, I never heard. Such a firing out of the old year, and such a firing in of the new! Fourth of July in Boston is nothing compared to it. The continual discharge of guns and pistols prevented my reading or writing in peace, and I took refuge in bed; but every five minutes a lurid flash darted athwart the walls, followed by the hateful crash of fire-arms. If any good thing is expressed by that sharp voice, it lies beyond the power of my imagination to discover it; why men should choose it for the utterance of joy, is more than I can tell.

The racket of these powder-devilkins kept me awake till two o'clock. At five, I was roused by a stout Hibernian voice,[5] almost under my window, shouting "Pa-ther!" "Pa-ther!" Peter did not answer, and——off went a pistol. Upon this, Peter was fain to put his head out of the window, and inquire what was wanted. "A bright New Year to ye, Pa-ther. Get up and open the door."

The show in the shop-windows, during the week between Christmas and New-Year's, was splendid, I assure you. All that Parisian taste, or English skill could furnish, was spread out to tempt the eye. How I did want the wealth of Rothschild, that I might make all the world a present! and then, methinks, I could still long for another world to endow. The happiness of Heaven must consist in loving and giving. What else is there worth living for? I have often involuntarily applied to myself a remark made by Madam Roland.[6] "Reflecting upon what part I was fitted to perform in the world," says she, "I could never think of any that quite satisfied me, but that of Divine Providence." To some this may sound blasphemous; it was, however, merely the spontaneous and child-like utterance of a loving and liberal soul.

Though no great observer of times and season, I do like the universal custom of ushering in the new year with gifts and gladsome wishes. I will not call these returning seasons notches cut in a stick, to count our prison hours, but rather a garlanding of mile-stones on the way to our Father's mansion.

In New-York, they observe this festival after the old Dutch fashion; and the Dutch, you know, were famous lovers of good eating. No lady, that *is* a lady, will be out in the streets on the first of January. Every woman, that *is* "anybody," stays at home, dressed in her best, and by her side is a table covered with cakes, preserves, wines, oysters, hot coffee, &c.; and as every gentleman is in honor bound to call on every lady, whose acquaintance he does not intend to cut, the amount of eating and drinking done by some fashionable beaux must of course be very considerable. The number of calls is a matter of pride and boasting among ladies, and there is, of course, considerable rivalry in the magnificence and variety of the eating tables. This custom is eminently Dutch in its character, and will pass away before a higher civilization.

To furnish forth this treat, the shops vied with each other to the utmost. Confectionary abounded in the shape of every living thing; beside many things nowhere to be found, not even among gnomes, or fairies, or uncouth merrows of the sea. Cakes were of every conceivable shape—pyramids, obelisks, towers, pagodas, castles, &c. Some frosted loaves nestled lovingly in a pretty basket of sugar eggs; others were garlanded with flowers, or surmounted by cooing doves, or dancing cupids. Altogether, they made a pretty show in Broadway—too pretty—since the object was to minister to heartless vanity, or tempt a sated appetite.

But I will not moralize. Let us all *have* virtue, and then there will be no further need to *talk* of it, as the German wisely said.

There is one lovely feature in this annual festival. It is a season when all past neglect, all family feuds, all heart-burning and estrangement among friends may be forgotten and laid aside for ever. They who have not spoken for years may renew acquaintance, without any unpleasant questions asked, if they signify a wish to do so by calling on the first of January. Wishing all may copy this warm bit of colouring in our social picture, I bid you farewell, with my heart's best blessing, and this one scrap of morals: May you treat every human being as you would treat him, and speak of every one as you would speak, if sure that death would part you before next New-Year's Day.[7]

Letter XIII [1]
January 20, 1842

Is your memory a daguerreotype machine,[2] taking instantaneous likenesses of whatsoever the light of imagination happens to rest upon? I wish mine were not; especially in a city like this—unless it would be more select in its choice, and engrave only the beautiful. Though I should greatly prefer the green fields, with cows, chewing the cud, under shady trees, by the side of deep, quiet pools—still I would find no fault, to have my gallery partly filled with the palaces of our "merchant princes," built of the sparkling Sing Sing marble, which glitters in the sunlight, like fairy domes; but the aforesaid daguerreotype will likewise engrave an ugly, angular building, which stands at the corner of Division-street, protruding its sharp corners into the midst of things, determined that all the world shall see it, whether it will or no, and covered with signs from cellar to garret, to blazen forth *all* it contains. 'Tis a caricature likeness of the nineteenth century; and like the nineteenth century it plagues me; I would I could get quit of it.

I know certain minds, imbued with poetic philosophy who earnestly seek all forms of outward beauty in this world, believing that their images become deeply impressed on the soul that loves them, and thus constitute its scenery through eternity. If I had faith in this theory, that large and many-labelled thing of bricks and mortar, at the corner of Division-street, would almost drive me mad; for though the spirit of beauty can witness that I love it not, its lines are branded into my mind with most disagreeable distinctness. I know not why it is so; for assuredly this is not a sinner above many other structures, built by contract, and inhabited by trade.

Luckily, no forms can re-appear in another world, which are not *within* the soul. The sublime landscape *there* belongs to him who has spiritually retired apart into high places to pray; not to the cultivated traveller with his mind's portfolio filled with images of Alpine scenery, or of huge Plinlimmon[3] veiled in clouds. The gardens *there* are not for nabobs, who exchange rupees for rare and fragrant roses; but for humble, loving souls, who cherish those sweet charities of life, that lie, "scattered at the feet of man like flowers." Thanks be to Him who careth for all he hath made, the poor child running about naked in the miserable abodes at Five Points, though the whole of his mortal life should be of hardship and privation, may by the grace of God, fashion for himself as beautiful an eternity, as Victoria's son;[4] nay, perchance his situation, bad as it is, involves even less danger of losing that beauty which alone remains, when the world, and all images thereof, pass away, like mist before the rising sun. The outward is but a seeming and a show; the inward alone is permanent and real.

That men have small faith in this, is witnessed by their doings. Parents shriek with terror to see a beloved child on the steep roof of lofty buildings, lest his body should fall a mutilated heap upon the pavement; but they can, without horror, send him to grow rich by trade, in such places as Havana or New Orleans, where his soul is almost sure to fall, battered and crushed, till scarcely one feature of God's image remains to be recognised. If heaven were to them as real as earth, they could not thus make contracts with Satan, to buy the shadow for the substance.

Alas, how few of us, even the wisest and the best, believe in Truth, and are willing to trust it altogether.—How we pass through life in simulation and false shows! In our pitiful anxiety how we shall appear before men, we forget how we appear before angels. Yet is *their* "public opinion" somewhat that concerns us most nearly. Passing by the theatre, I saw announced for performance a comedy, called the "Valley de Sham." That simple sentence of mis-spelled French brought to my mind a whole rail-road train of busy thought. I smiled as I read it, and said within myself, Is not that comedy New-York? Nay, is not the whole world a Valley of Sham? Are not you, and I, and every other mortal, the "valet" of some "sham" or other?

> "I scorn this hated scene
> Of masking and disguise,
> Where men on men still gleam,
> With falseness in their eyes;
> Where all is counterfeit,
> And truth hath never say;
> Where hearts themselves do cheat,
> Concealing hope's decay;
> And writhing at the stake,
> Themselves do liars make."

> "Go search thy heart, poor fool,
> And mark its passions well;
> 'Twere time to go to school—
> 'Twere time the *truth* to tell—
> 'Twere time this world should cast
> Its infant slough away,
> And hearts burst forth at last,
> Into the light of day:—
> 'Twere time all learned to be
> Fit for Eternity."

My friend, hast thou ever thought how pleasant, and altogether lovely, would be a life of entire sincerity, married to perfect love? The wildest stories of magic skill, or fairy power, could not equal the miracles that would be wrought by such a life; for it would change this hollow masquerade of veiled and restless souls into a place of divine communion.

Oh, let us no longer utter false, squeaking voices, through our stifling masks. If we have attained so far as to *speak* no lie, let us make the nobler effort to *live* none. Art thou troubled with vain fears concerning to-day's bread and to-morrow's garment? Let thy every word and act be perfect truth, uttered in genuine love; and though thou mayest ply thy spiritual trades all unconscious of their results, yet be assured that thus, and thus only, canst thou weave royal robes of eternal beauty, and fill ample storehouses, to remain long after Wall-street and State-street have crumbled into dust.

Be true to thyself. Let not the forms of business, or the conventional arrangements of society, seduce thee into falsehood. Have no fears of the harshness of sincerity. Truth is harsh, only when divorced from Love. There is no refinement like holiness; "for which humility is the other name." Politeness is but a parrot mockery of her heavenly tones, which the world lisps and stammers, to imitate, as best she can, the pure language known to us only in beautiful fragments. Not through the copy shall the fair original ever be restored.

Above all, be true to thyself in religious utterance, or remain for ever silent. Speak only according to thy own genuine, inward experience; and look well to it, that thou repeatest no phrase prescribed by creeds, or familiarly used by sects, unless that phrase really conveys some truth into thine own soul. There is far too much of this muttering of dead language. Indeed, the least syllable of it is too much, for him who has faith in the God of truth. Wouldst thou give up thy plain, expressive English, to mumble Greek phrases, without the dimmest perception of their meaning, because schools and colleges have taught that they mean thus and so? Or wilt thou maintain a blind reverence for words, which really have no more life for thee than old garments stuffed with chaff? Multitudes who make no "profession of religion," as the phrase is, are passively driven in the traces of a blind sectarism from which they lack either the energy or the courage to depart. When I see such startled by an honest inquiry what is really meant by established forms, or current phrases, I am reminded of the old man in the play, who said, "I speak no Greek, though I love the sound on't; it goes so thundering, as it conjured devils."

Not against any form, or phrase, do I enter a protest; but only against its unmeaning use. If to thy soul it really embodies truth, to thee it should be most sacred. But spiritual dialects, learned and spoken by rote, are among the worst of mockeries. "The man who claims to speak as books enable, as synods use, as fashion guides, or as interest commands, babbles. Let him hush."

Be true to thy friend. Never speak of his faults to another, to show thy own discrimination; but open them all to him, with candor and true gentleness. *Forgive* all his errors and his sins, be they ever so many; but do not *excuse* the slightest deviation from rectitude. Never forbear to dissent from a false opinion, or a wrong practice, from mistaken motives of kindness; nor seek thus to have thy own weakness sustained; for these things cannot be done without injury to the soul. "God forbid," says Emerson,[5] "that when I look to friendship as a firm rock to sustain me in moral emergencies, I should find it nothing but a mush of concession. Better be a nettle in the side of my friend, than to be merely his echo."

As thou wouldst be true to thy friend, be so likewise to thy country. Love her, with all her faults; but on the faults themselves pour out thy honest censure. Thus shalt thou truly serve her, and best rebuke the hirelings that would make her lose her freedom for the tickling of her ears.

Lastly, be true to the world. Benevolence, like music, is a universal language. It cannot freely utter itself in dialects, that belong to a nation, or a clan. In its large significance, the human race is to thee a brother and a friend. Posterity needs much at thy hands, and will receive much, whether thou art aware of it, or not. Thou mayest deem thyself without influence, and altogether unimportant. Believe it not. Thy simplest act, thy most casual word, is cast into "the great seed-field of human thought, and will re-appear, as poisonous weed, or herb-medicinal after a thousand years."[6]

Many live as if they were not ashamed to adopt practically the selfish creed, uttered in folly or in fun, "Why should I do anything for posterity? Posterity has done nothing for me." Ay; but the Past has done much for thee, and has given the Future an order upon thee for the payment. If thou hast received counterfeit coin, melt out the dross, and return true metal.

Letter XIV [1]
February 17, 1842

I was always eager for the spring-time, but never so much as now.

Patience yet a little longer! and I shall find delicate bells of the trailing arbutus, fragrant as an infant's breath, hidden deep, under their coverlid of autumn leaves, like modest worth in this pretending world. My spirit is weary for rural rambles. It is sad walking in the city. The streets shut out the sky, even as commerce comes between the soul and heaven. The busy throng, passing and repassing, fetter freedom, while they offer no sympathy. The loneliness of the soul is deeper, and far more restless, than in the solitude of the mighty forest. Wherever are woods and fields I find a home; each tinted leaf and shining pebble is to me a friend; and wherever I spy a wild flower, I am ready to leap up, clap my hands, and exclaim, "Cockatoo! he know me very well!" as did the poor New Zealander, when he recognised a bird of his native clime, in the menageries of London.

But amid these magnificent masses of sparkling marble, hewn *in prison,* I am all alone. For eight weary months, I have met in the crowded streets but two faces I had ever seen before. Of some, I would I could say that I should never see them again; but they haunt me in my sleep, and come between me and the morning. Beseeching looks, begging the comfort and the hope I have no power to give.

Hungry eyes, that look as if they had pleaded long for sympathy, and at last gone mute in still despair. Through what woful, what frightful masks, does the human soul look forth, leering, peeping, and defying, in this thoroughfare of nations. Yet in each and all lie the capacities of an archangel; as the majestic oak lies enfolded in the acorn that we tread carelessly under foot, and which decays, perchance, for want of soil to root in.

The other day, I went forth for exercise merely, without other hope of enjoyment than a farewell to the setting sun, on the now deserted Battery, and a fresh kiss from the breezes of the sea, ere they passed through the polluted city, bearing healing on their wings. I had not gone far, when I met a little ragged urchin, about four years old, with heap of newspapers, "more big as he could carry," under his little arm, and another clenched in his small, red fist. The sweet voice of childhood was prematurely cracked into shrillness, by screaming street cries, at the top of his lungs; and he looked blue, cold, and disconsolate.[2] May the angels guard him! How I wanted to warm him in my heart. I stood, looking after him, as he went shivering along. Imagination followed him to the miserable cellar where he probably slept on dirty straw; I saw him flogged, after his day of cheerless toil, because he had failed to bring home pence enough for his parents' grog; I saw wicked ones come muttering and beckoning between his young soul and heaven; they tempted him to steal, to avoid the dreaded beating. I saw him, years after, bewildered and frightened, in the police-office, surrounded by hard faces. Their law-jargon conveyed no meaning to his ear, awakened no slumbering moral sense, taught him no clear distinction between right and wrong; but from their cold, harsh tones, and heartless merriment, he drew the inference that they were enemies; and, as such, he hated them. At that moment, one tone like a mother's voice might have wholly changed his earthly destiny; one kind word of friendly counsel might have saved him—as if an angel, standing in the genial sunlight, had thrown to him one end of a garland, and gently diminishing the distance between them, had drawn him safely out of the deep and tangled labyrinth, where false echoes and winding paths conspired to make him lose his way.

But watchmen and constables were around him, and they have small fellowship with angels. The strong impulses that might have become overwhelming love for his race, are perverted to the bitterest hatred. He tries the universal resort of weakness against force; if they are too strong for *him,* he will be too cunning for *them. Their* cunning is roused to detect *his* cunning: and thus the gallows-game is played, with interludes of damnable merriment from police reports, whereat the heedless multitude laugh; while angels weep over the slow murder of a human soul.

When, oh when, will men learn that society makes and cherishes the very crimes it so fiercely punishes, and *in* punishing reproduces?

> "The key of knowledge first ye take away,
> And then, because ye've robbed him, ye enslave;

Ye shut out from him the sweet light of day,
And then, because he's in the dark, ye pave
The road, that leads him to his wished-for grave,
With stones of stumbling: then, if he but tread
Darkling and slow, ye call him "fool" and "knave"—
Doom him to toil, and yet deny him bread:
Chains round his limbs ye throw, and curses on his head."

God grant the little shivering carrier-boy a brighter destiny than I have fore-seen for him.

A little further on, I encountered two young boys fighting furiously for some coppers, that had been given them and had fallen on the pavement. They had matted black hair, large, lustrous eyes, and an olive complexion. They were evi-dently foreign children, from the sunny clime of Italy or Spain, and nature had made them subjects for an artist's dream. Near by on the cold stone steps, sat a ragged, emaciated woman, whom I conjectured, from the resemblance of her large, dark eyes, might be their mother; but she looked on their fight with languid indifference, as if seeing, she saw it not. I spoke to her, and she shook her head in a mournful way, that told me she did not understand my language. Poor, forlorn wanderer! would I could place thee and thy beautiful boys under shelter of sun-ripened vines, surrounded by the music of thy mother-land! Pence I will give thee, though political economy reprove the deed. They can but appease the hunger of the body; they cannot soothe the hunger of thy heart; that I obey the kindly impulse may make the world none the better—perchance some iota the worse; yet I must needs follow it—I cannot otherwise.

I raised my eyes above the woman's weather-beaten head, and saw behind the window, of clear, plate glass, large vases of gold and silver, curiously wrought. They spoke significantly of the sad contrasts in this disordered world; and excited in my mind whole volumes, not of political, but of angelic economy. "Truly," said I, "if the Law of Love prevailed, vases of gold and silver might even more abound—but no homeless outcast would sit shivering beneath their glittering mockery. All would be richer, and no man the poorer. When will the world learn its best wisdom? When will the mighty discord come into heavenly harmony?" I looked at the huge stone structures of commercial wealth, and they gave an an-swer that chilled my heart. Weary of city walks, I would have turned homeward; but nature, ever true and harmonious, beckoned to me from the Battery, and the glowing twilight gave me friendly welcome. It seemed as if the dancing Spring Hours had thrown their rosy mantles on old silvery winter in the lavishness of youthful love.

I opened my heart to the gladsome influence, and forgot that earth was not a mirror of the heavens. It was but for a moment; for there under the leafless trees, lay two ragged little boys, asleep in each other's arms. I remembered having read in the police reports, the day before, that two little children, thus found, had been taken up as vagabonds. They told, with simple pathos, how both their mothers had been dead for months; how they had formed an intimate friendship, had begged together, ate together, hungered together, and together slept uncovered beneath the steel-cold stars.

The twilight seemed no longer warm; and brushing away a tear, I walked hastily homeward. As I turned into the street where God has provided me with a friendly shelter, something lay across my path. It was a woman, apparently dead; with garments all draggled in New-York gutters, blacker than waves of the infernal rivers. Those who gathered around, said she had fallen in intoxication, and was rendered senseless by the force of the blow. They carried her to the watch-house, and the doctor promised she should be well attended. But, alas, for watch-house charities to a breaking heart! I could not bring myself to think otherwise than that hers *was* a breaking heart. Could she but give a full revelation of early emotions checked in their full and kindly flow, of affections repressed, of hopes blighted, and energies misemployed through ignorance, the heart would kindle and melt, as it does when genius stirs its deepest recesses.

It seemed as if the voice of human wo was destined to follow me through the whole of that unblest day. Late in the night I heard the sound of voices in the street, and raising the window, saw a poor, staggering woman in the hands of a watchman. My ear caught the words, "Thank you kindly, sir. I should *like* to go home." The sad and humble accents in which the simple phrase was uttered, the dreary image of the watch-house, which that poor wretch dreamed was her *home*, proved too much for my overloaded sympathies. I hid my face in the pillow, and wept; for "my heart was almost breaking with the misery of my kind."

I thought, then, that I would walk no more abroad, till the fields were green. But my mind and body grow alike impatient of being inclosed within walls; both ask for the free breeze, and the wide, blue dome that overarches and embraces *all*. Again I rambled forth under the February sun, as mild and genial as the breath of June. Heart, mind, and frame grew glad and strong, as we wandered on, past the old Stuyvesant church, which a few years agone was surrounded by fields and Dutch farm-houses, but now stands in the midst of peopled streets;—and past the trim, new houses, with their green verandahs, in the airy suburbs. Following the railroad, which lay far beneath our feet, as we wound our way over the hills, we came to the burying-ground of the poor. Weeds and brambles grew along the sides, and the stubble of last year's grass waved over it, like dreary memories of the past; but the sun smiled on it, like God's love on the desolate soul. It was inexpressibly touching to see the frail memorials of affection, placed there by hearts crushed under the weight of poverty. In one place was a small rude cross of wood, with the initials J. S. cut with a penknife, and apparently filled with ink. In another a small hoop had been bent into the form of a heart, painted green, and nailed on a stick at the head of the grave. On one upright shingle was painted only "MUTTER;" the German word for MOTHER. On another was scrawled, as if with

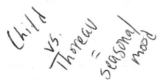

charcoal, "*So ruhe wohl, du unser liebes kind.*" (Rest well, our beloved child.) One recorded life's brief history thus: "H. G. born in Bavaria; died in New-York." Another short epitaph, in French, told that the sleeper came from the banks of the Seine.

The predominance of foreign epitaphs affected me deeply. Who could now tell with what high hopes those departed ones had left the heart-homes of Germany, the sunny hills of Spain, the laughing skies of Italy, or the wild beauty of Switzerland? Would not the friends they had left in their childhood's home, weep scalding tears to find them in a pauper's grave, with their initials rudely carved on a fragile shingle? Some had not even these frail memorials. It seemed there was none to care whether they lived or died. A wide, deep trench was open; and there I could see piles of unpainted coffins heaped one upon the other, left uncovered with earth, till the yawning cavity was filled with its hundred tenants.

Returning homeward, we passed a Catholic burying-ground. It belonged to the upper classes, and was filled with marble monuments, covered with long inscriptions. But none of them touched my heart like that rude shingle, with the simple word "Mutter" inscribed thereon. The gate was open, and hundreds of Irish, in their best Sunday clothes, were stepping reverently among the graves, and kissing the very sods. Tenderness for the dead is one of the loveliest features of their nation and their church.

The evening was closing in, as we returned, thoughtful, but not gloomy. Bright lights shone through crimson, blue, and green, in the apothecaries' windows, and were reflected in prismatic beauty from the dirty pools in the street. It was like poetic thoughts in the minds of the poor and ignorant; like the memory of pure aspirations in the vicious; like a rainbow of promise, that God's spirit never leaves even the most degraded soul. I smiled, as my spirit gratefully accepted this love-token from the outward; and I thanked our heavenly Father for a world beyond this.

Letter XV [1]
March 17, 1842

It may seem strange to you that among the mass of beings in this great human hive, I should occupy an entire letter with one whose life was like a troubled and fantastic dream; apparently without use to himself or others. Yet he was one who has left record on the public heart, and will not soon be forgotten. For several years past the eccentricities of Macdonald Clarke [2] have been the city talk, and almost every child in the street was familiar with his countenance. In latter years the record of inexpressible misery was written there; but he is said to have had rather an unusual portion of beauty in his youth; and even to the last, the heart looked out from his wild eyes with most friendly earnestness. I saw him but twice;

and now mourn sincerely that the pressure of many avocations prevented my seeking to see him oftener. So many forms of unhappiness crowd upon us in this world of perversion and disorder, that it is impossible to answer all demands. But stranger as poor Clarke was, it now makes me sad that I did not turn out of my way to utter the simple word of kindness, which never failed to rejoice his suffering and childlike soul.

I was always deeply touched by the answer of the poor, heart-broken page in Hope Leslie:[3] "Yes, lady, I *have* lost my way!" How often do I meet with those who, on the crowded pathway of life, have lost their way. With poor Clarke it was so from the very outset. Something that was not quite insanity, but was nigh akin to it, marked his very boyhood.

He was born in New London, Connecticut, and was school-mate with our eloquent friend, Charles C. Burleigh,[4] who always speaks of him as the most kindhearted of boys, but even then characterized by the oddest vagaries. His mother died at sea, when he was twelve years old; being on a voyage for her health. He says—

> "One night as the bleak October breeze
> Was sighing a dirge through the leafless trees,
> She was borne by rough men in the chilly dark,
> Down to the wharf-side, where a bark
> Waited for its precious freight.
> I watched the ship-lights long and late;
> When I could see them no more for tears,
> I turned drooping away,
> And felt that mine were darkening years."

And darkened indeed they were. "That delicate boy," as he describes himself, "an only son, having been petted to a pitiable unfitness for the sterner purposes of life, went forth alone, to struggle with the world's unfriendliness, and front its frowns."

He was in Philadelphia, at one period; but all we ever heard of him there was, that he habitually slept in the grave-yard, on Franklin's monument. In 1819, he came to New-York, where he wrote for newspapers, and struggled as he could with poverty; assisted from time to time by benevolence which he never sought. A sad situation for one who, like him, had a nerve protruding at every pore.

In New-York he became in love with a handsome young actress, of seventeen, by the name of Brundage. His poverty, and obvious incapacity to obtain a livelihood, made the match objectionable in the eyes of her mother; and they eloped. The time chosen was as wild and inopportune as most of his movements. On the very night she was to play Ophelia, on her way to the Park theatre, she absconded with her lover, and was married.[5] Of course, the play could not go on; the audience were disappointed, and the manager angry. The mother of the young lady, a strong, masculine woman, was so full of wrath, that she pulled her daughter out of bed at midnight, and dragged her home. The bridegroom tried to pacify the manager by the most polite explanations; but received nothing but kicks in return, with orders never to show his face within the building again. The young couple were strongly attached to each other, and of course were not long kept separated. But Macdonald, who had come of a wealthy family, was too proud to have his wife appear on the stage again; and the remarkable powers of his own mind were rendered useless by the jar that ran through them all; of course, poverty came upon them like an armed man. They suffered greatly, but still clung to each other with the most fervid affection. Sometimes they slept in the deserted market-house; and when the weather would permit, under the shadow of the trees. One dreadful stormy night, they were utterly without shelter, and in the extremity of their need, sought the residence of her mother. They knocked and knocked in vain; at last, the suffering young wife proposed climbing a shed, in order to enter the window of a chamber she used to occupy. To accomplish this purpose, Macdonald placed boards across a rain-water hogshead, at the corner of the shed. He mounted first, and drew her up after him; when suddenly the boards broke, and both fell into the water. Their screams brought out the strong-handed and unforgiving mother. She seized her offending daughter by the hair, and plunged her up and down in the water several times, before she would help her out. She finally took her into the house, and left Macdonald to escape as he could. They were not allowed to live together again, and the wife seemed compelled to return to the stage, as a means of obtaining bread. She was young and pretty, her affections were blighted, she was poor, and her profession abounded with temptations. It was a situation much to be pitied; for it hardly admitted of other result than that which followed. They who had loved so fondly, were divorced to meet no more. Whenever Macdonald alluded to this part of his strange history, as he often did to a very intimate friend, he always added, "I never blamed her; though it almost broke my heart. She was driven to it, and I always pitied her."

This lady is now an actress of considerable reputation in England; by the name of Burrows, I think.

From this period, the wildness of poor Clarke's nature increased; until he came to be generally known by the name of the "Mad Poet." His strange productions bore about the same relation to poetry that *grotesques,* with monkey faces jabbering out of lily cups, and gnarled trees with knot-holes twisted into hag's grimaces, bear to graceful *arabesques,*[6] with trailing vines and intertwisted blossoms. Yet was the undoubted presence of genius always visible. Ever and anon a light from another world shone on his innocent soul, kindling the holiest aspirations, which could find for themselves no form in his bewildered intellect, and so fell from his pen in uncouth and jagged fragments, still sparkling with the beauty of the region whence they came.[7] His metaphors were at times singularly fanciful. He thus describes the closing day:—

> "Now twilight lets her curtain down,
> And pins it with a star."

And in another place, he talks of memory that shall last

> *"Whilst the ear of the earth hears the hymn of the ocean."*

M. B. Lamar, late President of Texas, once met this eccentric individual at the room of William Page, the distinguished artist.[8] The interview led to the following very descriptive lines from Lamar:

> Say, have you seen Macdonald Clarke,
>   The poet of the Moon?
> He is a d——eccentric lark
>   As famous as Zip Coon.[9]
>
> He talks of Love and dreams of Fame,
>   And lauds his minstrel art;
> He has a kind of zig-zag brain—
>   But yet a straight-line heart.
>
> Sometimes his strains so sweetly float,
>   His harp so sweetly sings,
> You'd almost think the tuneful hand
>   Of Jubal[10] touched the strings.
>
> But soon, anon, with failing art,
>   The strain as rudely jars,
> As if a driver tuned the harp,
>   In cadence with his cars.

He was himself well aware that his mind was a broken instrument. He described himself as

> "A poet comfortably crazy—
> As pliant as a weeping-willow—
> Loves most everybody's girls; an't lazy—
> Can write an hundred lines an hour,
> With a rackety, whackety railroad power."

From the phrase, "loves most everybody's girls," it must not be inferred that he was profligate. On the contrary, he was innocent as a child. He talked of love continually; but it was of a mystic union of souls, whispered to him by angels, heard imperfectly in the lonely, echoing chambers of his soul, and uttered in phrases learned on earth, all unfit for the holy sentiment. Like the philosopher of the East,[11] he knew, by inward revelation, that his soul

> "In parting from its warm abode,
> Had lost its partner on the road,
> And never joined their hands."

His whole life was in fact a restless seeking for his other half. This idea continually broke from him in plaintive, wild, imploring tones.

> "I have met so much of scorn
> From those to whom my thoughts were kind,
> I've fancied there was never born
> On earth, for me, one kindred mind."

Again he says:

> "The soul that now is cursed and wild,
> In one fierce, wavering, ghastly flare,
> Would be calm and blest as a sleeping child,
> That dreams its mother's breast is there;
> Calm as the deep midsummer's air—
> Calm as that brow so mild and fair—
> Calm as God's angels everywhere—
> For all is Heaven—if Mary's there."

This restless idea often centred itself upon some young lady, whom he followed for a long time, with troublesome but guileless enthusiasm. The objects of his pursuit were sometimes afraid of him; but there was no occasion for this. As a New-York editor very happily said, "He pursued the little Red Riding Hoods of his imagination to bless and not to devour."

Indeed, in all respects, his nature was most kindly; insomuch that he suffered continual torture in this great Babel[12] of misery and crime. He wanted to relieve all the world, and was frenzied that he could not. All that he had—money, watch, rings, were given to forlorn street wanderers, with a compassionate, and even deferential gentleness, that sometimes brought tears to their eyes. Often, when he had nothing to give, he would snatch up a ragged, shivering child in the street, carry it to the door of some princely mansion, and demand to see the lady of the house. When she appeared, he would say, "Madam, God has made you one of the trustees of his wealth. It is His, not yours. Take this poor child, wash it, feed it, clothe it, comfort it—in God's name."

Ladies stared at such abrupt address, and deemed the natural action of the heart sufficient proof of madness; but the little ones were seldom sent away uncomforted.

Clarke was simple and temperate in all his habits; and in his deepest poverty always kept up the neat appearance of a gentleman; if his coat was thread-bare, it was never soiled. His tendency to refinement was shown in the church he chose to worship in. It was Grace church, the plainest, but most highly respectable of the Episcopal churches in this city. He was a constant attendant, and took comfort in the devotional frame of mind excited by the music. He was confirmed at that church but a few weeks before his death; and commemorated the event in lines, of which the following are an extract:

> "Calmly circled round the altar,
>   The children of the Cross are kneeling.
> Forward, brother—do not falter,
>   Fast the tears of sin are stealing;
> Washing memory bright and clean
>   Making futurity serene."

During the past winter, he raved more than usual. The editor of the Aurora [13] says he met him at his simple repast of apples and milk, in a public house, on last Christmas evening. He was absolutely mad. "You think I am Macdonald Clarke," said he; "but I am not. The mad poet dashed out his brains, last Thursday night, at the foot of Emmet's monument. The storm that night was the tears Heaven wept over him. God animated the body again. I am not now Macdonald Clarke, but Afara, an archangel of the Almighty.

"I went to Grace church to-day. Miss——sat in the seat behind me, and I tossed this velvet bible, with its golden clasps, into her lap. What do you think she did? A moment she looked surprised, and then she tossed it back again. So they all treat me. All I want is some religious people, that love God and love one another, to treat me kindly. One sweet smile of Mary——would make my mind all light and peace; and I would write such poetry as the world never saw.

"Something ought to be done for me," said he; "I can't take care of myself. I ought to be sent to the asylum; or wouldn't it be better to die? The moon shines through the willow trees on the graves in St. Paul's church-yard, and they look all covered with diamonds—don't you think they look like diamonds? Then there is a lake in Greenwood Cemetery; *that* would be a good cool place for me—I am not afraid to die. The stars of heaven look down on that lake, and it reflects their brightness."

The Mary to whom he alluded, was a wealthy young lady of this city; one of those whom his distempered imagination fancied was his lost half. Some giddy young persons, with thoughtless cruelty, sought to excite him on this favourite idea, by every species of joke and trickery. They made him believe that the young lady was dying with love for him, but restrained by her father; they sent him let-

ters, purporting to be from her hand; and finally led him to the house, on pre-
tence of introducing him, and then left him on the door-step. The poor fellow
returned to the Carlton House, in high frenzy. The next night but one, he was
found in the streets, kneeling before a poor beggar, to whom he had just given all
his money. The beggar, seeing his forlorn condition, wished to return it, and said,
"Poor fellow, you need it more than I." When the watchman encountered them,
Clarke was writing busily on his knee, the history of his companion, which he
was beseeching him to tell. The cap was blown from his head, on which a pitiless
storm was pelting. The watchman could make nothing of his incoherent talk, and
he was taken to the Egyptian Tombs; a prison where vagabonds and criminals
await their trial.

In the morning he begged that the book-keeper of the Carlton House might be
sent for; saying that he was his only friend. This gentleman conveyed him to the
Lunatic Asylum, on Blackwell's Island. Two of my friends, who visited him there,
found him as comfortable as his situation allowed. He said he was treated with
great kindness, but his earnest desire to get out rendered the interview very heart-
trying. He expressed a wish to recover, that he might write hymns and spiritual
songs all the rest of his life. In some quiet intervals, he complained of the jokes
that had been practised on him, and said it was not kind; but he was fearfully
delirious most of the time — calling vociferously for "Water! Water!" and complaining that his brain was all on fire.

He died a few days after, aged about 44. His friend of the Carlton House took
upon himself the charge of his funeral; and it is satisfactory to think that it was all
ordered, just as the kind and simple-hearted being would have himself desired.
The body was conveyed to Grace church, and the funeral service performed in the
presence of a few who had loved him. Among these was Fitz-Greene Halleck,[14]
who it is said often befriended him in the course of his suffering life. Many children were present; and one, with tearful eyes, brought a beautiful little bunch of
flowers, which a friend laid upon his bosom with reverent tenderness. He was
buried at Greenwood Cemetery, under the shadow of a pine tree, next to the grave
of a little child — a fitting resting place for the loving and childlike poet.

He had often expressed a wish to be buried at Greenwood. Walking there with
a friend of mine, they selected a spot for his grave; and he seemed pleased as a
boy, when told of the arrangements that should be made at his funeral. "I hope
the children will come," said he, "I want to be buried by the side of children. Four
things I am sure there will be in heaven; music, plenty of little children, flowers,
and pure air."

They are now getting up a subscription for a marble monument. It seems out
of keeping with his character and destiny. It were better to plant a rose-bush by
his grave, and mark his name on a simple white cross, that the few who loved him
might know where the gentle, sorrowing wanderer sleeps.

Letter XVI[1]
April 7, 1842

Were you ever near enough to a great fire to be in immediate danger! If you were not, you have missed one form of keen excitement, and awful beauty. Last week, we had here one of the most disastrous conflagrations that have occurred for a long time. It caught, as is supposed, by a spark from a furnace falling on the roof of a wheelwright's shop. A single bucket of water, thrown on immediately, would have extinguished it; but it was not instantly perceived, roofs were dry, and the wind was blowing a perfect March gale. Like slavery in our government, it was not put out in the day of small beginnings, and so went on increasing in its rage, making a great deal of hot and disagreeable work.

It began at the corner of Chrystie-street, not far from our dwelling; and the blazing shingles that came flying through the air, like a storm in the infernal regions, soon kindled our roof. We thought to avert the danger by buckets of water, until the block opposite us was one sheet of fire, and the heat like that of the furnace which tried Shadrach, Meshach and Abednego.[2] Then we began to pack our goods, and run with them in all haste to places of safety; an effort more easily described than done—for the streets all round were filled with a dense mass of living beings, each eager in playing the engines, or saving the *lares* of his own hearth-stone.

Nothing surprised me so much as the rapidity of the work of destruction. At three o'clock in the afternoon, there stood before us a close neighbourhood of houses, inhabited by those whose faces were familiar, though their names were mostly unknown; at five the whole was a pile of smoking ruins. The humble tenement of Jane Plato, the coloured woman, of whose neatly-kept garden and whitewashed fences I wrote you last summer, has passed away forever. The purple iris, and yellow daffodils, and variegated sweet-williams, were all trampled down under heaps of red-hot mortar. I feel a deeper sympathy for the destruction of Jane's little garden, than I do for those who have lost whole blocks of houses; for I have known and loved flowers, like the voice of a friend—but with houses and lands I was never cumbered. In truth, I am ashamed to say how much I grieve for that little flowery oasis in a desert of bricks and stone. My beautiful trees, too—the Ailanthus, whose graceful blossoms, changing their hue from month to month, blessed me the live-long summer; and the glossy young Catalpa, over which it threw its arms so lovingly and free—there they stand, scorched and blackened; and I know not whether nature, with her mighty healing power, can ever make them live again.

The utilitarian and the moralist will rebuke this trifling record, and remind me that one hundred houses were burned, and not less than two thousand persons deprived of shelter for the night.[3] Pardon my childish lamentations. Most gladly would I give a home to all the destitute; but I cannot love two thousand persons;

and I *loved* my trees. Insurance stocks are to me an abstraction; but stock gilli-
flowers a most pleasant reality.

Will your kind heart be shocked that I seem to sympathize more with Jane Plato
for the destruction of her little garden-patch, than I do with others for loss of
houses and furniture?[4]

Do not misunderstand me. It is simply my way of saying that money is not
wealth. I know the universal opinion of mankind is to the contrary; but it is nevertheless a mistake. Our real losses are those in which the *heart* is concerned. An
autograph letter from Napoleon Bonaparte might sell for fifty dollars; but if I
possessed such a rare document, would I save it from the fire, in preference to a
letter from a beloved and deceased husband, filled with dear little household
phrases? Which would a mother value most, the price of the most elegant pair of
Parisian slippers, or a little worn-out shoe, once filled with a precious infant foot,
now walking with the angels?

Jane Plato's garden might not be worth much in dollars and cents; but it was
to her the endeared companion of many a pleasant hour. After her daily toil, she
might be seen, till twilight deepened into evening, digging round the roots, prun-
ing branches, and training vines. I know by experience how very dear inanimate
objects become under such circumstances. I have dearly loved the house in which
I *lived,* but I could not love the one I merely *owned.* The one in which the *purse*
had interest might be ten times more valuable in the market; but let me calculate
as I would, I should mourn most for the one in which the *heart* had invested
stock. The common wild-flower that I have brought to my garden, and nursed,
and petted, till it has lost all home-sickness for its native woods, is *really* more
valuable than the costly exotic, purchased in full bloom from the conservatory.
Men of princely fortunes never know what wealth of happiness there is in a
garden.

> "The rich man in his garden walks,
>   Beneath his garden trees;
> Wrapped in a dream of other things,
>   He seems to take his ease.
> One moment he beholds his flowers,
>   The next they are forgot;
> He eateth of his rarest fruits,
>   As though he ate them not.
> It is not with the poor man so;
>   He knows each inch of ground,
> And every single plant and flower,
>   That grows within its bound.
> And though his garden-plot is small,
>   Him doth it satisfy;

For there's no inch of all his ground,
    That does not fill his eye.
It is not with the rich man thus;
    For though his grounds are wide,
He looks beyond, and yet beyond,
    With soul unsatisfied.
Yes, in the poor man's garden grow
    Far more than herbs and flowers;
Kind thoughts, contentment, peace of mind,
    And joy for weary hours."

The reason of this difference is easily explained:

"The rich man has his gardeners—
    His gardeners young and old;
He never takes a spade in hand,
    Nor worketh in the mould.
It is not with the poor man so—
    Wealth, servants, he has none;
And all the work that's done for him,
    Must by *himself* be done."

I have said this much to prove that money is *not* wealth, and that *God's* gifts are equal;[5] though joint-stock companies and corporations do their worst to prevent it.

And all the highest *truths,* as well as the genuine *good,* are universal. Doctrinal dogmas may be hammered out on theological anvils, and appropriated to spiritual corporations, called sects. But those high and holy truths, which make the soul at one with God and the neighbour, are by their very nature universal— open to all who wish to receive. Outward forms are always in harmonious correspondence with inward realities; therefore the material types of highest truths defy man's efforts to monopolize. Who can bottle up the sunlight, to sell at retail? or issue dividends of the ocean and the breeze?

This great fire,[6] like all calamities, public or private, has its bright side. A portion of New-York, and that not a small one, is for once thoroughly cleaned; a wide space is opened for our vision, and the free passage of the air. True, it looks desolate enough now; like a battle-field, when waving banners and rushing steeds, and fife and trumpet all are gone; and the dead alone remain. But the dreary sight ever brings up images of those hundred volcanoes spouting flame, and of the scene at midnight, so fearful in its beauty. Where houses so lately stood, and welcome feet passed over the threshold, and friendly voices cheered the fireside, there arose the lurid gleam of mouldering fires, with rolling masses of smoke, as if watched by giants from the nether world; and between them all lay the thick darkness. It was strikingly like Martin's pictures.[7] The resemblance renewed my old impression, that if the arts are cultivated in the infernal regions, of such are their galleries formed; not without a startling beauty, which impresses, while it disturbs the mind, because it embodies the idea of Power, and its discords bear harmonious relation to each other.

If you wanted to see the real, unqualified beauty of fire, you should have stood with me, in the darkness of evening, to gaze at a burning house nearly opposite. Four long hours it sent forth flame in every variety. Now it poured forth from the windows, like a broad banner on the wind; then it wound round the door-posts like a brilliant wreath; and from the open roof there ever went up a fountain of sparks, that fell like a shower of gems. I watched it for hours, and could not turn away from it. In my mind there insensibly grew up a respect for that house; because it defied the power of the elements, so bravely and so long. It must have been built of sound timber, well-jointed; and as the houses round it had fallen, its conflagration was not hastened by excessive heat, as the others had been.[8] It was one o'clock at night when the last tongue of flame flickered and died reluctantly. The next day, men came by order of the city authorities, to pull down the walls. This, too, the brave building resisted to the utmost. Ropes were fastened to it with grappling irons, and a hundred men tugged, and tugged at it, in vain. My respect for it increased, till it seemed to me like an heroic friend. I could not bear that it should fall. It seemed to me, if it did, I should no longer feel sure that J. Q. Adams and Giddings would stand on their feet against Southern aggression.[9] I sent up a joyous shout when the irons came out, bringing away only a few bricks, and the men fell backward from the force of the shock. But at last the walls reeled, and came down with a thundering crash. Nevertheless, I will trust Adams and Giddings, tug at them as they may.

By the blessing of heaven on the energy and presence of mind of those who came to our help, our walls stand unscathed, and nothing was destroyed in the tumult; but our hearts are aching; for all round us comes a voice of wailing from the houseless and the impoverished.[10]

Letter XVII [1]
April 14, 1842

In looking over some of my letters, my spirit stands reproved for its sadness. In this working-day world, where the bravest have need of all their buoyancy and strength, it is sinful to add our sorrows to the common load. Blessed are the missionaries of cheerfulness!

> "Tis glorious to have one's own proud will,
> And see the crown acknowledged, that we earn;
> But nobler yet, and nearer to the skies,

To feel one's self, in hours serene and still,
One of the spirits chosen by Heaven to turn
The *sunny* side of things to human eyes."

The fault was in my own spirit rather than in the streets of New-York. "Who *has* no inward beauty, none *perceives,* though all around is beautiful." Had my soul been at one with Nature and with God, I should not have seen *only* misery and vice in my city rambles. To-day, I have been *so* happy in Broadway! A multitude of doves went careering before me. Now wheeling in graceful circles, their white wings and breasts glittering in the sunshine; now descending within the shadow of the houses, like a cloud; now soaring high up in the sky, till they seemed immense flocks of dusky butterflies; and ever as I walked they went before me, with most loving companionship. If they had anything to say to me, I surely understood their language, though I heard it not; for through my whole frame there went a feathery buoyancy, a joyous uprising from the earth, as if I too had wings, with conscious power to use them. Then they brought such sweet images to my mind! I remembered the story of the pirate hardened in blood and crime, who listened to the notes of a turtle-dove in the stillness of evening. Perhaps he had never before heard the soothing tones of love. They spoke to his inmost soul, like the voice of an angel; and wakened such response there, that he thenceforth became a holy man. Then I thought how I would like to have this the mission of *my* spirit; to speak to hardened and suffering hearts, in the tones of a turtle-dove.

My flying companions brought before me another picture which has had a place in the halls of memory for several years. I was once visiting a friend in prison for debt; and through the grated window, I could see the outside of the criminals' apartments. On the stone ledges, beneath their windows, alighted three or four doves; and hard hands were thrust out between the iron bars, to sprinkle crumbs for them. The sight brought tears to my eyes. Hearts that still loved to feed doves must certainly contain somewhat that might be reached by the voice of kindness. I had not then reasoned on the subject; but I felt, even then, that prisons were not such spiritual hospitals as ought to be provided for the erring brothers. The birds themselves were not of snowy plumage; their little, rose-coloured feet were spattered with mud, and their feathers were soiled, as if they, too, were jail birds. The outward influences of a city had passed over them, as the inward had over those who fed them; nevertheless, they are doves, said I, and have all a dove's instincts. It was a significant lesson, and I laid it to my heart.

But these Broadway doves, ever wheeling before me in graceful eddies, why did their aerial frolic produce such joyous elasticity in my physical frame? Was it sympathy with nature, so intimate that her motions became my own? Or was it a revealing that the spiritual body had wings, wherewith I should hereafter fly?

The pleasant, buoyant sensation recalled to my mind a dream which I read, many years ago, in Doddridge's Life and Correspondence.[2] I will not vouch for it, that my copy is a likeness of the original. If anything is added, I know not where I obtained it, unless Doddridge himself has since told me. I surely have no *intention* to add any thing of my own. I do not profess to give anything like the language; for the words have passed from my memory utterly. As I remember the dream, it was thus:

Dr. Doddridge had been spending the evening with his friend, Dr. Watts. Their conversation had been concerning the future existence of the soul. Long and earnestly they pursued the theme; and both came to the conclusion, (rather a remarkable one for theologians of that day to arrive at) that it could not be they were to sing through all eternity; that each soul must necessarily be an individual, and have its appropriate employment for thought and affection. As Doddridge walked home, his mind brooded over these ideas, and took little cognizance of outward matters. In this state he laid his head upon the pillow and fell asleep. He dreamed that he was dying; he saw his weeping friends round his bedside, and wanted to speak to them, but could not. Presently there came a nightmare sensation. His soul was about to leave the body; but how would it get out? More and more anxiously rose the query, how could it get out? This uneasy state passed away; and he found that the soul *had* left his body. He himself stood beside the bed, looking at his own corpse, as if it were an old garment, laid aside as useless. His friends wept round the mortal covering, but could not see *him*.

While he was reflecting upon this, he passed out of the room, he knew not how; but presently he found himself floating over London, as if pillowed on a cloud borne by gentle breezes. Far below him, the busy multitude were hurrying hither and thither, like rats and mice scampering for crumbs. "Ah," thought the emancipated spirit, "how worse than foolish appears this feverish scramble. For what do they toil? and what do they obtain?"

London passed away beneath him, and he found himself floating over green fields and blooming gardens. How is it that I am borne through the air? thought he. He looked, and saw a large purple wing; and then he knew that he was carried by an angel. "Whither are we going?" said he. "To Heaven," was the reply. He asked no more questions; but remained in delicious quietude, as if they floated on a strain of music. At length they paused before a white marble temple, of exquisite beauty. The angel lowered his flight, and gently placed him on the steps. "I thought you were taking me to Heaven," said the spirit. "This is Heaven," replied the angel. "This! Assuredly this temple is of rare beauty; but I could imagine just such built on earth." "Nevertheless, it is Heaven," replied the angel.

They entered a room just within the temple. A table stood in the centre, on which was a golden vase, filled with sparkling wine. "Drink of this," said the angel, offering the vase; "for all who would know spiritual things, must first drink of spiritual wine." Scarcely had the ruby liquid wet his lips, when the Saviour of men stood before him, smiling most benignly. The spirit instantly dropped on his knees, and bowed down his head before Him. The holy hands of the Purest were folded over him in blessing; and his voice said, "You will see me seldom now; hereafter, you will see me more frequently. In the meantime, *observe well the wonders of this temple!*"

The sounds ceased. The spirit remained awhile in stillness. When he raised his head, the Saviour no longer appeared. He turned to ask the angel what this could mean; but the angel had departed also. The soul stood alone, in its own unveiled presence! "Why did the Holy One tell me to observe well the wonders of this temple?" thought he. He looked slowly round. A sudden start of joy and wonder! *There, painted on the walls, in most marvellous beauty, stood recorded the whole of his spiritual life!* Every doubt, and every clear perception, every conflict and every victory, were there before him! and though forgotten for years, he knew them at a glance. Even thus had a sunbeam pierced the darkest cloud, and thrown a rainbow bridge from the finite to the infinite; thus had he slept peacefully in green valleys, by the side of running brooks; and such had been his visions from the mountain tops. He knew them all. They had been always painted within the chambers of his soul; but now, for the first time, was the veil removed.

To those who *think* on spiritual things, this remarkable dream is too deeply and beautifully significant ever to be forgotten.

> "We shape *ourselves* the joy or fear
>   Of which the coming life is made,
> And fill our Future's atmosphere
>   With sunshine or with shade.
> Still shall the soul around it call
>   The shadows which it gathered *here*,
> And painted on the eternal wall
>   The Past shall reappear."

I do not mean that the *paintings*, and *statues*, and *houses*, which a man has made on earth, will form his environment in the world of souls; this would monopolize Heaven for the wealthy and the cultivated. I mean that the *spiritual* combats and victories of our pilgrimage, write themselves there above, in infinite variations of form, colour, and tone; and thus shall every word and thought be brought unto judgment. Of these things inscribed in Heaven, who can tell what may be the action upon souls newly born into time? Perhaps all lovely forms of Art are mere ultimates of *spiritual* victories in individual souls. It may be that all *genius* derives its life from some *holiness*, which preceded it, in the attainment of another spirit. Who shall venture to assert that Beethoven *could* have produced his strangely powerful music, had not souls gone before him on earth, who with infinite struggling against temptation, aspired toward the Highest, and in some degree realized their aspiration? The music thus brought from the eternal world kindles still higher spiritual aspirations in mortals, to be realized in this life, and

again written above, to inspire anew some gifted spirit, who stands a ready recipient in the far-off time. Upon this ladder, how beautifully the angels are seen
ascending and descending![3]

Letter XVIII[1]
May 26, 1842

The Battery is growing charming again, now that Nature has laid aside her pearls,
and put on her emeralds. The worst of it is, crowds are flocking there morning
and evening; yet I am ashamed of that anti-social sentiment. It does my heart
good to see the throng of children trundling their hoops and rolling on the grass;
some, with tattered garments and dirty hands, come up from narrow lanes and
stifled courts, and others with pale faces and weak limbs, the sickly occupants of
heated drawing-rooms. But while I rejoice for their sakes, I cannot overcome my
aversion to a multitude. It is so pleasant to run and jump, and throw pebbles, and
make up faces at a friend, without having a platoon of well-dressed people turn
round and stare, and ask, "Who *is* that strange woman, that acts so like a child?"
Those who are truly enamoured of Nature, love to be alone with her. It is with
them as with other lovers; the intrusion of strangers puts to flight a thousand
sweet fancies, as fairies are said to scamper at the approach of a mortal footstep.

I rarely see the Battery, without thinking how beautiful it must have been
before the white man looked upon it; when the tall, solemn forest came down to
the water's edge, and bathed in the moonlight stillness. The solitary Indian[2] came
out from the dense shadows, and stood in the glorious brightness. As he leaned
thoughtfully on his bow, his crest of eagles' feathers waved slowly in the gentle
evening breeze; and voices from the world of spirits spoke into his heart, and
stirred it with a troubled reverence, which he felt, but could not comprehend. To
us, likewise, they are ever speaking through many-voiced Nature: the soul, in its
quiet hour, listens intently to the friendly entreaty, and strives to guess its meaning. All round us, on hill and dale, the surging ocean and the evening cloud, they
have spread open the illuminated copy of their scriptures—revealing all things,
if we could but learn the language!

The Indian did not *think* this; but he *felt* it, even as I do. What have we gained
by civilization? It is a circling question, the beginning and end of which everywhere touch each other. One thing is certain; they who pass through the ordeal
of high civilization, with garments unspotted by the crowd, will make far higher
and holier angels; will love more, and know more, than they who went to their
Father's house through the lonely forest-path. But looking at it only in relation to
this earth, there is much to be said in favour of that wild life of savage freedom,
as well as much against it. It would be so pleasant to get rid of that nightmare of

civilized life—"What will Mrs. Smith say?" and "Do you suppose folks will think strange?" It is true that phantom troubles *me* but little; having snapped my fingers in its face years ago, it mainly vexes me by keeping me for ever from a full insight into the souls of others.

Should I have learned more of the spirit's life, could I have wandered at midnight with Pocahontas, on this fair island of Manhattan? I should have, at least, learned *all*; the soul of Nature's child might have lisped, and stammered in broken sentences, but it would not have muttered through a mask.

The very name of this island brings me back to civilization, by a most unpleasant path. It was in the autumn of 1609 that the celebrated Hudson[3] first entered the magnificent river that now bears his name, in his adventurous yacht, The Half Moon. The simple Indians were attracted by the red garments and bright buttons of the strangers; and as usual, their new friendship was soon sealed with the accursed "fire-water." On the island where the city now stands, they had a great carouse; and the Indians, in commemoration thereof, named it Manahachtanienks, abbreviated, by rapid speech, to Manhattan. The meaning of it is, *"The Place where all got Drunk Together."*[4] As I walk through the crowded streets, I am sometimes inclined to think the name is by no means misapplied at the present day.

New-York is beautiful now, with its broad rivers glancing in the sunbeams, its numerous islands, like fairy homes, and verdant headlands jutting out in graceful curves into its spacious harbour, where float the vessels of a hundred nations. But oh, how beautiful it must have been, when the thick forest hung all round Hudson's lonely bark! When the wild deer bounded through paths where swine now grunt and grovel! *That* chapter of the world's history was left unrecorded here below; but historians above have it on their tablets; for it wrote itself there in daguerreotype.

Of times far less ancient, the vestiges are passing away; recalled sometimes by names bringing the most contradictory association. Maiden-lane is now one of the busiest of commercial streets; the sky shut out with bricks and mortar; gutters on either side, black as the ancients imagined the rivers of hell; thronged with sailors and draymen; and redolent of all wharf-like smells. Its name, significant of innocence and youthful beauty, was given in the olden time, when a clear, sparking rivulet here flowed from an abundant spring, and the young Dutch girls went and came with baskets on their heads, to wash and bleach linen in the flowing stream, and on the verdant grass.

Greenwich-street, which now rears its huge masses of brick, and shows only a long vista of dirt and paving-stones, was once a beautiful beach, where boys and horses went in to bathe. In the middle of what is now the street, was a large rock, on which was built a rude summer-house, from which the merry bathers loved to jump, with splash and ringing shouts of laughter.

I know not from what Pearl-street derives its name; but, in more senses than one, it is now obviously a "pearl cast before swine."[5]

The Bowery, with name so flowery, where the discord of a thousand wheels is overtopped by shrill street-cries, was a line of orchards and mowing-land, in rear of the olden city, called in Dutch, the Bouwerys, or Farms; and in popular phrase, "The High Road to Boston." In 1631, old Governor Stuyvesant bought the "Bouwerys," (now so immensely valuable, in the market sense,) for 6,400 guilders, or 1,066; houses, barn, six cows, two horses, and two young negro slaves, were included with the land. He built a Reformed Dutch church at his own expense, on his farm, within the walls of which was the family vault. The church of St. Mark now occupies the same site, and on the outside wall stands his original grave stone, thus inscribed:

> "In this vault lies buried Petrus Stuyvesant, late Captain-General and Commander-in-Chief of Amsterdam in New-Netherland, now called New-York, and the Dutch West India Islands. Died August, A.D. 1682, aged 80 years."[6]

A pear tree stands without the wall, still vigorous, though brought from Holland and planted there by the governor himself. His family, still among the wealthiest of our city aristocracy, have preserved some curious memorials of their venerable Dutch ancestor. A portrait in armour, well executed in Holland, probably while he was admiral there, represents him as a dark complexioned man, with strong, bold features, and moustaches on the upper lip. They likewise preserve the shirt in which he was christened; of the finest Holland linen, edged with narrow lace.

Near the Battery is an inclosure, called the Bowling Green, where once stood a leaden statue of George II.;[7] an appropriate metal for the heavy house of Hanover. During the revolution, the poor king was pulled down and dragged irreverently through the streets, to be melted into bullets for the war. He would have deemed this worse than being

> "Turned to clay,
> To stop a hole to keep the wind away."

However, the purpose to which his image was applied, would probably have been less abhorrent to him, than it would be to the apostles to know the uses to which *they* are applied by modern Christians.[8]

The *antiquities*[9] of New-York! In this new and ever-changing country, what ridiculous associations are aroused by that word! For us, tradition has no desolate arches, no dim and cloistered aisles. People change their abodes so often, that, as Washington Irving wittily suggests, the very ghosts, if they are disposed to keep up an ancient custom, don't know where to call upon them.

This newness, combined with all surrounding social influences, tends to make us an irreverential people. It was the frequent remark of Mr. Combe,[10] that of all nations, whose heads he had ever had an opportunity to observe, the Americans had the organ of veneration the least developed. No wonder that it is so. Instead of moss-grown ruins, we have trim brick houses; instead of cathedrals, with their "dim, religious light," we have new meeting-houses, built on speculation, with four-and-twenty windows on each side, and at both ends, for the full enjoyment of cross-lights; instead of the dark and echoing recesses of the cloister, we have ready-made coffins in the shop-windows; instead of the rainbow halo of poetic philosophy, we have Franklin's maxims for "Poor Richard;"[11] and in lieu of kings divinely ordained, or governments heaven-descended, we have administrations turned in and out of office at every whirl of the ballot-box.

"This democratic experiment will prove a failure," said an old-fashioned federalist; "before fifty years are ended, we shall be governed by a king in this country." "And where will you get the *blood?*" inquired an Irishman, with earnest simplicity; "sure you will have to send over the water to get some of the blood." Whereupon, irreverent listeners laughed outright, and asked wherein a king's blood differed from that of an Irish ditch-digger. The poor fellow was puzzled. Could he have comprehended the question, I would have asked, "And if we could import the kingly blood, how could we import the sentiment of loyalty?"

The social world, as well as the world of matter, must have its centrifugal as well as centripetal force; and we Americans must perform that office; an honourable and useful one it is, yet not the most beautiful, nor in all respects the most desirable. Reverence is the highest quality of man's nature; and that individual, or nation, which has it slightly developed, is so far unfortunate. It is a strong spiritual instinct, and seeks to form channels for itself where none exists; thus Americans, in the dearth of other objects to worship, fall to worshipping themselves.

Now don't laugh, if you can help it, at what I bring forth as *antiquities.* Just keep the Parthenon, the Alhambra, and the ruins of Melrose out of your head, if you please; and pay due respect to my *American* antiquities.[12] At the corner of Bayard and Bowery, you will see a hotel, called the North American; and on the top thereof you may spy a wooden image of a lad with ragged knees and elbows, whose mother doesn't know they're out. That image commemorates the history of a Yankee boy, by the name of David Reynolds. Some fifty years ago, he came here at the age of twelve or fourteen, without a copper in his pocket. I think he had run away; at all events, he was alone and friendless. Weary and hungry, he leaned against a tree, where the hotel now stands; every eye looked strange upon him, and he felt utterly forlorn and disheartened. While he was trying to devise some honest means to obtain food, a gentleman inquired for a boy to carry his trunk to the wharf; and the Yankee eagerly offered his services. For this job he received twenty-five cents; most of which he spent in purchasing fruit to sell again. He stationed himself by the friendly tree, where he had first obtained employment, and soon disposed of his little stock to advantage. With increased capital

he increased his stock. He must have managed his business with Yankee shrewdness, or perhaps he was a cross of Scotch and Yankee; for he soon established a
respectable fruit stall under the tree; and then he bought a small shop, that stood
within its shade; and then he purchased a lot of land, including several buildings
round; and finally he pulled down the old shop, and the old houses, and built the
large hotel which now stands there. The old tree seemed to him like home. There
he had met with his first good luck in a strange city; and from day to day, and
month to month, those friendly boughs had still looked down upon his rising
fortune. He would not desert that which had stood by him in the dreary days of
poverty and trial. It must be removed, to make room for the big mansion; but it
should not be destroyed. From its beloved trunk he caused his image to be
carved, as a memento of his own forlorn beginnings, and his grateful recollections. That it might tell a truthful tale, and remind him of early struggles, the rich
citizen of New-York caused it to be carved, with ragged trowsers, and jacket out
at elbows.

There is a curious relic of bygone days over the door of a public house in Hudson street, between Hamersley street and Greenwich Bank, of which few guess
the origin. It is the sign of a fish, with a ring in its mouth. Tradition says, that in
the year 1743, a young nobleman, disguised as a sailor, won the heart of a beautiful village maiden, on the western coast of England. It is the old story of woman's
fondness, and woman's faith. She trusted him, and he deceived her. At their parting, they exchanged rings of betrothal. Time passed on, and she heard no more
from him; till at last there came the insulting offer of money, as a remuneration
for her ruined happiness, and support for herself and child. Some time after, she
learned, to her great surprise, that he was a nobleman of high rank in the royal
navy, and that his ship was lying near the coast. She sought his vessel, and conjured him by all recollections of her confiding love, and of his own earnest protes-
tations, to do her justice. At first, he was moved; but her pertinacity vexed him,
until he treated her with angry scorn, for presuming to think she could ever become his wife. "God forgive you," said the weeping beauty; "let us exchange our
rings again; give me back the one I gave you. It was my mother's; and I could not
have parted with it to any but my betrothed husband. There is your money; not
a penny of it will I ever use; it cannot restore my good name, or heal my broken
heart. I will labour to support your child." In a sudden fit of anger, he threw the
ring into the sea, saying, "When you can recover that bauble from the fishes, you
may expect to be the wife of a British nobleman. I give you my word of honour
to marry you then, and not till then."

Sadly and wearily the maiden walked home with her poor old father. On their
way, the old man bought a fish that was offered him, just taken from the sea.
When the fish was prepared for supper that night, lo! the ring was found in its
stomach!

When informed of this fact, the young nobleman was so strongly impressed with the idea that it was a direct interposition of Providence, that he did not venture to break the promise he had given. He married the village belle, and they lived long and happily together. When he died, an obelisk was erected to his memory, surmounted by the effigy of a fish with a ring in its mouth. Such a story was of course sung and told by wandering beggars and travelling merchants, until it became universal tradition. Some old emigrant brought it over to this country; and there in Hudson street hang the Fish and the Ring, to commemorate the loves of a past century.

Now laugh if you will; I think I have made out quite a respectable collection of American antiquities. If I seem to you at times to look back too lovingly on the Past, do not understand me as quarrelling with the Present. Sometimes, it is true, I am tempted to say of the Nineteenth Century, as the exile from New Zealand did of the huge scramble in London streets, "Me no like London. Shove me about."

Often, too, I am disgusted to see men trying to pull down the false, not for love of the true, but for their own selfish purposes. But notwithstanding these drawbacks, I gratefully acknowledge my own age and country as pre-eminently marked by activity and progress. Brave spirits are everywhere at work for freedom, peace, temperance, and education. Everywhere the walls of caste and sect are melting before them; everywhere dawns the golden twilight of universal love! Many are working for all these things, who have the dimmest insight into the infinity of their relations, and the eternity of their results; some, perchance, could they perceive the relation that each bears to all, would eagerly strive to undo what they are now doing; but luckily, heart and hand often work for better things than the head wots of.

Letter XIX [1]
June 2, 1842

You seem very curious to learn what I think of recent phenomena in animal magnetism, or mesmerism, which you have described to me. They have probably impressed your mind more than my own; because I was ten years ago convinced that animal magnetism was destined to produce great changes in the science of medicine, and in the whole philosophy of spirit and matter. The reports of French physicians, guarded as they were on every side by the scepticism that characterizes their profession and their country, contained amply enough to convince me that animal magnetism was not a nine-days' wonder. That there has been a great deal of trickery, collusion and imposture, in connection with this subject, is obvious enough. Its very nature renders it peculiarly liable to this; whatsoever relates to spiritual existence cannot be explained by the laws of matter, and therefore becomes at once a powerful temptation to deception. For this reason, I have taken too little interest in public exhibitions of animal magnetism ever to attend one; I should always observe them with distrust.[2] But it appears to me that nothing can be more unphilosophic than the ridicule attached to a belief in mesmerism. Phenomena of the most extraordinary character have occurred, proved by a cloud of witnesses. If these things have really happened, (as thousands of intelligent and rational people testify,) they are governed by laws as fixed and certain as the laws that govern matter. We call them miracles, simply because we do not understand the causes that produce them; and what *do* we fully understand? Our knowledge is exceedingly imperfect, even with regard to the laws of matter; though the world has had the experience of several thousand years to help its investigations. We cannot see that the majestic oak lies folded up in the acorn; still less can we tell how it came there. We have observed that a piece of wood decays in the damp ground, while a nut generates and becomes a tree; and we say it is because there is a principle of vitality in the nut, which is not in the wood; but explain, if you can, what *is* a principle of vitality? and how *came* it in the acorn?

They, who reject the supernatural, claim to be the only philosophers, in these days, when, as Peter Parley[3] says, "every little child knows all about the rainbow." Satisfied with the tangible inclosures of their own penfold, these are not aware that whosoever *did* know *all* about the rainbow, would know enough to make a world. *Super*natural simply means *above* the natural. Between the laws that govern the higher and the lower, there is doubtless the most perfect harmony; and this we should perceive and understand, if we had the enlarged faculties of angels.

There is something exceedingly arrogant and short-sighted in the pretensions of those who ridicule everything not capable of being proved to the senses. They are like a man who holds a penny close to his eye, and then denies that there is a glorious firmament of stars, because *he* cannot see them. Carlyle gives the following sharp rebuke to this annoying class of thinkers:—"Thou wilt have no mystery and mysticism? Wilt walk through the world by the sunshine of what thou callest logic? Thou wilt *explain* all, *account* for all, or believe nothing of it? Nay, thou wilt even attempt laughter?"

"Whoso recognises the unfathomable, all-pervading domain of mystery, which is everywhere under our feet and among our hands; to whom the universe is an *oracle* and a *temple*, as well as *kitchen* and *cattle-stall*—he shall be called a mystic, and delirious? To him thou, with sniffing charity, wilt protrusively proffer thy hand-lamp, and shriek, as one injured, when he kicks his foot through it?[4] Wert thou not *born?* Wilt thou not *die?* Explain me all *this*—or do one of two things: retire into private places with thy foolish cackle; or, what were better, give it up; and weep not that the reign of wonder is done, and God's world all disembellished and prosaic, but that thou thyself art hitherto a sand-blind pedant."

But if there be any truth in the wonders of animal magnetism, why has not the world heard of them before? asks the inquirer. The world *did* hear of them, centuries ago; and from time to time they have re-appeared, and arrested local and temporary attention; but not being understood, and not being conveyed to the human mind through the medium of religious belief, they were soon rejected as fabulous stories, or idle superstitions; no one thought of examining them, as phenomena governed by laws which regulate the universe.

It is recorded that when the plague raged in Athens, in the days of Plato, many recovered from it with a total oblivion of all *outward* things; they seemed to themselves to be living among other scenes, which were as real to them, as the material world was to others. The wisdom of angels, perchance, perceived it to be far *more* real.

Ancient history records that a learned Persian Magus[5] who resided among the mountains that overlooked Taoces, recovered from the plague with a perpetual oblivion of all outward forms, while he often had knowledge of the thoughts passing in the minds of those around him. If an unknown scroll were placed before him, he would read it, though a brazen shield were interposed between him and the parchment; and if figures were drawn on the water, he at once recognised the forms, of which no visible trace remained.

In Taylor's Plato,[6] mention is made of one Clearchus, who related an experiment tried in the presence of Aristotle and his disciples at the Lyceum. He declares that a man, by means of moving a wand up and down, over the body of a lad, "led the soul out of it," and left the form perfectly rigid and senseless; when he afterward led the soul back, it told, with wonderful accuracy, all that had been said and done.

This reminds me of a singular circumstance which happened to a venerable friend of mine. I had it from her own lips. She was taken suddenly ill one day, and swooned. To all appearance, she was entirely lifeless; insomuch that her friends feared she was really dead. A physician was sent for and a variety of experiments tried, before there were any symptoms of returning animation. She herself was merely aware of a dizzy and peculiar sensation, and then she found herself standing by her own lifeless body, watching all their efforts to resuscitate it. It seemed to her strange, and she was too confused to know whether she were in that body, or out of it. In the mean time, her anxious friends could not make the slightest impression on the rigid form, either by sight, hearing, touch, taste, or smell; it was to all appearance dead. The five outward gates of entrance to the soul were shut and barred. Yet when the body revived, she told everything that had been done in the room, every word that had been said, and the very expression of their countenances. The soul had stood by all the while, and observed what was done to the body. How did it see when the eyes were closed, like a corpse? Answer that, before you disbelieve a thing because you cannot understand it. Could I comprehend how the simplest violet came into existence, I too would urge that plea. It were as wise for a child of four years old to deny that the planets move round the sun, because its infant mind cannot receive the explanation, as for you and me to ridicule arcana of the soul's connection with the body, because we cannot comprehend them, in this imperfect state of existence. Beings so ignorant, should be more humble and reverential; this frame of mind has no affinity whatever with the greedy superstition that is eager to believe everything, merely *because* it is wonderful.

It is deemed incredible that people in magnetic sleep[7] can describe objects at a distance, and scenes which they never looked upon while waking; yet nobody doubts the common form of somnambulism, called sleep walking. You may singe the eye-lashes of a sleep walker with a candle, and he will perceive neither you nor the light. His eyes have no expression; they are like those of a corpse. Yet he will walk out in the dense darkness, avoiding chairs, tables and all other obstructions; he will tread the ridge-pole of a roof, far more securely than he could in a natural state, at mid-day; he will harness horses, pack wood, make shoes, &c. all in the darkness of midnight. Can you tell me with what *eyes* he sees to do these things? and what *light* directs him? If you cannot, be humble enough to acknowledge that God governs the universe by many laws incomprehensible to you; and be wise enough to conclude that these phenomena are not deviations from the divine order of things, but occasional manifestations of principles always at work in the great scale of being, made visible at times, by causes as yet unrevealed.

Allowing very largely for falsehood, trickery, superstitious fear, and stimulated imagination, I still believe most fully that many things now rejected as foolish superstitions, will hereafter take their appropriate place in a new science of spiritual philosophy.[8] From the progress of animal magnetism, there may perhaps be evolved much that will throw light upon old stories of oracles, witchcraft, and second-sight. A large portion of these stories are doubtless falsehoods, fabricated for the most selfish and mischievous purposes; others may be an honest record of things as they actually seemed to the narrator. Those which are true, assuredly have a *cause;* and are miraculous only as our whole being is miraculous. Is not *life* itself the highest miracle? Everybody can tell you what it *does,* but where is the wise man who can explain what it *is? When* did the infant receive that mysterious gift? *Whence* did it come? *Whither* does it go, when it leaves the body?

Scottish legends abound with instances of second-sight, oftentimes supported by a formidable array of evidence; but I have met only one individual who was the subject of such a story.

She is a woman of plain practical sense, very unimaginative, intelligent, extremely well-informed, and as truthful as the sun. I tell the story as she told it to me. One of her relatives was seized with rapid consumption. He had for some weeks been perfectly resigned to die; but one morning, when she called upon him, she found his eyes brilliant, his cheeks flushed with an unnatural bloom, and his mind full of belief that he should recover health. He talked eagerly of voyages he would take, and of the renovating influence of warmer climes. She listened to him with sadness; for she was well acquainted with his treacherous disease, and in all these things she saw symptoms of approaching death. She said this to her mother and sisters, when she returned home. In the afternoon of the same day, as she sat sewing in the usual family circle, she accidently looked up—and gave a sudden start, which immediately attracted attention and inquiry. She replied, "Don't you see cousin——?"

They thought she had been dreaming; but she said, "I certainly am not asleep. It is strange you do not see him; he is there." The next thought was that she was seized with sudden insanity; but she assured them that she was never more rational in her life: that she could not account for the circumstance, any more than they could; but her cousin certainly was there, and looking at her with a very pleasant countenance. Her mother tried to turn it off as a delusion; but nevertheless, she was so much impressed by it, that she looked at her watch, and immediately sent to inquire how the invalid did. The messenger returned with news that he was dead, and had died at that moment.

My friend told me that at first she saw only the bust; but gradually the whole form became visible, as if some imperceptible cloud, or veil, had slowly rolled away; the invisible veil again rose, till only the bust remained; and then that vanished.

She said the vision did not terrify her at the time; it simply perplexed her, as a thing incomprehensible. Why *she* saw it, she could explain no better than why her mother and sisters did *not* see it. She simply told it to me just as it appeared to her; as distinct and real as any other individual in the room.

Men would not be afraid to see spirits, if they were better acquainted with their own. It is because we live so entirely in the body, that we are startled at a revelation of the soul.

Animal magnetism will come out from all the shams and quackery that have made it ridiculous, and will yet be acknowledged as an important aid to science, an additional proof of immortality, and a means, in the hands of Divine Providence, to arrest the progress of materialism.

For myself, I am deeply thankful for *any* agency, that even momentarily blows aside the thick veil between the Finite and the Infinite, and gives me never so hurried and imperfect a glimpse of realities which lie beyond this valley of shadows.

Letter XX [1]
June 9, 1842

There is nothing which makes me feel the imprisonment of a city, like the absence of birds. Blessings on the little warblers! Lovely types are they of all winged and graceful thoughts. Dr. Follen [2] used to say, "I feel dependent for a vigorous and hopeful spirit on now and then a kind word, the loud laugh of a child, or the silent greeting of a flower." Fully do I sympathize with this utterance of his gentle, and loving spirit; but more than the benediction of the flower, more perhaps than even the mirth of childhood, is the clear, joyous note of the bird, a refreshment to my soul.

> "The birds! the birds of summer hours
>   They bring a gush of glee,
> To the child among the fragrant flowers,
>   To the sailor on the sea.
> We hear their thrilling voices
>   In their swift and airy flight,
> And the inmost heart rejoices
>   With a calm and pure delight.
> Amid the morning's fragrant dew,
>   Amidst the mists of even,
> They warble on, as if they drew
>   Their music down from Heaven.
> And when their holy anthems
>   Come pealing through the air,
> Our hearts leap forth to meet them,
>   With a blessing and a prayer."

But alas! like the free voices of fresh youth, they come not on the city air. Thus should it be; where mammon imprisons all thoughts and feelings that would fly upward, their winged types should be in cages too. Walk down Mulberry street,[3] and you may see, in one small room, hundreds of little feathered songsters, each hopping about restlessly in his gilded and garlanded cage, like a dyspeptic merchant in his marble mansion. I always turn my head away when I pass; for the sight of the little captives goes through my heart like an arrow. The darling little creatures have such visible delight in freedom;

> "In the joyous song they sing;
>   In the liquid air they cleave;
> In the sunshine; in the shower;
>   In the nests they weave."

I seldom see a bird encaged, without being reminded of Petion,[4] a truly great man, the popular idol of Haiti, as Washington is of the United States.

While Petion administered the government of the island, some distinguished foreigner sent his little daughter a beautiful bird, in a very handsome cage. The child was delighted, and with great exultation exhibited the present to her father. "It is indeed very beautiful, my daughter," said he; "but it makes my heart ache to look at it. I hope you will never show it to me again."

With great astonishment, she inquired his reasons. He replied, "When this island was called St. Domingo, we were all slaves. It makes me think of it to look at that bird; for *he* is a slave."

The little girl's eyes filled with tears, and her lips quivered, as she exclaimed, "Why, father! he has such a large, handsome cage; and as much as ever he can eat and drink."

"And would *you* be a slave," said he, "if you could live in a great house, and be fed on frosted cake?"

After a moment's thought, the child began to say, half reluctantly, "Would he be happier, if I opened the door of his cage?" "He would be *free!*" was the emphatic reply. Without another word, she took the cage to the open window, and a moment after, she saw her prisoner playing with the humming-birds among the honey-suckles.

One of the most remarkable cases of instinctive knowledge in birds was often related by my grandfather, who witnessed the fact with his own eyes. He was attracted to the door, one summer day, by a troubled twittering, indicating distress and terror. A bird, who had built her nest in a tree near the door, was flying back and forth with the utmost speed, uttering wailing cries as she went. He was at first at a loss to account for her strange movements; but they were soon explained by the sight of a snake slowly winding up the tree.

Animal magnetism was then unheard of; and whosoever had dared to mention it, would doubtless have been hung on Witch's Hill,[5] without benefit of clergy. Nevertheless, marvellous and altogether unaccountable stories had been told of the snake's power to charm birds. The popular belief was that the serpent charmed the bird by *looking steadily at it; and that such a sympathy was thereby established, that if the snake were struck, the bird felt the blow, and writhed under it.*[6]

These traditions excited my grandfather's curiosity to watch the progress of things; but, being a humane man, he resolved to kill the snake before he had a chance to despoil the nest. The distressed mother meanwhile continued her rapid movements and troubled cries; and he soon discovered that she went and came continually, with something in her bill, from one particular tree—a white ash. The snake wound his way up; but the instant his head came near the nest, his folds relaxed, and he fell to the ground rigid, and apparently lifeless. My grandfather made sure of his death by cutting off his head, and then mounted the tree to examine into the mystery. The snug little nest was filled with eggs, and covered with leaves of white ash!

That little bird knew, if my readers do not, that contact with the white ash is deadly to a snake. This is no idle superstition, but a veritable fact in natural history. The Indians are aware of it, and twist garlands of white ash leaves about their ankles, as a protection against rattlesnakes. Slaves often take the same precaution when they travel through swamps and forests, guided by the north star; or to the cabin of some poor white man, who teaches them to read and write by the light of pine splinters, and receives his pay in "massa's" corn or tobacco.

I have never heard any explanation of the effect produced by the white ash; but I know that settlers in the wilderness like to have these trees round their log houses, being convinced that no snake will voluntarily come near them. When touched with the boughs, they are said to grow suddenly rigid, with strong convulsions; after a while they slowly recover, but seem sickly for some time.

The following well authenticated anecdote has something wonderfully human about it:

A parrot had been caught young, and trained by a Spanish lady, who sold it to an English sea-captain. For a time the bird seemed sad among the fogs of England, where birds and men all spoke to her in a foreign tongue. By degrees, however, she learned the language, forgot her Spanish phrases, and seemed to feel at home. Years passed on, and found Pretty Poll the pet of the captain's family. At last her brilliant feathers began to turn gray with age; she could take no food but soft pulp, and had not strength enough to mount her perch. But no one had the heart to kill the old favourite, she was entwined with so many pleasant household recollections. She had been some time in this feeble condition, when a Spanish gentleman called one day to see her master. It was the first time she had heard the language for many years. It probably brought back to memory the scenes of her youth in that beautiful region of vines and sunshine. She spread forth her wings with a wild scream of joy, rapidly ran over the Spanish phrases, which she had not uttered for years, and fell down dead.

There is something strangely like reason in this. It makes one want to know whence comes the bird's soul, and whither goes it.

There are different theories on the subject of instinct. Some consider it a special revelation to each creature; others believe it is founded on traditions handed down among animals, from generation to generation, and is therefore a matter of education. My own observation, two years ago, tends to confirm the latter theory. Two barn-swallows came into our wood-shed in the spring time. Their busy, earnest twitterings led me at once to suspect that they were looking out on a building-spot; but as a carpenter's bench was under the window, and frequent hammering, sawing, and planing were going on, I had little hope they would choose a location under our roof. To my surprise, however, they soon began to build in the crotch of a beam, over the open door-way. I was delighted, and spent more time watching them, than "penny-wise" people would have approved. It was, in fact, a beautiful little drama of domestic love. The mother-bird was *so* busy, and *so* important; and her mate was *so* attentive! Never did any newly-married couple take more satisfaction with their first nicely-arranged drawer of baby-clothes, than these did in fashioning their little woven cradle.

The father-bird scarcely ever left the side of the nest. There he was, all day long, twittering in tones that were most obviously the outpourings of love. Sometimes he would bring in a straw, or a hair, to be inwoven in the precious little fabric. One day my attention was arrested by a very unusual twittering, and I saw him circling round with a large downy feather in his bill. He bent over the unfinished nest, and offered it to his mate with the most graceful and loving air imaginable;

and when she put up her mouth to take it, he poured forth *such* a gush of glad-some sound! It seemed as if pride and affection had swelled his heart, till it was almost too big for his little bosom. The whole transaction was the prettiest piece of fond coquetry, on both sides, that it was ever my good luck to witness.

It was evident that the father-bird had formed correct opinions on "the woman question;"[7] for during the process of incubation he volunteered to per-form his share of household duty. Three or four times a day would he, with coax-ing twitterings, persuade his patient mate to fly abroad for food; and the moment she left the eggs, he would take the maternal station, and give a loud alarm when-ever cat or dog came about the premises. He certainly performed the office with far less ease and grace than she did; it was something in the style of an old bach-elor tending a babe; but nevertheless it showed that his heart was kind, and his principles correct, concerning division of labour. When the young ones came forth, he pursued the same equalizing policy, and brought at least half the food for his greedy little family.

But when they became old enough to fly, the veriest misanthrope would have laughed to watch their manoeuvres! Such chirping and twittering! Such diving down from the nest, and flying up again! Such wheeling round in circles, talking to the young ones all the while! Such clinging to the sides of the shed with their sharp claws, to show the timid little fledgelings that there was no need of falling!

For three days all this was carried on with increasing activity. It was obviously an infant flying school. But all their talking and fussing was of no avail. The little downy things looked down, and then looked up, and alarmed at the infinity of space, sunk down into the nest again. At length the parents grew impatient, and summoned their neighbours. As I was picking up chips one day, I found my head encircled with a swarm of swallows. They flew up to the nest, and chatted away to the young ones; they clung to the walls, looking back to tell how the thing was done; they dived, and wheeled, and balanced, and floated, in a manner perfectly beautiful to behold.

The pupils were evidently much excited. They jumped up on the edge of the nest, and twittered, and shook their feathers, and waved their wings; and then hopped back again, saying, "It's pretty sport, but we can't do it."

Three times the neighbours came in and repeated their graceful lessons. The third time, two of the young birds gave sudden plunge downward, and then flut-tered and hopped, till they alighted on a small upright log. And oh, such praises as were warbled by the whole troop! The air was filled with their joy! Some were flying round, swift as a ray of light; others were perched on the hoe-handle, and the teeth of the rake; multitudes clung to the wall, after the fashion of their pretty kind; and two were swinging, in most graceful style, on a pendant hoop. Never while memory lasts, shall I forget that swallow party! I have frolicked with blessed Nature much and often; but this, above all her gambols, spoke into my inmost heart, like the glad voices of little children. That beautiful family continued to be our playmates, until the falling leaves gave token of approaching winter. For some time, the little ones came home regularly to their nest at night. I was ever on the watch to welcome them, and count that none were missing. A sculptor might have taken a lesson in his art, from those little creatures perched so gracefully on the edge of their clay-built cradle, fast asleep, with heads hidden under their folded wings. Their familiarity was wonderful. If I hung my gown on a nail, I found a little swallow perched on the sleeve. If I took a nap in the afternoon, my waking eyes were greeted by a swallow on the bed-post; in the summer twilight, they flew about the sitting-room in search of flies, and sometimes lighted on chairs and tables. I almost thought they knew how much I loved them. But at last they flew away to more genial skies, with a whole troop of relations and neighbours. It was a deep pain to me, that I should never know them from other swallows, and that they would have no recollection of me. We had lived so friendly together, that I wanted to meet them in another world, if I could not in this; and I wept, as a child weeps at its first grief.

There was somewhat, too, in their beautiful life of loving freedom which was a reproach to me. Why was not *my* life as happy and as graceful as theirs? Because they were innocent, confiding, and unconscious, they fulfilled all the laws of their being without obstruction.

> "Inward, inward to thy heart,
>   Kindly Nature, take me;
> Lovely, even as thou art,
>   Full of loving, make me.
> *Thou* knowest nought of dead-cold forms,
>   Knowest nought of littleness;
> Lifeful truth *thy* being warms,
>   Majesty and earnestness."

The old Greeks observed a beautiful festival, called "The Welcome of the Swallows." When these social birds first returned in the spring-time, the children went about in procession, with music and garlands; receiving presents at every door, where they stopped to sing a welcome to the swallows, in that graceful old language, so melodious even in its ruins, that the listener feels as if the brilliant azure of Grecian skies, the breezy motion of their olive groves, and the gush of their silvery fountains, had all passed into a monument of liquid and harmonious sounds.

Letter XXI [1]
June 16, 1842

If you want refreshment for the eye, and the luxury of pure breezes, go to Staten Island. This beautiful little spot, which lies so gracefully on the waters, was sold by the Indians to the Dutch, in 1657, for ten shirts, thirty pairs of stockings, ten guns, thirty bars of lead for balls, thirty pounds of powder, twelve coats, two pieces of duffil, thirty kettles, thirty hatchets, twenty hoes, and a case of knives and awls. This was then considered a fair compensation for a tract eighteen miles long, and seven broad; and compared with most of our business transactions with the Indians, it will not appear illiberal. The facilities for fishing, the abundance of oysters, the pleasantness of the situation, and old associations, all endeared it to the natives. They lingered about the island, like reluctant ghosts, until 1670; when, being urged to depart, they made a new requisition of four hundred fathoms of wampum, and a large number of guns and axes; a demand which was very wisely complied with, for the sake of a final ratification of the treaty.

On this island is a quarantine ground,[2] unrivalled for the airiness of its situation and the comfort and cleanliness of its arrangements. Of the foreigners from all nations which flood our shores, an immense proportion here take their first footstep on American soil; and judging from the welcome Nature gives them, they might well believe they had arrived in Paradise. From the high grounds, three hundred feet above the level of the sea, may be seen a most beautiful variety of land and sea, of rural quiet, and city splendor. Long Island spreads before you her vernal forests, and fields of golden grain; the North and East rivers sparkle in the distance; and the magnificent Hudson is seen flowing on in joyful freedom. The city itself seems clean and bright in the distance—its deformities hidden, and its beauties exaggerated, like the fame of far-off heroes. When the sun shines on its steeples, windows, and roofs of glittering tin, it is as if the Fire Spirits had suddenly created a city of fairy palaces. And when the still shadows creep over it, and the distant lights shine like descended constellations, twinkling to the moaning music of the sea, there is something oppressive in its solemn beauty. Then comes the golden morning light, as if God suddenly unveiled his glory! There on the bright waters float a thousand snowy sails, like a troop of beautiful sea birds; and imagination, strong in morning freshness, flies off through the outlet to the distant sea, and circles all the globe with its wreath of flowers.

Amid these images of joy, reposes the quarantine burying-ground; bringing sad association, like the bass-note in a music-box. How many who leave their distant homes, full of golden visions, come here to take their first and last look of the promised land. What to them are all the fair, broad, acres of this new world? They need but the narrow heritage of a grave. But every soul that goes hence, apart from friends and kindred, carries with it a whole unrevealed epic of joy and sorrow, of gentle sympathies and passion's fiery depths. O, how rich in more than Shakspearean beauty would be the literature of that quarantine ground, if all the images that pass in procession before those dying eyes, would write themselves in daguerreotype!

One of the most interesting places on this island, is the Sailor's Snug Harbor.[3] A few years ago, a gentleman by the name of Randall, left a small farm, that rented for two or three hundred dollars, at the corner of Eleventh-street and Broadway, for the benefit of old and worn-out sailors. This property increased in value, until it enabled the trustees to purchase a farm on Staten Island, and erect a noble stone edifice, as a hospital for disabled seamen; with an annual income of nearly thirty thousand dollars. The building has a very handsome exterior, and is large, airy, and convenient. The front door opens into a spacious hall, at the extremity of which flowers and evergreens are arranged one above another, like the terrace of a conservatory; and from the entries above, you look down into this pretty nook of "greenery." The whole aspect of things is extremely pleasant—with the exception of the sailors themselves. There is a sort of torpid resignation in countenance and movement, painful to witness. They reminded me of what some one said of the Greenwich pensioners:[4] "They seem to be waiting for death." No outward comfort seemed wanting, except the constant prospect of the sea: but they stood *alone* in the world—no wives, no children. Connected by no link with the ever-active Present, a monotonous Future stretched before them, made more dreary by its contrast with the keen excitement and ever-shifting variety of their Past life of peril and pleasure. I have always thought too little provision was made for this lassitude of the mind, in the most benevolent institutions. Men accustomed to excitement, cannot do altogether without it. It is a necessity of nature, and should be ministered to in all innocent forms. Those poor old tars should have sea-songs and instrumental music, once in a while, to stir their sluggish blood; and a feast might be given on great occasions, to younger sailors from temperance boarding-houses, that the Past might have a chance to hear from the Present. We perform but a half charity, when we comfort the body and leave the soul desolate.

Within the precincts of the city, too, are pleasant and safe homes provided for sailors; spacious, well-ventilated, and supplied with libraries and museums.[5]

After all, this nineteenth century, with all its turmoil and clatter, has some lovely features about it. If evil spreads with unexampled rapidity, good is abroad, too, with miraculous and omnipresent activity. Unless we are struck by the tail of a comet, or swallowed by the sun meanwhile, we certainly shall get the world right side up, by and by.[6]

Among the many instrumentalities at work to produce this, increasing interest in the sailor's welfare is a cheering omen. Of all classes, except the negro slaves, they have been the most neglected and the most abused. The book of judgement can alone reveal how much they have suffered on the wide, deep ocean, with no door to escape from tyranny, no friendly forest to hide them from the hunter; doomed, at their best estate, to suffer almost continued deprivation of *home*, that worst feature in the curse of Cain; their minds shut up in caves of ignorance so deep, that if religion enters with a friendly lamp, it too frequently terrifies them with the shadows it makes visible. Religious they *must* be, in some sense, even when they know it not; for no man with a human soul within him, can be unconscious of the Divine Presence, with infinite space round him, the blue sky overhead, with its million world-lamps, and everywhere, beneath and around him,

> "Great ocean, strangest of creation's sons!
> Unconquerable, unreposed, untired!
> That rolls the wild, profound, eternal bass
> In Nature's anthem, and makes music such
> As pleaseth the ear of God."

Thus circumstanced, the sailor cannot be ignorant, without being superstitious too. The Infinite comes continually before him, in the sublimest symbols of sight and sound. He does not know the language, but he feels the tone. Goethe has told us, in most beautiful allegory, of two bridges, whereby earnest souls pass from the Finite to the Infinite. One is a rainbow, which spans the dark river; and this is Faith; the other is a shadow cast quite over by the giant Superstition, when he stands between the setting sun and the unknown shore.

Blessings on all friendly hands that are leading the sailor to the rainbow bridge. His spirit is made reverential in the great temple of Nature, resounding with the wild voices of the winds, and strange music of the storm-organ; too long has it been left trembling and shivering on the bridge of shadows. For him, too, the rainbow spans the dark stream, and becomes at last a bridge of gems.

Letter XXII [1]
June 23, 1842

The highest gifts my soul has received, during its world-pilgrimage, have often been bestowed by those who were poor, both in money and intellectual cultivation. Among these donors, I particularly remember a hard-working, uneducated mechanic, from Indiana or Illinois. He told me that he was one of thirty or forty New Englanders, who, twelve years before, had gone out to settle in the western wilderness. They were mostly neighbours; and had been drawn to unite together in emigration from a general unity of opinion on various subjects. For some years previous, they had been in the habit of meeting occasionally at each others' houses, to talk over their duties to God and man, in all simplicity of heart. Their library was the gospel, their priesthood the inward light. There were then no anti-slavery societies; but thus taught, and reverently willing to learn, they had no need of such agency, to discover that it was wicked to enslave.[2] The efforts of peace societies had reached this secluded band only in broken echoes, and non-resistance societies had no existence.[3] But with the volume of the Prince of Peace, and hearts open to his influence, what need had they of preambles and resolutions?

Rich in spiritual culture,[4] this little band started for the far West. Their inward homes were blooming gardens; they made their outward in a wilderness. They were industrious and frugal, and all things prospered under their hands. But soon wolves came near the fold, in the shape of reckless, unprincipled adventurers; believers in force and cunning, who acted according to their creed. The colony of practical Christians spoke of their depredations in terms of gentlest remonstrance, and repaid them with unvarying kindness. They went farther—they openly announced, "You may do us what evil you choose, we will return nothing but good." Lawyers came into the neighbourhood, and offered their services to settle disputes. They answered, "We have no need of you. As neighbours, we receive you in the most friendly spirit; but for us, your occupation has ceased to exist." "What will you do, if rascals burn your barns, and steal your harvests?" "We will return good for evil. We believe this is the highest truth, and therefore the best expediency."

When the rascals heard this, they considered it a marvellous good joke, and said and did many provoking things, which to them seemed witty. Bars were taken down in the night, and cows let into the cornfields. The Christians repaired the damage as well as they could, put the cows in the barn, and at twilight drove them gently home, saying, "Neighbour, your cows have been in my field. I have fed them well during the day, but I would not keep them all night, lest the children should suffer for their milk."

If this was fun, they who planned the joke found no heart to laugh at it. By degrees, a visible change came over these troublesome neighbours. They ceased to cut off horses' tails, and break the legs of poultry. Rude boys would say to a younger brother, "Don't throw that stone, Bill! When I killed the chicken last week, didn't they send it to mother, because they thought chicken-broth would be good for poor Mary? I should think you'd be ashamed to throw stones at *their* chickens." Thus was evil overcome with good, till not one was found to do them wilful injury.

Years passed on, and saw them thriving in worldly substance, beyond their neighbours, yet beloved by all. From them the lawyer and the constable obtained no fees. The sheriff stammered and apologized, when he took their hard-earned goods in payment for the war-tax. They mildly replied, "'Tis a bad trade, friend. Examine it in the light of conscience and see if it be not so." But while they refused to pay such fees and taxes, they were liberal to a proverb in their contributions for all useful and benevolent purposes.

At the end of ten years, the public lands, which they had chosen for their farms, were advertised for sale by auction. According to custom, those who had settled and cultivated the soil, were considered to have a right to bid it in at the government price; which at that time was $1,25 per acre. But the fever of land-speculation then chanced to run unusually high. Adventurers from all parts of the country were flocking to the auction; and capitalists in Baltimore, Philadelphia, New-York, and Boston, were sending agents to buy up western lands. No one supposed that custom, or equity, would be regarded. The first day's sale showed that speculation ran to the verge of insanity. Land was eagerly bought in, at seventeen, twenty-five, and thirty dollars an acre. The Christian colony had small hope of retaining their farms. As first settlers, they had chosen the best land; and persevering industry had brought it into the highest cultivation. Its market-value was much greater than the acres already sold, at exorbitant prices. In view of these facts, they had prepared their minds for another remove into the wilderness, perhaps to be again ejected by a similar process. But the morning their lot was offered for sale, they observed, with grateful surprise, that their neighbours were everywhere busy among the crowd, begging and expostulating: "Don't bid on *these* lands! These men have been working hard on them for ten years. During all that time, they never did harm to man or brute. They are always ready to do good for evil. They are a blessing to any neighbourhood. It would be a sin and a shame to bid on *their* lands. Let them go, at the government price."

The sale came on; the cultivators of the soil offered $1,25; intending to bid higher if necessary. But among all that crowd of selfish, reckless speculators, *not one bid over them!* Without an opposing voice, the fair acres returned to them! I do not know a more remarkable instance of evil overcome with good. The wisest political economy lies folded up in the maxims of Christ.

With delighted reverence, I listened to this unlettered backwoodsman, as he explained his philosophy of universal love. "What would you do," said I, "if an idle, thieving vagabond came among you, resolved to stay, but determined not to work?" "We would give him food when hungry, shelter him when cold, and always treat him as a brother." "Would not this process attract such characters? How would you avoid being overrun with them?" "Such characters would either reform, or not remain with us. We should never speak an angry word, or refuse to minister to their necessities; but we should invariably regard them with the deepest sadness, as we would a guilty, but beloved son. This is harder for the human soul to bear, than whips or prisons. They could not stand it; I am sure they could not. It would either melt them, or drive them away. In nine cases out of ten, I believe it would melt them."

I felt rebuked for my want of faith, and consequent shallowness of insight. That hard-handed labourer brought greater riches to my soul than an Eastern merchant laden with pearls. Again I repeat, money is *not* wealth.

Letter XXIII [1]
July 7, 1842

It has been my fortune, in the course of a changing life, to meet with many strange characters; but I never, till lately, met with one altogether unaccountable.

Some six or eight years ago, I read a very odd pamphlet, called "The Patriarchal System of Society, as it exists under the name of Slavery; with its necessity and advantages. By an inhabitant of Florida."[2] The writer assumes that "the patriarchal system constitutes the bond of social compact; and is better adapted for strength, durability, and independence, than any state of society hitherto adopted."

"The prosperous state of our northern neighbours," says he, "proceeds, in many instances, indirectly from southern slave labour; though they are not aware of it." This was written in 1829; read in these days of universal southern bankruptcy, it seems ludicrous; as if it had been intended for sarcasm, rather than sober earnest.

But the main object of this singular production is to prove that *colour* ought not to be the badge of degradation; that the only distinction should be between *slave* and *free*—not between *white* and *coloured*. That the free people of colour, instead of being persecuted, and driven from the Southern States, ought to be made eligible to all offices and means of wealth. This would form, he thinks, a grand chain of security, by which the interests of the two castes would become united, and the slaves be kept in permanent subordination. Intermarriage between the races he strongly advocates; not only as strengthening the bond of union between castes that otherwise naturally war upon each other, but as a great improvement of the human race. "The intermediate grades of colour," says he, "are not only healthy, but, when condition is favourable, they are improved in shape, strength, and beauty. Daily experience shows that there is no natural antipathy between the castes on account of colour. It only requires to repeal laws as impolitic as they are unjust and unnatural—laws which confound beauty, merit, and condition, in one state of infamy and degradation on account of complexion. It is only required to leave nature to find out a safe and wholesome remedy for evils, which of all others are the most deplorable, because they are morally irreconcileable with the fundamental principles of happiness and self-preservation."

I afterwards heard that Z. Kinsley, the author of this pamphlet, lived with a coloured wife, and treated her and her children with kindness and consideration. A traveller, writing from Florida, stated that he visited a planter, whose coloured wife sat at the head of the table, surrounded by healthy and handsome children. That the parlour was full of portraits of African beauties, to which the gentleman drew his attention, with much exultation; dwelling with great earnestness on the superior physical endowments of the coloured race, and the obvious advantages of amalgamation. I at once conjectured that this eccentric planter was the author of the pamphlet on the patriarchal system.

Soon after, it was rumoured that Mr. Kinsley had purchased a large tract of land of the Haitien government; that he had carried his slaves there, and given them lots. Then I heard that it was a colony, established for the advantage of his own mulatto sons; that the workmen were in a qualified kind of slavery, by consent of the government; and that he still held a large number of slaves in Florida.

Last week, this individual, who had so much excited my curiosity, was in the city; and I sought an interview. I found his conversation entertaining, but marked by the same incongruity, that characterizes his writings and his practice. His head is a peculiar one; it would, I think, prove as great a puzzle to phrenologists, as he himself is to moralists and philosophers.

I told him of the traveller's letter, and asked if he were the gentleman described.

"I never saw the letter;" he replied: "but from what you say, I have no doubt that I am the man. I always thought and said, that the coloured race were superior to us, physically and morally. They are more healthy, have more graceful forms, softer skins,[3] and sweeter voices. They are more docile and affectionate, more faithful in their attachments, and less prone to mischief, than the white race. If it were not so, they could not have been kept in slavery."

"It is a shameful and a shocking thought," said I, "that we should keep them in slavery by reason of their very virtues."

"It is so, ma'am; but, like many other shameful things, it is true."

"Where did you obtain your portraits of coloured beauties?"

"In various places. Some of them I got on the coast of Africa. If you want to see beautiful specimens of the human race, you should see some of the native women there."

"Then you have been on the coast of Africa?"

"Yes, ma'am; I carried on the slave trade several years."

"You announce that fact very coolly," said I. "Do you know that, in New England, men look upon a slave-trader with as much horror as they do upon a pirate?"

"Yes; and I am glad of it. They will look upon a slaveholder just so, by and by. Slave trading was very respectable business when I was young. The first merchants in England and America were engaged in it. Some people hide things which they think other people don't like. I never conceal anything."

"Where did you become acquainted with your wife?"

"On the coast of Africa, ma'am. She was a new nigger, when I first saw her."

"What led you to become attached to her?"

"She was a fine, tall figure, black as jet, but very handsome. She was very capable, and could carry on all the affairs of the plantation in my absence, as well as I could myself. She was affectionate and faithful, and I could trust her. I have fixed her nicely in my Haitien colony. I wish you would go there. She would give you the best in the house. You *ought* to go, to see how happy the human race can be. It is in a fine, rich valley, about thirty miles from Port Platte; heavily timbered with mahogany all round; well watered; flowers so beautiful; fruits in abundance, so delicious that you could not refrain from stopping to eat, till you could eat no more. My son has laid out good roads, and built bridges and mills; the people are improving, and everything is prosperous. I am anxious to establish a good school there. I engaged a teacher; but somebody persuaded him it was mean to teach niggers, and so he fell off from his bargain."

"I have heard that you hold your labourers in a sort of qualified slavery; and some friends of the coloured race have apprehensions that you may sell them again."

"My labourers in Haiti are not slaves. They are a kind of indented apprentices. I give them land, and they bind themselves to work for me. I have no power to take them away from that island; and you know very well that I could not sell them there."

"I am glad you have relinquished the power to make slaves of them again. I had charge of a fine, intelligent fugitive, about a year ago. I wanted to send him to your colony; but I did not dare to trust you."

"You need not have been afraid, ma'am. I should be the last man on earth to give up a runaway. If my own were to run away, I wouldn't go after 'em."[4]

"If these are your feelings, why don't you take *all* your slaves to Haiti?"

"I have thought that subject all over, ma'am; and I have settled it in my own mind. All we can do in this world is to balance evils. I want to do great things for Haiti; and in order to do them, I must have money. If I have no negroes to cultivate my Florida lands, they will run to waste; and then I can raise no money from them for the benefit of Haiti. I do all I can to make them comfortable, and they love me like a father. They would do any thing on earth to please me. Once I stayed away longer than usual, and they thought I was dead. When I reached home, they overwhelmed me with their caresses; I could hardly stand it."

"Does it not grieve you to think of leaving these faithful, kind-hearted people, to the cruel chances of slavery?"

"Yes, it does; but I hope to get all my plans settled in a few years."

"You tell me you are seventy-six years old; what if you should die before your plans are completed?"

"Likely enough I shall. In that case, my heirs would break my will, I dare say, and my poor niggers would be badly off."

"Then manumit them now; and avoid this dreadful risk."

"I have thought that all over ma'am; and I have settled it that I can do more good by keeping them in slavery a few years more. The best we can do in this world is to balance evils judiciously."

"But you do not balance wisely. Remember that all the descendants of your slaves, through all coming time, will be affected by your decision."

"So will all Haiti be affected, through all coming time, if I can carry out my plans. To do good in the world, we *must* have money. That's the way I reasoned when I carried on the slave trade. It was very profitable then."

"And do you have no remorse of conscience, in recollecting that bad business?"

"*Some* things I do not like to remember; but they were not things in which I was to blame; they were inevitably attendant on the trade."

I argued that any trade must be wicked, that *had* such inevitable consequences. He admitted it; but still clung to his balance of evils. If that theory is admitted in morals at all, I confess that his practice seems to me a legitimate, though an extreme result. But it was altogether vain to argue with him about fixed principles of right and wrong; one might as well fire small shot at the hide of a rhinoceros. Yet were there admirable points about him;—perseverance, that would conquer the world; an heroic candour, that avowed all things, creditable and discreditable; and kindly sympathies too—though it must be confessed that they go groping and floundering about in the strangest fashion.

He came from Scotland; no other country, perhaps, except New-England, could have produced such a character. His father was a Quaker; and he still loves to attend Quaker meetings; particularly silent ones, where he says he has planned some of his best bargains.[5] To complete the circle of contradictions, he likes the abolitionists, and is a prodigious admirer of George Thompson.[6]

"My neighbours call me an abolitionist," said he; "I tell them they may do so, in welcome; for it is a pity they shouldn't have *one* case of amalgamation to point at."

This singular individual has been conversant with all sorts of people, and seen almost all parts of the world. "I have known the Malay and the African, the North American Indian and the European,"[7] said he; "and the more I've seen of the world, the less I understand it. It's a queer place; that's a fact."

Probably this mixture with people of all creeds and customs, combined with the habit of looking *outward* for his guide of action, may have bewildered his moral sense, and produced his system of "balancing evils!" A theory obviously absurd, as well as slippery in its application; for none but God *can* balance evils; it requires omniscience and omnipresence to do it.

His conversation produced great activity of thought on the subject of conscience, and of that "light that lighteth every man who cometh into the world." Whether this utilitarian remembers it or not, he must have stifled many convictions before he arrived at his present state of mind. And so it must have been with "the pious John Newton,"[8] whose devotional letters from the coast of Africa, while he was slave-trading there, record "sweet seasons of communion with his God." That *he* was not left without a witness within him, is proved by the fact, that in his journal he expresses gratitude to God for opening the door for him to leave the slave trade, by providing other employment. The monitor *within* did not deceive him; but his education was at war with its dictates, because it taught him that whatever was *legalized* was *right*. Plain as the guilt of the slave trade now is, to every man, woman, and child, it was not so in the time of Clarkson;[9] had it been otherwise, there would have been no need of his labours. He was accused of planning treason and insurrection, plots were laid against his life, and the difficulty of combating his obviously just principles, led to the vilest misrepresentations and the most false assumptions.[10] Thus it must always be with those who attack a very corrupt public opinion.

The slave *trade,* which all civilized laws now denounce as piracy, was defended in precisely the same spirit that *slavery* is now. Witness the following remarks from Boswell,[11] the biographer of Dr. Johnson, whose opinions echo the tone of genteel society:

"I beg leave to enter my most solemn protest against Dr. Johnson's general doctrine with respect to the slave trade. I will resolutely say that his unfavourable notion of it was owing to prejudice, and imperfect or false information. The *wild* and *dangerous* attempt which has for some time been persisted in, to obtain an act of our legislature to abolish so very *important and necessary a branch of commercial interest,* must have been crushed at once, had not the *insignificance* of the zealots, who vainly took the lead in it, made the vast body of planters, merchants, and others, whose immense properties are involved in that trade, reasonably enough suppose that there could be no danger. The encouragement which the attempt has received, excites my wonder and indignation; and though some men of superior abilities have supported it, (whether from a love of temporary popularity when prosperous, or a love of general mischief when desperate,) my opinion is unshaken. To abolish a status which in all ages *God has sanctioned,* and man continued, would not only be robbery to an innumerable class of our fellow subjects, but it would be extreme cruelty to African savages; a portion of whom it saves from massacre, or intolerable bondage in their own country, and introduces into a much happier state of life; especially now, when their passage to the West Indies, and their treatment there, is humanely regulated. *To abolish that trade, would be to shut the gates of mercy on mankind.*"

These changes in the code of morals adopted by society, by no means unsettle my belief in eternal and unchangeable principles of right and wrong; neither do they lead me to doubt that in all these cases men inwardly know better than they act. The slaveholder, when he manumits on his death-bed, thereby acknowledges that he has known he was doing wrong. Public opinion expresses what men *will* to do; not their inward *perceptions.* All kinds of crimes have been countenanced by public opinion, in some age or nation; but we cannot as easily show how far they were sustained by reason and conscience in each individual. I believe the lamp never goes out, though it may shine dimly through a foggy atmosphere.

This consideration should renew our zeal to purify public opinion; to let no act or word of ours help to corrupt it, in the slightest degree. How shall we fulfil this sacred trust, which each holds for the good of all? Not by calculating consequences; not by balancing evils; but by reverent obedience to our own highest convictions of individual duty.[12]

Few men ask concerning right and wrong of their *own* hearts. Few listen to the oracle *within,* which can only be heard in the stillness. The merchant seeks his moral standard on 'Change—a fitting name for a thing so fluctuating; the sectary in the opinion of his small theological department; the politician in the tumultuous echo of his party; the worldling in the buzz of saloons. In a word, each man inquires of *his* public; what wonder, then, that the answers are selfish as trading interest, blind as local prejudice, and various as human whim?

A German drawing-master once told me of a lad who wished to sketch landscapes from nature. The teacher told him that the first object was to choose some *fixed point of view*. The sagacious pupil chose a cow grazing beneath the trees. Of course, his *fixed point* soon began to move hither and thither, as she was attracted by the sweetness of the pasturage; and the lines of his drawing fell into strange confusion.

This is a correct type of those who choose public opinion for their moral fixed point of view. It moves according to the provender before it, and they who trust to it have but a whirling and distorted landscape.

Coleridge [13] defines public opinion as "the average prejudices of the community." Wo unto those who have no safer guide of principle and practice than this "average of prejudices." Wo unto them in an especial manner, in these latter days, when "The windows of heaven are opened, and *therefore* the foundations of the earth do *shake!*"

Feeble wanderers are they, following a flickering Jack-o' lantern, when there is a calm, bright pole-star for ever above the horizon, to guide their steps, if they would but look to it.

Letter XXIV [1]
July 28, 1842

When the spirit is at war with its outward environment, because it is not inwardly dwelling in trustful obedience to its God, how often does some very slight incident bring it back, humble, and repentant, to the Father's footstool! A few days since, cities seemed to me such hateful places, that I deemed it the greatest of hardships to be pent up therein. As usual, the outward grew more and more detestable, as it reflected the restlessness of the inward. Piles of stones and rubbish, left by the desolating fire, looked more hot and dreary than ever; they were building brick houses between me and the sunset—and in my requiring selfishness, I felt as if it were *my* sunset, and no man had a *right* to shut it out; and then to add the last drop to my vexation, they painted the roof of house and piazza as fierce a red as if the mantle of the great fire, that destroyed its predecessor, had fallen over them.[2] The wise course would have been, to try to find something agreeable in a red roof, since it suited my neighbour's convenience to have one. But the head was not in a mood to be wise, because the heart was not humble and obedient; so I fretted inwardly about the red roof, more than I would care to tell in words; I even thought to myself, that it would be no more than just and right if people with such bad taste should be sent to live by themselves on a quarantine island. Then I began to think of myself as a most unfortunate and ill-used indi vidual, to be for ever pent up within brick walls without even a dandelion to gaze upon; from that I fell to thinking of many fierce encounters between my will and necessity, and how will had always been conquered, chained, and sent to the treadmill to work. The more I thought after this fashion, hotter glared the bricks, and fiercer glowed the red roof, under the scorching sun. I was making a desert within, to paint its desolate likeness on the scene without.

A friend found me thus, and having faith in Nature's healing power, he said, "Let us seek green fields and flowery nooks." So we walked abroad; and while yet amid the rattle and glare of the city, close by the iron railway, I saw a very little, ragged child stooping over a small patch of stinted, dusty grass. She rose up with a broad smile over her hot face, for she had found a white clover! The tears were in my eyes. "God bless thee, poor child!" said I; "thou hast taught my soul a lesson, which it will not soon forget. Thou, poor neglected one, canst find blossoms by the dusty wayside, and rejoice in thy hard path, as if it were a mossy bank strewn with violets." I felt humbled before that ragged, gladsome child. Then saw I plainly that walls of brick and mortar did not, and could not, hem me in. I thought of those who loved me, and every remembered kindness was a flower in my path; I thought of intellectual gardens, where this child might perchance never enter, but where I could wander at will over acres broad as the world; and if even there, the restless spirit felt a limit, lo, poetry had but to throw a ray thereon, and the fair gardens of earth were reflected in the heavens like the *fata morgana*[3] of Italian skies, in a drapery of rainbows. Because I was poor in spirit, straightway there was none so rich as I. Then was it revealed to me that only the soul which gathers flowers by the dusty wayside can truly love the fresh anemone by the running brook, or the trailing arbutus hiding its sweet face among the fallen leaves. I returned home a better and wiser woman, thanks to the ministry of that little one. I saw that I was not ill-used and unfortunate, but blessed beyond others; one of Nature's favourites, whom she ever took to her kindly heart, and comforted in all seasons of distress and waywardness. Though the sunset was shut out, there still remained the roseate flush of twilight, as if the sun, in answer to my love, had written to me a farewell message on the sky. The red piazza stood there, blushing for him who painted it; but it no longer pained my eyesight; I thought what a friendly warmth it would have, seen through the wintry snows. Oh, blessed indeed are little children! Mortals do not understand half they owe them; for the good they do us is a spiritual gift, and few perceive how it intertwines the mystery of life. They form a ladder of garlands on which the angels descend to our souls; and without them, such communication would be utterly lost. Let us strive to be like little children.

As I mused on the altered aspect of the outward world, according to the state of him who looked upon it, I raised to my eye a drop from a broken chandelier. That glass fragment was like a fairy wand, or Aladdin's wondrous lamp. The line of tumbling wooden shantees, which I had often blamed the capricious fire for sparing, the piles of lime and stones that wearied my eyesight, were at once changed to rainbows; even the offensive red roof smiled upon me in the softened beauty of purple and gold. Not earth, but the medium through which earth is seen, produces beauty. I said to myself, "Whereunto shall I liken this angular bit of glass?" The answer came to me in music—in words and tones of song: "The faith touching all things with hues of heaven." Then prayed I earnestly for that faith, as a perpetual gift. Prayer, earnest and true, rose from that fragment of broken glass; thus from things most common and trivial, spring the highest and the holiest.

I thought then that I would never again look on outward circumstances, except in the cheerful light of a trusting and grateful heart. Yet within a week, came the restless comparing of *me* with *thee*. If I could only be situated as such an one was, how good I could *be,* and how much good I would *do.* I said within myself, "This must not be. If I indulge this train of thought, the walls will again crowd upon me, and the bricks glare worse than ever." So I walked to the Battery, to look at moonlight on the water; in full faith that "Nature never did betray the heart that loved her." The moon had not yet risen; but softly from the recesses of Castle Garden came tones of music, welcome to my soul as a mother's voice. We walked in, thinking only to hear the band, and lounge quietly on a seat overhanging the water. All pleasure in this world is but the cessation of some pain; and they only who work unto weariness, in mind or body, can fully enjoy the luxury of repose. And this repose was so perfect, so strengthening! Instead of the pent-up, stifling air of the central city, was a cool, evening breeze, gentle as if a thousand winged messengers fanned one's cheeks for love; below, the ever-flowing water laved the stones with a refreshing sound; round us floated music, so plaintive and so shadowy! It sung "The light of other days"—the very voice of moonlight, soft and trembling over the dim waters of the Past; and then, as if the atmosphere were not already bathed in sufficient beauty, slowly rose the mild, majestic moon; and the water-spirits hailed her presence with mazy, undulating dance, as if rejoicing in the glittering wealth of jewelry she gave. At such an hour, beyond all others, does nature seem to be filled with an inward, hidden life; in serious and beseeching tones, she seems to say, "Lo I reveal unto you a great mystery, lying at the foundation of all being. I speak it in all tones, I write it in all colours. When will the mortal arise who understands my language?" And a sacred voice answers, "When His will is done on *earth,* as it is done in *heaven.*" In the midst of such communion, the soul feels that

"This visible nature and this common world,
Is all too narrow."

Wings wave in the air, voices speak through the sea, and the rustling trees are whispering spirits. It was this yearning after the spiritual that pervades all things, whose presence, never found, is constantly revealed in so many echoes—it is this dim longing, which of old "peopled space with life and mystical predominance;" this filled the grove with dryads, the waves with nymphs, the earth with fairies, the sky with angels. The external and the sensual call this the ravings of Imagination; and they know not that she is the priestess of high Truth.

All this I did not *think* of, as I leaned over the waters of Castle Garden; but this, and far more, was spoken into my *heart;* and I shall find it all recorded in rainbow letters, on my journal there beyond.

In such listening mood, when the outward lay before me, in hieroglyphic symbols of a volume so infinite, I turned with a feeling of sadness toward a painted representation of Vera Cruz,[4] which the bill proclaimed was to be taken by the French fleet that evening, for the amusement of spectators. The imitation of a distant city was certainly good, speaking according to the theatrical standard: but it seemed to me desecration, that Art should thus intrude her delusions into the sanctuary of Nature. In a mood less elevated, I might have scorned her pretensions, with a proud impatience; but as it was, I simply felt sad at the incongruity. I looked at the moon in her serene beauty, at the little boats, here floating across the veil of silver blonde, which she had thrown over the dancing waves, and there, with lanterns, gliding like fire-flies among the deep distant shadows; and I said if Art ventures into this presence, let her come only as the Greek Diana, or marble nymph sleeping on her urn.

But Art revenged herself for the slight estimation in which I held her. She could not satisfy me with beauty harmonious with Nature; but she charmed with the brilliancy of contrast. Opposite me I saw a light mildly splendid, as if seen through an atmosphere of motionless water. It had a fairy look, and I could not otherwise than observe it, from time to time, though the moonbeams played so gracefully and still. Anon, with a whizzing sound, it became a wheel of fire; then it changed to a hexagon, set with emeralds, topaz, and rubies; then circles of orange, white, and crimson light revolved swiftly round a resplendent centre of amethyst; then it became flowers made of gems; and after manifold changes of unexpected beauty, it revolved a large star, set with jewels of all rainbow hues, over which there fell a continual fountain of golden rain. It was called the kaleidescope; and its fairy splendour far exceeded anything I ever imagined of fireworks. I asked pardon of insulted Art, and thanked *her,* too, for the pleasure she had given me.

I turned again to moonlight and silence, and my happy spirit carried no discord there. Even when I thought of returning to the hot and crowded city, I said, "This too will I do in cheerfulness. I will learn of Nature to love all, and do all." Slowly, and with loving reluctance, we turned away from the moon-lighted waters; then came across the waves the liquid melody of a flute; it called us back with such friendly, sweet intreaty, that we could not otherwise than stop to listen to its last silvery cadence. Again we turned away, and had nearly made our escape, when an accordion from a distant boat, in softened accents begged us still to linger. Then a band on board the newly-arrived French frigate struck up the Cra-covienne, the expressive dance of Poland, bringing with it images of romantic grace, and strange, deep thoughts of the destiny of nations.—We lingered and lingered. Nature and Art seemed to have conspired that night to do their best to please us. At last, the sounds died away; and stepping to their echo in our memories, we passed out; the iron gate of the Battery clanked behind us; the streets reared their brick walls between us and the loveliness of earth and heaven. But they could not shut it out; for it had passed *into* our souls.

You will smile, and say the amount of all this romancing is a confession that I was a tired and wayward child, needing moonlight and a show to restore my serenity. And what of that? If I am not too perfect to *be* in a wayward humour, I surely will not be too dignified to *tell* of it. I say, as Bettine does to Gunderode: "How glad I am to be so insignificant. I need not fork up discreet thoughts when I write to thee, but just narrate how things are. Once I thought I must not write unless I could give importance to the letter by a bit of moral, or some discreet thought; now I think not to chisel out, or glue together my thoughts. Let others do that. If I must write so, I cannot think." [5]

Letter XXV [1]
August 4, 1842

Last week, for a single day, I hid myself in the green sanctuary of Nature; and from the rising of the sun till the going down of the moon, took no more thought of cities, than if such excrescences never existed on the surface of the globe. A huge wagon, traversing our streets, under the midsummer sun, bearing in immense letters, the words, ICE FROM ROCKLAND LAKE, had frequently attracted my attention, and become associated with images of freshness and romantic beauty. Therefore, in seeking the country for a day, I said our course should be up the Hudson, to Rockland Lake. The noontide sun was scorching, and our heads were dizzy with the motion of the boat; but these inconveniences, so irksome at the moment, are faintly traced on the tablet of memory. She engraves only the beautiful in lasting characters; for beauty alone is immortal and divine.

We stopped at Piermont, on the widest part of Tappan bay, where the Hudson extends itself to the width of three miles. On the opposite side, in full view from the Hotel, is Tarrytown, where poor Andre was captured. Tradition says, that a very large white-wood tree, under which he was taken, was struck by lightning, on the very day that news of Arnold's death was received at Tarrytown. As I sat gazing on the opposite woods, dark in the shadows of moonlight, I thought upon how very slight a circumstance often depends the fate of individuals, and the destiny of nations. In the autumn of 1780, a farmer chanced to be making cider at a mill, on the east bank of the Hudson, near that part of Haverstraw Bay, called

"Mother's Lap." Two young men, carrying muskets, as usual in those troubled times, stopped for a draught of sweet cider, and seated themselves on a log to wait for it. The farmer found them looking very intently on some distant object, and inquired what they saw. "Hush! hush!" they replied; "The red-coats are yonder, just within the Lap," pointing to an English gunboat, with twenty-four men, lying on their oars. Behind the shelter of a rock they fired into the boat, and killed two persons. The British returned a random shot; but ignorant of the number of their opponents, and seeing that it was useless to waste ammunition on a hidden foe, they returned whence they came, with all possible speed. This boat had been sent to convey Major Andre to the British sloop-of-war, Vulture, then lying at anchor off Teller's point. Shortly after, Andre arrived, and finding the boat gone, he, in attempting to proceed through the interior, was captured.[2] Had not those men stopped to drink sweet cider, it is probable that Andre would not have been hung; the American revolution might have terminated in quite different fashion;[3] men now deified as heroes, might have been handed down to posterity as traitors; our citizens might be proud of claiming descent from tories; and slavery have been abolished eight years ago, by virtue of our being British colonies. So much may depend on a draught of cider! But would England herself have abolished slavery, had it not been for the impulse given to free principles by the American revolution? Probably not. It is not easy to calculate the consequences involved even in a draught of cider; for no fact stands alone; each has infinite relations.

A very pleasant ride at sunset brought us to Orangetown, to the lone field where Major Andre was executed. It is planted with potatoes, but the plough spares the spot on which was once his gallows and his grave. A rude heap of stones, with the remains of a dead fir tree in the midst, are all that mark it; but tree and stones are covered with names. It is on an eminence, commanding a view of the country for miles. I gazed on the surrounding woods, and remembered that on this self-same spot, the beautiful and accomplished young man walked back and forth, a few minutes preceding his execution, taking an earnest farewell look of earth and sky. My heart was sad within me. Our guide pointed to a house in full view, at half a mile's distance, which he told us was at that time the head-quarters of General Washington. I turned my back suddenly upon it. The last place on earth where I would wish to think of Washington, is at the grave of Andre. I know that military men not only sanction, but applaud the deed; and reasoning according to the maxims of war, I am well aware how much can be said in its defence. That Washington considered it a duty, the discharge of which was most painful to him, I doubt not.[4] But, thank God, the instincts of my childhood are unvitiated by any such maxims. From the first hour I read of the deed, until the present day, I never did, and never could, look upon it as otherwise than cool, deliberate murder. That the theory and practice of war commends the transaction, only serves to prove the infernal nature of war itself.

Milton (stern moralist as he was, in many respects) maintains, in his "*Chris-*

tian Doctrine,"[5] that falsehoods are sometimes not only allowable, but necessary. "It is scarcely possible," says he, "to execute any of the artifices of war without openly uttering the greatest untruths, with the undisputable intention of deceiving." And because *war* requires lies, we are told by a *Christian* moralist that lies must, therefore, be lawful! It is observable that Milton is obliged to defend the necessity of falsehoods in the same way that fighting is defended; he makes many references to the *Jewish* scriptures, but none to the *Christian*. Having established his position, that wilful, deliberate deception was a necessary ingredient of war, it is strange, indeed, that his enlightened mind did not at once draw the inference that war itself must be evil. It would have been so, had not the instincts of heart and conscience been perverted by the maxims of men, and the customs of that fierce period.

The soul may be brought into military drill service, like the limbs of the body; and such a one, perchance, might stand on Andre's grave, and glory in his capture; but I would rather suffer his inglorious death, than attain to such a state of mind.

A few years ago, the Duke of York requested the British consul to send the remains of Major Andre to England. At that time, two thriving firs were found near the grave, and a peach tree, which a lady in the neighbourhood had planted there, in the kindness of her heart. The farmers, who came to witness the interesting ceremony, generally evinced the most respectful tenderness for the memory of the unfortunate dead; and many of the women and children wept. A few loafers, educated by militia trainings, and Fourth of July declamation, began to murmur that the memory of General Washington was insulted by any respect shown to the remains of Andre; but the offer of a treat lured them to the tavern, where they soon became too drunk to guard the character of Washington. It was a beautiful day: and these disturbing spirits being removed, the impressive ceremony proceeded in solemn silence. The coffin was in good preservation, and contained all the bones, with a small quantity of dust. The roots of the peach tree had entirely interwoven the skull with their fine network. His hair, so much praised for its uncommon beauty, was tied, on the day of his execution, according to the fashion of the times. When his grave was opened, half a century afterward, the ribbon was found in perfect preservation, and sent to his sister in England. When it was known that the sarcophagus, containing his remains, had arrived in New-York, on its way to London, many ladies sent garlands, and emblematic devices, to be wreathed around it, in memory of the "beloved and lamented Andre." In their compassionate hearts, the teachings of nature were unperverted by maxims of war, or that selfish jealousy, which dignifies itself with the name of patriotism. Blessed be God, that custom forbids women to electioneer or fight. May the sentiment remain, till war and politics have passed away. Had not women and children been kept free from their polluting influence, the medium of communication between earth and heaven would have been completely cut off.

At the foot of the eminence where the gallows had been erected, we found an old Dutch farm-house, occupied by a man who witnessed the execution, and whose father often sold peaches to the unhappy prisoner. He confirmed the accounts of Andre's uncommon personal beauty; and had a vivid remembrance of the pale, but calm, heroism with which he met his untimely death. Everything about this dwelling was antiquated. Two prim pictures of George III and his homely queen, taken at the period when we owed allegiance to them, as "the government ordained of God," marked plainly the progress of Art since that period; for the portraits of Victoria on our cotton-spools, are graceful in comparison.[6] An ancient clock, which has ticked uninterrupted good time on the same ground for more than a hundred years, stood in one corner of the little parlour. It was brought from the East Indies, by an old Dutch sea captain, great grandfather of the present owner. In those nations, where *opinions* are transmitted unchanged, the outward *forms* and *symbols* of thought remain so likewise. The gilded figures, which entirely cover the body of this old clock, are precisely the same, in perspective, outline, and expression, as East India figures of the present day.

My observations, as a traveller, are limited to a very small portion of the new world; and therefore, it has never been my lot to visit scenes so decidedly bearing the impress of former days, as this Dutch county.

"Life, on a soil inhabited in olden time, and once glorious in its industry, activity, and attachment to noble pursuits, has a peculiar charm," says Novalis.[7] "Nature seems to have become there more human, more rational; a dim remembrance throws back, through the transparent present, the images of the world in marked outline; and thus you enjoy a two-fold world, purged by this very process from the rude and disagreeable, and made the magic poetry and fable of the mind. Who knows whether also an indefinable influence of the former inhabitants, now departed, does not conspire to this end?"

The solemn impression, so eloquently described by Novalis, is what I have desired above all things to experience; but the times seen through "the transparent present" of these thatched farm-houses, and that red Dutch church, are not far *enough* in the distance; far removed from us, it is true; but still farther from mitred priest, crusading knight, and graceful troubadour. "An indefinable influence of the former inhabitants," is indeed most visible; but then it needs no ghost to tell us that these inhabitants were thoroughly Dutch. Since the New-York and Erie railroad passed through their midst, careful observers say, that the surface of the stagnant social pool begins to ripple, in very small whirlpools, as if an insect stirred the waters. But *before* that period, a century produced no visible change in theology, agriculture, dress, or cooking. They were the very type of conservatism; immoveable in the midst of incessant change. The same family lived on the same homestead, generation after generation. Brothers married, and came home to father's to live, so long as the old house would contain wives and swarming children; and when house and barn were both overrun, a new tenement, of the self-same construction, was put up, within a stone's throw. To *sell* an acre of land received from their fathers, would be downright desecration. It is now literally impossible for a stranger to buy of them at any price. A mother might be coaxed to sell her babies, as easily as they to sell their farms. Consider what consternation such a people must have been in, when informed that the New-York and Erie railroad was to be cut straight through their beloved hereditary acres! They swore, by "donner and blitzen," that not a rail should ever be laid on their premises. The railroad company, however, by aid of chancery, compelled them to acquiesce; and their grief was really pitiful to behold. Neighbours went to each others' "stoops," to spend a *social* evening; and, as their wont had ever been, they sat and smoked at each other, without the unprofitable interruption of a single word of conversation: but *not* according to custom, they now grasped each other's hands tightly at parting, and tears rolled down their weather-beaten cheeks. The iron of the railroad had entered their souls. And well it might; for it not only divided orchards, pastures, and gardens; but, in many instances, cut right through the old homesteads. Clocks that didn't know how to tick, except on the sinking floor where they had stood for years, were now removed to other premises and went mute with sorrow. Heavy old tables, that hadn't stirred one of their countless legs for half a century, were now compelled to budge: and potatoes, whose grandfathers and great grandfathers had slept together in the same bed, were now removed beyond nodding distance. Joking apart, it was a cruel case. The women and children wept, and some of the old settlers actually died of a broken heart. Several years have elapsed since the fire-king first went whizzing through on his wings of steam; but the Dutch farmers have not yet learned to look on him without a muttered curse; with fear and trembling, they guide their sleek horses and slow-and-sure wagons over the crossings, expecting, every instant, to be reduced to impalpable powder.[8]

Poor old men! what will they say when railroads are carried through all their old seed-fields of opinion, theological and political? As yet, there are no twilight fore-shadowings of such possibilities; but assuredly, the day will come, when ideas, like potatoes, will not be allowed to sprout up peaceably in the same hillock where their venerable progenitors vegetated from time immemorial.

As yet, no rival spires here point to the same heaven. There stands the Dutch Reformed Church, with its red body, and low white tower, just where stood the small stone church, in which Major Andre was tried and sentenced. The modern church (I mean the *building*) is larger than the one of olden time; but creed and customs, somewhat of the sternest, have not changed one hair's breadth. I thought of this, as I looked at the unsightly edifice; and suddenly there rose up before me the image of some of our modern disturbers,[9] stalking in among these worshipping antediluvians, and pricking their ears with the astounding intelligence, that they were "a den of thieves," and "a hill of hell."[10] 'Tis a misfortune to have an imagination too vivid. I cannot think of that red Dutch church, without a crowd of images that make me laugh till the tears come.

Not far from the church is a small stone building, used as a tavern. Here they showed me the identical room where Andre was imprisoned. With the exception of new plastering, it remains the same as then. It is long, low, and narrow, and being without furniture or fireplace, it still has rather a jail-like look. I was sorry for the new plastering; for I hoped to find some record of prison thoughts cut in the walls. Two doves were cuddled together on a bench in one corner, and looked in somewhat melancholy mood. These mates were all alone in that silent apartment, where Andre shed bitter tears over the miniature of his beloved. Alas for mated human hearts! This world is too often for them a pilgrimage of sorrow.

The miniature, which Andre made such strong efforts to preserve, when everything else was taken from him, and which he carried next his heart till the last fatal moment, is generally supposed to have been a likeness of the beautiful, graceful, and highly-gifted Honora Sneyd, who married Richard Lovel Edgeworth, and thus became step-mother to the celebrated Maria Edgeworth.[11] A strong youthful attachment existed between her and Major Andre; but for some reason or other they separated. He entered the army, and died the death of a felon. *Was* he a felon? No. He was generous, kind, and brave. His noble nature was perverted by the maxims of war; but the act he committed for the British army was what an American officer would have gloried in doing for his own. Washington *employed* spies; nor is it probable that he, or any other military commander, would have hesitated to *become* one, if by so doing so he could get the enemy completely into his power. It is not therefore a sense of justice, but a wish to inspire terror, which leads to the execution of spies. War is a game, in which the devil plays at nine-pins with the souls of men.

Early the next morning, we rose before the sun, and took a wagon ride, of ten miles, to Rockland Lake. The road was exceedingly romantic. On one side, high, precipitous hills, covered with luxuriant foliage, or rising in perpendicular masses of stone, singularly like the facade of some ruined castle; on the other side, almost near enough to dip our hands in its waters, flowed the broad Hudson, with a line of glittering light along its edge, announcing the coming sun. Our path lay straight over the high hills, full of rolling stones, and innumerable elbows; for it went round about to avoid every rock, as a good, old-fashioned Dutch path should, in prophetic contempt of railroads. But all around was verdure, abundance, and beauty; and we could have been well content to wind round and round among those picturesque hills, like Peter Rugg,[12] in his everlasting ride, had not the advancing sun given premonitory symptoms of the fiercest heat. We plainly saw that he was pulling the corn up by the hair of its head, and making the grass grow with a forty horse power. At last, the lake itself opened upon us, with whole troops of lilies. This pure sheet of water, more than a mile long, is inclosed by a most graceful sweep of hills, verdant with foliage, and dotted with golden grain. It is as beautiful a scene as my eye ever rested on. "A piece of heaven let fall to earth." At the farm where we lodged, a summer house was placed on a verdant curve, which swelled out into the lake, as if a breeze had floated it there in play. There I sat all day long, too happy to talk. Never did I thus throw myself on the bosom of Nature, as it were on the heart of my dearest friend. The cool rippling of the water, the whirring of a humming-bird, and the happy notes of some little warbler, tending her nest directly over our heads, was all that broke silence in that most beautiful temple.

After a while, our landlord came among us. He had been a sailor, soldier, Indian doctor, and farmer; but the incidents of his changing life had for him no deeper significance than the accumulation of money.

I sighed, that man alone should be at discord with the harmony of nature. But the bird again piped a welcome to her young; and no other false note intruded on the universal hymn of earth, and air, and sky.

At twilight, we took boat, and went paddling about among the shadows of the green hills. I wept when I gave a farewell look to Rockland Lake; for I had no hope that I should ever again see her lovely face, or listen to her friendly voice; and none but Him, who speaks through Nature, can ever know what heavenly things she whispered in my ear, that happy summer's day.

Letter XXVI[1]
September 1, 1842

From childhood, I have had a most absorbing passion for flowers. What unheard of quantities of moss and violets have I trailed from their shady birthplace, to some little nook, which fate allowed me, for the time being, to call my home! And then, how I have pitied the poor things, and feared they would not be so happy, as if I had left them alone. Yet flowers ever seemed to thrive with me, as if they knew I loved them. Perchance they *did;* for invisible radii, inaudible language, go forth from the souls of all things. Nature ever sees and hears it; as man would, were it not for his *self-listening.*

The flowers have spoken to me more than I can tell in written words. They are the hieroglyphics of angels, loved by all men for the beauty of the character, though few can decypher even fragments of their meaning. Minerals, flowers, and birds, among a thousand other tri-une ideas, ever speak to me of the Past, the Present, and the Future. The Past, like minerals, with their fixed forms of gorgeous but unchanging beauty; the Present, like flowers, growing and ever changing—bud, blossom, and seed-vessel—seed, bud, and blossom, in endless progression; the Future, like birds, with winged aspirations, and a voice that sings into the clouds. Not separate are past, present, and future; but one evolved from the other, like the continuous, ever-rising line of the spiral: and not separate are minerals, vegetables, and animals. The same soul pervades them all; they are but higher and higher types of the self-same Ideas; spirally they rise, one out of the other. Strike away one curve in the great growth of the universe, and the stars themselves would fall. Some glimpses of these arcana were revealed to the ancients; hence the spiral line occurs frequently among the sacred and mysterious emblems in their temples.

There is an astronomical theory that this earth, by a succession of spiral movements, is changing its position, until its poles will be brought into harmonious relation with the poles of the heavens; then sunshine will equally overspread the globe, and Spring become perpetual. I know not whether this theory be correct; but I think it is—for reasons not at all allied with astronomical knowledge. If the millenium, so long prophesied, ever comes, if the lion and the lamb ever lie down together within the souls of men, the outward world must likewise come into divine order, and the poles of the earth will harmonize with the poles of the heavens; then shall universal Spring reign without, the emblem and offspring of universal Peace within.

Everywhere in creation, we find visible types of these ascending series. Everything is interlinked; each reaches one hand upward and one downward, and touching palms, each is interclasped with all above and all below. Plainly is this truth written on the human soul, both in its individual and universal progress; and *therefore* it is inscribed on all material forms. But yesterday, I saw a plant called the Crab Cactus, most singularly like the animal from which it takes its name. My companion said it was "a strange freak of Nature." But I knew it was no *freak*. I saw that the cactus and the crab meant the same thing—one on a higher plane than the other. The singular plant was the point where fish and vegetable touched palms; where the ascending spiral circles passed into each other. There is another Cactus that resembles the Sea Urchin; and another, like the Star-fish. In fact, they all seem allied to the crustaceous tribe of animals; and from the idea, which this embodies, sprung the fancy that fairies of the earth sometimes formed strange union with merrows of the sea. Every fancy, the wildest and the strangest, is somewhere in the universe of God, a fact.

Another indication of interlinking series is found in the zoophytes, the strangest of all links between the vegetable and animal world; sometimes growing from a stem like a plant, and radiating like a blossom, yet devouring insects and digesting them, like an animal. Behold minerals in their dark mines! how they strive toward efflorescence, in picturesque imitation of foliage and tendrils, and roots, and tangled vines. Such minerals are approaching the circle of creation that lies above them, and from which they receive their life; mineral and vegetable here touch palms, and pass the electric fluid that pervades all life.

As the approach of different planes in existence is indicated in forms, so is it in character and uses. Among minerals, the magnet points ever to the North; so is there a plant in the prairies, called by travellers the Polar Plant, or Indian Compass, because the plane of its leaf points due North and South, without other variation than the temporary ruffling of the breeze.

If these secrets were clearly read, they might throw much light on the science of healing, and perhaps reconcile the clashing claims of mineral and vegetable medicines. Doubtless every substance in Nature is an antidote to some physical evil; owing to some spiritual cause, as fixed as the laws of mathematics, but not as easily perceived. The toad, when bitten by a spider, goes to the plantain leaf, and is cured; the bird, when stung by the yellow serpent, flies to the Guaco plant, and is healed. If we knew what spiritual evil was represented by the spider's poison, and what spiritual good by the plantain leaf, we should probably see the mystery revealed. Good always overcomes the evil, which is its perverted form; thus love casteth out hatred, truth overcomes falsehood, and suspicion cannot live before perfect frankness. Always and everywhere is evil overcome with good; and because it is so in the soul of man, it is and must be so in all the laws and operations of Nature.

> "There are influences yet unthought, and virtues, and many inventions,
> And uses, above and around, which man hath not yet regarded.
> —There be virtues yet unknown in the wasted foliage of the elm,
> In the sun-dried harebell of the downs, and the hyacinth drinking in the
>   meadows;
> In the sycamore's winged fruit, and the facet-cut cones of the cedar;
> And the pansy and bright geranium live not alone for beauty,
> Nor the waxen flower of the arbute, though it dieth in a day;
> Nor the sculptured crest of the fir, unseen but by the stars;
> And the meanest weed of the garden serveth unto many uses;
> The salt tamarisk, and juicy flag, the freckled arum, and the daisy.
> For every green herb, from the lotus to the darnel,
> Is rich with delicate aids to help incurious man."

> "There is a final *cause* for the aromatic gum, that congealeth the moss
>   around a rose;
> A *reason* for each blade of grass, that reareth its small spire.
> How knoweth discontented man what a train of ills might follow,
> If the lowest menial of nature knew not her secret office?
> In the perfect circle of creation not an atom could be spared,
> From earth's magnetic zone to the bindweed round a hawthorn.
> The briar and the palm have the wages of life, rendering secret service."

I did not *intend* to write thus mystically; and I feel that these are thoughts that should be spoken into your private ear, not published to the world. To some few they may, perchance, awaken a series of aspiring thoughts, till the highest touch the golden harps of heaven, and fill the world with celestial echoes. But to most they will seem an ambitious attempt to write something, which is in fact nothing. Be it so. I have spoken in a language which few understand, and none can teach or learn. It writes itself in sunbeams, on flowers, gems, and an infinity of forms.

I know it at a glance; but I learned it in no school. When I go home and shut the door, it speaks to me, as if it were a voice; but amid the multitude, the sound is hushed.

This which people call the real world, is not real to me; all its sights seem to me shadows, all its sounds echoes. I live at service in it, and sweep dead leaves out of paths, and dust mirrors, and do errands, as I am bid; but glad am I when work is done, to go *home* to rest. Then do I enter a golden palace, with light let in only from above; and all forms of beauty are on the walls, from the seraph before God's throne, to the rose-tinted shell on the sea-shore.

I strove *not* to speak in mysticism; and lo, here I am, as the Germans would say, "up in the blue" again. I know not how it is, my thoughts to-day are like birds of paradise; they have no feet, and will not light on earth.

I began to write about flowers with the utmost simplicity; not meaning to twine of them a spiral ladder of garlands from earth to heaven. The whole fabric arose from my looking into the blue eyes of my German Forget-me-not, which seems so much like a babe just wakening from a pleasant dream. Then my heart blessed flowers from its inmost depths. I thought of the beautiful story of the Italian child laid on the bed of death with a wreath among his golden ringlets, and a bouquet in his little cold hand. They had decked him thus for the angels; but when they went to place him in his coffin, lo, the little cherub was sitting up playing with the flowers.

How the universal heart of man blesses flowers! They are wreathed round the cradle, the marriage altar, and the tomb. The Persian in the far East, delights in their perfume, and writes his love in nosegays, while the Indian child of the far west clasps his hands with glee, as he gathers the abundant blossoms—the illuminated scripture of the prairies. The Cupid of the ancient Hindoos tipped his arrows with flowers, and orange buds are the bridal crown with us, a nation of yesterday. Flowers garlanded the Grecian altar, and they hang in votive wreaths before the Christian shrine.

All these are appropriate uses. Flowers should deck the brow of the youthful bride, for they are in themselves a lovely type of marriage. They should twine round the tomb, for their perpetually renewed beauty is a symbol of the resurrection. They should festoon the altar, for their fragrance and their beauty ascend in perpetual worship, before the Most High.[2]

Letter XXVII [1]
September 8, 1842

It is curious to observe by what laws ideas are associated; how, from the tiniest seed of thought, rises the umbrageous tree, with moss about its foot, blossoms on its head, and birds among its branches. Reading my last letter, concerning the spiral series of the universe, some busy little spirit suggested that there should, somewhere in creation, be a flower that made music. But I said, do they not *all* make melody? The Persians write their music in *colours;* and perchance in the arrangement of flowers, angels may perceive songs and anthems. The close relationship between light and music has been more or less dimly perceived by the human mind everywhere. The Persian, when he gave to each *note* a *colour,* probably embodied a greater mystery than he understood. The same undefined perception makes us talk of the *harmony* of colours, and the *tone* of a picture; it led the blind man to say that his idea of red was like the sound of a trumpet; and it taught Festus[2] to speak of "a rainbow of sweet sounds." John S. Dwight[3] was inspired with the same idea, when he eloquently described music as "a prophecy of what life is to be; the rainbow of promise, translated out of *seeing* into *hearing.*"

But I must not trust myself to trace the beautiful analogy between light and music. As I muse upon it, it is like an opening between clouds, so transparent, and so deep, *deep,* that it seems as if one could see through it beyond the farthest star—if one *could* but gaze long and earnestly enough.

"Every flower writes music on the air;" and every tree that grows enshrines a tone within its heart. Do you doubt it? Try the willow and the oak, the elm and the poplar, and see whether each has not its own peculiar sound, waiting only for the master's hand to make them discourse sweet music. One of the most remarkable instruments ever invented gives proof of this. M. Guzikow was a Polish Jew;[4] a shepherd in the service of a nobleman. From earliest childhood, music seemed to pervade his whole being. As he tended his flocks in the loneliness of the fields, he was for ever fashioning flutes and reeds from the trees that grew around him. He soon observed that the tone of the flute varied according to the wood he used; by degrees he came to know every tree by its sound; and the forests stood round him a silent oratorio. The skill with which he played on his rustic flutes attracted attention. The nobility invited him to their houses, and he became a favourite of fortune. Men never grew weary of hearing him. But soon it was perceived that he was pouring forth the fountains of his life in song. Physicians said he must abjure the flute, or die. It was a dreadful sacrifice; for music to him *was* life. His old familiarity with tones of the forest came to his aid. He took four round sticks of wood, and bound them closely together with bands of straw; across these he arranged numerous pieces of round, smooth wood, of different kinds. They were arranged irregularly to the eye, though harmoniously to the ear; for some jutted beyond the straw-bound foundation at one end, and some at the other; in and out, in apparent confusion. The whole was lashed together with twine, as men would fasten a raft. This was laid on a common table, and struck with two small ebony sticks. Rude as the instrument appeared, Guzikow brought from it such rich and liquid melody, that it seemed to take the heart of man on its wings, and bear it aloft to the throne of God. They who have heard it, describe it as far exceeding even the miraculous warblings of Paganini's violin.[5] The emperor of Austria heard it, and forthwith took the Polish peasant into his own especial service. In some of the large cities, he now and then gave a concert, by royal permission; and on such an occasion he was heard by a friend of mine at Hamburg.

The countenance of the musician was very pale and haggard, and his large dark eyes wildly expressive. He covered his head, according to the custom of the Jews; but the small cap of black velvet was not to be distinguished in colour from the jet black hair that fell from under it, and flowed over his shoulders in glossy, natural ringlets. He wore the costume of his people, an ample robe, that fell about him in graceful folds. From head to foot all was black, as his own hair and eyes, relieved only by the burning brilliancy of a diamond on his breast. The butterflies of fashion were of course attracted by the unusual and poetic beauty of his appearance; and ringlets *à la Guzikow* were the order of the day.

Before this singularly gifted being stood a common wooden table, on which reposed his rude-looking invention. He touched it with his ebony sticks. At first you heard a sound as of wood; the orchestra rose higher and higher, till it drowned its voice; then gradually subsiding, the wonderful instrument rose above other sounds, clear-warbling, like a nightingale; the orchestra rose higher, like the coming of the breeze—but above them all, swelled the sweet tones of the magic instrument, rich, liquid, and strong, like a sky-lark piercing the heavens! They who heard it listened in delighted wonder, that the trees could be made to speak thus under the touch of genius.

There is something pleasant to my imagination in the fact that every tree has its own peculiar note, and is a performer in the great concert of the universe, which for ever rises before the throne of Jehovah. But when the idea is applied to *man,* it is painful in the extreme. The emperor of Russia is said to have an imperial band, in which each man is doomed all his life long to sound *one* note, that he may acquire the greatest possible perfection. The effect of the whole is said to be admirable; but nothing would tempt me to hear this human musical machine. A *tree* is a *unit* in creation; though, like everything else, it stands in relation to all things. But every human *soul* represents the *universe.* There is horrible profanation in compelling a living spirit to utter but one note. Theological sects strive to do this continually; for they *are* sects because they magnify some *one* attribute of deity, or see but *one* aspect of the divine government. To me, their fragmentary echoes are most discordant; but doubtless the angels listen to them as a *whole,* and perhaps they hear a pleasant chorus.

Music, whether I listen to it, or try to analyse it, ever fills me with thoughts which I cannot express—because I cannot *sing;* for nothing but music can express the emotions to which it gives birth. Language, even the richest flow of metaphor, is too poor to do it. That the universe moves to music, I have no doubt; and could I but penetrate this mystery, where the finite passes into the infinite, I should surely know how the world was created. Pythagoras supposed that the heavenly bodies, in their motion, produced music inaudible to mortal ears. These motions he believed conformed to certain fixed laws, that could be stated in *numbers*, corresponding to the numbers which express the harmony of sounds. This "music of the spheres" has been considered an idea altogether fanciful; but the immortal Kepler applied the Pythagorean theory of numbers, and musical intervals, to the distances of the planets; and a long time after, Newton discovered and acknowledged the importance of the application.[6] Said I not that the universe moved to music? The planets dance before Jehovah; and music is the echo of their motions. Surely the ear of Beethoven had listened to it, when he wrote those misnamed "waltzes" of his, which, as John S. Dwight says, "remind us of no dance, unless it be the dances of the heavenly systems in their sublime career through space."

Have you ever seen Retzsch's illustration of Schiller's Song of a Bell?[7] If you have, and know how to appreciate its speaking gracefulness, its earnest depth of life, you are richer than Rothschild or Astor; for a vision of beauty is an everlasting inheritance. Perhaps none but a German, would have thus entwined the sound of a bell with the whole of human life; for with them the bell mingles with all of mirth, sorrow, and worship. Almost all of the German and Belgian towns are provided with chiming bells, which play at noon and evening. There was such a set of musical bells on the church of St. Nicholas, at Hamburg. The bell-player was a gray-headed man, who had for many years rung forth the sonorous chimes, that told the hours to the busy throng below. When the church was on fire, either from infirmity, or want of thought, the old man remained at his post. In the terrible confusion of the blazing city, no one thought of him, till the high steeple was seen wreathed with flame. As the throng gazed upward, the firm walls of the old church, that had stood for ages, began to shake. At that moment the bells sounded the well-known German Choral, which usually concludes the Protestant service, "Nun danket alle Gott"—"Now all thank God." Another moment, and there was an awful crash! The bells, which had spoken into the hearts of so many generations, went silent for ever. They and the old musician sunk together into a fiery grave; but the echo of their chimes goes sounding on through the far eternity.

They have a beautiful custom at Hamburg. At ten o'clock in the morning, when the men are hurrying hither and yon in the great whirlpool of business, from the high church tower comes down the sound of sacred music, from a large and powerful horn appropriated to that service. It is as if an angel spake from the clouds, reminding them of immortality.

You have doubtless heard of the mysterious music that peals over the bay at West Pascagoula. It has for a long time been one of the greatest wonders of the Southwest. Multitudes have heard it, rising as it were from the water, like the drone of a bagpipe, then floating away—away—away—in the distance—soft, plaintive, and fairy-like, as if Æolian harps[8] sounded with richer melody through the liquid element; but none have been able to account for the beautiful phenomenon.

"There are several legends touching these mysterious sounds. One of them relates to the extinction of the Pascagoula tribe of Indians;[9] the remnant of which, many years ago, it is said, deliberately entered the waters of the bay and drowned themselves, to escape capture and torture, when attacked by a neighbouring formidable tribe. There is another legend, as well authenticated as traditionary history can well be, to the effect, that about one hundred years ago, three families of Spaniards, who had provoked the resentment of the Indians, were beset by the savages, and to avoid massacre and pollution, marched into the bay, and were drowned—men, women, and children. Tradition adds, that the Spaniards went down to the waters following a drum and pipe, and singing, as enthusiasts are said to do, when about to commit self-immolation. Slaves in the neighbourhood believe that the sounds, which sweep with mournful cadence over the bay, are uttered by the spirits of those hapless families; nor will any remonstrance against the superstition abate their terror, when the wailing is heard." Formerly, neither threats nor blows could induce them to venture out after night; and to this day, it is exceedingly difficult to induce one of them to go in a boat alone upon the quiet waters of Pascagoula Bay. One of them, being asked by a recent traveller what he thought occasioned that music, replied:

"Wall, I tinks it's dead folks come back agin; dat's what I does. White people say it's dis ting and dat ting; but it's noting, massa, but de ghosts of people wat didn't die nat'rally in dere beds, long time ago—Indians or Spaniards, I believes dey was."

"But does the music never frighten you?"

"Well, it does. Sometimes wen I'se out alone on de bay in a skiff, and I hears it about, I always finds myself in a perspiration; and de way I works my way home, is of de fastest kind. I declare, de way I'se frightened sometimes, is so bad, I doesn't know myself."

But in these days, few things are allowed to *remain* mysterious. A correspondent of the Baltimore Republican thus explains the music of the water-spirits:

"During several of my voyages on the Spanish main, in the neighbourhood of 'Paraguay,' and San Juan de Nicaragua, from the nature of the coast, we were compelled to anchor at a considerable distance from the shore; and every evening, from dark to late night, our ears were delighted with Æolian music, that could be heard beneath the counter of our schooner. At first, I thought it was the sea-breeze sweeping through the strings of my violin, (the bridge of which I had inadvertently left standing;) but after examination, I found it was not so. I then placed my ear on the rail of the vessel, when I was continually charmed with the most heavenly strains that ever fell upon my ear. They did not sound as close to us, but were sweet, mellow, and aerial; like the soft breathings of a thousand lutes, touched by fingers of the deep sea-nymphs, at an immense distance.

"Although I have considerable 'music in my soul,' one night I became tired, and determined to fish. My luck in half an hour was astonishing; I had half filled my bucket with the finest white cat-fish I ever saw; and it being late, and the cook asleep, and the moon shining, I filled my bucket with water, and took fish and all into my cabin for the night.

"I had not yet fallen asleep, when the same sweet notes fell upon my ear; and getting up, what was my surprise to find my 'cat fish' discoursing sweet sounds to the sides of my bucket.

"I examined them closely, and discovered that there was attached to each lower lip an excrescence, divided by soft, wiry fibres. By the pressure of the upper lip thereon, and by the exhalation and discharge of breath, a vibration was created, similar to that produced by the breath on the tongue of the jew's-harp."

So you see the Naiads have a band to dance by. I should like to have the mocking-bird try his skill at imitating this submarine melody. You know the Bob-o'link with his inimitable strain of "linked sweetness, long drawn out?" At a farm-house occupied by my father-in-law, one of these rich warblers came and seated himself on a rail near the window, and began to sing. A cat-bird (our New England mocking-bird) perched near, and began to imitate the notes. The short, quick, "bob-a-link," "bob-a-link," he could master very well; but when it came to the prolonged trill of gushing melody, at the close of the strain—the imitator stopped in the midst. Again the bob-o'-link poured forth his soul in song; the mocking-bird hopped nearer, and listened most intently. Again he tried; but it was all in vain. The bob-o'-link, as if conscious that none could imitate his God-given tune, sent forth a clearer, stronger, richer strain than ever. The mocking-bird evidently felt that his reputation was at stake. He warbled all kinds of notes in quick succession. You would have thought the house was surrounded by robins, sparrows, whippowills, black-birds, and linnets. Having shown off his ac-complishments, he again tried his powers on the all-together inimitable trill. The effort he made was prodigious; but it was mere talent trying to copy genius. He couldn't do it. He stopped, gasping, in the midst of the prolonged melody, and flew away abruptly, in evident vexation.

Music, like everything else, is now passing from the few to the many. The art of printing has laid before the multitude the written wisdom of ages, once locked up in the elaborate manuscripts of the cloister. Engraving and daguerreotype spread the productions of the pencil before the whole people. Music is taught in our common schools, and the cheap accordion brings its delights to the hum-blest class of citizens. All these things are full of prophecy. Slowly, slowly, to the measured sound of the spirit's music, there goes round the world the golden band of brotherhood; slowly, slowly, the earth comes to its place, and makes a chord with heaven.

Sing on, thou true-hearted, and be not discouraged! If a harp be in perfect tune, and a flute, or other instrument of music, be near it, and in perfect tune also, thou canst not play on one without wakening an answer from the other. Behold, thou shalt hear its sweet echo in the air, as if played on by the invisible. Even so shall other spirits vibrate to the harmony of thine. Utter what God giveth thee to say. In the sunny West Indies, in gay and graceful Paris, in frozen Iceland, and the deep stillness of the Hindoo jungle, thou wilt wake a slumbering echo, to be carried on for ever through the universe. In word and act sing thou of united truth and love; another voice shall take up the strain over the waters; soon it will become a WORLD CONCERT;—and thou above there, in that realm of light and love, well pleased wilt hear thy early song, in earth's sweet vibration to the harps of heaven.

Letter XXVIII [1]
September 29, 1842

I wish I could walk abroad without having misery forced on my notice, which I have no power to relieve. The other day, I looked out of my window, and saw a tall, gaunt-looking woman leading a little ragged girl, of five or six years old. The child carried a dirty little basket, and I observed that she went up to every door, and stood on tiptoe to reach the bell. From every one, as she held up her little basket, she turned away, and came down the steps so wearily, and looked so sad— so very sad. I saw this repeated at four or five doors, and my heart began to swell within me. "I cannot endure this," thought I: "I must buy whatever her basket contains." Then prudence answered, "Where's the use? Don't you meet twenty objects more wretched every day? Where can you stop?" I moved from my window; but as I did so, I saw my guardian angel turn away in sorrow. I felt that neither incense nor anthem would rise before God from that selfish second thought. I went to the door. Another group of suffering wretches were coming from the other end of the street; and I turned away again, with the feeling that there was no use in attending to the hopeless mass of misery around me. I should have closed the door, perhaps, but as the little girl came near, I saw on her neck a cross, with a rudely carved image of the crucified Saviour. Oh, blessed Jesus! friend of the poor, the suffering, and the guilty, who is like thee to guide the erring soul, and soften the selfish heart? The tears gushed to my eyes. I bought from the little basket a store of matches for a year. The woman offered me change; but I could not take it in sight of that cross. "In the Saviour's name, take it all," I said, "and buy clothes for that little one." A gleam lighted up the woman's hard features; she looked surprised and grateful. But the child grabbed at the money, with a hungry avarice, that made my very heart ache. Hardship, privation, and perchance severity, had changed the genial heart-warmth, the gladsome thoughtlessness of childhood, into the grasping sensuality of a world-trodden soul. It seemed to me the saddest thing, that in all God's creation there should be one such little child. I almost feared they had driven the angels away from her. But it is not so. *Her* angel, too, does always stand before the face of her Father, who is in Heaven.

This time, I yielded to the melting of my heart; but a hundred times a week, I drive back the generous impulse, because I have not the means to gratify it. This is the misery of a city like New-York, that a kindly spirit not only suffers continual pain, but is obliged to do itself perpetual wrong. At times, I almost fancy I can feel myself turning to stone by inches. Gladly, oh, how gladly, do I hail any little sunbeam of love, that breaks through this cloud of misery and wrong.

The other day, as I came down Broome-street, I saw a street musician, playing near the door of a genteel dwelling. The organ was uncommonly sweet and mellow in its tones, the tunes were slow and plaintive, and I fancied that I saw in the woman's Italian face an expression that indicated sufficient refinement to prefer the tender and the melancholy, to the lively "trainer tunes" in vogue with the populace. She looked like one who had suffered much, and the sorrowful music seemed her own appropriate voice. A little girl clung to her scanty garments, as if afraid of all things but her mother. As I looked at them, a young lady of pleasing countenance opened the window, and began to sing like a bird, in keeping with the street organ. Two other young girls came and leaned on her shoulder; and still she sang on. Blessings on her gentle heart! It was evidently the spontaneous gush of human love and sympathy. The beauty of the incident attracted attention. A group of gentlemen gradually collected round the organist; and ever as the tune ended, they bowed respectfully toward the window, waved their hats, and called out, "More, if you please!" One, whom I knew well for the kindest and truest soul, passed round his hat; hearts were kindled, and the silver fell in freely. In a minute, four or five dollars were collected for the poor woman. She spoke no word of gratitude, but she gave *such* a look! "Will you go to the next street, and play to a friend of mine?" said my kind-hearted friend. She answered, in tones expressing the deepest emotion, "No, sir, God bless you all—God bless you *all*," (making a courtesy to the young lady, who had stept back, and stood sheltered by the curtain of the window,) "I will play no more to-day; I will go *home*, now." The tears trickled down her cheeks, and as she walked away, she ever and anon wiped her eyes with the corner of her shawl. The group of gentlemen lingered a moment to look after her, then turning toward the now closed window, they gave three enthusiastic cheers, and departed, better than they came. The pavement on which they stood had been a church to them; and for the next hour, at least, their hearts were more than usually prepared for deeds of gentleness and mercy. Why are such scenes so uncommon? Why do we thus repress our sympathies, and chill the genial current of nature, by formal observances and restraints?

I thank my heavenly Father for every manifestation of human love. I thank him for all experiences, be they sweet or bitter, which help me to forgive all things, and to enfold the whole world with blessing. "What shall be our reward," says Swedenborg,[2] "for loving our neighbour *as* ourselves in this life? That when we become angels, we shall be enabled to love him *better* than ourselves." This is a reward pure and holy; the only one, which my heart has not rejected, whenever offered as an incitement to goodness. It is this chiefly which makes the happiness of lovers more nearly allied to heaven, than any other emotions experienced by the human heart. Each loves the other better than himself; each is willing to sacrifice all to the other—nay, finds joy therein. This it is that surrounds them with a golden atmosphere, and tinges the world with rose-colour. A mother's love has the same angelic character; more completely unselfish, but lacking the charm of perfect reciprocity.

The cure for all the ills and wrongs, the cares, the sorrows, and the crimes of humanity, all lie in that one word, LOVE. It is the divine vitality that everywhere produces and restores life. To each and every one of us it gives the power of working miracles, if we will.

"Love is the story without an end, that angels throng to hear;
The word, the king of words, carved on Jehovah's heart."

From the highest to the lowest, all feel its influence, all acknowledge its sway. Even the poor, despised donkey is changed by its magic influence. When coerced and beaten, he is vicious, obstinate, and stupid. With the peasantry of Spain, he is a petted favourite, almost an inmate of the household. The children bid him welcome home, and the wife feeds him from her hands. He knows them all, and he loves them all, for he feels in his inmost heart that they all love him. He will follow his master, and come and go at his bidding, like a faithful dog; and he delights to take the baby on his back, and walk him round, gently, on the greensward. His intellect expands, too, in the sunshine of affection; and he that is called the stupidest of animals becomes sagacious. A Spanish peasant had for many years carried milk into Madrid, to supply a set of customers. Every morning, he and his donkey, with loaded panniers, trudged the well-known round. At last, the peasant became very ill, and had no one to send to market. His wife proposed to send the faithful old animal by himself. The panniers were accordingly filled with cannisters of milk; an inscription, written by the priest, requested customers to measure their own milk, and return the vessels; and the donkey was instructed to set off with his load. He went, and returned in due time with empty cannisters; and this he continued to do for several days. The house bells in Madrid are usually so constructed that you pull downward to make them ring. The peasant afterward learned that his sagacious animal stopped before the door of every customer, and after waiting what he deemed a sufficient time, pulled the bell with his mouth. If affectionate treatment will thus idealize the jackass, what may it not do? Assuredly there is no limit to its power. It can banish crime, and make this earth an Eden.

The best tamer of colts that was ever known in Massachusetts, never allowed whip or spur to be used; and the horses he trained never *needed* the whip. Their spirits were unbroken by severity, and they obeyed the slightest impulse of the voice or rein, with the most animated promptitude; but rendered obedient to affection, their vivacity was always restrained by graceful docility. He said it was with horses as with children; if accustomed to beating, they would not obey without it. But if managed with untiring gentleness, united with consistent and very equable firmness, the victory once gained over them, was gained for ever.

In the face of all these facts, the world goes on manufacturing whips, spurs, the gallows, and chains; while each one carries within his own soul a divine substitute for these devil's inventions, with which he *might* work miracles, inward and outward, if he *would*.[3] Unto this end let us work with unfaltering faith. Great is the strength of an individual soul, true to its high trust;—mighty is it even to the redemption of a world.

A German, whose sense of sound was exceedingly acute, was passing by a church, a day or two after he had landed in this country, and the sound of music attracted him to enter, though he had no knowledge of our language. The music proved to be a piece of nasal psalmody, sung in most discordant fashion; and the sensitive German would fain have covered his ears. As this was scarcely civil, and might appear like insanity, his next impulse was to rush into the open air, and leave the hated sounds behind him. "But this, too, I feared to do," said he, "lest offence might be given; so I resolved to endure the torture with the best fortitude I could assume; when lo! I distinguished, amid the din, the soft clear voice of a woman singing in perfect tune. She made no effort to drown the voices of her companions, neither was she disturbed by their noisy discord; but patiently and sweetly she sang in full, rich tones: one after another yielded to the gentle influence; and before the tune was finished, all were in perfect harmony."

I have often thought of this story as conveying an instructive lesson for reformers. The spirit that *can* thus sing patiently and sweetly in a world of discord, must indeed be of the strongest, as well as the gentlest kind. One scarce can hear his own soft voice amid the braying of the multitude; and ever and anon comes the temptation to sing louder than they, and drown the voices that cannot thus be *forced* into perfect tune. But this were a pitiful experiment; the melodious tones, cracked into shrillness, would only increase the tumult.

Stronger, and more frequently, comes the temptation to stop singing, and let discord do its own wild work. But blessed are they that endure to the end— singing patiently and sweetly, till all join in with loving acquiescence, and universal harmony prevails, without forcing into submission the free discord of a single voice.

This is the hardest and the bravest task, which a true soul has to perform amid the clashing elements of time. But *once* has it been done perfectly, unto the end; and that voice, so clear in its meekness, is heard above all the din of a tumultuous world; one after another chimes in with its patient sweetness; and, through infinite discords, the listening soul can perceive that the great tune is slowly coming into harmony.

Letter XXIX [1]
October 6, 1842

I went last week to Blackwell's island, in the East river, between the city and Long Island. The environs of the city are unusually beautiful, considering how far Autumn has advanced upon us. Frequent rains have coaxed vegetation into abundance, and preserved it in verdant beauty. The trees are hung with a profusion of vines, the rocks are dressed in nature's green velvet of moss, and from every little cleft peeps the rich foliage of some wind-scattered seed. The island itself presents a quiet loveliness of scenery, unsurpassed by anything I have ever witnessed; though Nature and I are old friends, and she has shown me many of her choicest pictures, in a light let in only from above. No form of gracefulness can compare with the bend of flowing waters all round and round a verdant island. The circle typifies Love; and they who read the spiritual alphabet, will see that a circle of *waters* must needs be very beautiful. Beautiful it *is*, even when the language it speaks is an unknown tongue. Then the green hills beyond look so very pleasant in the sunshine, with *homes* nestling among them, like dimples on a smiling face. The island itself abounds with charming nooks—open wells in shady places, screened by large weeping willows; gardens and arbors running down to the river's edge, to look at themselves in the waters; and pretty boats, like white-winged birds, chased by their shadows, and breaking the waves into gems.

But man has profaned this charming retreat. He has brought the screech-owl, the bat, and the vulture, into the holy temple of Nature. The island belongs to government; and the only buildings on it are penitentiary, mad-house, and hospital; with a few dwellings occupied by people connected with those institutions. The discord between man and nature never before struck me so painfully; yet it is wise and kind to place the erring and the diseased in the midst of such calm, bright influences. Man may curse, but Nature for ever blesses. The guiltiest of her wandering children she would fain enfold within her arms to the friendly heart-warmth of a mother's bosom. She speaks to them ever in the soft, low tones of earnest love; but they, alas, tossed on the roaring, stunning surge of society, forget the quiet language.

As I looked up at the massive walls of the prison, it did my heart good to see doves nestling within the shelter of the deep, narrow, grated windows. I thought what blessed little messengers of heaven they would appear to me, if I were in prison; but instantly a shadow passed over the sunshine of my thought. Alas, doves do not speak to *their* souls, as they would to *mine;* for they have lost their love for child-like, and gentle things. *How* have they lost it? Society with its unequal distribution, its perverted education, its manifold injustice, its cold neglect, its biting mockery, has taken from them the gifts of God. They are placed here, in the midst of green hills, and flowing streams, and cooing doves, after the heart is petrified against the genial influence of all such sights and sounds.

As usual, the organ of justice (which phrenologists say is unusually developed in my head) was roused into great activity by the sight of prisoners. "Would you have them prey on society?" said one of my companions. I answered, "I am troubled that society has preyed upon *them.* I will not enter into an argument about the right of society to punish these sinners; but I say she *made* them sinners. How much I have done toward it, by yielding to popular prejudices, obeying false customs, and suppressing vital truths, I know not; but doubtless I have done, and am doing, my share. God forgive me. If He dealt with us, as we deal with our brother, who could stand before Him?"

While I was there, they brought in the editors of the Flash, the Libertine, and the Weekly Rake.[2] My very soul loathes such polluted publications; yet a sense of justice again made me refractory. These men were perhaps trained to such service by all the social influences they had ever known. They dared to *publish* what nine-tenths of all around them *lived* unreproved. Why should they be imprisoned, while————flourished in the full tide of editorial success, circulating a paper as immoral, and perhaps more dangerous, because its indecency is slightly veiled? Why should the Weekly Rake be shut up, when daily rakes walk Broadway in fine broadcloth and silk velvet?

Many more than half the inmates of the penitentiary were women; and of course a large proportion of them were taken up as "street-walkers."[3] The men who made them such, who, perchance, caused the love of a human heart to be its ruin, and changed tenderness into sensuality and crime—these men live in the "ceiled houses" of Broadway, and sit in council in the City Hall, and pass "regulations" to clear the streets they have filled with sin. And do you suppose their poor victims do not *feel* the injustice of society thus regulated? Think you they respect the *laws?* Vicious they are, and they may be both ignorant and foolish; but, nevertheless, they are too wise to respect such laws. Their whole being cries out that it is a mockery; all their experience proves that society is a game of chance, where the cunning slip through, and the strong leap over. The criminal *feels* this, even when incapable of *reasoning* upon it. The laws do not secure his reverence, because he sees that their operation is unjust. The secrets of prisons, so far as they are revealed, all tend to show that the prevailing feeling of criminals, of all grades, is that they are *wronged.* What we call *justice,* they regard as an unlucky *chance;* and whosoever looks calmly and wisely into the foundations on which society rolls and tumbles, (I cannot say on which it *rests,* for its foundations heave like the sea,) will perceive that they *are* victims of chance.

For instance, everything in school-books, social remarks, domestic conversation, literature, public festivals, legislative proceedings, and popular honours, all teach the young soul that it is noble to retaliate, mean to forgive an insult, and unmanly not to resent a wrong. Animal instincts, instead of being brought into subjection to the higher powers of the soul, are thus cherished into more than natural activity. Of three men thus educated, one enters the army, kills a hundred

Indians, hangs their scalps on a tree, is made major general, and considered a fitting candidate for the presidency.[4] The second goes to the Southwest to reside; some "roarer" calls him a rascal—a phrase not misapplied, perhaps, but necessary to be resented; he agrees to settle the question of honour at ten paces, shoots his insulter through the heart, and is hailed by society as a brave man. The third lives in New-York; a man enters his office, and, true or untrue, calls him a knave. He fights, kills his adversary, is tried by the laws of the land, and hung. These three men indulged the same passion, acted from the same motives, and illustrated the same education; yet how different their fate!

With regard to dishonesty, too—the maxims of trade, the customs of society, and the general unreflecting tone of public conversation, all tend to promote it. The man who has made "good bargains," is wealthy and honoured; yet the details of those bargains few would dare to pronounce good. Of two young men nurtured under such influences, one becomes a successful merchant; five thousand dollars are borrowed of him; he takes a mortgage on a house worth twenty thousand dollars; in the absence of the owner, when sales are very dull, he offers the house for sale, to pay his mortgage; he bids it in himself, for four thousand dollars; and afterwards persecutes and imprisons his debtor for the remaining thousand. Society calls him a shrewd business man, and pronounces his dinners excellent; the chance is, he will be a magistrate before he dies.—The other young man is unsuccessful; his necessities are great; he borrows some money from his employer's drawer, perhaps resolving to restore the same; the loss is discovered before he has a chance to refund it; and society sends him to Blackwell's island, to hammer stone with highway robbers. Society made both these men thieves; but punished the one, while she rewarded the other. That criminals so universally *feel* themselves victims of injustice, is one strong proof that it is true; for impressions entirely without foundation are not apt to become universal. If society does make its own criminals, how shall she cease to do it? It can be done only by a change in the structure of society, that will diminish the temptations to vice, and increase the encouragements to virtue. If we can abolish *poverty,* we shall have taken the greatest step towards the abolition of *crime;* and this will be the final triumph of the gospel of Christ. Diversities of gifts will doubtless always exist; for the law written on spirit, as well as matter, is infinite variety. But when the kingdom of God comes "on earth, as it is in heaven," there will not be found in any corner of it that poverty which hardens the heart under the severe pressure of physical suffering, and stultifies the intellect with toil for mere animal wants. When public opinion regards wealth as a *means,* and not as an *end,* men will no longer deem penitentiaries a necessary evil; for society will then cease to be a great school for crime. In the meantime, do penitentiaries and prisons increase or diminish the evils they are intended to remedy?

The superintendent at Blackwell told me, unasked, that ten years' experience had convinced him that the whole system tended to *increase* crime. He said of the lads who came there, a large proportion had already been in the house of refuge; and a large proportion of those who left, afterward went to Sing Sing.[5] "It is as regular a succession as the classes in a college," said he, "from the house of refuge to the penitentiary, and from the penitentiary to the State prison." I remarked that coercion tended to rouse all the bad passions in man's nature, and if long continued, hardened the whole character. "I know that," said he, "from my own experience; all the devil there is in me rises up when a man attempts to compel me. But what can I do? I am *obliged* to be very strict. When my feelings tempt me to unusual indulgence, a bad use is almost always made of it. I see that the system fails to produce the effect intended; but I cannot change the result."

I felt that his words were true. He could not change the influence of the system while he discharged the duties of his office; for the same reason that a man cannot be at once slave-driver and missionary on a plantation. I allude to the necessities of the office, and do not mean to imply that the character of the individual was severe. On the contrary, the prisoners seemed to be made as comfortable as was compatible with their situation. There were watch-towers, with loaded guns, to prevent escape from the island; but they conversed freely with each other as they worked in the sunshine, and very few of them looked wretched. Among those who were sent under guard to row us back to the city, was one who jested on his own situation, in a manner which showed plainly enough that he looked on the whole thing as a game of chance, in which he *happened* to be the loser. Indulgence cannot benefit such characters. What is wanted is, that no human being should grow up without deep and friendly interest from the society round him; and that none should feel himself the victim of injustice, because society punishes the very sins which it teaches, nay drives men to commit. The world would be in a happier condition if legislators spent half as much time and labour to *prevent* crime, as they do to *punish* it.[6] The poor need houses of *encouragement;* and society gives them houses of *correction.* Benevolent institutions and reformitory societies perform but a limited and temporary use. They do not reach the ground-work of evil; and it is reproduced too rapidly for them to keep even the surface healed. The natural, spontaneous influences of society should be such as to supply men with healthy motives, and give full, free play to the affections, and the faculties. It is horrible to see our young men goaded on by the fierce, speculating spirit of the age, from the contagion of which it is almost impossible to escape, and then see them tortured into madness, or driven to crime, by fluctuating changes of the money-market. The young soul is, as it were, entangled in the great merciless machine of a falsely-constructed society; the steam he had no hand in raising, whirls him hither and thither, and it is altogether a lottery-chance whether it crushes or propels him.

Many, who are mourning over the too obvious diseases of the world, will smile contemptuously at the idea of *reconstruction.* But let them reflect a moment upon the immense changes that have already come over society. In the middle ages, both noble and peasant would have laughed loud and long at the prophecy of such a state of society as now exists in the free States of America; yet here we are!

I by no means underrate modern improvements in the discipline of prisons, or progressive meliorations in the criminal code. I rejoice in these things as facts, and still more as prophecy. Strong as my faith is that the time will come when war and prisons will both cease from the face of the earth, I am by no means blind to the great difficulties in the way of those who are honestly striving to make the best of things as they *are*. Violations of right, continued generation after generation, and interwoven into the whole structure of action and opinion, will continue troublesome and injurious, even for a long time after they are outwardly removed. Legislators and philanthropists may well be puzzled to know what to do with those who have become hardened in crime; meanwhile, the highest wisdom should busy itself with the more important questions.—How did these men *become* criminals? Are not social influences largely at fault? If society is the criminal, were it not well to reform society?

It is common to treat the inmates of penitentiaries and prisons as if they were altogether unlike ourselves—as if they belonged to another race; but this indicates superficial thought and feeling. The passions which carried those men to prison exist in your own bosom, and have been gratified, only in a less degree: perchance, if you look inward, with enlightened self-knowledge, you will perceive that there have been periods in your own life when a hair's-breadth further in the wrong would have rendered you amenable to human laws; and that you were prevented from moving over that hair's-breadth boundary by outward circumstances, for which you deserve no credit.

If reflections like these make you think lightly of sin, you pervert them to a very bad use. They *should* teach you that every criminal has a human heart, which *can* be reached and softened by the same means that will reach and soften your own. In all, even the most hardened, love lies folded up, perchance buried; and the voice of love calls it forth, and makes it gleam like living coals through ashes. This influence, if applied in season, would assuredly *prevent* the hardness, which it has so much power to soften.

That most tender-spirited and beautiful book, entitled "My Prisons, by Sylvio Pellico,"[7] abounds with incidents to prove the omnipotence of kindness. He was a gentle and a noble soul, imprisoned merely for reasons of state, being suspected of republican notions. Robbers and banditti, confined in the same building, saluted him with respect as they passed him in the court; and he always returned their salutations with brotherly cordiality. He says, "One of them once said to me, 'Your greeting, signore, does me good. Perhaps you see something in my face that is not very bad? An unhappy passion led me to commit a crime; but oh, signore, I am not, indeed I am not a villain.' And he burst into tears. I held out my hand to him, but he could not take it. My guards, not from bad feeling, but in obedience to orders, repulsed him."

In the sight of God, perchance their repulse was a heavier crime than that for which the poor fellow was imprisoned; perhaps it *made* him "a villain," when the genial influence of Sylvio Pellico might have restored him a blessing to the human family. If these things *are* so, for what a frightful amount of crime are the coercing and repelling influences of society responsible![8]

I have not been happy since that visit to Blackwell's island. There is something painful, yea, terrific, in feeling myself involved in the great wheel of society, which goes whirling on, crushing thousands at every turn. This relation of the individual to the mass is the sternest and most frightful of all the conflicts between necessity and free will. Yet here, too, conflict *should* be harmony, and *will* be so. Put far away from thy soul all desire of retaliation, all angry thoughts, all disposition to overcome or humiliate an adversary, and be assured thou hast done much to abolish gallows, chains, and prisons, though thou hast never written or spoken a word on the criminal code.

God and good angels alone know the vast, the incalculable influence that goes out into the universe of spirit, and thence flows into the universe of matter, from the conquered evil, and the voiceless prayer, of one solitary soul. Wouldst thou bring the world unto God? Then live near to him thyself. If divine life pervade thine own soul, every thing that touches thee will receive the electric spark, though thou mayest be unconscious of being charged therewith. This surely would be the highest, to strive to keep near the holy, not for the sake of our own reward here or hereafter, but that through love to God we might bless our neighbour. The human soul can perceive this, and yet the beauty of the earth is everywhere defaced with jails and gibbets! Angelic natures can never deride, else were there loud laughter in heaven at the discord between man's perceptions and his practice.

At Long Island Farms I found six hundred children, supported by the public. It gives them wholesome food, comfortable clothing, and the common rudiments of education. For this it deserves praise. But the aliment which the spirit craves, the *public* has not to give. The young heart asks for *love,* yearns for love—but its own echo returns to it through empty halls, instead of answer.

The institution is much lauded by visiters, and not without reason; for every thing looks clean and comfortable, and the children appear happy. The drawbacks are such as inevitably belong to their situation, as children of the public. The oppressive feeling is, that there are no *mothers* there. Every thing moves by machinery, as it always must with masses of children, never subdivided into families. In one place, I saw a stack of small wooden guns, and was informed that the boys were daily drilled to military exercises, as a useful means of forming habits of order, as well as fitting them for the future service of the state. Their infant school evolutions partook of the same drill character; and as for their religion, I was informed that it was "beautiful to see them pray; for at the first tip of the whistle, they all dropped on their knees." Alas, poor childhood, thus doth "church and state" provide for thee! The state arms thee with wooden guns, to play the future murderer, and the church teaches thee to pray in platoons, "at the first tip of the whistle." Luckily they cannot drive the angels from thee, or most assuredly they would do it, *pro bono publico.*[9]

The sleeping-rooms were clean as a Shaker's apron.[10] When I saw the long rows of nice little beds, ranged side by side, I inquired whether there was not a merry buzz in the morning. "They are not permitted to speak at all in the sleeping apartments," replied the superintendent. The answer sent a chill through my heart. I acknowledged that in such large establishments the most exact method was necessary, and I knew that the children had abundant opportunity for fun and frolic in the sunshine and the open fields, in the after part of the day; but it is so natural for all young things to crow and sing when they open their eyes to the morning light, that I could not bear to have the cheerful instinct perpetually repressed.

The hospital for these children is on the neighbouring island of Blackwell. This establishment, though clean and well supplied with outward comforts, was the most painful sight I ever witnessed. About one hundred and fifty children were there, mostly orphans, inheriting every variety of disease from vicious and sickly parents. In beds all of a row, or rolling by dozens over clean matting on the floor, the poor little pale, shrivelled, and blinded creatures were waiting for death to come and release them. Here the absence of a mother's love was most agonizing; not even the patience and gentleness of a saint could supply its place; and saints are rarely hired by the public. There was a sort of resignation expressed in the countenances of some of the little ones, which would have been beautiful in maturer years, but in childhood it spoke mournfully of a withered soul. It was pleasant to think that a large proportion of them would soon be received by the angels, who will doubtless let them sing in the morning.

That the law of Love may cheer and bless even *public* establishments, has been proved by the example of the Society of Friends.[11] They formerly had an establishment for their own poor, in the city of Philadelphia, on a plan so simple and so beautiful, that one cannot but mourn to think it has given place to more common and less brotherly modes of relief. A nest of small households enclosed, on three sides, an open space devoted to gardens, in which each had a share. Here each poor family lived in separate rooms, and were assisted by the Society, according to its needs. Sometimes a widow could support herself, with the exception of rent; and in that case, merely rooms were furnished gratis. An aged couple could perhaps subsist very comfortably, if supplied with house and fuel; and the friendly assistance was according to their wants. Some needed entire support; and to such it was ungrudgingly given. These paupers were oftentimes ministers and elders, took the highest seats in the meeting-house, and had as much influence as any in the affairs of the Society. Everything conspired to make them retain undiminished self-respect. The manner in which they evinced this would be considered impudence in the tenets of our modern alms-houses. One old lady being supplied with a load of wood at her free lodgings, refused to take it, saying, that it did not suit her; she wanted dry, small wood. "But," remonstrated the man, "I was ordered to bring it here." "I can't help that. Tell 'em the best wood is the best economy. I do not want such wood as that." Her orders were obeyed, and the old lady's wishes were gratified. Another, who took great pride and pleasure in the neatness of her little garden, employed a carpenter to make a trellis for her vines. Some objection was made to paying this bill, it being considered a mere superfluity. But the old lady maintained that it was necessary for her comfort; and at meetings and all public places, she never failed to rebuke the elders. "O *you* profess to do unto others as you would be done by, and you have never paid that carpenter his bill." Worn out by her perseverance, they paid the bill, and she kept her trellis of vines. It probably was more necessary to her comfort than many things *they* would have considered as not superfluous.

The poor of this establishment did not feel like dependents, and were never regarded as a burden. They considered themselves as members of a family, receiving from brethren the assistance they would have gladly bestowed under a reverse of circumstances. This approaches the gospel standard. Since the dawn of Christianity, no class of people have furnished an example so replete with a most wise tenderness, as the Society of Friends, in the days of its purity. Thank God, nothing good or true ever dies. The lifeless form falls from it, and it lives elsewhere.

Letter XXX [1]
November 13, 1842

Oh, who that has not been shut up in the great prison-cell of a city, and made to drink of its brackish springs, can estimate the blessings of the Croton Aqueduct? clean, sweet, abundant water! Well might they bring it thirty miles under-ground, and usher it into the city with roaring cannon, sonorous bells, waving flags, floral canopies, and a loud chorus of song! [2]

I shall never forget my sensations when I first looked upon the Fountains. My soul jumped, and clapped its hands, rejoicing in exceeding beauty. I am a novice, and easily made wild by the play of graceful forms; [3] but those accustomed to the splendid displays of France and Italy, say the world offers nothing to equal the magnificence of the New-York *jets*. There is such a head of water, that it throws the column sixty feet into the air, and drops it into the basin in a shower of diamonds. The one in the Park, opposite the Astor house, consists of a large central pipe, with eighteen subordinate jets in a basin a hundred feet broad. By shifting the plate on the conduit pipe, these fountains can be made to assume various shapes: The Maid of the Mist, the Croton Plume, the Vase, the Dome, the Bouquet, the Sheaf of Wheat, and the Weeping-willow. As the sun shone on the sparkling drops, through mist and feathery foam, rainbows glimmered at the sides, as if they came to celebrate a marriage between Spirits of Light and Water Nymphs.

The fountain in Union Park is smaller, but scarcely less beautiful. It is a weeping willow of crystal drops; but one can see that it weeps for *joy*. Now it leaps and sports as gracefully as Undine[4] in her wildest moods, and then sinks into the vase under a veil of woven pearl, like the undulating farewell courtesy of her fluid relations. On the evening of the great Croton celebration, they illuminated this Fountain with coloured fireworks, kindling the cloud of mist with many-coloured gems; as if the Water Spirits had had another wedding with Fairies of the Diamond Mines.

I went out to Harlaem,[5] the other day, to see the great jet of water, which there rises a hundred feet into the air, and falls through a belt of rainbows. Water *will* rise to its level, as surely as the morality of a nation, or a sect, rises to its idea of God. They to whom God is the Almighty, rather than the Heavenly *Father,* do not understand that the highest ideal of Justice is perfect and universal Love. They *cannot* perceive this: for both spiritually and naturally water never rises above the level of its source. But how sublimely it rushes upward to *find* its level! As I gazed in loving wonder on that beautiful column, it seemed to me a fitting type of those pure, free spirits, who, at the smallest opening, spring upward to the highest, revealing to all mankind the true level of the religious idea of their age. But, alas, here is the stern old conflict between Necessity and Freewill. The column, by the law of its being, would rise *quite* to the level of its source; but as the impulse, that sent it forth in such glorious majesty, expends itself, the *lateral pressure* overpowers the leaping waters, and sends them downward in tears.

If we had a tube high enough to defend the struggling water from surrounding pressure, it *would* rise to its level. Will society ever be so constructed as to enable us to do this spiritually? It *must* be so, before, "Holiness to the Lord," is written on the bells of the horses.

I told my beloved friends, as we stood gazing on that magnificent jet of water, that its grandeur and its gracefulness revealed much, and promised more. They smiled, and reminded me that it was a canon of criticism, laid down by Blair, never to liken the natural to the spiritual.[6] I have no dispute with those who let down an iron-barred portcullis between matter and spirit. The winged soul flies over, and sees the whole as one fair region, golden with the same sunlight, fresh with the same breezes from heaven.

But I must not offer sybilline leaves in the market. Who will buy them? The question shows that *my* spirit likewise feels the *lateral pressure.* Would I could turn downward as gracefully as the waters! uniting the upward and the downward tendency in an arch so beautiful, and every drop sparkling as it falls into the common reservoir, whence future fountains shall gush in perpetual beauty.

I am again violating Blair's injunction. His iron gate rolls away like a stage curtain, and lo, the whole region of spiritual progress opens in glorious perspective! How shall I get back to the actual, and *stay* there? If the doctrine of transmigration of souls were true, I should assuredly pass into a bird of Paradise, which forever floats in the air, or if it touches the earth for a moment, is impatient to soar again.

Strange material this for a reformer! And I tell you plainly that reforming work lies around me like "the ring of Necessity," and ever and anon Freewill bites at the circle. But this necessity is only another name for conscience; and that is the voice of God. I would not unchain Freewill, if I could; for if I did, the planets would fly out of their places; for they, too, in their far off splendour, are linked with every fragment we perceive of truth and duty.[7]

But there is a *false* necessity with which we industriously surround ourselves; a circle that never expands; whose iron never changes to ductile gold. This is the pressure of public opinion; the intolerable restraint of conventional forms. Under this despotic influence, men and women check their best impulses, suppress their noblest feelings, conceal their highest thoughts. Each longs for full communion with other souls, but dares not give utterance to its yearnings. What hinders? The fear of what Mrs. Smith, or Mrs. Clark, will say; or the frown of some sect; or the anathema of some synod; or the fashion of some clique; or the laugh of some club; or the misrepresentation of some political party. Oh, thou foolish soul! Thou art afraid of thy neighbour, and knowest not that he is equally afraid of thee. He has bound thy hands, and thou hast fettered his feet. It were wise for both to snap the imaginary bonds, and walk onward unshackled. If thy heart yearns for love, *be* loving; if thou wouldst free mankind, *be* free; if thou wouldst have a brother frank to thee, *be* frank to him.

> "*Be* noble! and the nobleness that lies
> In other men, *sleeping* but never *dead,*
> Will rise in majesty to meet thine own."

"But what will people say?"

Why does it concern thee *what* they say? Thy life is not in *their* hands. They can give thee nothing of real value, nor take from thee anything that is worth the having. Satan may *promise* thee all the kingdoms of the earth, but he has not an acre of it to give. He may *offer* much, as the price of his worship, but there is a flaw in all his title deeds. Eternal and sure is the promise, "Blessed are the meek, for *they* shall inherit the earth." Only have faith in this, and thou wilt live high above the rewards and punishments of that spectral giant, which men call Society.

"But I shall be misunderstood—misrepresented."

And what if thou art? They who throw stones at what is above them, receive the missiles back again, by the law of gravity; and lucky are they, if they bruise not their own faces.

Would that I could persuade all who read this to be truthful and free; to say what they think, and act what they feel; to cast from them, like ropes of sand, *all* fear of sects, and parties, and clans, and classes. Most earnestly do I pray to be bound only by my own conscience, in that circle of duties, which widens ever, till it enfolds all being, and touches the throne of God.

What is there of joyful freedom in our social intercourse? We meet to see each other; and not a peep do we get under the thick, stifling veil which each carries about him. We visit to enjoy ourselves; and our host takes away all our freedom, while we destroy his own. If the host wishes to work or ride, he dare not, lest it seem unpolite to the guest; if the guest wishes to read or sleep, he dare not, lest it seem unpolite to the host; so they both remain slaves, and feel it a relief to part company. A few individuals, mostly in foreign lands, arrange this matter with wiser freedom. If a visiter arrives, they say, "I am busy to-day; but if you wish to ride, there are horse and saddle in the stable; if you wish to read, there are books in the library; if you are inclined to music, flute and piano are in the parlour; if you want to work, the men are raking hay in the fields; if you want to romp, the children are at play in the court; if you want to talk with me, I can be with you at such an hour. Go when you please, and while you stay do as you please."

At some houses in Florence, large parties meet, without invitation, and with the slightest preparation. It is understood that on some particular evening of the week, a lady or gentleman always receive their friends. In one room are books, and busts, and flowers; in another, pictures and engravings; in a third, music; couples are ensconced in some sheltered alcove, or groups dotted about the rooms in mirthful or serious conversation. No one is required to speak to his host, either entering or departing. Lemonade and baskets of fruit stand here and there on the side-tables, that all may take who like; but *eating,* which constitutes so large a part of all American entertainments, is a slight and almost unnoticed incident in these festivals of intellect and taste. Wouldst thou like to see such social freedom introduced here? Then do it. But the first step must be complete indifference to Mrs. Smith's assertion, that you were mean enough to offer only one kind of cake to your company, and to put less shortening in the under-crust of your pies than the upper. Let Mrs. Smith talk according to her gifts; be thou assured that all *living* souls love freedom better than cake or under-crust.

Of *perfect* social freedom I never knew but one instance. Doctor H——of Boston,[8] coming home to dine one day, found a very bright-looking handsome mulatto on the steps, apparently about seven or eight years old. As he opened the door, the boy glided in, as if it were his home. "What do you want?" said the doctor. The child looked up with smiling confidence, and answered, "I am a little boy that run away from Providence; and I want some dinner; and I thought maybe you would give me some." His radiant face, and child-like freedom operated like a charm. He had a good dinner, and remained several days, becoming more and more the pet of the whole household. He said he had been cruelly treated by somebody in Providence, and had run away; but the people he described could not be found. The doctor thought it would not do to have him growing up in idleness, and he tried to find a place where he could run errands, clean knives, &c., for his living. An hour after this was mentioned, the boy was missing. In a few weeks, they heard of him in the opposite part of the city, sitting on a door-step at dinner-time. When the door opened, he walked in, smiling, and said, "I am a little boy that run away from Providence; and I want some dinner, and I thought maybe you would give me some." He was not mistaken this time either. The heart that trusted so completely received a cordial welcome. After a time, it was again proposed to find some place at service; and straight way this human butterfly was off, no one knew whither.

For several months no more was heard of him. But one bright winter day, his first benefactor found him seated on the steps of a house in Beacon-street.[9] "Why, Tom, where did you come from?" said he. "I came from Philadelphia." "How upon earth did you get there?" "I heard folks talk about New-York, and I thought I should like to see it. So I went on board a steamboat; and when it put off, the captain asked me who I was; and I told him that I was a little boy that run away from Providence, and I wanted to go to New-York, but I hadn't any money. 'You little rascal,'[10] says he, 'I'll throw you overboard.' 'I don't believe you will,' said I; and he didn't. I told him I was hungry, and he gave me something to eat, and made up a nice little bed for me. When I got to New-York, I went and sat down on a door-step; and when the gentleman came home to dinner, I went in, and told him that I was a little boy that run away from Providence, and I was hungry. So they gave me something to eat, and made up a nice little bed for me, and let me stay there. But I wanted to see Philadelphia; so I went into a steamboat; and when they asked me who I was, I told them that I was a little boy that run away from Providence. They said I had no business there, but they gave me an orange. When I got to Philadelphia, I sat down on a door-step, and when the gentleman came home to dinner, I told him I was a little boy that run away from Providence, and I thought perhaps he would give me something to eat. So they gave me a good dinner, and made me up a nice little bed. Then I wanted to come back to Boston; and everybody gave me something to eat, and made me up a nice little bed. And I sat down on this door-step, and when the lady asked me what I wanted, I told her I was a little boy that run away from Providence, and I was hungry. So she gave me something to eat, and made me up a nice little bed; and I stay here, and do her errands sometimes. Every body is very good to me, and I like everybody."

He looked up with the most sunny gayety, and striking his hoop as he spoke, went down the street like an arrow. He disappeared soon after, probably in quest of new adventures. I have never heard of him since; and sometimes a painful fear passes through my mind that the kidnappers, prowling about all our large towns, have carried him into slavery.

The story had a charm for me, for two reasons. I was delighted with the artless freedom of the winning, wayward child; and still more did I rejoice in the perpetual kindness, which everywhere gave it such friendly greeting. Oh, if we *would* but dare to throw ourselves on each other's hearts, how the image of heaven would be reflected all over the face of this earth, as the clear blue sky lies mirrored in the waters.

Letter XXXI [1]
November 19, 1842

To-day, I cannot write of beauty; for I am sad and troubled. Heart, head, and conscience, are all in battle-array against the savage customs of my time. By and by, the law of love, like oil upon the waters, will calm my surging sympathies, and make the current flow more calmly, though none the less deep or strong. But to-day, do not ask me to love governor, sheriff or constable, or any man who defends capital punishment. I ought to do it; for genuine love enfolds even murderers with its blessing. By to-morrow, I think I can remember them without bitterness; but to-day, I cannot love them; on my soul, I cannot.

We were to have had an execution yesterday; but the wretched prisoner avoided it by suicide. The gallows had been erected for several hours, and with a cool refinement of cruelty, was hoisted before the window of the condemned; the hangman was all ready to cut the cord: marshals paced back and forth, smoking and whistling; spectators were waiting impatiently to see whether he would "die game." Printed circulars had been handed abroad to summon the number of witnesses required by law: "You are respectfully invited to witness the execution of John C. Colt." [2] I trust some of them are preserved for museums. Specimens should be kept, as relics of a barbarous age, for succeeding generations to wonder at. They might be hung up in a frame; and the portrait of a New Zealand Chief, picking the bones of an enemy of his tribe, would be an appropriate pendant.

This bloody insult was thrust into the hands of *some* citizens, who carried hearts under their vests, and they threw it in tattered fragments to the dogs and swine, as more fitting witnesses than human beings. It was cheering to those who have faith in human progress, to see how many viewed the subject in this light. But as a general thing, the very spirit of murder was rife among the dense crowd, which thronged the place of execution. They were swelling with revenge, and eager for blood. One man came all the way from New Hampshire, on purpose to witness the entertainment; thereby showing himself a likely subject for the gallows, whoever he may be. *Women* deemed themselves not treated with becoming gallantry, because tickets of admittance were denied *them;* and I think it showed injudicious partiality; for many of them can be taught murder by as short a lesson as any man, and sustain it by arguments from Scripture, as ably as any theologian. However, *they* were not admitted to this edifying exhibition in the great school of public morals; and had only the slim comfort of standing outside, in a keen November wind, to catch the first toll of the bell, which would announce that a human brother had been sent struggling into eternity by the hand of violence. But while the multitude stood with open watches, and strained ears to catch the sound, and the marshals smoked and whistled, and the hangman walked up and down, waiting for his prey, lo! word was brought that the criminal was found dead in his bed! He had asked one half hour alone to prepare his mind for departure; and at the end of that brief interval, he was found with a dagger thrust into his heart. The tidings were received with fierce mutterings of disappointed rage.[3] The throng beyond the walls were furious to see him with their own eyes, to be sure that he was dead. But when the welcome news met *my* ear, a tremendous load was taken from my heart. I had no chance to analyze right and wrong; for over all thought and feeling flowed impulsive joy, that this "Christian" community were cheated of a hanging. They who had assembled to commit legalized murder, in cold blood, with strange confusion of ideas, were unmindful of their own guilt, while they talked of his suicide as a crime equal to that for which he was condemned. I am willing to leave it between him and his God. For myself, I would rather have the burden of it on my own soul, than take the guilt of those who would have executed a fellow-creature. *He* was driven to a fearful extremity of agony and desperation.[4] He was precisely in the situation of a man on board a burning ship, who being *compelled* to face death, jumps into the waves, as the least painful mode of the two. But they, who thus drove him "to walk the plank," made cool, deliberate preparations to take life, and with inventive cruelty sought to add every bitter drop that *could* be added to the dreadful cup of vengeance.

To me, human life seems so sacred a thing, that its violent termination always fills me with horror, whether perpetrated by an individual or a crowd; whether done contrary to law and custom, or according to law and custom. Why John C. Colt should be condemned to an ignominious death for an act of resentment altogether unpremeditated, while men, who deliberately, and with malice aforethought, go out to murder another for some insulting word, are judges, and senators in the land, and favourite candidates for the President's chair, is more than I can comprehend. There is, to say the least, a strange inconsistency in our customs.

At the same moment that I was informed of the death of the prisoner, I heard that the prison was on fire. It was soon extinguished, but the remarkable coincidence added not a little to the convulsive excitement of the hour. I went with a friend to look at the beautiful spectacle; for it was exceedingly beautiful. The fire had kindled at the very top of the cupola, the wind was high, and the flames rushed upward, as if the angry spirits below had escaped on fiery wings. Heaven forgive the feelings that, for a moment, mingled with my admiration of that beautiful conflagration! Society had kindled all around me a bad excitement, and one of the infernal sparks fell into my own heart. If this was the effect produced on me, who am by nature tender-hearted, by principle opposed to all retaliation, and by social position secluded from contact with evil, what must it have been on the minds of rowdies and desperadoes? The effect of executions on *all* brought within their influence is evil, and nothing but evil. For a fortnight past, this whole city has been kept in a state of corroding excitement, either of hope or fear. The stern pride of the prisoner left little in his peculiar case to appeal to the sympathies of society; yet the instincts of our common nature rose up against the sanguinary spirit manifested toward him. The public were, moreover, divided in opinion with regard to the legal construction of his crime; and in the keen discussion of *legal* distinctions, *moral* distinctions became wofully confused. Each day, hope and fear alternated; the natural effect of all this, was to have the whole thing regarded as a game, in which the criminal might, or might not, become the winner; and every experiment of this kind shakes public respect for the laws, from centre to circumference. Worse than all this was the horrible amount of diabolical passion excited. The hearts of men were filled with murder; they gloated over the thoughts of vengeance, and were rabid to witness a fellow-creature's agony. They complained loudly that he was not to be hung high enough for the crowd to *see* him. "What a pity!" exclaimed a woman, who stood near me, gazing at the burning tower; "they will have to give him two hours more to live." "Would you feel so, if he were your *son?*" said I. Her countenance changed instantly. She had not before realized that every criminal was *somebody's* son.[5]

As we walked homeward, we encountered a deputy sheriff; not the most promising material, certainly, for lessons on humanity; but to him we spoke of the crowd of savage faces, and the tones of hatred, as obvious proofs of the bad influence of capital punishment. "I know that," said he; "but I don't see how we could dispense with it. Now suppose we had fifty murderers shut up in prison for life, instead of hanging 'em; and suppose there should come a revolution; what an awful thing it would be to have fifty murderers inside the prison, to be let loose upon the community!" "There is another side to that proposition," we answered; "for every criminal you execute, you make a hundred murderers *outside* the prison, each as dangerous as would be the one inside." He said perhaps it was so; and went his way.

As for the punishment and the terror of such doings, they fall most keenly on the best hearts in the community. Thousands of men, as well as women, had broken and startled sleep for several nights preceding that dreadful day. Executions always excite a universal shudder among the innocent, the humane, and the wisehearted. It is the voice of God, crying aloud within us against the wickedness of this savage custom. Else why is it that the instinct is so universal?

The last conversation I had with the late William Ladd[6] made a strong impression on my mind. While he was a sea-captain, he occasionally visited Spain, and once witnessed an execution there. He said that no man, however low and despicable, would consent to perform the office of hangman; and whoever should dare to suggest such a thing to a decent man, would be likely to have his brains blown out. This feeling was so strong, and so universal, that the only way they could procure an executioner, was to offer a condemned criminal his own life, if he would consent to perform the vile and hateful office on another. Sometimes executions were postponed for months, because there was no condemned criminal to perform the office of hangman. A fee was allotted by law to the wretch who did perform it, but no one would run the risk of touching his polluted hand by giving it to him; therefore, the priest threw the purse as far as possible; the odious being ran to pick it up, and hastened to escape from the shuddering execrations of all who had known him as a hangman. Even the poor animal that carried the criminal and his coffin in a cart to the foot of the gallows, was an object of universal loathing. He was cropped and marked, that he might be known as the "Hangman's Donkey." No man, however great his needs, would use this beast, either for pleasure or labour; and the peasants were so averse to having him pollute their fields with his footsteps, that when he was seen approaching, the boys hastened to open the gates, and drive him off with hisses, sticks, and stones. Thus does the human heart cry out aloud against this wicked practice! [7]

A tacit acknowledgment of the demoralizing influence of executions is generally made, in the fact that they are forbidden to be *public,* as formerly. The scene is now in a prison yard, instead of open fields, and no spectators are admitted but officers of the law, and those especially invited. Yet a favourite argument in favour of capital punishment has been the terror that the spectacle inspires in the breast of evil doers. I trust the two or three hundred, singled out from the mass of New-York population, by particular invitation, especially the judges and civil officers, will feel the full weight of the compliment. During the French Revolution, public executions seemed too slow, and Fouquier proposed to put the guillotine under cover, where batches of a hundred might be despatched with few spectators. "Wilt thou *demoralize the guillotine?*" asked Callot, reproachfully. [8]

That bloody guillotine was an instrument of *law,* as well as our gallows; and what, in the name of all that is villanous, has *not* been established by law? [9] Nations, clans, and classes, engaged in fierce struggles of selfishness and hatred, made laws to strengthen each other's power, and revenge each other's aggressions. By slow degrees, always timidly and reluctantly, society emerges out of the barbarisms with which it thus became entangled. It is but a short time ago that men were hung in this country for stealing. The last human brother who suffered under this law, in Massachusetts, was so wretchedly poor, that when he hung on the gallows his rags fluttered in the wind. What think you was the comparative guilt, in the eye of God, between him and those who hung him? Yet, it was *according to law;* and men cried out as vociferously then as they now do, that it was not *safe* to have the law changed. Judge McKean, [10] governor of Pennsylvania, was strongly opposed to the abolition of death for stealing, and the disuse of the pillory and whipping-post. He was a very humane man, but had the common fear of changing old customs. "It will not do to abolish these salutary restraints," said the old gentleman; "it will break up the foundations of society." Those relics of barbarism were banished long ago; but the foundations of society are in nowise injured thereby.

The testimony from all parts of the world is invariable and conclusive, that crime diminishes in proportion to the mildness of the laws.[11] The *real* danger is in having laws on the statute-book at variance with universal instincts of the human heart, and thus tempting men to continual evasion. The *evasion,* even of a bad law, is attended with many mischievous results; its *abolition* is always safe.[12]

In looking at Capital Punishment in its practical bearings on the operation of justice, an observing mind is at once struck with the extreme *uncertainty* attending it. The balance swings hither and thither, and settles, as it were, by chance. The strong instincts of the heart teach juries extreme reluctance to convict for capital offences. They will avail themselves of every loophole in the evidence, to avoid the bloody responsibility imposed upon them. In this way, undoubted criminals escape all punishment, until society becomes alarmed for its own safety, and insists that the next victim *shall* be sacrificed. It was the misfortune of John C. Colt to be arrested at the time when the popular wave of indignation had been swelling higher and higher, in consequence of the impunity with which Robinson, White, and Jewell, had escaped.[13] The wrath and jealousy which they had excited was visited upon him, and his chance for a merciful verdict was greatly diminished. The scale now turns the other way; and the next offender will probably receive very lenient treatment, though he should not have half so many extenuating circumstances in his favour.

Another thought which forces itself upon the mind in consideration of this subject is the danger of convicting the innocent. Murder is a crime which must of course be committed in secret, and therefore the proof must be mainly circumstantial. This kind of evidence is in its nature so precarious, that men have learned great timidity in trusting to it. In Scotland, it led to so many terrible mistakes, that they long ago refused to convict any man of a capital offence, upon circumstantial evidence.

A few years ago, a poor German came to New-York, and took lodgings, where he was allowed to do his cooking in the same room with the family. The husband and wife lived in a perpetual quarrel. One day, the German came into the kitchen with a clasp knife and a pan of potatoes, and began to pare them for his dinner. The quarrelsome couple were in a more violent altercation than usual; but he sat with his back toward them, and being ignorant of their language, felt in no danger of being involved in their disputes. But the woman, with a sudden and unexpected movement, snatched the knife from his hand, and plunged it in her husband's heart. She had sufficient presence of mind to rush into the street, and scream murder. The poor foreigner, in the meanwhile, seeing the wounded man reel, sprang forward to catch him in his arms, and drew out the knife. People from the street crowded in, and found him with the dying man in his arms, the knife in his hand, and blood upon his clothes. The wicked woman swore, in the most positive terms, that he had been fighting with her husband, and had stabbed him with a knife he always carried. The unfortunate German knew too little English to understand her accusation, or to tell his own story. He was dragged off to prison, and the true state of the case was made known through an interpreter; but it was not believed. Circumstantial evidence was exceedingly strong against the accused, and the real criminal swore unhesitatingly that she saw him commit the murder. He was executed, notwithstanding the most persevering efforts of his lawyer, John Anthon, Esq.,[14] whose convictions of the man's innocence were so painfully strong, that from that day to this, he has refused to have any connection with a capital case. Some years after this tragic event, the woman died, and, on her death-bed, confessed her agency in the diabolical transaction; but her poor victim could receive no benefit from this tardy repentance; society had wantonly thrown away its power to atone for the grievous wrong.

Many of my readers will doubtless recollect the tragical fate of Burton, in Missouri, on which a novel was founded, which still circulates in the libraries. A young lady, belonging to a genteel and very proud family, in Missouri, was beloved by a young man named Burton; but unfortunately, her affections were fixed on another less worthy. He left her with a tarnished reputation.[15] She was by nature energetic and high-spirited, her family were proud, and she lived in the midst of a society which considered revenge a virtue, and named it honour. Misled by this false popular sentiment, and her own excited feelings, she resolved to repay her lover's treachery with death. But she kept her secret so well, that no one suspected her purpose, though she purchased pistols, and practised with them daily. Mr. Burton gave evidence of his strong attachment by renewing his attentions when the world looked most coldly upon her. His generous kindness won her bleeding heart, but the softening influence of love did not lead her to forego the dreadful purpose she had formed. She watched for a favourable opportunity, and shot her betrayer, when no one was near, to witness the horrible deed. Some little incident excited the suspicion of Burton, and he induced her to confess to him the whole transaction. It was obvious enough that suspicion would naturally fasten upon him, the well-known lover of her who had been so deeply injured. He was arrested, but succeeded in persuading her that he was in no danger. Circumstantial evidence was fearfully against him, and he soon saw that his chance was doubtful; but with affectionate magnanimity, he concealed this from her. He was convicted and condemned. A short time before the execution, he endeavoured to cut his throat; but his life was saved, for the cruel purpose of taking it away according to the cold-blooded barbarism of the law. Pale and wounded, he was hoisted to the gallows before the gaze of a *Christian* community.

The guilty cause of all this was almost frantic, when she found that he had thus sacrificed himself to save her. She immediately published the whole history of her wrongs, and her revenge. Her keen sense of wounded honour was in accordance with public sentiment, her wrongs excited indignation and compassion, and the knowledge that an innocent and magnanimous man had been so brutally treated, excited a general revulsion of popular feeling. No one wished for another victim, and she was left unpunished, save by the dreadful records of her memory.

Few know how numerous are the cases where it has subsequently been discovered that the innocent suffered instead of the guilty. Yet one such case in an age is surely enough to make legislators pause before they cast a vote against the abolition of Capital Punishment.[16]

But many say, "the Old Testament requires blood for blood." So it requires that a woman should be put to death for adultery; and men for doing work on the Sabbath; and children for cursing their parents; and "If an ox were to push with his horn, in time past, and it hath been testified to his owner, and he hath not kept him in, but that he hath killed a man or a woman, the ox shall be stoned, and his owner also shall be put to death." The commands given to the Jews, in the old dispensation, do not form the basis of any legal code in Christendom. They *could* not form the basis of any civilized code. If *one* command is binding on our consciences, *all* are binding; for they all rest on the same authority. They who feel bound to advocate capital punishment for murder, on account of the law given to Moses, ought, for the same reason, to insist that children should be executed for striking or cursing their parents.

"It was said by them of *old* time, an eye for an eye, and a tooth for a tooth; but *I* say unto you resist not evil." If our "eyes were lifted up," we should see, not Moses and Elias, but *Jesus only.*

Letter XXXII [1]
November 26, 1842

Every year of my life I grow more and more convinced that it is wisest and best to fix our attention on the beautiful and good, and dwell as little as possible on the evil and the false. Society has done my spirit grievous wrong, for the last few weeks, with its legal bull-baitings, and its hired murderers. They have made me ashamed of belonging to the human species; and were it not that I struggled hard against it, and prayed earnestly for a spirit of forgiveness, they would have made me hate my race. Yet feeling thus, I did wrong to *them.* Most of them had merely caught the contagion of murder, and really were not aware of the nature of the fiend they harboured. Probably there was not a single heart in the community, not even the most brutal, that would not have been softened, could it have entered into confidential intercourse with the prisoner, as Dr. Anthon[2] did. All would then have learned that he was a human being, with a heart to be melted, and a conscience to be roused, like the rest of us; that under the turbid and surging tide of proud, exasperated feelings, ran a warm current of human affections, which, with more genial influences, might have flowed on deeper and stronger, mingling its waters with the river of life. All this each one would have known, could he have looked into the heart of the poor criminal as God looketh. But his whole life was judged by a desperate act, done in the insanity of passion; and the motives and the circumstances were revealed to the public only through the cold barbarisms of the law, and the fierce exaggerations of an excited populace; therefore he seemed like a wild beast, walled out from human sympathies,—not as a fellow-creature, with like passions and feelings as themselves.

Carlyle, in his French Revolution,[3] speaking of one of the three bloodiest judges of the Reign of Terror, says: "Marat too, had a brother, and natural affections; and was wrapt once in swaddling-clothes, and slept safe in a cradle, like the rest of us." We are too apt to forget these gentle considerations when talking of public criminals.

If we looked into our souls with a more wise humility, we should discover in our own ungoverned anger the germ of murder; and meekly thank God that we, too, had not been brought into temptations too fiery for our strength. It is sad to think how the records of a few evil days may blot out from the memory of our fellow-men whole years of generous thoughts and deeds of kindness; and this, too, when each one has before him the volume of his own broken resolutions, and oft-repeated sins. The temptation which most easily besets you, needed, perhaps, to be only a *little* stronger; you needed only to be surrounded by circumstances a *little* more dangerous and exciting, and perhaps you, who now walk abroad in the sunshine of respectability, might have come under the ban of human laws, as you have into frequent disobedience of the divine; and then that one foul blot would have been regarded as the hieroglyphic symbol of your whole life. Between you and the inmate of the penitentiary, society sees a difference so great, that you are scarcely recognized as belonging to the same species; but there is One who judgeth not as man judgeth.

When Mrs. Fry spoke at Newgate, she was wont to address both prisoners and visiters as sinners. When Dr. Channing alluded to this practice, she meekly replied, "In the sight of God, there is not, perhaps, so much difference as men think."[4] In the midst of recklessness, revenge and despair, there is often a glimmering evidence that the divine spark is not quite extinguished. Who can tell into what a holy flame of benevolence and self-sacrifice it might have been kindled, had the man been surrounded from his cradle by an atmosphere of love?[5]

Surely these considerations should make us judge mercifully of the sinner, while we hate the sin with tenfold intensity, because it is an enemy that lies in wait for us all. The highest and holiest example teaches us to *forgive* all crimes, while we *palliate* none.

Would that we could learn to be kind—always and everywhere kind! Every jealous thought I cherish, every angry word I utter, every repulsive tone, is helping to build penitentiaries and prisons, and to fill them with those who merely carry the same passions and feelings farther than I do. It is an awful thought; and the more it is impressed upon me, the more earnestly do I pray to live in a state of perpetual benediction.

"Love hath a longing and a power to save the gathered world,
And rescue universal man from the hunting hell-hounds of his doings."[6]

And so I return, as the old preachers used to say, to my first proposition; that we should think gently of all, and claim kindred with all, and include all, without exception, in the circle of our kindly sympathies. I would not thrust out even the hangman, though methinks if I were dying of thirst, I would rather wait to receive water from another hand than his. Yet what is the hangman but a servant of the law? And what is the law but an expression of public opinion? And if public opinion be brutal, and thou a component part thereof, art *thou* not the hangman's accomplice? In the name of our common Father, sing *thy* part of the great chorus in the truest time, and thus bring this crashing discord into harmony!

And if at times, the discord proves too strong for thee, go out into the great temple of Nature, and drink in freshness from her never-failing fountain. The devices of men pass away as a vapour; but she changes never. Above all fluctuations of opinion, and all the tumult of the passions, she smiles ever, in various but unchanging beauty. I have gone to her with tears in my eyes, with a heart full of the saddest forebodings, for myself and all the human race; and lo, she has shown me a babe plucking a white clover, with busy, uncertain little fingers, and the child walked straight into my heart, and prophesied as hopefully as an angel; and I believed her, and went on my way rejoicing. The language of nature, like that of music, is universal; it speaks to the heart, and is understood by all. *Dialects* belong to clans and sects; *tones* to the universe. High above all language, floats music on its amber cloud. It is not the exponent of *opinion,* but of *feeling.* The *heart* made it; therefore it is infinite. It reveals more than language can ever utter, or thoughts conceive. And high as music is above mere dialects—winging its godlike way, while verbs and nouns go creeping—even so, sounds the voice of Love, that clear, treble-note of the universe, into the heart of man, and the ear of Jehovah.

In sincere humility do I acknowledge that if I am less guilty than some of my human brothers, it is mainly because I have been *beloved.* Kind emotions and impulses have not been sent back to me, like dreary echoes, through empty rooms. All around me, at this moment, are tokens of a friendly heart-warmth. A sheaf of dried grasses brings near the gentle image of one who gathered them for love; a varied group of the graceful lady-fern tells me of summer rambles in the woods, by one who mingled thoughts of me with all her glimpses of nature's beauty. A rose-bush, from a poor Irish woman, speaks to me of her blessings. A bird of paradise, sent by friendship, to warm the wintry hours with thoughts of sunny Eastern climes, cheers me with its floating beauty, like a fairy fancy. Flower-tokens from the best of neighbours, have come all summer long, to bid me a blithe good morning, and tell me news of sunshine and fresh air. A piece of sponge, graceful as if it grew on the arms of the wave, reminds me of Grecian seas, and of Hylas[7] borne away by water-nymphs. It was given me for its uncommon beauty; and who will not try harder to be good, for being deemed a fit recipient of the beautiful? A root, which promises to bloom into fragrance, is sent by an old Quaker lady, whom I know not, but who says, "I would fain minister to thy love of flowers." Affection sends childhood to peep lovingly at me from engravings, or stand in classic grace, embodied in the little plaster cast. The far-off and the near, the past and the future, are with me in my humble apartment. True, the mementoes cost little of the world's wealth; for they are of the simplest kind; but they express the universe—because they are thoughts of love, clothed in forms of beauty.

Why do I mention these things? From vanity? Nay, verily; for it often humbles me to tears, to think how much I am loved more than I deserve; while thousands, far nearer to God, pass on their thorny path, comparatively uncheered by love and blessing. But it came into my heart to tell you how much these things helped me to be *good;* how they were like roses dropped by unseen hands, guiding me through a wilderness-path unto our Father's mansion. And the love that helps *me* to be good, I would have you bestow upon all, that *all* may become good.[8] To love others is greater happiness than to be beloved by them; to *do* good is more blessed than to *receive.* The heart of Jesus was so full of love, that he called little children to his arms, and folded John upon his bosom; and this love made him capable of such divine self-renunciation, that he could offer up even his life for the good of the world. The desire to be beloved is ever restless and unsatisfied; but the love that flows out upon others is a perpetual well-spring from on high. *This* source of happiness is within the reach of all; here, if not elsewhere, may the stranger and the friendless satisfy the infinite yearnings of the human heart, and find therein refreshment and joy.

Believe me, the great panacea for all the disorders in the universe, is Love. For thousands of years the world has gone on perversely, trying to overcome evil *with* evil; with the worst results, as the condition of things plainly testifies. Nearly two thousand years ago, the prophet of the Highest proclaimed that evil could be overcome only with *good.* But "when the Son of Man cometh, shall he find *faith* on the earth?" If we *have* faith in this holy principle, where is it written on our laws or our customs?

Write it on thine own life; and men reading it shall say, lo, something greater than vengeance is here; a power mightier than coercion. And thus the individual faith shall become a social faith; and to the mountains of crime around us, it will say, "Be thou removed, and cast into the depths of the sea!" and they *will* be removed; and the places that knew them shall know them no more.

This hope is coming toward us, with a halo of sunshine round its head; in the light it casts before, let us do works of zeal with the spirit of love. Man *may* be redeemed from his thraldom! He *will* be redeemed. For the mouth of the Most High hath spoken it. It is inscribed in written prophecy, and He utters it to our hearts in perpetual revelation. To you, and me, and each of us, He says, "Go, bring my people out of Egypt, into the promised land."

To perform this mission, we must love both the evil and the good, and shower blessings on the just as well as the unjust. Thanks to our Heavenly Father, I have had much friendly aid on my own spiritual pilgrimage; through many a cloud has pierced a sunbeam, and over many a pitfall have I been guided by a garland. In gratitude for this, fain would I help others to be good, according to the small measure of my ability. My spiritual adventures are like those of the "little boy that run away from Providence."[9] When troubled or discouraged, my soul seats itself on some door-step — there is ever some one to welcome me in, and make "a nice little bed" for my weary heart. It may be a young friend, who gathers for me flowers in Summer, and grasses, ferns, and red berries in the Autumn; or it may be sweet Mary Howitt, whose mission it is "to turn the *sunny* side of things to human eyes;" or Charles Dickens, who looks with such deep and friendly glance into the human heart, whether it beats beneath embroidered vest, or tattered jacket; or the serene and gentle Fenelon; or the devout Thomas à Kempis; or the meek-spirited John Woolman; or the eloquent hopefulness of Channing; or the cathedral tones of Keble, or the saintly beauty of Raphael, or the clear melody of Handel.[10] All speak to me with friendly greeting, and have somewhat to give my thirsty soul. Fain would I do the same, for all who come to *my* door-step, hungry, and cold, spiritually or naturally. To the erring and the guilty, above all others, the door of my heart shall never open outward. I have too much *need* of mercy. Are we not all children of the same Father? and shall we not pity those who among pitfalls lose their way home?

Letter XXXIII [1]
December 8, 1842

I went, last Sunday, to the Catholic Cathedral, a fine-looking Gothic edifice, which impressed me with that feeling of reverence so easily inspired in my soul by a relic of the past. I have heard many say that their first visit to a Catholic church filled them with laughter, the services seemed so absurd a mockery. It was never thus with me. I know not whether it is that Nature endowed me so largely with imagination and with devotional feelings, or whether it is because I slept for years with "Thomas à Kempis's Imitation of Christ"[2] under my pillow, and found it my greatest consolation, and best outward guide, next to the New-Testament; but so it is, that holy old monk is twined all about my heart with loving reverence, and the forms which had so deep spiritual significance to him, could never excite in me a mirthful feeling. Then the mere circumstance of antiquity is impressive to a character inclined to veneration. There stands the image of what was once a living church. A sort of Congress of Religions is she; with the tiara of the Persian priest, the staff of the Roman augur, and the embroidered mantle of the Jewish rabbi. This is all natural;[3] for the Christian Idea was a resurrection from deceased Heathenism and Judaism, and rose encumbered with the grave-clothes and jewels of the dead. The Greek and Roman, when they became Christian, still clung fondly to the reminiscences of their early faith. The undying flame on Apollo's shrine reappeared in ever-lighted candles on the Christian altar; and the same idea that demanded vestal virgins for the heathen temple, set nuns apart for the Christian sanctuary. Tiara and embroidered garments were sacred to the imagination of the converted Jew; and conservatism, which in man's dual nature ever keeps innovation in check, led him to adopt them in his new worship. Thus did the spirituality of Christ come to us loaded with forms, not naturally and spontaneously flowing therefrom. The very cathedrals, with their clustering columns and intertwining arches, were architectural models of the groves and "high-places," sacred to the mind of the Pagans, who from infancy had therein worshipped their "strange gods." The days of the Christian week took the names of heathen deities, and statues of Venus were adored as Virgin Mothers. The bronze image of St. Peter, at Rome, whose toe has been kissed away by devotees, was once a statue of Jupiter. An English traveller took off his hat to it as Jupiter, and asked him, if he ever recovered his power, to reward the only individual that ever bowed to him in his adversity.

Let us not smile at this odd commingling of religious faiths and forms. It is most natural; and must ever be, when a new idea evolves itself from the old. The Reformers,[4] to evade this tendency, destroyed the churches, the paintings, and the statues, which habit had so long endeared to the hearts and imaginations of men; yet while they flung away, with ruthless hand, all the poetry of the old establishment, they were themselves so much the creatures of education, that they brought into the new order of things many cumbrous forms of theology, the mere results of tradition; and the unpretending fisherman, and tent-maker, still remained *Saint* Peter, and *Saint* Paul.

Protestants make no *images* of Moses; but many divide the homage of Christ with him, and *spiritually* kiss his toe. Thus will the glory of a coming church walk in the shadow of our times, casting a radiance over that which it cannot quite dispel.

I think it is Mosheim,[5] who says, "After Christianity became incorporated with the government, it is difficult to determine whether Heathenism was most Christianized, or Christianity most heathenized."

Wo for the hour, when moral truth became wedded to politics, and religion was made to subserve purposes of State! That prostration of reason to authority still fetters the extremest Protestant of the nineteenth century, after the lapse of more than a thousand years, and a succession of convulsive efforts to throw it off. That boasted "triumph of Christianity" came near being its destruction. The old fable of the Pleiad fallen from the sky, by her marriage with an earth-born prince, is full of significance, in many applications; and in none more so, than the attempt to advance a spiritual principle by political machinery. Constantine[6] legalized Christianity, and straightway the powers of this world made it their tool. To this day, two-thirds of Christians look outward to ask whether a thing is *law,* and not inward to ask whether it is *right.* They have mere legal consciences; and do not perceive that human law is sacred only when it is the expression of a divine principle. To them, the slave trade is justifiable while the *law* sanctions it, and becomes piracy when the law pronounces it so. The moral principle that changes laws, never emanates from them. It acts *on* them, but never *with* them. They *through* whom it acts, constitute the real church of the world, by whatsoever name they are called.[7]

The Catholic church is a bad foundation for liberty, civil or religious. I deprecate its obvious and undeniable tendency to enslave the human mind;[8] but I marvel not that the imaginations of men are chained and led captive by this vision of the Past; for it is encircled all around with poetry, as with a halo; and within its fantastic pageantry there is much that makes it *sacred* poetry.

At the present time, indications are numerous that the human mind is tired out in the gymnasium of controversy, and asks earnestly for repose, protection, mystery, and undoubting faith. This tendency betrays itself in the rainbow mysticism of Coleridge, the patriarchal tenderness of Wordsworth, the infinite aspiration of Beethoven.[9] The reverential habit of mind varies its forms, according to temperament and character. In some minds, it shows itself in a superstitious fondness for all *old* forms of belief; the Church which is proved to their minds to resemble the apostolic, in its ritual, as well as its creed, is therefore the true Church. In other minds, veneration takes a form less obviously religious; it is shown by a strong affection for everything antique; they worship shadowy legends, architectural ruins, and ancient customs. This habit of thought enabled Sir Walter to conjure up the guardian spirit of the house of Avenel, and re-people the regal halls of Kenilworth.[10] His works were the final efflorescence of feudal grandeur; that system had passed away from political forms, and no longer had a home in human reason; but it lingered with a dim glory in the imagination, and blossomed thus.

Another class of minds rise to a higher plane of reverence; their passion for the past becomes mingled with earnest aspiration for the holy. Such spirits walk in a golden fog of mysticism, which leads them far, often only to bring them back in a circling path to the faith of childhood, and the established laws of the realm.[11]

To such, Puseyism[12] comes forward, like a fine old cathedral made visible by a gush of moonlight. It appeals to the ancient, the venerable, and the moss-grown. It promises permanent repose in the midst of endless agitation. The young, the poetic, and the mystical, are charmed with "the dim religious light" from its painted oriels; they enter its Gothic aisles, resounding with the echoes of the past; and the solemn glory fills them with worship. Episcopacy rebukes, and dissenters argue; but that which ministers to the sentiment of reverence, will have power over many souls, who hunt in vain for truth through the mazes of argument.[13] To the ear that loves music, and sits listening intently for the voice that speaks while the dove descends from heaven, how discordant, how altogether unprofitable, is this hammering of sects!—this coopering and heading up of empty barrels, so industriously carried on in theological schools! When I am stunned by the loud, and many-tongued jargon of sect, I no longer wonder that men are ready to fall down and worship Romish absurdities, dressed up in purple robes and golden crown; the marvel rather is, that they have not returned to the worship of the ancient graces, the sun, the moon, the stars, or even the element of fire.

But be not disturbed by Pope or Pusey. They are but a part of the check-and-balance system of the universe, and in due time will yield to something better.[14] Modes of faith last just as long as they are needed in the order of Providence, and not a day longer. Let the theologian fume and fret as he may, truth cannot be *forced* above its level, any more than its great prototype, water. Of what avail are sectarian efforts, and controversial words? Live thou a holy life—let thy utterance be that of a free, meek spirit! Thus, and not by ecclesiastical machinery, wilt thou help to prepare the world for a wiser faith and a purer worship.

Meanwhile, let us hope and trust; and respect sincere devotion, wheresoever found.[15] A wise mind never despises aught that flows from a feeling heart. Nothing would tempt me to disturb, even by the rustle of my garments, the Irish servant girl, kneeling in the crowded aisle. Blessed be any power, which, even for a moment, brings the human soul to the foot of the cross, conscious of its weakness and its ignorance, its errors and its sins! We may call it superstition if we will, but the zealous faith of the Catholic is everywhere conspicuous above that of the Protestant. A friend from Canada lately told me an incident which deeply impressed this fact upon his mind. When they cut new roads through the woods, the priests are in the habit of inspecting all the places where villages are to be laid out. They choose the finest site for a church, and build thereon a high, strong cross, with railings round it, about three feet distant from each other. The inner enclosure is usually more elevated than the outer; a mound being raised about the foot of the Cross. Inserted in the main timber is a small image of the crucified Saviour, defended from the atmosphere by glass. In Catholic countries, this is called a *Calvare*. In the village called *Petit Brulé* (because nearly all the dwellings of the first settlers had been consumed by fire) was one of these tall Calvares, rendered conspicuous by its whiteness among the dense foliage of the forest. My friend had been riding for a long time in silence and solitude, and twilight was fast deepening into evening, when his horse suddenly reared, and showed signs of fear. Thinking it most prudent to understand the nature of the danger that awaited him, he stopped the horse and looked cautiously round. The tall white Cross stood near, in distinct relief against the dark back-ground of the forest, and at the foot were two Irishmen kneeling to say their evening prayers. They were poor, labouring men, employed in making the road. There was no human habitation for miles. From their own rude shantees, they must have walked at least two or three miles, after their severe daily toil, thus to bow down and worship the Infinite, in a place they deemed holy!

Let those who can, ridicule the superstition that prompted such an act. Hereafter, may angels teach what remained unrevealed to them on earth, that Christ is truly worshipped, "neither on this mountain, nor yet at Jerusalem."

I love the Irish. Blessings on their warm hearts, and their leaping fancies! Clarkson records that while opposition met him in almost every form, not a single Irish member of the British Parliament ever voted against the abolition of the slave-trade; and how is the heart of that generous island now throbbing with sympathy for the American slave!

Creatures of impulse and imagination, their very speech is poetry. "What are you going to kill?" said I to one of the most stupid of Irish serving-maids, who seemed in great haste to crush some object in the corner of the room. "A black *boog*, ma'am," she replied. "That is a cricket," said I. "It does no harm, but makes a friendly chirping on the hearth stone."

"Och, and is it a cricket it is? And when the night is abroad, will it be *spaking?* Sure, I'll not be after killing it, at all."

The most faithful and warm-hearted of Irish labourers, (and the good among them are the best on earth) urged me last spring not to fail, by any means, to rise before the sun on Easter morning. "The Easter sun always dances when it rises," said he. Assuredly he saw no mockery in my countenance, but perhaps he saw incredulity; for he added, with pleading earnestness, "And why should it *not* dance, by reason of rejoicement?" In his believing ignorance, he had small cause to envy me the superiority of my reason; at least I felt so for the moment. Beautiful is the superstition that makes all nature hail the holy; that sees the cattle all kneel at the hour Christ was born, and the sun dance, "by reason of rejoicement," on the morning of his resurrection; that believes the dark Cross, actually found on the back of every Ass, was first placed there when Jesus rode into Jerusalem with Palm-branches strewed before him.

Not in vain is Ireland pouring itself all over the earth. Divine Providence has a mission for her children to fulfil; though a mission unrecognized by political economists. There is ever a moral balance preserved in the universe, like the vibrations of the pendulum. The Irish, with their glowing hearts and reverent credulity, are needed in this cold age of intellect and scepticism.

Africa furnishes another class, in whom the heart ever takes guidance of the head; and all over the world the way is opening for them among the nations.

Hayti and the British West Indies; Algiers, settled by the French; British colonies, spreading over the west and south of Africa; and emancipation urged throughout the civilized world.

Women, too, on whose intellect ever rests the warm light of the affections, are obviously coming into a wider and wider field of action.

All these things prophesy of physical force yielding to moral sentiment; and they all are agents to fulfil what they prophesy. God speed the hour.

Letter XXXIV [1]
January, 1843

You ask what are my opinions about "Women's Rights." [2] I confess, a strong distaste to the subject, as it has been generally treated. On no other theme, probably, has there been uttered so much of false, mawkish sentiment, shallow philosophy, and sputtering, farthing-candle wit. If the style of its advocates has often been offensive to taste, and unacceptable to reason, assuredly that of its opponents has been still more so. College boys have amused themselves with writing dreams, in which they saw women in hotels, with their feet hoisted, and chairs tilted back, or growling and bickering at each other in legislative halls, or fighting at the polls, with eyes blackened by fisticuffs. But it never seems to have occurred to these facetious writers, that the proceedings which appear so ludicrous and improper in *women,* are also ridiculous and disgraceful in *men.* It were well that *men* should learn not to hoist their feet above their heads, and tilt their chairs backward, not to growl and snap in the halls of legislation, or give each other black eyes at the polls.

Maria Edgeworth says, "We are disgusted when we see a woman's mind overwhelmed with a torrent of learning; that the tide of literature has passed over it should be betrayed only by its fertility." This is beautiful and true; but is it not likewise applicable to man? The truly great never seek to display themselves. If they carry their heads high above the crowd, it is only made manifest to others by accidental revelations of their extended vision. "Human duties and proprieties do not lie so very far apart," said Harriet Martineau; "if they did, there would be two gospels, and two teachers, one for man, and another for woman." [3]

It would seem, indeed, as if men were willing to give women the exclusive benefit of gospel-teaching. "*Women* should be gentle," say the advocates of subordination; but when Christ said, "Blessed are the meek," did he preach to women only? "*Girls* should be modest," is the language of common teaching, continually uttered in words and customs. Would it not be an improvement for men, also, to be scrupulously pure in manners, conversation, and life? Books addressed to young married people abound with advice to the *wife,* to control her temper, and never to utter wearisome complaints, or vexatious words, when the husband comes home fretful or unreasonable, from his out-of-door conflicts with the world. Would not the advice be as excellent and appropriate, if the husband were advised to conquer *his* fretfulness, and forbear *his* complaints, in consideration of his wife's ill-health, fatiguing cares, and the thousand disheartening influences of domestic routine? In short, whatsoever can be named as loveliest, best, and most graceful in woman, would likewise be good and graceful in man. You will perhaps remind me of courage. If you use the word in its highest signification, I answer that woman, above others, has abundant need of it, in her pilgrimage; and the true woman wears it with a quiet grace. If you mean mere animal courage, *that* is not mentioned in the Sermon on the Mount,[4] among those qualities which enable us to inherit the earth, or become the children of God. That the feminine ideal approaches much nearer to the gospel standard, than the prevalent idea of manhood, is shown by the universal tendency to represent the Saviour and his most beloved disciple with mild, meek expression, and feminine beauty. None speak of the bravery, the might, or the intellect of Jesus; but the devil is always imagined as a being of acute intellect, political cunning, and the fiercest courage. These universal and instinctive tendencies of the human mind reveal much.

That the present position of women in society is the result of physical force, is obvious enough; whosoever doubts it, let her reflect why she is afraid to go out in the evening without the protection of a man. What constitutes the danger of aggression? Superior physical strength, uncontrolled by the moral sentiments. If physical strength were in complete subjection to moral influence, there would be no need of outward protection. That animal instinct and brute force now govern the world, is painfully apparent in the condition of women everywhere; from the Morduan Tartars,[5] whose ceremony of marriage consists in placing the bride on a mat, and consigning her to the bridegroom, with the words, "Here, wolf, take thy lamb,"—to the German remark, that "stiff ale, stinging tobacco, and a girl in her smart dress, are the best things." The same thing, softened by the refinements of civilization, peeps out in Stephen's remark, that "woman never looks so interesting, as when leaning on the arm of a soldier": and in Hazlitt's[6] complaint that "it is not easy to keep up a conversation with women in company. It is thought a piece of rudeness to differ from them; it is not quite fair to ask them a *reason* for what they say."[7]

This sort of politeness to women is what men call gallantry; an odious word to every sensible woman, because she sees that it is merely the flimsy veil which foppery throws over sensuality, to conceal its grossness. So far is it from indicating sincere esteem and affection for women, that the profligacy of a nation may, in general, be fairly measured by its gallantry. This taking away *rights*, and *condescending* to grant *privileges*, is an old trick of the physical force principle; and with the immense majority, who only look on the surface of things, this mask effectually disguises an ugliness, which would otherwise be abhorred. The most inveterate slaveholders are probably those who take most pride in dressing their household servants handsomely, and who would be most ashamed to have the name of being *unnecessarily* cruel. And profligates, who form the lowest and most sensual estimate of women, are the very ones to treat them with an excess of outward deference.

There are few books, which I can read through, without feeling insulted as a woman; but this insult is almost universally conveyed through that which was intended for praise. Just imagine, for a moment, what impression it would make on men, if women authors should write about *their* "rosy lips," and "melting eyes," and "voluptuous forms," as they write about *us!* That women in general do not feel this kind of flattery to be an insult, I readily admit; for, in the first place, they do not perceive the gross chattel-principle, of which it is the utterance; moreover, they have, from long habit, become accustomed to consider themselves as household conveniences, or gilded toys. Hence, they consider it feminine and pretty to abjure all such use of their faculties, as would make them co-workers with man in the advancement of those great principles, on which the progress of society depends. "There is perhaps no *animal*," says Hannah More, "so much indebted to subordination, for its good behaviour, as woman." Alas, for the animal age, in which such utterance could be tolerated by public sentiment!

Martha More, sister of Hannah, describing a very impressive scene at the funeral of one of her Charity School teachers, says: "The spirit within seemed struggling to speak, and I was in a sort of agony; but I recollected that I had heard, somewhere, a woman must not speak in the *church*. Oh, had she been buried in the church *yard*, a messenger from Mr. Pitt[8] himself should not have restrained me; for I seemed to have received a message from a higher Master within."

This application of theological teaching carries its own commentary.

I have said enough to show that I consider prevalent opinions and customs highly unfavourable to the moral and intellectual development of women: and I need not say, that, in proportion to their true culture, women will be more useful and happy, and domestic life more perfected. True culture, in them, as in men, consists in the full and free development of individual character, regulated by their *own* perceptions of what is true, and their *own* love of what is good.

This individual responsibility is rarely acknowledged, even by the most refined, as necessary to the spiritual progress of women. I once heard a very beautiful lecture from R. W. Emerson, on Being and Seeming.[9] In the course of many remarks, as true as they were graceful, he urged women to *be*, rather than *seem*. He told them that all their laboured education of forms, strict observance of genteel etiquette, tasteful arrangement of the toilette, &c., all this *seeming* would not *gain hearts* like *being* truly what God made them; that earnest simplicity, the sincerity of nature, would kindle the eye, light up the countenance, and give an inexpressible charm to the plainest features.

The advice was excellent, but the motive, by which it was urged, brought a flush of indignation over my face. *Men* were exhorted to *be,* rather than to *seem,* that they might fulfil the sacred mission for which their souls were embodied; that they might, in God's freedom, grow up into the full stature of spiritual manhood; but *women* were urged to simplicity and truthfulness, that they might become more *pleasing.*

Are we not all immortal beings? Is not each one responsible for himself and herself? There is no measuring the mischief done by the prevailing tendency to teach women to be virtuous as a duty to *man,* rather than to *God*—for the sake of pleasing the creature, rather than the Creator. "*God* is thy law, *thou* mine," said Eve to Adam. May Milton be forgiven for sending that thought "out into everlasting time" in such a jewelled setting. What weakness, vanity, frivolity, infirmity of moral purpose, sinful flexibility of principle—in a word, what soul-stifling, has been the result of thus putting man in the place of God! [10]

But while I see plainly that society is on a false foundation, and that prevailing views concerning women indicate the want of wisdom and purity, which they serve to perpetuate—still, I must acknowledge that much of the talk about Women's Rights offends both my reason and my taste. I am not of those who maintain there is no sex in souls; nor do I like the results deducible from that doctrine.[11] Kinmont, in his admirable book, called the Natural History of Man,[12] speaking of the warlike courage of the ancient German women, and of their being respectfully consulted on important public affairs, says: "You ask me if I consider all this right, and deserving of approbation? or that women were here engaged in their appropriate tasks? I answer, yes; it is just *as* right that they should take this interest in the honour of their country, as the other sex. Of course, I do not think that women were *made* for war and battle; neither do I believe that *men* were. But since the fashion of the times had made it so, and settled it that war was a necessary element of greatness, and that no safety was to be procured without it, I argue that it shows a healthful state of feeling in other respects, that the feelings of both sexes were *equally* enlisted in the cause; that there was no *division* in the house, or the State; and that the serious pursuits and objects of the one were also the serious pursuits and objects of the other." [13]

The nearer society approaches to divine order, the less separation will there be in the characters, duties, and pursuits of men and women. Women will not become less gentle and graceful, but men will become more so. Women will not neglect the care and education of their children, but men will find themselves ennobled and refined by sharing those duties with them; and will receive, in return, co-operation and sympathy in the discharge of various other duties, now deemed inappropriate to women. The more women become rational companions, partners in business and in thought, as well as in affection and amusement, the more highly will men appreciate *home*—that blessed word, which opens to the human heart the most perfect glimpse of Heaven, and helps to carry it thither, as on an angel's wings.

> "Domestic bliss,
> That can, the world eluding, be itself
> A world enjoyed; that wants no witnesses
> But its own sharers, and approving heaven;
> That, like a flower deep hid in rocky cleft,
> Smiles, though 'tis looking only at the sky."

Alas, for these days of Astor houses, and Tremonts, and Albions! where families exchange comfort for costliness, fireside retirement for flirtation and flaunting, and the simple, healthful, cozy meal, for gravies and gout, dainties and dyspepsia. There is no characteristic of my countrymen which I regret so deeply, as their slight degree of adhesiveness to home. Closely intertwined with this instinct, is the religion of a nation. The Home and the Church bear a near relation to each other. The French have no such word as home in their language, and I believe they are the least reverential and religious of all the Christian nations. A Frenchman had been in the habit of visiting a lady constantly for several years, and being alarmed at a report that she was sought in marriage, he was asked why he did not marry her himself. "*Marry* her!" exclaimed he; "Good heavens! *where should I spend my evenings?*" The idea of domestic happiness was altogether a foreign idea to his soul, like a word that conveyed no meaning. Religious sentiment in France leads the same roving life as the domestic affections; breakfasting at one restaurateur's and supping at another's. When some wag in Boston reported that Louis Philippe had sent over for Dr. Channing to manufacture a religion for the French people, the witty significance of the joke was generally appreciated.

There is a deep spiritual reason why all that relates to the domestic affections should ever be found in close proximity with religious faith. The age of chivalry was likewise one of unquestioning veneration, which led to the crusade for the holy sepulchre. The French Revolution, which tore down churches, and voted that there was no God, likewise annulled marriage; and the doctrine that there is no sex in souls has usually been urged by those of infidel tendencies. Carlyle says: "But what feeling it was in the ancient, devout, deep soul, which of marriage made a *sacrament,* this, of all things in the world, is what Diderot will think of for aeons without discovering; unless, perhaps, it were to increase the *vestry fees.*" [14]

The conviction that woman's present position in society is a false one, and therefore re-acts disastrously on the happiness and improvement of man, is pressing, by slow degrees, on the common consciousness, through all the obstacles of bigotry, sensuality, and selfishness. As man approaches to the truest life, he will perceive more and more that there is no separation or discord in their mutual duties. They will be one; but it will be as affection and thought are one; the treble and bass of the same harmonious tune.

Letter XXXV[1]

February, 1843

A book has been lately published called the Westover Manuscripts, written more than a hundred years ago, by Col. William Byrd,[2] an old Virginian cavalier, residing at Westover, on the north bank of James river. He relates the following remarkable circumstance, which powerfully arrested my attention, and set in motion thoughts that flew beyond the stars, and so I lost sight of them, till they again come within my vision, in yonder world, where, as the German beautifully expresses it, "we shall find our dreams, and only lose our sleep." The writer says:

"Of all the effects of lightning that ever I heard of, the most amazing happened in this country, in the year 1736. In the summer of that year, a surgeon of a ship, whose name was Davis, came ashore at York, to visit a patient. He was no sooner got into the house, but it began to rain, with many terrible claps of thunder. When it was almost dark, there came a dreadful flash of lightning, which struck the surgeon dead, as he was walking about the room, but hurt no other person, though several were near him. At the same time, it made a large hole in the trunk of a pine tree, which grew about ten feet from the window. But what was most surprising in this disaster was, that *on the breast of the unfortunate man that was killed, was the figure of a pine tree, as exactly delineated as any limner in the world could draw it; nay, the resemblance went so far as to represent the colour of the pine, as well as the figure.* The lightning must probably have passed through the tree first, before it struck the man, and by that means have printed the icon of it on his breast. But whatever may have been the cause, the effect was certain, and can be attested by a cloud of witnesses, who had the curiosity to go and see this wonderful phenomenon."

This lightning daguerreotype aroused within me the old inquiry, "What *is* electricity?[3] Of what spiritual essence is it the form and type?" Questions that again and again have led my soul in such eager chase through the universe, to find an answer, that it has come back weary, as if it had carried heavy weights, and traversed Saturn's rings, in magnetic sleep. Thick clouds come between me and this mystery, into which I have searched for years; but I see burning lines of light along the edges, which significantly indicate the glory it veils.

I sometimes think electricity is the medium which puts man into relation with all things, enabling him to act on all, and receive from all. It is now well established as a scientific fact, though long regarded as an idle superstition, that some men can ascertain the vicinity of water, under ground, by means of a divining rod. Thouvenel,[4] and other scientific men in France, account for it by supposing that "the water forms with the earth above it, and the fluids of the human body, a *galvanic circle.*" The human body is said to be one of the best conductors yet discovered, and nervous or debilitated persons to be better conductors than those in sound health. If the body of the operator be a very good conductor, the rod in his hand will be forcibly drawn toward the earth, whenever he approaches a vein of water, that lies near the surface. If silk gloves or stockings are worn, the attraction is interrupted; and it varies in degree, according as any substances between the water and the hand of the operator are more or less good conductors of the galvanic fluid.

Everybody knows what a frightful imitation of life can be produced in a dead body by the galvanic battery.[5]

The animal magnetizer often feels as if strength had gone out of him; and it is very common for persons in magnetic sleep to speak of bright emanations from the fingers which are making passes over them.

What *is* this invisible, all-pervading essence, which thus has power to put man into communication with all? That man contains the universe within himself, philosophers conjectured ages ago; and therefore named him "the microcosm." If man led a true life, he would, doubtless, come into harmonious relation with all forms of being,[6] and thus his instincts would be universal, and far more certain and perfect, than those of animals. The bird knows what plant will cure the bite of a serpent; and if man led a life as true to the laws of *his* being, as the bird does to *hers*, he would have no occasion to study medicine, for, he would at once perceive the medicinal quality of every herb and mineral. His *inventions* are, in fact, only *discoveries;* for all existed, before he applied it, and called it his own. The upholsterer-bee had a perfect cutting instrument, ages before scissors were invented; the mason-bee cemented pebbles together, for his dwelling, centuries before houses were built with stone and mortar; the wasp of Cayenne made her nest of beautiful white card paper, cycles before paper was invented; the lightning knew how to print images, aeons before Monsieur Daguerre found out half the process; viz: the *form* without the *colour;*[7] the bee knew how to take up the least possible room in the construction of her cells, long before mathematicians discovered that she had worked out the problem perfectly; and I doubt not fishes had the very best of submarine reflectors, before Mrs. Mather[8] invented her ocean telescope, which shows a pin distinctly on the muddy bottom of the bay.

I cannot recall the name of the ancient philosopher, who spent his days in watching insects and other animals, that he might gather hints to fashion tools; but the idea has long been familiar to my mind, that every conceivable thing which has been, or will be invented, already exists in nature, in some form or other. Man alone can reproduce all things of creation; because he contains the WHOLE in himself, and all forms of being flow into his, as a common centre.

Of what spiritual thing is electricity the type? Is there a universal medium by which all things of spirit act on the soul, as matter on the body by means of electricity? And is that medium the WILL, whether of angels or of men? Wonderful stories are told of early Friends,[9] how they were guided by a sudden and powerful impulse, to avoid some particular bridge, or leave some particular house, and subsequent events showed that danger was there. Many people consider this fanaticism; but I have faith in it. I believe the most remarkable of these accounts give but a faint idea of the perfection to which man's moral and physical instincts might attain, if his life were obedient and true.[10]

Though in vigorous health, I am habitually affected by the weather. I never indulge gloomy thoughts; but resolutely turn away my gaze from the lone stubble waving in the autumn wind, and think only of the ripe, golden seed which the sower will go forth to sow. But when to the dreariness of departing summer is added a week of successive rains; when day after day, the earth under foot is slippery mud, and the sky over head like gray marble, then my nature yields itself prisoner to utter melancholy. I am ashamed to confess it, and hundreds of times have struggled desperately against it, unwilling to be conquered by the elements, looking at me with an "evil eye." But so it is—a protracted rain always convinces me that I never did any good, and never can do any; that I love nobody, and nobody loves me. I have heard that Dr. Franklin[11] acknowledges a similar effect on himself, and philosophically conjectures the physical cause. He says animal spirits depend greatly on the presence of electricity in our bodies; and during long-continued rain, the dampness of the atmosphere absorbs a large portion of it; for this reason, he advises that a silk waistcoat be worn next the skin; silk being a nonconductor of electricity. Perhaps this precaution might diminish the number of suicides in the foggy month of November, "when Englishmen are so prone to hang and drown themselves."

Animal magnetism is connected, in some unexplained way, with electricity. All those who have tried it, are aware that there is a *metallic* feeling occasioned by the magnetic passes—a sort of attraction, as one might imagine the magnet and the steel to feel when brought near each other. The magnetizer passes his hands over the subject, without touching, and at the end of each operation shakes them, precisely as if he were conducting off electric fluid. If this is the actual effect, the drowsiness, stupor, and final insensibility, may be occasioned by a cause similar to that which produces heaviness and depression of spirits in rainy weather. *Why* it should be so, in either case, none can tell. The most learned have no knowledge what electricity *is;* they can only tell *what* it does, not *how* it does it.

That the state of the atmosphere has prodigious effect on human temperament, is sufficiently indicated by the character of nations. The Frenchman owes his sanguine hopes, his supple limbs, his untiring vivacity, to a genial climate; to this too, in a great measure, the Italian owes his pliant gracefulness and impulsive warmth. The Dutchman, on his level marshes, could never dance La Sylphide; nor the Scotch girl, on her foggy hills, become an improvisatrice. The French dance into everything, on everything, and over everything; for they live where the breezes dance among vines, and the sun showers down gold to the piper; and dance they must, for gladsome sympathy. We call them of *"mercurial"* temperament; according to Dr. Franklin's theory, they are surcharged with *electricity.*

In language, too, how plainly one perceives the influence of climate! Languages of northern origin abound in consonants, and sound like clanging metals, or the tipping up of a cart-load of stones. The southern languages flow like a rill that moves to music; the liquid vowels so sweetly melt into each other. This difference is observable even in the dialect of our northern and southern tribes of Indians. At the north, we find such words as Carratunk, Scowhegan, Norridgewock, and Memphremagog; at the south, Pascagoula, Santee, and that most musical of all names, Oceola.[12]

Climate has had its effect, too, on the religious ideas of nations. How strongly do the bloody Woden and the thundering Thor, of northern mythology, contrast with the beautiful Graces and gliding Nymphs of Grecian origin. As a general rule, (sometimes affected by local causes,) southern nations cling to the pictured glory of the Catholic church, while the northern assimilate better with the severe plainness of the Protestant.

If I had been reared from infancy under the cloudless sky of Athens, perhaps I might have bounded over the earth, as if my "element were air, and music but the echo of my steps;" the caution that looks where it treads, might have been changed for the ardent gush of a Sappho's song;[13] the sunbeam might have passed into my soul, and written itself on the now thoughtful countenance in perpetual smiles.

Do you complain of this, as you do of phrenology, and say that it favours fatalism too much? I answer, no matter what it favours, if it be truth. No two truths ever devoured each other, or ever can. Look among the families of your acquaintance—you will see two brothers vigorous, intelligent, and enterprising; the third was like them, till he fell on his head, had fits, and was ever after puny and stupid. There are two sunny-tempered, graceful girls—their sister might have been as cheerful as they, but their father died suddenly, before her birth, and the mother's sorrow chilled the fountains of her infant life, and she is nervous, deformed, and fretful. Is there no fatality, as you call it, in this? Assuredly, we are all, in some degree, the creatures of outward circumstance; but this in nowise disturbs the scale of moral responsibility, or prevents equality of happiness. Our responsibility consists in the *use* we make of our possessions, not on their *extent*. Salvation comes to all through obedience to the light they have, be it much or little. Happiness consists not in having much, but in wanting no more than we have. The idiot is as happy in playing at Jack Straws, or blowing bubbles all the livelong day, as Newton was in watching the great choral dance of the planets. The same universe lies above and around both. "The mouse can drink no more than his fill at the mightiest river;" yet he enjoys his draught as well as the elephant. Thus are we all unequal, yet equal. That we *are,* in part, creatures of necessity, who that has tried to exert free will, can doubt? But it is a necessity which has power only over the outward, and can never change evil into good, or good into evil. It may compel us to postpone or forbear the good we would fain do, but it cannot compel us to commit the evil.

If a consideration of all these outward influences teach us charity for the deficiencies of others, and a strict watch over our own weaknesses, they will perform their appropriate office.

"There is so much of good among the worst, so much of evil in the best,
Such seeming partialities in Providence, so many things to lessen and expand,
Yea, and with all man's boast, so little real freedom of his will,
That to look a little lower than the surface, garb, or dialect, or fashion,
Thou shalt feebly pronounce for a saint, and faintly condemn for a sinner." [14]

Letter XXXVI [1]
March, 1843

I went, a few evenings ago, to the American Museum,[2] to see fifteen Indians, fresh from the western forest. Sacs, Fox, and Iowas;[3] really important people in their respective tribes. Nan-Nouce-Fush-E-To, which means the Buffalo King, is a famous Sac chief, sixty years old, covered with scars, and grim as a Hindoo god, or pictures of the devil on a Portuguese contribution box, to help sinners through purgatory. It is said that he has killed with his own hand one hundred Osages, three Mohawks, two Kas, two Sioux, and one Pawnee; and if we may judge by his organ of destructiveness, the story is true; a more enormous bump I never saw in that region of the skull. He speaks nine Indian dialects, has visited almost every existing tribe of his race, and is altogether a remarkable personage. Mon-To-Gah, the White Bear, wears a medal from President Monroe, for certain services rendered to the whites. Wa-Con-To-Kitch-Er, is an Iowa chief, of grave and thoughtful countenance, held in much veneration as the Prophet of his tribe. He sees visions, which he communicates to them for their spiritual instruction. Among the squaws is No-Nos-See, the She Wolf, a niece of the famous Black Hawk,[4] and very proud of the relationship; and Do-Hum-Me, the Productive Pumpkin, a very handsome woman, with a great deal of heart and happiness in her countenance.

"Smiles settled on her sun-flecked cheeks,
Like noon upon the mellow apricot." [5]

She was married about a fortnight ago, at Philadelphia, to Cow-Hick-He, son of the principal chief of the Iowas, and as noble a specimen of manhood as I ever looked upon. Indeed I have never seen a group of human beings so athletic, well-proportioned, and majestic. They are a keen satire on our civilized customs, which produce such feeble forms and pallid faces. The unlimited pathway, the broad horizon, the free grandeur of the forest, has passed into their souls, and so stands revealed in their material forms.

We who have robbed the Indians of their lands, and worse still, of *themselves,* are very fond of proving their inferiority. We are told that the *facial angle*[6] in the

Caucasian race is	85	degrees.
Asiatic	78	"
American Indian	73	"
Ethiopian	70	"
Ourang Outang	67	"

This simply proves that the Caucasian race, through a succession of ages, has been exposed to influences eminently calculated to develop the moral and intellectual faculties. That they started *first* in the race, might have been owing to a finer and more susceptible nervous organization, originating in climate, perhaps, but serving to bring the physical organization into more harmonious relation with the laws of spiritual reception. But by whatever agency it might have been produced, the nation, or race that perceived even one spiritual idea in advance of others, would necessarily go on improving in geometric ratio, through the lapse of ages. For *our* Past, we have the oriental fervour, gorgeous imagery, and deep reverence of the Jews, flowing from that high fountain, the perception of the oneness and invisibility of God. From the Greeks we receive the very Spirit of Beauty, flowing into all forms of Philosophy and Art, encircled by a golden halo of Platonism, which

> "Far over many a land and age hath shone,
> And mingles with the light that beams from God's own throne."

These have been transmitted to us in their own forms, and again reproduced through the classic strength and high cultivation of Rome, and the romantic minstrelsy and rich architecture of the middle ages. Thus we stand, a congress of ages, each with a glory on its brow, peculiar to itself, yet in part reflected from the glory that went before.

But what have the African savage, and the wandering Indian for *their* Past? To fight for food, and grovel in the senses, has been the employment of *their* ancestors. The Past reproduced in them, mostly belongs to the animal part of our mixed nature. They have indeed come in contact with the race on which had dawned higher ideas; but *how* have they come in contact? As *victims,* not as *pupils.* Rum, gunpowder, the horrors of slavery, the unblushing knavery of trade, these have been their teachers! And because these have failed to produce a high degree of moral and intellectual cultivation, we coolly declare that the negroes are made for slaves, that the Indians cannot be civilized; and that when either of the races come in contact with us, they must either consent to be our beasts of burden, or be driven to the wall, and perish.

That the races of mankind are different, spiritually as well as physically, there is, of course, no doubt; but it is as the difference between trees of the same forest, not as between trees and minerals. The facial angle and shape of the head, is various in races and nations; but these are the *effects* of spiritual influences, long operating on character, and in their turn becoming *causes;* thus intertwining, as Past and Future ever do.

But it is urged that Indians who have been put to schools and colleges, still remained attached to a roving life; away from all these advantages,

"His blanket tied with yellow strings, the Indian of the forest went."

And what if he did? Do not white, young men who have been captured by savages in infancy, show an equally strong disinclination to take upon themselves the restraints of civilized life? Does anybody urge that this well-known fact proves the *white* race incapable of civilization?

You ask, perhaps, what becomes of my theory that races and individuals are the product of ages, if the influences of half a life produce the same effects on the Caucasian and the Indian? I answer, that white children brought up among Indians, though they strongly imbibe the habits of the race, are generally prone to be the geniuses and prophets of their tribe. The organization of nerve and brain has been changed by a more harmonious relation between the animal and the spiritual; and this comparative harmony has been produced by the influences of Judea, and Greece, and Rome, and the age of chivalry; though of all these things the young man never heard.

Similar influences brought to bear on the Indians or the Africans, as a race, would gradually change the structure of their skulls, and enlarge their perceptions of moral and intellectual truth. The *same* influences cannot be brought to bear upon them; for *their* Past is not *our* Past; and of course never can be. But let ours mingle with theirs, and you will find the result variety, without inferiority. They will be flutes on different notes, and so harmonize the better.

And how is this elevation of all races to be effected? By that which worketh *all* miracles, in the name of Jesus—The LAW OF LOVE. We must not teach as superiors; we must *love as brothers.* Here is the great deficiency in all our efforts for the ignorant and the criminal. We stand apart from them, and expect them to feel grateful for our condescension in noticing them at all. We do not embrace them warmly with our sympathies, and put our souls into their soul's stead.

But even under this great disadvantage; accustomed to our smooth, deceitful talk, when we want their lands, and to the cool villany with which we break treaties when our purposes are gained; receiving gunpowder and rum from the very hands which retain from them all the better influences of civilized life; cheated by knavish agents, cajoled by government, and hunted with bloodhounds—still, under all *these* disadvantages, the Indians have shown that they *can* be civilized. Of this, the Choctaws and Cherokees are admirable proofs.[7] Both these tribes have a regularly-organized, systematic government, in the democratic form, and a printed constitution. The right of trial by jury, and other principles of a free government, are established on a permanent basis. They have good farms, cotton-gins, saw-mills, schools, and churches. Their dwellings are generally comfort-able, and some of them are handsome. The last annual message of the chief of the Cherokees is a highly-interesting document, which would not compare dis-advantageously with any of our governors' messages. It states that more than $2,500,000 are due to them from the United States; and recommends that this sum be obtained, and in part distributed among the people; but that the interest of the school fund be devoted to the maintenance of schools, and the diffusion of knowledge.

There was a time when *our* ancestors, the ancient Britons, went nearly without clothing, painted their bodies in fantastic fashion, offered up human victims to uncouth idols, and lived in hollow trees, or rude habitations, which we should now consider unfit for cattle. Making all due allowance for the different state of the world, it is much to be questioned whether they made more rapid advance-ment than the Cherokees and Choctaws.

It always fills me with sadness to see Indians surrounded by the false environ-ment of civilized life; but I never felt so deep a sadness, as I did in looking upon these western warriors; for they were evidently the noblest of their dwindling race, unused to restraint, accustomed to sleep beneath the stars. And here they were, set up for a two-shilling show, with monkeys, flamingoes, dancers, and buffoons! If they understood our modes of society well enough to be aware of their degraded position, they would doubtless quit it, with burning indignation at the insult. But as it is, they allow women to examine their beads and children to play with their wampum, with the most philosophic indifference. In their imperturbable coun-tenances, I thought I could once or twice detect a slight expression of scorn at the eager curiosity of the crowd. The Albiness, a short woman, with pink eyes, and hair like white floss, was the only object that visibly amused them. The young chiefs nodded to her often, and exchanged smiling remarks with each other, as they looked at her. Upon all the buffooneries and ledgerdermain tricks of the Museum, they gazed as unmoved as John Knox[8] himself could have done. I would have given a good deal to know their thoughts, as mimic cities, and fairy grottoes, and mechanical dancing figures, rose and sunk before them. The me-chanical figures were such perfect imitations of life, and went through so many wonderful evolutions, that they might well surprise even those accustomed to the marvels of mechanism. But Indians, who pay religious honours to venerable rocks, and moss-grown trees, who believe that brutes have souls, as well as men, and that all nature is filled with spirits, might well doubt whether there was not here some supernatural agency, either good or evil. I would suffer almost any-thing, if my soul could be transmigrated into the She Wolf, or the Productive Pumpkin, and their souls pass consciously into my frame, for a few days, that I might experience the fashion of their thoughts and feelings. Was there ever such a foolish wish! The soul *is* ME, and *is* Thee. I might as well put on their blankets, as their bodies, for purposes of spiritual insight. In that other world, shall we be enabled to know exactly how heaven, and earth, and hell, appear to other persons, nations, and tribes? I would it might be so; for I have an intense desire for such revelations. I do not care to travel to Rome, or St. Petersburg, because I can only look *at* people; and I want to look *into* them, and *through* them; to know how things appear to *their* spiritual eyes, and sound to *their* spiritual ears. This is a universal want; hence the intense interest taken in autobiography, by all classes of readers. Oh, if any one had but the courage to write the *whole* truth of himself, undisguised, as it appears before the eye of God and angels, the WORLD would read it, and it would soon be translated into all the dialects of the universe.

But these children of the forest do not even give us glimpses of their inner life; for they consider that the body was given to *conceal* the emotions of the soul. The stars look down into their hearts, as into mind, the broad ocean, glittering in the moonbeams, speaks to them of the Infinite; and doubtless the wild flowers and the sea-shells, "talk to them a thought." But *what* thoughts, *what* revelations of the infinite? This would I give the world to know; but the world cannot buy an answer.

How foreign is my soul to that of the beautiful Do-Hum-Me! How helpless should I be in situations where she would be a heroine; and how little could she comprehend my eager thought, which seeks the creative three-in-one throughout the universe, and finds it in every blossom, and every mineral. Between Wa-Con-To-Kitch-Er, and the German Herder,[9] what a distance! Yet are they both prophets; and though one looks through nature with the pitch-pine torch of the wilderness, and the other is lighted by a whole constellation of suns, yet have both learned, in their degree, that matter is only the time-garment of the spirit. The stammering utterance with which the Iowa seer reveals this, it were worth a kingdom to hear, if we could but borrow the souls of his tribe, while they listen to his visions.

It is a general trait with the Indian tribes to recognise the Great Spirit in every little child. They rarely refuse a child anything. When their revenge is most implacable, a little one is often sent to them, adorned with flowers and shells, and taught to lisp a prayer that the culprit may be forgiven; and such mediation is rarely without effect, even on the sternest warrior. This trait alone is sufficient to establish their relationship with Herder, Richter,[10] and other spirits of angel-stature. Nay, if we could look back a few centuries, we should find the ancestors of Shakspeare, and the fastidiously-refined Goethe, with painted cheeks, wolves' teeth for jewels, and boars' hides for garments. Perhaps the universe could not have passed before the vision of those star-like spirits, except through the forest life of such wild ancestry.

Some theorists say that the human brain, in its formation, "changes with a steady rise, through a likeness to one animal and then another, till it is perfected in that of man, the highest animal." It seems to be so with the nations, in their progressive rise out of barbarism. I was never before so much struck with the animalism of Indian character, as I was in the frightful war-dance of these chiefs. Their gestures were as furious as wild-cats, they howled like wolves, screamed like prairie dogs, and tramped like buffaloes. Their faces were painted fiery red, or with cross-bars of green and red, and they were decorated with all sorts of uncouth trappings of hair, and bones, and teeth. That which regulated their movements, in lieu of music, was a discordant clash; and altogether they looked and acted more like demons from the pit, than anything I ever imagined. It was the natural and appropriate language of War. The wolfish howl, and the wild-cat leap, represent it more truly than graceful evolutions, and the Marseilles hymn. *That* music rises above mere brute vengeance; it breathes, in fervid ecstacy the *soul's* aspiration after freedom—the struggle of will with fate. It is the Future setting sail from old landings, and merrily piping all hands on board. It is too noble a voice to belong to physical warfare; the shrill howl of old Nan-Nouce-Fush-E-To is good enough for such brutish work; it clove the brain like a tomahawk, and was hot with hatred.

In truth, that war-dance was terrific both to eye and ear. I looked at the door, to see if escape were easy, in case they really worked themselves up to the scalping point. For the first time, I fully conceived the sacrifices and perils of Puritan settlers. Heaven have mercy on the mother who heard those dreadful yells, when they really foreboded murder! or who suddenly met such a group of grotesque demons in the loneliness of the forest!

But instantly I felt that I was wronging them in my thought. Through paint and feathers, I saw gleams of right honest and friendly expression; and I said, we are children of the same Father, seeking the same home. If the Puritans suffered from their savage hatred, it was because they met them with savage weapons, and a savage spirit. Then I thought of William Penn's treaty with the Indians; "the only one ever formed without an oath, and the only one that was never broken." I thought of the deputation of Indians, who, some years ago, visited Philadelphia, and knelt with one spontaneous impulse around the monument of Penn.

Again I looked at the yelling savages in their grim array, stamping through the war-dance, with a furious energy that made the floor shake, as by an earthquake; and I said, These, too, would bow, like little children, before the persuasive power of Christian love! Alas, if we had but faith in this divine principle, what mountains of evil might be removed into the depths of the sea.

P.S.
Alas, poor Do-Hum-Me is dead; so is No-See, Black Hawk's niece; and several of the chiefs are indisposed. Sleeping by hot anthracite fires, and then exposed to the keen encounters of the wintry wind; one hour, half stifled in the close atmosphere of theatres and crowded saloons, and the next, driving through snowy streets and the midnight air; this is a process which kills civilized people by inches, but savages at a few strokes.

Do-Hum-Me was but nineteen years old, in vigorous health, when I saw her a few days since, and obviously so happy in her newly wedded love, that it ran over at her expressive eyes, and mantled her handsome face like a veil of sunshine. Now she rests among the trees, in Greenwood Cemetery; not the trees that whispered to her childhood. Her coffin was decorated according to Indian custom, and deposited with the ceremonies peculiar to her people. Alas, for the handsome one, how lonely she sleeps here! Far, far away from him, to whom her eye turned constantly, as the sunflower to the light!

Sick, and sad at heart, this noble band of warriors, with melancholy steps, left the pestilential city last week, for their own broad prairies in the West. Do-Hum-Me was the pride and idol of them all. The old Iowa chief, the head of the deputation, was her father; and notwithstanding the stoicism of Indian character, it is said that both he and the bereaved young husband were overwhelmed with an agony of grief. They obviously loved each other most strongly. May the Great Spirit grant them a happy meeting in their "fair hunting grounds" beyond the sky.[11]

Letter XXXVII [1]
March, 1843

When I began to write these letters, it was simply as a safety-valve for an expanding spirit, pent up like steam in a boiler. I told you they would be of every fashion, according to my changing mood; now a mere panorama of passing scenes, then childlike prattle about birds or mosses; now a serious exposition of facts, for the reformer's use, and then the poet's path, on winged Pegasus,[2] far up into the blue.

To-day I know not what I shall write; but I *think* I shall be off to the sky; for my spirit is in that mood when smiling faces peep through chinks in the clouds, and angel fingers beckon and point upward. As I grow older, these glimpses into the spiritual become more and more clear, and all the *visible* stamps itself on my soul, a daguerreotype image of the *invisible*, written with sunbeams.

I sometimes ask myself, Will it continue to be so? For coming age casts its shadow before; and the rarest of attainments is to grow old happily and gracefully. When I look around among the old people of my acquaintance, I am frightened to see how large a proportion are a burden to themselves, and an annoyance to others. The joyfulness of youth excites in them no kindlier feeling than gloom, and lucky is it, if it does not encounter angry rebuke or supercilious contempt. The happiness of lovers has a still worse effect; it frets them until they become like the man with a toothache, whose irritation impelled him to kick poor puss, because she was sleeping so comfortably in the sunshine.

If this state were an inevitable attendant upon advanced years, then indeed would long life be an unmitigated curse. But there *is* no such necessity imposed upon us. We make old age cheerless and morose, in the same way that we pervert all things; and that is, by *selfishness*. We allow ourselves to think more of our own convenience and comfort, in little matters, than we do of the happiness and improvement of others; and thus we lose the habit of sympathizing with love and joy. I pray God to enable me to guard against this. May I be ever willing to promote the innocent pleasure of others, in their *own* way, even if it be not *my* way. Selfishness can blight even the abundant blossoms of youth; and if carried into age, it leaves the soul like a horse enclosed within an arid and stony field, with plenty of verdant pastures all around him.

Childhood itself is scarcely more lovely than a cheerful, kind, sunshiny old age.

> "How I love the mellow sage,
> Smiling through the veil of age!
> And whene'er this man of years
> In the dance of joy appears,
> Age is on his temples hung,
> But his heart—*his heart is young!*"

Here is the great secret of a bright and green old age. When Tithonus[3] asked for an eternal life in the body, and found, to his sorrow, that immortal *youth* was not included in the bargain, it surely was because he forgot to ask the perpetual gift of loving and sympathizing.

Next to this, is an intense affection for nature, and for all simple things. A human heart can never grow old, if it takes a lively interest in the pairing of birds, the re-production of flowers, and the changing tints of autumn-ferns. Nature, unlike other friends, has an exhaustless meaning, which one sees and hears more distinctly, the more they are enamoured of her. Blessed are they who *hear* it; for through tones comes the most inward perceptions of the spirit. Into the ear of the soul, which reverently *listens*, Nature whispers, speaks, or warbles, most heavenly arcana.

And even they who seek her only through science, receive a portion of her own tranquillity, and perpetual youth. The happiest old man I ever saw, was one who knew how the mason-bee builds his cell, and how every bird lines her nest; who found pleasure in a sea-shore pebble, as boys do in new marbles; and who placed every glittering mineral in a focus of light, under a kaleidescope of his own construction. The effect was like the imagined riches of fairy land; and when an admiring group of happy young people gathered round it, the heart of the good old man leapt like the heart of a child. The laws of nature, as manifested in her infinitely various operations, were to him a perennial fountain of delight; and, like her, he offered the joy to all. Here was no admixture of the bad excitement attendant upon ambition or controversy; but all was serenely happy, as are an angel's thoughts, or an infant's dreams.

Age, in its outward senses, returns again to childhood; and thus should it do spiritually. The little child enters a rich man's house, and loves to play with the things that are new and pretty; but he thinks not of their market value, nor does he pride himself that another child cannot play with the same. The farmer's home will probably delight him more; for he will love living squirrels better than marble greyhounds, and the merry bob o' lincoln better than stuffed birds from Araby the blest;[4] for *they* cannot sing into his heart. What *he* wants is life and love—the power of giving and receiving joy. To this estimate of things, wisdom returns, after the intuitions of childhood are lost. Virtue is but innocence on a higher plane, to be attained only through severe conflict. Thus life completes its circle; but it is a circle that *rises* while it revolves; for the path of spirit is ever spiral, containing *all* of truth and love in each revolution, yet ever tending upward. The virtue which brings us back to innocence, on a higher plane of wisdom, may be the childhood of another state of existence; and through successive conflicts, we may again complete the ascending circle, and find it holiness.

The ages, too, are rising spirally; each containing all, yet ever ascending. Hence, all our new things are old, and yet they are new. Some truth known to the ancients meets us on a higher plane, and we do not recognise it, because it is like a child of earth, which has passed upward and become an angel. Nothing of true beauty ever passes away. The youth of the world, which Greece embodied in immortal marble, will return in the circling Ages, as innocence comes back in virtue; but it shall return filled with a higher life; and that, too, shall point upward. Thus shall the Arts be glorified. Beethoven's music prophesies all this, and struggles after it continually; therefore, whosoever hears it, (with the *inward,* as well as the *outward* ear,) feels his soul spread its strong pinions, eager to pass "the flaming bounds of time and space," and circle all the infinite.

It is a beautiful conception of Fourier's, that the Aurora borealis is the *Earth's aspiration* after its glorious future; and that when the moral and intellectual world are brought into order by the right construction of society, these restless, flashing northern lights will settle into an intensely radiant circle round the poles, melt all the ice, and bring into existence new flowers of unknown beauty.[5]

Astronomers almost contemporary with Fourier, and probably unacquainted with his theory of re-constructing society, have suggested the idea of progressive changes in the earth's motions, till her poles shall be brought into exact harmony with the poles of the heavens, and thus perpetual spring pervade the whole earth.

It is a singular fact, too, that the groups and series of Fourier's plan of society are in accordance with Swedenborg's description of the order in heaven. It is said that Fourier never read Swedenborg; yet has he embodied his spiritual order in political economy, as perfectly as if he had been sent to answer the prayer, "Thy kingdom come on *earth,* as it is in *heaven.*"

Visions! idle visions! exclaims the man of mere facts. Very well, friend; walk by the light of thy lantern, if it be sufficient for thee. I ask thee not to *believe* in these visions; for peradventure thou canst not. But said I not truly that their faces *smile* through chinks in the clouds, and that their fingers beckon and *point upward*?

Letter XXXVIII [1]
March 17, 1843

Here it is the 17th of March, and I was rejoicing that winter had but a fortnight longer to live, and imagination already began to stir its foot among last year's fallen leaves, in search of the hidden fragrant treasures of the trailing arbutus— when lo, there comes a snow-storm, the wildest and most beautiful of the season! The snow-spirit has been abroad, careering on the wings of the wind, in the finest style imaginable; throwing diamonds and ermine mantles around him, with princely prodigality.

> "And when his hours are numbered, and the world
> Is all his own, retiring, as he were not,
> Leaves, when the sun appears, astonished Art
> To mimic, in slow structures, stone by stone,
> Built in an age, the mad wind's night work,
> The frolic architecture of the snow."

I had wealth of fairy splendor on my windows this morning. Alpine heights, cathedral spires, and glittering grottoes. It reminded me of the days of my youth, when on the shores of Kennebec I used to watch to see "the river go down," as the rafters expressed it.[2] A magnificent spectacle it was, in those seasons when huge masses of ice were loosened by sudden warmth, and came tumbling over the falls, to lie broken into a thousand fantastic shapes of beauty. Trees, mountains, turrets, spires, broken columns, went sailing along, glancing and glittering in the moonlight, like petrified Fata-Morgana of Italian skies, with the rainbows frozen out. And here I had it painted in crystal, by the wild artist whom I heard at his work in the night-time, between my dreams, as he went by with the whistling storm.

"Nature, dear goddess," is *so* beautiful! *always* so beautiful! Every little flake of the snow is such a perfect crystal; and they fall together so gracefully, as if fairies of the air caught water-drops, and made them into artificial flowers to garland the wings of the wind! Oh, it is the saddest of all things, that even one human soul should dimly perceive the Beauty, that is ever around us, "a perpetual benediction." Nature, that great missionary of the Most High, preaches to us for ever in all tones of love, and writes truth in all colours, on manuscripts illuminated with stars and flowers. But we are not in harmony with the *whole*, and so we understand her not.

Here and there, a spirit less at discord with Nature, hears semitones in the ocean and wind, and when the stars look into his heart, he is stirred with dim recollections of a universal language, which would reveal *all*, if he only remembered the alphabet. "When one stands alone at night, amidst unfettered Nature," says Bettine,[3] "it seems as though she were a spirit praying to man for release! And *should* man set Nature free? I must at some time reflect upon this: but I have already very often had this sensation, as if wailing Nature plaintively *begged* something of me; and it cut me to the heart, not to be able to understand what she would have. I must consider seriously of this; perhaps I may discover something which shall raise us above this earthly life."

Well may Nature beg plaintively of man; for all that disturbs her harmony flows from *his* spirit. Age after age, she has toiled patiently, manifesting in thunder and lightning, tempest and tornado, the evils which man produces, and thus striving to restore the equilibrium which *he* disturbs. Every thing else seeks earnestly to live according to the laws of its being, and therefore each has individual excellence, the best adapted of all things to its purpose. Because Nature is earnest, spontaneous, and true, she is perfect. Art, though it makes a fair show, produces nothing perfect. Look through a powerful microscope at the finest cambric needle that ever was manufactured, and it shall seem blunt as a crowbar; but apply the same test to the antennae of a beetle or a butterfly, and thou wilt see them taper to an invisible point. That man's best works should be such bungling imitations of Nature's infinite perfection, matters not much; but that he should make *himself* an imitation, this is the fact which Nature moans over, and deprecates beseechingly. Be spontaneous, be truthful, be free, and thus be individuals! is the song she sings through warbling birds, and whispering pines, and roaring waves, and screeching winds. She wails and implores, because man keeps her in captivity, and he alone can set her free. To those who rise above custom and tradition, and dare to trust their own wings never so little above the crowd, how eagerly does she throw her garland ladders to tempt them upward! How beautiful, how angelic, seems every fragment of life which is earnest and true! Every man can be really great, if he will only trust his own highest instincts, think his own thoughts, and say his own say. The stupidest fellow, if he would but reveal, with childlike honesty, how he feels, and what he thinks, when the stars wink at him, when he sees the ocean for the first time, when music comes over the waters, or when he and his beloved look into each others' eyes,—would he but *reveal* this, the world would hail him as a genius, in *his* way, and would prefer his story to all the epics that ever were written, from Homer to Scott.

"The commonest mind is full of thought, some worthy of the rarest;
And could it see them fairly writ, would wonder at its wealth."

Nay, there is truth in the facetious assertion of Carlyle, that the dog, who sits looking at the moon so seriously, would doubtless be a poet, if he could but find a *publisher*. Of this thing be assured, no romance was ever so interesting, as would be a right comprehension of that dog's relation to the moon, and of the relation of both to all things, and of all things to thyself, and of thyself, to God. Some glimmering of this mysterious relation of each to All may disturb the dog's mind with a strange solemnity, until he fancies he sees another dog in the moon, and howls thereat. Could his howl be translated and published, it might teach us somewhat that the wisest has not yet conjectured.

Let not the matter-of-fact reader imagine me to say that it is difficult for puppies to find publishers. The frothy sea of circulating literature would prove such assertion a most manifest falsehood. Nor do I assert that puerile and common-place minds are diffident about making books. There is babbling more than enough; but among it all, one finds little true speech, or true silence. The *dullest* mind has some beauty peculiarly its *own;* but it echoes, and does not speak *itself.* It strives to write as schools have taught, as custom dictates, or as sects prescribe; and so it stammers, and makes no utterance. Nature made us *individuals,* as she did the flowers and the pebbles; but we are afraid to be peculiar, and so our soci-ety resembles a bag of marbles, or a string of mould candles. Why should we all dress after the same fashion? The frost never paints my windows twice alike.

As I write, I look round for the sparkling tracery; it is gone, and I shall never see a copy. Well, I will not mourn for this. The sunshine has its own glorious beauty, and my spirit rejoices therein, even more than in the graceful pencilings of the snow. All kinds of beauty have I loved with fervent homage.[4] Above all, do I worship it in its highest forms; that of a sincere and loving soul. Even here in the city, amid bricks and mortar, and filth and finery, I find it in all its manifestations, from the animal to the godlike.

This morning our pavements were spread with jewelled ermine, more daintily prepared than the foot-cloth of an Eastern queen. But now the world has trav-elled through it, as it does through the heart of a politician, and every pure drift is mud-bespattered. But there is still the beauty of the bells, and the graceful little shell-like sleighs, and the swift motions. There is something exhilarating in the rapid whirl of life, abroad and joyous, in New-York, soon after a new-fallen snow. It excites somewhat of the triumphant emotion which one feels when riding a swift horse, or careering on the surging sea. It brings to my mind Lapland deer, and flashing Aurora, and moon-images in the sky, and those wonderful luminous snows, which clothe the whole landscape with phosphoric fire.

But there is beauty here far beyond rich furs, and Russian chimes, and noble horses, or imagination of the glorious refractions in arctic skies; for here are hu-man hearts, faithful and loving, amid the fiercest temptations; still genial and cheerful, though surrounded by storm and blight. Two little ragged girls went by the window just now, their scanty garments fluttering in the wind; but their little blue hands were locked in each other, and the elder tenderly lifted the younger through the snow-drift. It was but a short time ago, that I passed the same chil-dren in Broadway. One of them had rags bound round her feet, and a pair of bro-ken shoes. The other was barefoot, and she looked very red, for it was pinching cold. "Mary," said the other, in a gentle voice, "sit down on the door-step, here, and I will take off my rags and shoes. Your feet are cold, and you shall wear them the rest of the way." "Just a *little* while," replied the other; "for they *are* very cold; but you shall have them again, directly." They sat down, and made the friendly exchange; and away jumped the little one, her bare feet pattering on the cold stones, but glowing with a happy heart-warmth.

You say I must make up such incidents, because *you* never see humanity under such winning aspects, in the streets of New-York. Nay, my friend, I do *not* make up these stories; but I look on this ever-moving panorama of life, as Coleridge describes his Cupid:

> "What *outward* form and features are,
> He guesseth but in part;
> But what *within* is good and fair,
> *He seeth with the heart.*"

Letter XXXIX [1]
April 27, 1843

There is a fine engraving of Jean Paul Richter,[2] surrounded by floating clouds, all of which are angels' faces; but so soft and shadowy, that they must be sought for to be perceived. It was a beautiful idea thus to environ Jean Paul; for whosoever reads him, with an earnest thoughtfulness, will see heavenly features perpetually shining through the golden mists or rolling vapour.

But the picture interested me especially, because it embodied a great spiritual truth. In all clouds that surround the soul, there *are* angel faces, and we should *see* them if we were calm and holy. It is because we are impatient of our destiny, and do not understand its use in our eternal progression, that the clouds which envelope it seem like black masses of thunder, or cold and dismal obstructions of the sunshine. If man looked at his being as a whole, or had faith that all things were intended to bring him into harmony with the divine will, he would gratefully acknowledge that spiritual dew and rain, wind and lightning, cloud and sunshine, all help his growth, as their natural forms bring to maturity the flowers and the grain. "Whosoever quarrels with his fate, does not understand it," says Bettine; and among all her inspired sayings, she spake none wiser.

Misfortune is never mournful to the soul that accepts it; for such do always see that every cloud is an angel's face. Every man deems that he has precisely the trials and temptations which are the hardest of all others for him to bear; but they are so, simply because they are the very ones he most needs.[3]

I admit the truth of Bulwer's[4] assertion, that "long adversity usually leaves its prey somewhat chilled, and somewhat hardened to affection; passive and quiet of hope, resigned to the worst, as to the common order of events, and expecting little from the best, as an unlooked for incident in the regularity of human afflictions." But I apprehend this remark is mainly applicable to pecuniary difficulties, which, "in all their wretched and entangling minutiae, like the diminutive cords by which Gulliver[5] was bound, tame the strongest mind, and quell the most buoyant spirit."

These vexations are not man's natural destiny, and therefore are not healthy for his soul. They are produced by a false structure of society, which daily sends thousands of kind and generous hearts down to ruin and despair, in its great whirl of falsity and wrong. These are victims of a stinging grief, which has in it nothing divine, and brings no healing on its wings.

But the sorrow which God appoints is purifying and ennobling, and contains within it a serious joy. Our Father saw that disappointment and separation were necessary, and he has made them holy and elevating. From the sepulchre the stone is rolled away, and angels declare to the mourner, "He is not here; he is risen. Why seek ye the living among the dead?" And a voice higher than the angels, proclaims, "Because I live, ye shall live also."

> "There *is* no Death to those who know of life;
> No Time to those who see Eternity."

Blessed indeed are the ministrations of sorrow! Through it, we are brought into more tender relationship to all other forms of being, obtain a deeper insight into the mystery of eternal life, and feel more distinctly the breathings of the infinite. "All sorrow raises us above the civic, ceremonial law, and makes the prosaist a psalmist," says Jean Paul.

Whatsoever is highest and holiest is tinged with melancholy. The eye of genius has always a plaintive expression, and its natural language is pathos. A prophet is sadder than other men; and He who was greater than all prophets, was "a man of sorrows, and acquainted with grief."

Sorrow connects the soul with the invisible and the everlasting; and therefore all things prophesy it, before it comes to us. The babe weeps at the wail of music, though he is a stranger to grief; and joyful young hearts are saddened by the solemn brightness of the moon. When men try to explain the oppressive feelings inspired by moonlight and the ever silent stars, they say it is as if spirits were near. Thus Bettine writes to Gunderode: "In the night was something confidential, which allured me as a child; and before I ever *heard* of spirits, it seemed as if there was something living near me, in whose protection I trusted. So was it with me on the balcony, when a child three or four years old, when all the bells were tolling for the emperor's death. As it always grew more nightly and cool, and nobody with me, it seemed as if the air was full of bell-chimes, which surrounded me; then came a gloom over my little heart, and then again sudden composure, as if my guardian angel had taken me in his arms. What a great mystery is life, so closely embracing the soul, as the chrysalis the butterfly!"

The spiritual speaks ever to us, but we hear it at such moments, because the soul is silent and listening, and therefore the infinite pervades it.—All alone, alone, through deep shadows, thus only can ye pass to golden sunshine on the eternal shore! this is the prophetic voice, whose sad but holy utterance goes deep down into the soul when it is alone with moonlight and stars. Under its unearthly influence, childhood nestles closer to its mother's side, and the mirthful heart of youth melts into tears. It is as if the cross upreared its dark shadow before the vision of the infant Saviour.

As we grow older, this prophecy becomes experience. By the hand of Sorrow the finite is rolled away like a scroll, and we stand consciously in the presence of the infinite and the eternal. The wailing of the autumn wind, the lone stubble waving in the wintry field, the falling foliage, and the starry stillness, are no longer a luxury of sadness, as in the days of youthful imagination. The voice of wailing has been *within* us; our loved ones have left us, and *we* are like the lone stubble in the once blooming field; the leaves of our hopes are falling withered around us; and the midnight stillness is filled with dreary echoes of the past.

Oh, Father, how fearful is this pilgrimage!—Alone in the twilight, and voices from the earth, the air, and the sky, call, "Whence art thou?—Whither goest thou?" And none makes answer. Behind us comes the voice of the Past, like the echo of a bell travelling through space for a thousand years; and all it utters is, "As thou art, I was." Before us stands the Future, a shadow robed in vapour, with a far-off sunlight shining through. The Present is around us—passing away—passing away. And *we?* Oh, Father! fearful indeed is this earth pilgrimage, when the soul has learned that all its sounds are echoes,—all its sights are shadows.

But lo! the clouds open, and a face serene and hopeful looks forth, and says, Be thou as a little child, and thus shalt thou become a seraph. The shadows which perplex thee are all realities; the echoes are all from the eternal voice which gave to light its being. All the changing forms around thee are but images of the infinite and the true, seen in the mirror of time, as they pass by, each on a heavenly mission. Be thou as a little child. Thy Father's hand will guide thee home.

I bow my head in silent humility. I cannot pray that afflictions may not visit me. I know why it was that Mrs. Fletcher[6] said, "Such prayers never seem to have wings." I am willing to be purified through sorrow, and to accept it meekly as a blessing. I see that all the clouds are angels' faces, and their voices speak harmoniously of the everlasting chime.

Letter XL [1]
May 1, 1843

The first of May! How the phrase is twined all round with violets; and clumps of the small Housitania, (which remind me of a "Sylvania phalanx" of babies;) and slight anemones, nodding gracefully as blooming maidens, under the old moss-grown trees! How it brings up visions of fair young floral queens, and garlanded May-poles, and door-posts wreathed with flowers, and juvenile choirs hymning the return of the swallows, in the ancient time! The old French word *Mes,* signifies a garden; and in Lorraine, *Mai* still has that meaning; from which, perhaps, the word *maiden.* In Brittany, *Mae* signifies green, flourishing; the Dutch *Mooy,* means beautiful, agreeable; the Swedish *Mio* is small, pretty and pleasant; and the East India *Maya* is Goddess of Nature. Thus, have men shown their love of this genial month, by connecting its name with images of youth and loveliness.

In our climate, it happens frequently, that "Winter lingering, chills the lap of May," and we are often tantalized with promises unfulfilled. But though our Northern Indians named June "the month of flowers," yet with all her abundant beauty, I doubt whether she commends herself to the heart, like May, with her scanty love-tokens from the grave of the frosty past. They are like infancy, like resurrection, like everything new and fresh, and full of hopefulness and promise.

The *First*, and the *Last!* Ah, in all human things, how does one idea forever follow the other, like its shadow! The circling year oppresses me with its fulness of meaning. Youth, manhood, and old age, are its most external significance. It is symbolical of things far deeper, as every soul knows, that is travelling over steep hills, and through quiet valleys, unto the palace called Beautiful, like Bunyan's world-renowned Pilgrim.[2] Human life, in its forever-repeating circle, like Nature, in her perpetual self-restoring beauty, tells us that from the burial place of Winter, young Spring shall come forth to preach resurrection; and thus it must be in the outward and symbolical, because thus it is in the inward, spiritual progression of the soul.

> "Two children in two neighbour villages,
> Playing mad pranks along the heathy lees;
> Two strangers meeting at a festival;
> Two lovers whispering by an orchard wall;
> Two lives bound fast in one, with golden ease;
> Two graves grass-green beside a gray church-tower,
> Washed with still rains, and daisy-blossomed;
> Two children in one hamlet born and bred;
> So runs the round of life from hour to hour."

Blessings on the Spring-time, when Nature stands like young children hand in hand, in prophecy of future marriage!

May-day in New-York is the saddest thing, to one who has been used to hunting mosses by the brook, and paddling in its waters. Brick walls, instead of budding trees, and rattling wheels in lieu of singing birds, are bad enough; but to make the matter worse, all New-York *moves* on the first of May; not only moves about, as usual, in the everlasting hurry-scurry of business, but one house empties itself into another, all over the city.[3] The streets are full of loaded drays, on which tables are dancing, and carpets rolling to and fro. Small chairs, which bring up such pretty, cozy images of rolly-pooly mannikins and maidens, eating supper from tilted porringers, and spilling the milk on their night-gowns—these go ricketing along on the tops of beds and bureaus, and not unfrequently pitch into the street, and so fall asunder. Children are driving hither and yon, one with a flower-pot in his hand, another with work-box, band-box, or oil-canakin; each so intent upon his important mission, that all the world seems to him (as it does to many a theologian,) safely locked up within the little walls *he* carries. Luckily, both boy and bigot are mistaken, or mankind would be in a bad box, sure enough. The dogs seem bewildered with this universal transmigration of bodies; and as for the cats, they sit on the door-steps, mewing piteously, that they were not born in the middle ages, or at least, in the quiet old portion of the world. And I, who have almost as strong a love of localities as poor puss, turn away from the win-dows, with a suppressed anathema on the nineteenth century, with its perpetual changes. Do you want an appropriate emblem of this country, and this age? Then stand on the side-walks of New-York, and watch the universal transit on the first of May. The facility and speed with which our people change politics, and move from sect to sect, and from theory to theory, is comparatively slow and moss-grown; unless, indeed, one excepts the Rev. O. A. Brownson,[4] who seems to stay in any spiritual habitation a much shorter time than the New-Yorkers do in their houses. It is the custom here, for those who move out to leave the accumulated dust and dirt of the year, for them who enter to clear up. I apprehend it is some-what so with all the ecclesiastical and civil establishments, which have so long been let out to tenants in rotation. Those who enter them, must make a great sweeping and scrubbing, if they would have a clean residence.

That people should move so *often* in this city, is generally a matter of their own volition. Aspirations after the infinite, lead them to perpetual change, in the rest-less hope of finding something better and better still. But they would not raise the price of drays, and subject themselves to great inconvenience, by moving *all on one day,* were it not that the law compels everybody who intends to move at all, to quit his premises before twelve o'clock, on May morning. Failing to do this, the police will put him and his goods into the street, where they will fare much like a boy beside an upset hornet's nest. The object of this regulation is to have the Directory[5] for the year arranged with accuracy. For, as theologians, and some reformers, can perceive no higher mission for human souls than to arrange them-selves rank and file in sectarian platoons, so the civil authorities do not appre-hend that a citizen has any more important object for living, just at this season, than to have his name set in a well-ordered Directory.

However, human beings are such creatures of habit and imitation, that what is necessity soon becomes fashion, and each one wishes to do what everybody else is doing. A lady in the neighbourhood closed all her blinds and shutters, on May-day; being asked by her acquaintance whether she had been in the country, she answered, "I was *ashamed* not to be moving on the first of May; and so I shut up the house that the neighbours might not know it." One could not well imagine a fact more characteristic of the despotic sway of custom and public opinion, in the United States, and the nineteenth century. Elias Hicks'[6] remark, that it takes "*live* fish to swim *up* stream," is emphatically true of this age and country, in which liberty-caps abound, but no one is allowed to wear them.

I am by temperament averse to frequent changes, either in my spiritual or material abodes. I think I was made for a German; and that my soul in coming down to earth, got drifted away by some side-wind, and so was wafted into the United States, to take up its abode in New-York. Jean Paul,[7] speaking of the quiet habits of the Germans, says he does not believe they turn in their beds so often as the French do. O, for one of those old German homes, where the same stork, with his children and grandchildren, builds on the same roof, generation after generation; where each family knows its own particular stork, and each stork knows the family from all the world beside. Oh, for a quiet nook in good old Nuremberg, where still flourishes the lime tree, planted seven hundred years ago, by empress Cunegunde;[8] where the same family inhabits the same mansion for five centuries; where cards are still sold in the same house where cards were first manufactured; and where the great grandson makes watches in the same shop that was occupied by his watchmaking great-grandfather.

But after all, this is a foolish, whining complaint. A stork's nest is very pleasant, but there are better things. Man is moving to his highest destiny through manifold revolutions of spirit; and the outward must change with the inward.

It is selfish and unwise to quarrel with this spiritual truth or its ultimate results, however inconvenient they may be. The old fisherman, who would have exterminated steam-boats, because they frightened the fish away from the waters where he had baited them for years, was by no means profound in his social views, or of expansive benevolence.

If the world were filled with different tribes of Nurembergers, with their storks, what strangers should we brethren of the human household be to each other! Thanks to Carlyle, who has brought England and America into such close companionship with the mind of Germany. Thanks to Mary Howitt, who has introduced Frederika Bremer into our homes, like a sunbeam of spring, and thus changed Sweden from a snowy abstraction to a beautiful and healthy reality.[9] It is so pleasant to look into the hearts and eyes of those Northern brothers! To be conveyed to their firesides by a process so much swifter than steam!

Do you fear that the patriot will be lost in the cosmopolite? Never fear. We shall not love our own household less, because we love others more. In the beautiful words of Frederika: "The human heart is like Heaven; the more angels, the more room."

Appendix

Letter 12 [1]
December 2, 1841

I propose to fill this letter with an account of some remarkable individuals among the colored population. In the days of thoughtless romance, I might have smiled at such an idea, or have introduced it with some playful apology; such as the fact in natural history, that lions are black in Africa, and that she has her black swans also. But I have thought too deeply of this people's wrongs, and have discovered in them capabilities too high, to admit of merriment.

Among these lions, the brave Cinquez, and his thirty-four associates, are of course most prominent. Through the friendly thoughtfulness of Lewis Tappan,[2] I received notice of a farewell meeting of the Mendians, at Zion's church,[3] last week; and there I heard them for the first and last time.

I shall not give you a detailed account of the highly interesting services; for they were similar to those so often repeated in the newspapers; but I will glance at a few things which stand in most distinct relief on the tablet of my memory. Mr. A. T. Williams,[4] their teacher, to whom they seemed warmly attached, opened the meeting, by giving a brief account of them. His introductory remarks jarred slightly on my feelings; for they *seemed* like ministering to an unjust public sentiment, though I do not think they were so *intended*. He said he wished to do away [with] two errors, which had crept into the popular mind concerning these people. In the first place, they were not cannibals in their native country. In the next place, they did not rise against their masters, for cruel treatment; but in consequence of being tormented by the cook, who told them they would be cut up and salted for sale, as soon as they arrived in port. I would rather not have had the motive presented to my mind in such an unheroic form. It knocked in the head all my *romantic* associations with Cinquez, as a brave soul, prefering death to slavery. I thought of his speech, which, had it been uttered by an ancient hero, Plutarch[5] would have recorded as a gem. To a soul that could utter itself thus, it appeared to me that being sold salted must have appeared far preferable to being sold alive. However, I am not disposed to quarrel with fact, because it is not romance. But when it was explained, as if in apology, that they did not rise against their masters, I felt disturbed. I was strongly moved to ask, "By what standard are these strangers to be tried? By the gospel standard, of which they had then never heard? Or by the same standard that the world judges of Washington, Kosciusko, and William Tell?"[6] The latter was the standard, not *professed* merely, (like the gospel) but *practically* acknowledged by nearly all of every American audience. Why, then, should an assembly with such sentiments be assured, in tones of apology, that Cinquez had not done what Washington and Kosciusko would assuredly have done under similar circumstances? If any people on earth have a right to fight in self-defense, the captured and enslaved negro has most peculiarly that right; and the advocates of defensive war are neither consistent nor magnanimous in refusing to make this admission. I, of course, cannot make it; because I believe all war to be a violation of the gospel.

Mr. Williams bore testimony to the very scrupulous honesty of these Mendians, and to their remarkable adherence to truth; which they had never been known to violate, in a single instance, though there had some times been very strong temptation to do it, to escape from blame. This quality was conspicuous in the artlessness of their remarks, and their unwillingness to say anything that was not really *within* them. Hence, there was a very observable difference between their manner of answering questions connected with their own experience and knowledge, and those relating merely to speculative faith.

All these interesting strangers carried their heads as freemen are wont to do, and several of them had very expressive countenances. Next to Cinquez, the youthful Kinna appeared most intelligent and interesting. Alluding to the progress in their education, he said, "When in Hartford, good gentleman bring us book—we no care much about. We say what good? Maybe to-morrow we die. But when we go to Farmington, and they tell us we no die, then we read—like much. We will tell Mendi people all whites no bad. We think all whites be same. But we find there be darkness-white, him you call Spaniard—that be evil white. But the snow-white—the 'Meriky-white, that be much good."

Being asked if he could love his enemies, he replied, with a strong foreign accent, "Yes I love *him*. Can pray to God forgive *him*." "If Ruiz[7] should come to Mendi, and you should meet him alone in the bushes, what would you do?" "I let him *go*, I no touch *him*. But if him catch our children—him see what he catch!"

A loud shout of laughter and applause, from the crowded audience, here announced the universality of the instinct of retaliation; not could I refrain from smiling at the *naive* earnestness of the reply.

Some one asked him when he experienced a change of heart; to which he answered, with most refreshing simplicity: "In prison, at Hartford, I think much of wrong things I do. I remember many wrong thing. I no want to do no more wrong thing. I pray to God he forgive me, I no do no more wrong thing. Good man say Christ die for me. I thank Christ because he pray his Father to come die for me."

"How do you know the Bible is the word of God?"

Kinna looked perplexed at this question, as if it conveyed no definite idea to his mind. After listening intently, as it was a second time repeated, he said: "In prison, I think I die. I no die. Good man say God take me out of jaws of my enemy. I thank God. Bible tell 'bout God. Like read much."

"How will you *prove* to the Mendi people that the Bible is the word of God?"

Here was a poser, that might have perplexed deeper theologians than the untutored African. He seemed puzzled; but after a little thought, answered with the unpretending honesty of a little child: "I ask Mendi people, 'You ever know Mendi to come back to father and mother, when darkness-white man catch him?' They say, 'No, never came back. We never no more see him.' I say, 'We come back to Mendi. God put it in the hearts of good 'Meriky people. Bible tell 'bout God. You read Bible, you know 'bout God, that send us back to Mendi.'"

I thought these honest creatures would be vexatious materials, should any theological drill-serjeant try to substitute a routine of catechisms and creeds for the indwelling life. Spiritual murderers are all such—men who smother human souls—to whatever sect they may belong. May none such tarnish the truthful simplicity of these poor children of the sun.

James Covey,[8] the interpreter, after describing in his broken language, his introduction to the captives, and how he discovered that they spoke the same language as his father and mother, repeated some little incidents, one of which pleased me much. "One Sunday, when I go to prison, Cinquez hear the bell ring. He say 'what for bell ring?' I tell him when 'Meriky people go pray to God, they ring bell. He say, 'These people be fool. When want pray to God, what for ring bell?'"

Three or four of the company read quite tolerably; and the boy, Kali, spelled entire sentences of Scripture with great correctness. Five of them united in singing, "When I can read my title clear," to the tune of "Auld lang syne." Two songs were then sung in their native dialect; both decidedly pleasant to my ear, but the last particularly so. The first strongly resembled a German catch, which I have somewhere heard. The last was soft, melodious, and friendly in its sound; consisting of question and response, plainly marked in the emphasis and cadence of the tones.

I imagined it must be very like the Italian gondoliers, replying to each other in music across the Venetian waters. Their teacher explained that it was an African welcome to newly-arrived guests; the constantly-recurring chorus, which sounded like "Come——O? Come——O?" signified "Will you stay? Will you stay?" The answer, as often repeated, "I love you, and will stay with you."

Wm. W. Anderson, formerly Solicitor-General for Jamaica, made some interesting statements concerning the missionary spirit excited among the emancipated of that island, and gave a very satisfactory account of their rapid improvement in knowledge, morality, and religion.

Through all the services, Cinquez had remained seated among his brethren, in a quiet, unpretending manner, yet evidently the great man of the evening. Several of them whispered to him; to which he replied with a dignified bend of the head, not even turning his eyes. Toward the close of the evening he gave an account, in his native tongue, of taking the Amistad from their Spanish masters. His style of eloquence was perfectly electrifying. He moved rapidly about the pulpit, his eyes flashed, his tones were vehement, his motions graceful, and his gestures, though taught by nature, were in the highest style of dramatic art. He seemed to hold the hearts of his companions chained to the magic of his voice. During his narrative, they ever and anon broke forth into spontaneous responses, with the greatest animation. He illustrates perfectly the description given by Lander,[9] and other travellers, of the eloquent and exciting *palavers* of Africa.

Theodore Wright,[10] pastor of the African Presbyterian church, spoke very feelingly of the Mendian mission, as one that rejoiced the hearts of the colored people. It was the first one in which they had been able to unite with their whole souls. All other missions had been in partnership with colonization, that worst enemy of their persecuted race; or they had joined hands with the slaveholder, by consenting to accept from his treasury the price of African blood. But he thanked God the skirts of *this* mission were pure. Not a cent from those who bought or sold human beings would ever be allowed to pollute its funds.

There is beautiful propriety in the fact, that these interesting strangers, so wonderfully rescued from slavery, are the first occasion of *such* a mission. May it be wisely conducted, and abundantly blessed!

Above all people in the world, the African race are probably most susceptible of religious feeling, and have the strongest tendency to devotion. Swedenborg[11] speaks of them as being nearer to Christians in the spiritual world than any other heathen; by reason of their docility and reverence. He moreover makes the remarkable statement that the only church on earth, acknowledged by the angels as a true church, is in the centre of Africa unvisited and unknown to the rest of the world; and if I recollect aright, he implies that, by simplicity and obedience, they have preserved that visible intercourse with spiritual beings, which is recorded of the most ancient church.

Whether this be true or not, the world will probably find out some time or other; but of one thing I have long been assured—that a very prominent place among the nations must be assigned to the African race, whenever the age of Moral Sentiment arrives.[12] Creatures of affection and of faith, everything marks them peculiarly appropriate to represent a religious age, as the Anglo-Saxons were to represent an intellectual one.

Every idea that one has in these days, if they do not make great haste to utter it, is sure to come to them from a hundred other sources. Thus I found the thought so long familiar to my mind echoed by Kinmont, in his Lectures on Man.[13] Speaking of the civilization of Africa, he says: "It will be—indeed it must be—civilization of a peculiar stamp; perhaps we might venture to conjecture, not so much distinguished by *art* as a certain beautiful *nature*; not so marked or adorned by science, as exalted and refined by a new and lovely *theology*; a reflection of the light of heaven, more perfect and endearing than that which the intellects of the Caucasian race have ever yet exhibited. There is more of the *child*, of unsophisticated *nature*, in the negro race than in the European." And again: "The sweeter graces of the Christian religion appear almost too tropical and tender plants to grow in the soil of the Caucasian mind. They require a character of human nature, of which you can see the rude lineaments in the Ethiopian, to be implanted in and grow naturally and beautifully withal."

Dr. Channing[14] says, "A short residence among the negroes of the West Indies impressed me with their capacity of improvement. On all sides I heard of their religious tendencies, the noblest in human nature." Speaking of British emancipation,[15] he says: "History contains no record more touching than the account of the religious, tender thankfulness which this vast boon awakened in the negro breast."

A few evenings since, I went to Asbury-street church to hear a blind Methodist preacher, who had once been a slave. His countenance was good, but he had not that frank, noble bearing of the Haitian, or the African, fresh from his native deserts. This no man can attain to in a community that treats him as an inferior. His voice, like that of most Methodist preachers, sounded like a rasp going over hard wood; the result of their loud style of speaking, continued for an astonishing length of time without cadance of intonation. But there was a charm in his earnest, and evidently sincere feeling; and touches of real eloquence were interspersed here and there, like stars in a cloudy sky. He spoke of "Brother Paul," with a familiarity well suited to this most democratic of all sects. The picture he drew of

Paul and Silas in prison, showed great vividness of imagination. Speaking of the chains, he placed his hand upon his heart, and exclaimed, "But they couldn't chain him *here!* They might gag his mouth; but every whisper of his soul God would hear in Heaven."

This William Harden has the acute senses and strong memory common to the totally blind. Though he was never able to read, he can repeat the Bible from one end to the other, and give out any hymn in the book, from memory. In this interesting man I probably had a good sample of some of the slave preachers, addressing their fellow slaves from a stump in the forest, and often attracting the planters and their families by their untutored eloquence.

It is invidious to single out a few individuals, where many deserve commendation; but as I lately met with Hester Lane, I cannot forbear giving her a passing notice. Diligent, capable, and laborious, she has earned a great deal of money by washing and ironing. With these hard earnings she has purchased ten out of the house of bondage; in some cases receiving her pay by small instalments, in others receiving nothing. The heart of a king may dwell in a pedlar's breast, and right regal may be the soul of a washerwoman. I have another heroine to describe, but must reserve her for my next letter.—L.M.C.

Letter 14
December 16, 1841

I know not whether you take as much interest as I do in getting at the spiritual experience of human souls, in all their varieties. The desire to read the hearts of others is indeed intense and universal; and to this instinct autobiography owes its strong and peculiar charm. But after all, how little real insight do we obtain into each other's existence! Confessions are never full and free. Hypocrisy with its dead forms; tradition with its parrot language; pride with its fear of betraying ignorance; love of approbation, afraid to express doubts that may be deemed discreditable; all these, and many other things, tend to make that which should be a revelation of the inward, a mere unmeaning echo of the outward. Even where there is the best intention to be earnest and truthful, it is extremely difficult for souls to pass into each other's life. "Warmed by some signs of sympathy," says Emerson, "the soul springs forth to embrace another soul; but as the conversation proceeds, how soon it perceives that high mountains and wide rivers come between——lucky even if some *word* convey the same idea to both, and thus acts as a ferryman to convey them temporarily into each other's regions."

Yet such imperfect glimpses as we do get into each other's inward life, is the most powerful form of the preached word. "The lip, and thoughts, and heart of a living man must be brought into contact with the lip, and thoughts, and heart of a living man for the conversion of the world."*

All this is an involuntary preface to the religious experience of a poor, uneducated woman, once a slave, from whose lips I heard it told, with impassioned earnestness, in a humble apartment, in an obscure Court of Boston. I took it down verbatim, and have not added a word or thought.

She had been describing to me a severe flogging inflicted upon her brother, for attempting to run away. The circumstances attending this punishment were too harrowing to the feelings, and too revolting, to be here described. I never think of them without a creeping and shuddering of the flesh.

"Did your brother die?" I inquired. "No, ma'am; but he was all broke down after that. He seemed like an old man; though I don't think he could be more than eight and twenty." "Was your master a cruel man?" "I don't know nothing about him. He lived in England, and never set foot in Virginny. We was left to the care of overseers. I always *called* my master a good man; for when he died he give us all free." "Perhaps you were treated worse than you would have been, if your master had lived on his plantation." "May be so; but bad as it was, we had golden opportunities compared with some plantations round us. True enough, there is some kind masters, but you may go through a hundred to find one." "You were not quite destitute of privileges; for I remember you told me that you heard preaching sometimes." "Oh, yes, ma'am, there was Stephen used to preach to us, and it was a great comfort to hear him. There was a white gentleman came on a visit to the Great Hus, (great house) and they had Stephen up on the piazza, on purpose that he might hear him preach; and he said he never heard anything like it in all his life. He used to preach on a stump, in a little piece of woods, close by our field. They didn't like it, because so many come to hear him. I spose they thought there'd be a *rising*. They flogged him to make him stop preaching and praying. Oh, *how* they flogged him! But it all wouldn't do. As soon as ever they untied him, he was up on the stump again, praying for his tormentors. At last, they told him they'd shoot him if he didn't stop preaching; and one day the overseer got so mad, that he did shoot him, when he was standing on the stump; and the ball took off part of his cheek; but he tied a handkerchief over it, and preached away, with the blood streaming down his face. I shall never forget it; for he looked as white as one that had come up from the dead. Ah, *he* was a *real* preacher! Why, ma'am, you might have heard him from here to Cambridge bridge."

"And you think the slaves took comfort in their religion?" "Comfort! yes, indeed they did. Why I've known women, after they'd been working hard all day, walk five miles in the night, and back again, just to talk with some poor, perishing sister, that was inquiring the way to be saved." "What first led you to feel interested in religion?" "I had a cousin, who died mourning dreadfully because he wasn't religious. He said if he could only live to get well, he'd preach and pray, and call souls to Jesus, as long as he could speak. This took hold of me, and I tried to pray. I thought I did pray; but I hadn't give up my heart yet. I prayed kneeling, and I prayed *prosterate* on my face; but all wouldn't do, because I hadn't give up my heart yet. Everything called me a sinner. I well remember when I came to the brook to drink, the waters seemed too pure for me. The very brook cried out unworthy! unworthy! There was holes made in the ground by the hoofs of the cattle, as they passed over. I stooped down and dipped up some water from the holes, and drinked it out of my hand. Even that water seemed too holy for me. I go to the woods, and fall *prosterate* on my face, and pray. I come back and hoe awhile. (I was then head of a gang of eight.) I hear a voice, saying, 'Go to Jesus!' Again I go to the woods; I fall on my knees. Then I *could* give up my whole heart. I said, 'O Lord, do what thou wilt. I am in thy hand. If thou send me to hell, it will be justice.' That was the first time I prayed. I thought I had prayed before; but I didn't give up my heart till then. All at once, I feel my heart burst! I *hear* it burst! And a voice called to me, saying, 'I have washed thee in my blood. Nailed upon the cross, I have borne thy sins.' I said, 'Lord, is it I?' Again the voice answered, 'I have washed thee in my blood.' Then, in a lower whisper, (for my soul trembled) I said, 'Lord is it I?' The blessed voice repeated, 'I have washed thee in my blood.'

Then I felt as a feather in the air. I ran along, and met a sister in Christ. She gave me part of a loaf, and said, 'Hepsy, here is your bread.' I laid it down on a stump. I had other bread to eat. 'Sister,' said I, 'Jesus has washed me in his blood.' The tears ran down her cheeks when she heard me say so. Then I heard a voice, (I heard it just as plain as you hear me now) and it said, 'Little one, go and tell your mother what wonderful things the Lord has done for you.'

Off I went, like an arrow! Mother lived more than a mile off, on what we called the Upper Plantation. She cried and groaned, when I told her what had happened. 'Child,' said she, 'go home. The enemy will be before you, and you will get a flogging. Go to Aunt Polly, and ask her to pray that if this be God's work, it may stand; and that if it be of the devil, he will show it to be so.'

Off I went. I feared no enemy then; for I knew He that sent me would take care of me. A little child went smiling before me. I could see her white wings shining among the green trees. She sang,

> 'Broad is the way that leads to death,
> And thousands walk together there;
> But wisdom shows a narrow path,
> With here and there a traveller.'

Oh, how happy I was! Oh, such music as I heard! It seemed as if one note touched another note; and that touched a higher; and that a higher still; and then a lower; sometimes high, and sometimes low; as if ten thousand little children, with their sweet voices, sung in the air.

After that sweet season, I had some dark times. I heard folks talk about being *called*. I said, 'O, Lord, thou hast never called *me*.' This was from the arch enemy. But the Lord answered, 'Whenever thou hast laid a brother or sister in the ground, I have called thee. In the loud thunder I have called thee.'"

After a short pause, I said, "You remember all your impressions with wonderful distinctness." "Yes, indeed I do, ma'am. I shall never forget that time. I was about sixteen years old, and it was of a Wednesday morning, when I first received a hope. If I was to go back to old Virginny, I think I could find the very tree where I prayed my first real prayer. I hope to live to see old Virginny emancipated. If I do, may be I shall see that tree again, before I die."

"Can you read?" "No, ma'am, I can't read a word; and Stephen the preacher couldn't read a word; but if you tried to palm off anything upon him that wasn't in the Bible, I guess he's found it out quick enough."

This singular communication impressed me strangely; uttered as it was with great fervor, and liveliness of gesture. There was evidently an intermingling of tradition and imagination with her genuine impressions. I did not trouble myself to define the boundaries of each; for she evidently believed *all* that she said; and I felt no disposition to pronounce in what manner God might make himself manifest to souls as benighted as her own. The poetry of her vivid description struck me more than any other feature in it. It reminded me of Major Laing's description of the interior of Africa:[1] "Above all, the passion for poetry is nearly universal. As soon as the evening breeze begins to blow, the song resounds throughout all Africa. It cheers the despondency of the wanderer through the desert; it enlivens the social meeting; it inspires the dance; and even the lamentations of the mourner are poured forth in measured accents. Their poetry does not consist of studied and regular pieces; they are spontaneous effusions, in which the speaker gives utterance to his hopes and fears, his joys and sorrows."

Oh, how will Ethiopa plume her wings in the light of Wisdom and the warmth of Love! The day of her redemption will be, as the enthusiast described her own—"as if the voices of ten thousand children made music in the air."

It is our mission to speed the hour. Let us be faithful and true.—L.M.C.

*Memoirs of Harlan Page.[2]

Letter 18 [1]
March 3, 1842

A short time ago, I went over to Bergen Heights, about a mile from Jersey City, to look at the first beginnings of a most interesting and praiseworthy institution, called the Delevan Temperance Institute.[2] The large building was formerly a military store-house, belonging to the United States; and was purchased by Mr. G. M. Danforth, to be converted into a laboratory. Some changes in the tariff rendered this chemical establishment unprofitable; and the buiding has for some time remained empty. The owner being much interested in the management of a Sunday school, was grieved to find the religious influence on poor, ignorant children, lamentably counteracted by the misery and vise of their parents. This led him to visit their homes; if such a name could be applied to the miserable dens and dilapidated sheds at Five Points,[3] where they were huddled together like rats. He found them without food or fuel, almost without clothing, and in many instances without fire-places; yet striving to solace all their woes, and supply all their wants with Rum. They were dying of all manner of diseases, produced by want of sustenance, excess of alcoholic stimulus, and the slow agony of discouragement and despair. Yet even there, human nature was not altogether degraded; the secret spark had a smouldering life, under the heaps of dirt and ashes that society had thrown upon it. When Mr. Danforth urged them to sign the temperance pledge, many exclaimed, "Oh, most gladly would we do it; but we cannot keep it here. We have no employment, no home; and the devil is at our elbow all the time, tempting us to drink." The more he went among them, the more deeply was his heart moved, and the more earnest grew the entreaty, "Oh, take us away from here! Do take us away! We want to be good, indeed we do; but we never can be good in this dreadful place."

The uselessness of expending his means in temporary relief was obvious enough; and he could not leave human brothers to die there, physically and spiritually, of foul disease. Suddenly he bethought himself of his large laboratory; and that it was now lying empty, for the use of the Lord. He at once resolved to employ such pecuniary means as he had (which I believe were quite moderate) in fitting it up with partitions, fire-places, &c. to make it tolerably comfortable. Hither he invited the men and women, who wished to reform, and lead sober, industrious lives. They were to work for the benefit of the concern, and leave whenever they could do better. Many received the proposition with thankful joy. Fifty or sixty are now there, with their temperance medals about their necks, working according to their strength; though many of them are sick, infirm, and feeble. They are of all trades and capacities, and work in abundance can be procured for them. One is an excellent globe-maker, and he has received an order for five hundred globes; another makes washing-machines, on an excellent and improved plan, for which there is rapid sale. They seem contented and hopeful; though at present they are suffering many inconveniences, from want of clothing and furniture. Mr. Danforth has done to the extent of his means, and greatly needs the assistance of the benevolent. Let those who have old garments, expecially of woollen; or old chairs, bedsteads, pans, kettles, &c. stowed away as lumber, remember that any article which could be converted into use, would be thankfully accepted at the Delevan Institute. Still better would it be, if manufacturers would now and then send pieces of strong cotton, or coarse woollen. It would be an easy matter for them to satisfy themselves that such donations were honestly and judiciously appropriated.

My visit to this institution did my heart good, though it was at a dreary season of the year, and the unfinished state of the building gave it a cheerless aspect. It was beautiful to see, even under such forlorn circumstances, revelations of those genial emotions, which belong to our universal nature, and indicate our common godlike origin. One woman wept like the rain, when she informed me that her little boy, "as good a child as ever lived," was in the house of correction; being caught in the company of some young thieves. "He would not have been in their company, ma'am," said she, "if"—Her voice choked too much for utterance; but I well understood the unfinished sentence, and answered in words of consolation and encouragement. A bright-looking man told a most affecting story of the process by which he had been brought to sober reflection. On one occasion, when he returned to his miserable rookery, at Five Points, he found a woman half-burned up, but so drunk that she did not feel the fire. "Shall I ever come to *that?*" thought he; "perhaps I shall; for the bad appetite grows stronger and stronger, every day." On another occasion, he found in the court by his door, a drunken woman, with her head shockingly cut open, in some recent fight. Her blood flowed over the pavement; but she was in the deep stupor of intoxication. He turned away from the dreadful sight, sickened and sad; and when his eye rested on his little boy, a fine, bright child of four years old, it seemed as if his heart would break. His wife died; and at last the alms-house commissioners took the boy. Tears were in his eyes, as he told me this; and he added, with a stifled voice, "Oh, how much I thought of my blessed child; in the alms-house because I was not fit to take care of him. It cut me to the heart to remember how I had put him among drunkards and swearers, when I *should* have had the sweet little soul at my knee, teaching him his prayers, and the words of the blessed Jesus. For *his* sake I wanted to become a sober man; but if I took the pledge, how *could* I keep it in that place of sin? and where could I find employment and a home?" His countenance brightened, as he looked toward Mr. Danforth, and added, "But God has raised me up a friend; and he tells me, if I'll keep steady and industrious, my little boy shall come to live with me. By the blessing of God, I *will* keep the pledge; and one of these days, I'll go to the wicked haunts where I used to live, and I'll preach to them, and tell them what temperance has done for me; and I'll try to bring them away with me; for wasn't I thankful to find a friend that would bring *me* away? I feel strong at heart, ma'am. *The thought of that dear child keeps me strong.*"

Alas for earth,

> "'Mid its labors and its cares,
> 'Mid its sufferings and its snares,"

if it were not for these little ministering spirits, to link us with the angels! I rejoiced to see that this poor, unlearned man, had within his heart the same fountain of love, which in Mary Howitt gushed forth in these sweet words:

> "'Mid the mighty, 'mid the mean,
> *Little children* may be seen;
> Like the flowers that spring up fair,

> Bright and countless, every where!
> Blessings on them! they in me
> Move a kindly sympathy,
> With their wishes, hopes and fears;
> With their laughter and their tears;
> With their wonder so intense,
> And their small experience!"

This affectionate father is a capable mechanic, strong and industrious; and I doubt not his little boy will be trotting through the green fields by his side, next summer.

I saw at this institution one elderly woman, very much diseased. It was proposed to remove her to the hospital, on account of the difficulty of making her comfortable with their poor accommodations. But she fell on her knees and wept, imploring them not to carry her away. To all their explanations, she answered, "I will sleep anyhow—I'll eat anything—I'll be strong as quick as I can, and go to work. Oh, do let me stay here! I'm safe here. If they carry me away, I shall get to drinking again."

They yielded to her entreaties, and did the best they could for her comfort.

Delevan Institute stands on an airy elevation, in the midst of green fields, and commands an extensive prospect, comprising the North and East rivers, Elizabethtown, Newark, and Belleville. In summer, it must be a healthy and beautiful residence. Would that every arsenal in the country were thus employed.

A lady of intelligence and active benevolence has established a similar institution, on a similar scale, in 19th street, New-York, for poor widows, who from discouragement and other causes, have become more or less addicted to intemperance. The proceeds of their labor is sold for their support; and they have the advantage of a kind friend to obtain for them the patronage they could not obtain for themselves.

Blessings on these movements! John the Baptists are they all, making way in the desert for the Highest. Blessings on the Washington Temperance Society, of which these [are] offshoots. By applying love instead of force, encouragement instead of punishment, they are working miracles in the name of Jesus!

The brief experiment of Bergen Heights, already proves that the principle of association and voluntary industry may be made profitable in a pecuniary view. These people are now earning their own living, including that of the sick and infirm; though a good deal of their labor has been unavoidably bestowed on providing means of present comfort, and the necessary implements for employment. This gives a hint of what *ought* to be substituted for constables and Egyptian Tombs.* The poor need houses of *encouragement*; and society gives them houses of *correction*.

These things, moreover, point the same way with a thousand other indications, all teaching that a *reconstruction of society is necessary.* Our benevolent institutions and reformatory societies perform but a limited and temporary use. They do not reach the groundwork of evil; and it is reproduced too rapidly for them to keep even the surface healed. The natural, spontaneous influences of society should be such as to supply men with healthy motives, and give full, free play to the affections, and the faculties. It is horrible to see our young men goaded on by the fierce, speculating spirit of the age, from the contagion of which it is almost impossible to escape, and then see them tortured into madness, or driven to crime, by fluctuating changes of the money-market. The young soul is, as it were, entangled in the great merciless machine of a falsely-constructed society; the steam he had no hand in raising whirls him hither and thither, and it is altogether a lottery-chance whether it crushes or propels him.

Many, who are mourning over the too obvious diseases of the world, will smile contemptuously at the idea of *reconstruction*. But let them reflect a moment upon the immense changes that have already come over society. In the middle ages, both noble and peasant would have laughed loud and long at the prophecy of such a state of society as now exists in the free States of America; yet here we are!

Greater changes still lie imaged in the mirror of the future; and we are by no means certain that Charles Fourier[4] has not seen them with a clearer vision than any other man. At all events his system of association deserves candid and thoughtful consideration.—L.M.C.

*Name of a prison in New-York city.

Letter 24[1]
May 12, 1842

Miller[2] is preaching every evening here, and draws crowds to hear him. You know he founds his theory on the prophecy of Daniel;[3] and by comparing intervals between epochs, such as the Babylonish captivity, the coming of Christ, &c. he supposes that he has arrived at the exact meaning of "times and a time and a half a time." Like all theories founded on the literal interpretation of Scripture, it admits of much being said on both sides. The whole question would interest my mind so little, that I should find it difficult to give the argument a patient investigation. What matters it to me, whether the world is destroyed in 1843, or 18,443? For *me* it must soon cease to exist, even if nature pursues its usual course. And what will it concern my spirit in the realms beyond, whether this ball of earth and stones still continues its circling march through space, or falls into the bosom of the sun? Let spirit change forms as it will, I know that nothing is really lost. The human soul contains within itself the universe. If the stars are blotted out, and the heavens rolled up as a scroll, they are not lost. They have merely dropped the vesture that we saw them by. "Life never dies; matter dies off it, and it lives elsewhere."

My belief in spirit is so strong, that to me matter appears the illusion. My body never seems to me to be myself. Death never seems to me an end of life, but a beginning. I suppose it is owing to this vivid and realizing sense of spiritual existence, so that the destruction of the visible world would have so little power to affect me, even if I foresaw its approach. It would be but a new mode of passing into life. For the earth I have the same sort of affection that I have for a house in which I have dwelt; but it matters not to me whether I pass away from it, or we pass away together. If I live a true and humble life, I shall carry with me all its forms of love and beauty, safe from the touch of material fire. "What would you be doing?" said one to me, "if you knew that Miller's theory were certainly true?" "Just what I am now doing," I replied; "endeavoring to discharge my duty in the fear of God, and with love to my neighbor." Liable as we are to drop into the grave at every moment, it is strange that the idea of the end of the world should be so terrific as it is to many. It must be because we realize the existence of matter so much more distinctly than we do that of spirit.

Thousands of minds *are* in a state of intense alarm, in consequence of Miller's preaching; but I have heard of very few instances of stolen money restored, falsehoods acknowledged, &c. as a preparation for the dreaded event. One man of whom I bought some calico, took two cents a yard less than he asked. When I thanked him, he said, "I suppose you are surprised that I should diminish the price, after you have bought the article; but the fact is, I have been hearing Mr. Miller, and I believe he is in the right. If we are all to come to an end in '43, it is best to be pretty moderate and fair in our dealings." "But we cannot come to an end," said I. "Oh, I meant the world, and our bodies," he replied. "And if they come to an end in '98 instead of '43, is it not still best to be moderate and fair in our dealings?" He admitted the premises; but as one admits an abstraction.

A prophet who appeared in London, many years ago, and predicted the destruction of the world, from Scripture authority, produced a much more decided effect in driving people into good works. Under his preaching very large sums of money were restored, and seventy thousand persons were married, who had formed illicit connexions.

This reminds me of a fine old building, lately demolished in the north part of Boston. It was built by Sir Harry Falkland, who held a high office under the crown, in old colonial days. I think Cooper[4] has described it, in some of his early works. When I saw it, it was inhabited by several laboring families, and was in a poor state of preservation. But through all the dust and scratches, I could perceive that the tesselated floor, of various colored woods, with the baronet's coat of arms in the centre, had once been very beautiful. The pannels were a series of landscapes in gilded borders; and every now and then, in some closet or recess, one was startled by an owl, a falcon, or an eagle, done in fresco. Tradition said that Lady Falkland[5] required her daughters to dance on the variegated oaken floor, with waxed shoes, till it shone like a mirror. When one of the daughters was married, the little slave, who brought wine and cake on a silver salver, tripped on the smooth surface; whereupon she received a whipping; as have many other persons in this world, for tripping in paths made needlessly slippery.

Tradition further says that Lady Falkland was not always the wife of Sir Harry. She accompanied him when he was ambassador to Portugal, and lived with him without the sanction of the law, for several years. The great earthquake of 1755 came; and Lisbon reeled and tottered from its foundations. They saw houses crack asunder, and the earth yawn in the streets. They thought the end of the world had come; and the first thing they did was to run to a church, and beseech a priest to marry them, amid the heaving and trembling of the elements.

I wish Miller would go to the South. He would have numerous converts; for in the slave-holding region, both the master and his victim have a natural tendency to clothe religion in forms of superstition and terror; and if they believed his theory, they would emancipate by thousands; notwithstanding their parental fear that the poor creatures could not take care of themselves.—L.M.C.

Letter 33
August 18, 1842

It is curious how a single note in the great hymn of Nature sometimes recalls the memories of years—opens whole galleries of soul-painting, stretching far off into the remote perspective of the past. Rambling on the Brooklyn side of the ferry the other evening, I heard the note of a Katy-did. Instantly it flashed upon my recollection, under what impressive circumstances I, for the first time in my life, heard the singular note of that hand-some insect. Six years ago, George Thompson[1] accompanied us to New-York. It was August; a month which the persecuted abolitionists were wont to observe brought out a multitude of snakes and southerners. The comparison was made with no sectional hostil-ity, but in reference to the effects such visiters produced on the comfort and safety of our-selves and the colored population. When southern merchants and travellers abound in our cities, the chance is, mobs and kidnappers will abound also.

Times have changed since 1835. Thanks to the despised agency of anti-slavery societies, the abolition sentiment has now spread widely, and taken a firm hold of the sympathies of the people. Moreover, southern trade is in less esteem than it was then; and they who have made us "a nation of bankrupts," have now less to expend for eggs and brick-bats, or to hire the hands that throw them. In 1835, they were in the full tide of successful experiment, and the whole North trembled before them; with the exception of one small but un-daunted phalanx.[2] The steamboat, which brought us to New-York, was filled with our masters. We saw one after another pointing out George Thompson; and never has it been my fortune to witness such fierce manifestations of hatred written on the human counte-nance. Men, who a few moments before seemed like polished gentlemen, were suddenly transformed into demons. They followed close behind us, as we walked the deck, with clenched fists, and uttering the most fearful imprecations. One man, from Georgia, drew a sword from his cane, and swore he would kill whoever dared to say a word against slav-ery. It was our intention to stop at Newport, to visit a relative; and I was glad that it so hap-pened; for had we gone on, the boat would have arrived in New-York just at dark; and I, for one, had no inclination to land at that hour, with such a set of ferocious characters, to whom our persons were well known, and whom we had observed in whispered consulta-tion, ominous of mischief. We pursued our route the next day, without attracting atten-tion; and fearing that George Thompson would bring ruin to the dwelling of any ac-quaintance we might visit in the city, we crossed over to Brooklyn, to the house of a friend who had known and loved him in Europe. The katydids were then in full concert; and their name was legion. It was the first time I had ever heard them; and my mind was in that excited state, which made all sounds discordant. We were most hospitably received; yet it was evident that our host had much rather we had staid at home. He told us that the news of George Thompson's approach had preceded us, and that the most awful excite-ment prevailed in the city; it was as much as his house was worth, to have it known that the roof covered him. For his sake, we kept within doors, and avoided the front windows. The next day, he brought over from the city a placard which was posted up on posts, and at street-corners, throughout New-York. I have it now; and never look at it without seeing images of the French revolution. It ran thus:

> "That notorious English swindler and vagabond, George Thompson, is now in the city, and supposed to be at the house of Lewis Tappan,[3] No. 40 Rose street. I hereby order my trusty followers to bring him before me, without delay.   JUDGE LYNCH."[4]

Mr. Thompson seemed, as he did on all similar occasions, very little disturbed con-cerning his own danger; but our host was so obviously anxious, that it imparted a degree of uneasiness to us all. That night, I started at every sound; and when the harsh and un-usual notes of that army of katydids met my ear, I was again and again deceived by the impression that they were the shouts of a mob in the distance. I shall never be able to get rid of the image thus engraved; to my mind the katydid will forever speak of mobs. I am sorry for it; for it is a pretty creature, and meant me no such harm. The next day, Thompson returned to Boston by a 4 o'clock morning boat. We afterward learned that extensive preparation had been made to mob Lewis Tappan's house, in obedience to the commands of "Judge Lynch." A few southerners, probably those who came in the boat with us, had hired their "trusty followers" to have a ladder in readiness in rear of the building, and proceed in any way most likely to secure Thompson. Luckily, the agents of the intended mischief mentioned it to a political comrade, who had become somewhat infected with abolition himself. He gave information of names, dates, and places; upon which the mayor addressed letters to several gentlemen, warning them of the liabilities they would incur, by this mode of sustaining the "patriarchal institution." Finding their names were known to the authorities, they relinquished their design. Our host was by no means quite reassured, even when Thompson and my husband had both left. I was not of sufficient consequence to endanger anybody; but should I be recognized, it might naturally be reported that Thompson was in the same house. Resolving that no one should incur risk on my account, and being utterly without friends in New-York, I went to a hotel at Bath, and staid there alone. Never, before or since, have I experienced such utter desolation, as I did the few days I remained there. It seemed to me as if anti-slavery had cut me off from all the sympathies of my kind. As I sat there alone, watching the surging sea, I wrote the following lines, for George Thompson's magnificent album. They have been several times printed; but as my reminiscences are busy with him, I will repeat them:

> I've heard thee when thy powerful words
>   Were like the cataract's roar—
> Or like the ocean's mighty waves
>   Resounding on the shore.
> But even in reproof of sin,
>   Love brooded over all—
> As the mild rainbow's heavenly arch
>   Rests on the waterfall.
>
> I've heard thee in the hour of prayer,
>   When dangers were around:
> Thy voice was like the royal harp,
>   That breathed a charmed sound.
> The evil spirit felt its power,
>   And howling turned away;
> And some, perchance, "who came to scoff,
>   Remained with thee to pray."
> I've seen thee, too, in playful mood,
>   When words of magic spell
> Dropped from thy lips like fairy gems,
>   That sparkled as they fell.
> Still great and good in every change!
>   Magnificent and mild!
> As if a seraph's god-like power
>   Dwelt in a little child.

Among the various exciting recollections with which Thompson is associated, no one is impressed so deeply on my mind as the 1st of August, 1835. It was the first anniversary of emancipation in the British West Indies;[5] and the abolitionists of Boston proposed to hold a meeting in commemoration of that glorious event. The Tremont House was swarming with southerners; and they swore that George Thompson should not be allowed to speak. The meeting was, however, held at Julian Hall. Few people were there, and I had a chance to observe them all. Near the stairs, was a line of men in fine broadcloth, whom I saw at a glance were slaveholders; the fact was plainly enough written in the clenched fist, the fiercely compressed lip, and the haughty carriage of the head. In front of them were a dozen or more stout truckmen, in shirt sleeves, with faces red enough to make a rain-drop sizzle, if it should chance to fall upon them. Various nods and glances were exchanged between fine broadcloth and shirt sleeves; there seemed to be an understanding between them; they were in fact "the glorious Union." Near the front seats, in the midst of the abolitionists, was an ill-looking fellow, whose bloated countenance, so furious and so sensual, seemed a perfect embodiment of the French revolution. A genteel-looking young man, with nice gloves, and white fur hat, held frequent whispered consultations with this vile-looking personage. It seemed to me a strange alliance. I inquired who the white hat was, and was told that it was Mr. Stetson, bar-keeper of the Tremont. I mentioned this fact to my husband, who saw in it the same significance that I did.

Thompson came in late, while S. J. May[6] was speaking. Fine broadcloth pointed thumbs at him significantly, shirt sleeves nodded, and white hat whispered to M. Guillotine.[7] My heart throbbed violently; I saw that there were well-managed preparations for a savage mob. Thompson could not have been unconscious of this, even if violent threats had not reached him before he came. Yet he was perfectly self-collected; and such burning torrents of eloquence as he poured forth, I never before listened to! There was nothing vulgar or vindictive, but it scorched like the lightning. The southerners writhed under it; the truckmen were amazed. He described what the foul system *was* that had been destroyed in the British West Indies; what it was, and must be, in all countries, and under all governments.—He told of the negroes' gratitude, and of their midnight chorus of prayer and praise. Then, in tones deep and solemn, like an old cathedral bell, he added, slowly, "It is the death-knell of American slavery!"

Excited by the powerful eloquence, and goaded with rage, the southerners rose in a body, and with loud stamping, left the hall. The truckmen went tearing down stairs after them, like so many furies. When the noise subsided, Thompson, half smiling, said, "Since the gentlemen for whose especial benefit I have been speaking have withdrawn, I will soon finish my remarks." Their allies had not all withdrawn, however; for well do I remember the dark and threatening scowls that followed this cool declaration.

When the meeting closed, the heart of every abolitionist beat with a quickened pulse, for Thompson's safety. From time to time, the fierce, impatient faces of the truckmen, were seen above the staircase; their courage evidently reinforced by fresh supplies of rum, paid for by southern generosity. Abolitionists, who left the meeting, came back to tell that the stairway and entry were lined with desperate-looking fellows, brandishing clubs and cart-whips; and that a carriage, with the steps down, stood close to the door. I did not then know that a train was laid by our friends for Thompson's escape. All I could do, was to join with the women, who formed a dense circle around him; a species of troops in much requisition at that period, and well known by the name of "Quaker militia."[8] My husband, in the meantime, being acquainted with the bar-keeper of the Tremont, entered into conversation with him, and held him by the coat-button, to his most visible annoyance. Near the platform where the speakers had stood, was a private door, leading, by a flight of back stairs, into a store-room, that opened into another street than the front entrance. The mob were either ignorant of this entrance, or forgetful; but our friends were neither. One of our number held the key; a second had engaged a carriage, with swift horses, and a colored driver; a third made a signal from a window, for the carriage to approach the store communicating with the back passage. Holding Thompson in friendly chat, the women, as it were quite accidentally, approached the private door. The circle opened—the door opened—a volley of oaths from the truckmen, and a deafening rush down the front stairs—but where was *he?*

For a few agonizing moments, we who remained in the hall could not answer. But presently, S. J. May came to us, with a face like Carara marble, and breathed, rather than uttered, the welcome words, "Thank God! he's safe!"

Their carriage was in readiness, to convey him to a southern vessel, and an ignominious death; but he entered *our* carriage, and was off like the wind; though the mob turned the corner of the building quick enough to clutch at the wheels, as they started.

Much as southerners hated George Thompson, he was the very man they would have peculiarly admired, had any other subject than slavery been the theme of his eloquence. His bold frankness, his earnest enthusiasm, his rapid changes from the thrilling to the comic—the spontaneous heartiness of his whole character and manner, were all well calculated to please southern taste. Mr. Kingsley,[9] of Florida, fully concurred in this sentiment. "I've heard many public speakers in my lifetime," said he, "but I never but once heard eloquence to be compared to George Thompson. His only equal, in my estimation, was Sheridan, an emancipated slave, sent out to Africa, by the colonization society. The planters used to ride miles and miles to hear him; and all agreed that they never heard so great a natural orator. I used to tell them, 'Hear George Thompson, and he'll captivate you, in spite of your teeth.' "

No effort of Thompson's ever *surprised* me more than his discussion with R. R. Gurley,[10] in Boston. No one who had lived here from the first conception of the colonization society, could have brought a greater amount of information to bear on that treacherous scheme. It was a beautiful sight, to see his manly directness and eloquent sincerity, in contrast with Mr. Gurley's jesuitical evasions, hair-splitting subtlety, and cunning appeals to popular prejudice. I shall never forget the expressive beauty of his countenance, and the gracefulness of his unstudied attitude, as he stood with his cloak folded about him, like some fine old statue, and answered Mr. Gurley's reiterated sneers at England: "I rejoice to hear the guilt charged upon England. Yes, heap it upon erring, sinning England! Mountains on mountains, till it reaches to the skies! So much the more need that I, a humble representative of England, should strive to *atone* for the mischief she has done. As you have copied England in her *sin,* copy her in her *repentance!*"

This devoted friend of humanity is now exerting his admirable powers to the utmost, for the repeal of the corn laws,[11] and the oppressed in the East Indies. The respect and love of thousands of England's best and noblest spirits follow him wherever he goes. The proscribed of America is the idol of Great Britain. Yet he writes to me, "I long, impatiently and painfully, again to tread the shores of America; not merely to grasp those I love by the hand, but to share again the labors and sufferings of the devoted ones, who are still striving to sustain the standard of freedom and equality—to endure the *extra* persecution which would be awarded to me, the most obnoxious and hated being that ever stood on American soil. But my work is here; and I must not permit inclination to be my guide. Never, for a moment, think my zeal in your cause has abated. The links that bind me to you are as bright and strong as ever; and if God permits, I hope yet to realize the cherished wish of my heart, and see you again, though it be but for a short time. Oh, how distinct are the scenes we have passed through together. Your attendance at my lectures; the Gurley debate; those trying scenes at Brooklyn; the farewell, when Judge Lynch was announced at New-York. Oh, how vivid are all these memories, though seven years have rolled away! God bless you both, and those who labor with you to advance the best of causes."

I never saw George Thompson again, after that hurried farewell at morning twilight, when "Judge Lynch" was lying in wait for him. He left the country a few months after.— L.M.C.

Letter 40 [1]
November 3, 1842

The story called Catochus [2] on the last page, may be thought by many out of the limits of probability. Numerous cases are on record where people have recovered after every sign of death had been present for two or three days. Such cases are well known to physicians, under the term asphyxia. [3] But the disease described in the thrilling sketch to which I have alluded, where the subject is conscious of being alive, while all others suppose him dead, is new to me. It is the utmost horror which human imagination can conceive.

A remarkable case, unaccompanied with the consciousness of being alive, occurred in my own family. The yellow fever raged fearfully in Boston, the last part of the eighteenth century. The panic was so universal that wives forsook their dying husbands, in some cases, and mothers their children, to escape the contagious atmosphere of the city. Funeral rites were generally omitted. The "death-carts," sent into every part of the town, were so arranged as to pass through each street every half hour. At each house known to contain a victim of the fever, they rung a bell, and called, "Bring out your dead." When the lifeless forms were brought out, they were wrapped in tarred sheets, put into the cart, and carried to the burial-place, unaccompanied by relatives. In most instances, in fact, relatives had fled before the first approach of the fatal disease. One of my father's brothers, residing in Boston at that time, became a victim to the pestilence. When the first symptoms appeared, his wife sent the children into the country, and herself remained to attend upon him. Her friends warned her against such rashness. They told her it would be death to her, and no benefit to him; for he would soon be too ill to know who attended upon him. These arguments made no impression on her affectionate heart. She felt that it would be a life-long satisfaction to *her* to know who attended upon him, if he did not. She accordingly staid and watched him with unremitting care. This, however, did not avail to save him. He grew worse and worse, and finally died. Those who went round with the death-carts, had visited the chamber, and seen that the end was near. They now came to take the body. His wife refused to let it go. She told me that she never knew how to account for it, but though he was perfectly cold and rigid, and to every appearance quite dead, there was a powerful impression on her mind that life was not extinct. The men were overborne by the strength of her conviction, though their own reason was opposed to it. The half hour again came round, and again was heard the solemn words, "Bring out your dead." The wife again resisted their importunities; but this time the men were more resolute. They said the duty assigned them was a painful one; but the health of the city required punctual obedience to the orders they received; if they ever expected the pestilence to abate, it must be by a prompt removal of the dead, and immediate fumigation of the infected apartments. She pleaded and pleaded, and even knelt to them in an agony of tears; continually saying, "I am sure he is not dead." The men represented the utter absurdity of such an idea; but finally, overcome by her tears, again departed. With trembling haste she renewed her efforts to restore life. She raised his head, rolled his limbs in hot flannel, and placed hot onions on his feet. The dreaded half hour again came round, and found him as cold and rigid as ever. She renewed her intreaties so desperately, that the messengers began to think a little gentle force would be necessary. They accordingly attempted to remove the body against her will; but she threw herself upon it, and clung to it with such frantic strength, that they could not easily loosen her grasp. Impressed by the remarkable strength of her will, they relaxed their efforts. To all their remonstrances, she answered, "If you bury him, you shall bury me with him." At last, by dint of reasoning on the necessity of the case, they obtained from her a promise that if he showed no signs of life before they again came round, she would make no further opposition to the removal. Having gained this respite, she hung the watch up on the bedpost, and renewed her efforts with redoubled zeal. She placed kegs of hot water about him, forced brandy between his teeth, breathed into his nostrils, and held hartshorn to his nose; but still the body lay motionless and cold. She looked anxiously at the watch; in five minutes the promised half hour would expire, and those dreadful voices would be heard, passing through the street. Hopelessness came over her; she dropped the head she had been sustaining; her hand trembled violently; and the hartshorn she had been holding was spilled on the pallid face. Accidentally, the position of the head had become slightly tipped backward, and the powerful liquid flowed into his nostrils. Instantly there was a short, quick gasp—a struggle—his eyes opened and when the death-men again came, they found him sitting up in the bed. He is still alive, and has enjoyed unusually good health.

I should be sorry to awaken any fears, or excite unpleasant impressions, by the recital of this story; but I have ever thought that funerals were too much hurried in this country; particularly in the newly settled parts of it. It seems to me there ought to be as much delay as possible; especially in cases of sudden death. I believe no nation buries with such haste as Americans. The ancients took many precautions. They washed and anointed the body many successive times before it was carried to the burial. The Romans cut off a joint of the finger, to make sure that life was extinct, before they lighted the funeral pile. Doubtless it is very unusual for the body to remain apparently lifeless for several hours, unless it be really dead; but the mere possibility of such cases should make friends careful to observe undoubted symptoms of dissolution before interment.

If we have not improved upon the ancients in this respect, we surely have not in our impersonations of death. Ever since the 14th century, the friendly hand that leads mortals to a higher existence has been represented by Christians as a frightful, grinning skeleton. The Greeks, notwithstanding their shadowy faith in a future existence, represented death as a gentle and beautiful youth; sometimes as a sleeping winged child, with an inverted torch resting on a wreath of flowers. Even Samael, the awful death-angel of the Hebrews, resembling our popular ideas of the devil, was always said to take away the souls of the young by a kiss.

The gloom with which we invest everything connected with this step from one existence to another, reveals plainly enough the weakness, or at least the indistinctness, of our faith in immortality. If we indeed believed that they who have gone from us are as truly living, loving, and sentient beings as ourselves, we could not "hang the heavens with black" as we do. It would be more consonant with Christian faith to have the hearse garlanded with flowers, and supported by golden-winged angels, pointing upward.

Of all the absurd customs handed down to us from benighted ages, few appear to me so irrational and unchristian, as that of wearing mourning for those mortals who have passed into immortality. The torture of attending to new garments when the heart is really weighted down with sorrow; the mockery of assuming them when it is not; the additional strength it gives to the idea of separation, which is only apparent, not real; and the practical denial to our children of that cheerful faith, which we attempt to teach them by our maxims, are strong reasons why mourning should be abolished. That the poor cannot afford it, ought to be a sufficient reason to kind and sympathizing hearts; for a custom intended to impress affection and respect for our lost ones, is not a mere matter of pride; it comes home to the heart. To be sure it *is* no standard of respect for the departed; but while the world choose so to consider it, it will always occasion a pang to be compelled to nonconformity by poverty. Under the influence of a high and serene faith, it becomes easy for all classes to renounce this absurd and inconvenient custom. Thousands, of various sects, already begin to marvel why it has so long been allowed to cast its gloomy shadow over an enlightened age. "We wear no black garments," say the friends of the excellent Henry G. Chapman;[4] "for they would ill express our feelings."

Popular modes of speech are likewise wrong on this important subject. If we want our children to be impressed with a lively faith in immortality, we should not speak of people as dead, but as passed into another mode of existence. The body should be regarded as a suit of cast-off clothes, which the wearer has outgrown; consecrated indeed by the beloved being that used them for a season, but of no value within themselves.

Canova,[5] in his monument to the Stuarts, in St. Peters, at Rome, has restored the lovely Grecian image, and represented death as a serene and beautiful youth. The approach of a more cheerful faith is likewise indicated by the increasing tendency to place the cast-off "time-garments" of our beloved ones in the midst of blooming flowers, and gentle streams. Protestant ideas of death have been strikingly more gloomy than those of Catholics; if they are fairly indicated by their customs. I have never known how to account for this, except by the fact that there is not such a feeling of separation between those who live on this side the rainbow bridge, and those who live on the other. The masses said for the dead, the prayers to saints to help their passage through the intermediate state, which they call purgatory, and the affectionate custom of daily placing wreaths and baskets of flowers on the tomb—all these keep alive a feeling of nearness between the living and those called dead.

A friend of mine, walking on the beach in Brazil, overtook a colored woman with a tray upon her head. Being asked what she had to sell, she lowered the tray, and with reverent tenderness uncovered it. It was the lifeless form of her babe, covered with a neat white robe, with a garland round the head, and flowers within the little hands, that lay clasped upon its bosom. "Is that your child?" said the traveller. "It *was* mine a few days ago," she replied; "but the Madonna has it for her little angel now." "How beautifully you have laid it out!" said he. She answered cheerfully, "Ah, what is that, to the bright wings it wears in Heaven."

Thanks, thanks, for the light that falls from that other world on this. Let us no longer cast between us and it the ghastly shadow of a skeleton. Let our customs, as well as our oc- casional sermons, teach the little ones whom we train for immortality, that nothing but the garment lies in the grave. "He is not here; he is risen."—L.M.C.

Letter 44
December 8, 1842

In my visit to Blackwell's island,[1] few things interested me so much as the insane. In the penitentiary was one poor, Lascar youth,[2] who had been there ten years, because there was no one to claim him, and he was too mischievous to go at large. I know not why he was not placed in the insane hospital, near by; for it seemed a clear case of lunacy. He sits on the ground, in the sunshine, all the time, generally in a state of stupor, but at times snap- ping his fingers, and laughing at something which he sees or hears inwardly; for he takes no cognizance of what is going on around him. He is at all times averse to leaving the open air; and sometimes resists, with troublesome violence, all efforts to coax or carry him within walls. Poor fellow! he lost his way somewhere in the battle of life; the world will never know how or where. From his own memory the record is blotted, never to re-appear until he enters into that existence where every word is brought into judgment. That he has suffered grievous wrong, there is no doubt. Probably, the son of some vicious mother, who sold him to a sea-captain, to get rid of him; on ship-board, he learned sensuality and vio- lence; thence transferred to the penitentiary; doomed to live and die, without ever know- ing the restoring power of gentleness.

I did not go into the mad-house, for I lacked nerve to witness insanity in its most vio- lent forms; as I passed the building, I heard shrieks and groans, and laughter still more terrific. In the lunatic asylum, they generally seemed tranquil; and many of them happy. With the exception of intemperance, no cause of insanity is so prolific as that of religious excitement; a fact which betrays an exceedingly unnatural and false state of things in theo- logical teaching. But in this, more than in other things, it seems as if mankind were fated to exhaust every species of error, before they arrive at truth.

The most amusing form of insanity that came under my eye, was a diseased-enlargement of self-esteem. One woman, dressed in fantastic decorations, called herself Lady Mary, and pompously displayed her patent of nobility; another imagined herself the widow of Gen- eral Washington, and talked largely of the battles she had fought, and still would fight, if her troops would only rally round her; a third was rolling off Latin sentences with great volubility, and complaining of the mis-pronunciation of the vulgar.

Phrenology[3] has unquestionably been of great use in pointing out the causes of insan- ity, and in helping to give increased light on the subject of its treatment. I know many scholars entertain a strong contempt for this science, considering it the democracy of metaphysics; but I believe it will by no means prove a farthing rush-light in the history of disease and crime. A case of painful interest is said to have occurred a few years since in

Baltimore. A wealthy gentleman had a wife much observed for her beauty, and winning manners. She was quite an idol in general society, and much beloved by her acquaintance. Her husband was strongly attached to her, and very proud of her. Soon after the birth of her third child, she had a fever, which endangered her life. She recovered, however, and appeared the same as formerly. The first thing which excited attention to any change in her character, was the charge of having stolen a valuable lace veil from a store where she was purchasing other goods. Her husband indignantly repelled the accusation; but she, with a flood of tears, acknowledged that it was true. "But, my dear," said he, "what *could* have tempted you? You can have a hundred dollars, whenever you wish it." "I know that," she replied; "but it seemed as if something possessed me to take that veil, and as if I couldn't help it."

This disagreeable affair was settled by the payment of money; but it was not long before a similar case again occurred; and again, and again, and again; though each time the confession was made with an agony of tears, and the most fervent promises of amendment. She seemed keenly alive to the distress her proceedings occasioned a beloved husband, and the shame they would bring on her darling little children; but still the excuse was, that the temptation proved so strong at the moment, it seemed as if she were possessed. At last, the offense was committed against one, who insisted upon bringing it to trial. The case was accordingly brought into court, and much compassion excited by the pale countenance of the husband, and the agonized expression of the beautiful culprit. Her physician testified that, according to his belief, it was a case of partial insanity; that so far as could be ascertained by diligent inquiry, nothing of the kind had ever happened, from her childhood upward, until after that memorable fever. In one respect, her pilferings differed remarkably from usual theft: she attempted to make no concealment of her stolen goods, but with a sort of childish eagerness, would display them to every acquaintance who came in her way; telling the name of the store, and advising them to go and purchase of the same.

The sympathy excited was so great, that it produced a reaction among the populace; and they complained loudly that the crimes of the rich were very apt to be called insanity. She was reluctantly sentenced to the penitentiary, but in consequence of a petition, very numerously signed, was finally pardoned, and the whole family left the country.

I have heard of other cases similar to this; and when phrenologically examined, it was found that sickness had greatly enlarged the organ of acquisitiveness. Some are unwilling to be convinced of facts like these, because they say they tend to fatality. But is it not likewise a most unfortunate fatality, that men inherit insanity and nervous melancholy from their ancestors?

Among the inmates of the lunatic asylum were two crazy children. I had never happened to think of such a thing, and the sight struck me painfully. In both cases, the derangement was occasioned by fits; but one was loud and violent, the other quiet and idiotic. The latter came to me, with great joyfulness of look and tone, and displaying an apron full of chips, exclaimed, "I've got sticks in my lap!" The poor little thing had deep, affectionate eyes, and as she looked up into mine, I involuntarily folded her to my heart, and parted her hair tenderly. It was a transient movement, occasioned by an impulse of pity; but from that moment, she clung to my side, and followed me everywhere. To every word addressed to her, she answered only, "I've got sticks in my lap!" And this she repeated fifty times over, to every one that looked at her. At last one of the women superintendents came along, and somewhat sternly ordered her to give up her sticks. The child looked disappointed, but at once emptied her apron, and ceased to repeat her joyful phrase. It was a simple incident, but nothing I saw at Blackwell's island so cut me to the heart. The poor little diseased thing seemed so *happy* with her sticks! I inquired why they must be taken from her, and the reply was, that she would soon have them all over the floor. I thought to myself I would rather see her happy in building chip houses on the floor, than to see everything so elaborately neat. In all these great establishments, I apprehend that the temptation is great to attend more to the appearance of things to visitors, than to happiness of soul in the inmates. This building was beautifully airy and clean, and many of the rooms were decorated with evergreens and flowers. This is a great improvement upon the old *regime* of chains and scourges. The truth, that Love is omnipotent, is slowly dawning upon men's minds. They have discovered that even the violence of insanity is better guided by gentleness than by coercion. Reluctantly, fearing and doubting as they go, they will finally learn that the same thing is true of the moral insanity, which men call crime.—L.M.C.

Letter 45
December 22, 1842

It is somewhat humbling to this self-sufficing and boastful age, that we still find ourselves completely ignorant of even the simplest laws by which spirit is united to matter. The more remarkable and unusual phenomena, arising from this divine union, terrified those of the olden time, and were straightway ascribed by them to the direct intervention of supernatural powers; for they wist not that in the natural there *always* exists the *super-natural*. Their blind superstition was a temptation to jugglery and deception; and after ages mixed up true phenomena with the trickish imitations, and buried them all under the snow-drift of scepticism. It were wiser to admit that unaccountable things do occur, and doubtless owe their origin to established laws of the universe, of which we are as yet ignorant. For, much as we boast of our advancement, it may be said of man in the nineteenth century, as it was by Plato, in ages long past: "He is like one shut up in a cavern, who sees shadows of things on the wall, but cannot perceive the objects themselves."[1]

The story of the Persian Magus,[2] who could read a scroll through a brazen shield, has for centuries been considered as improbable as the fables of men and women gradually turning into trees and animals; but it is now known, beyond all power of dispute, that moderns, under the influence of animal magnetism,[3] perform the same exploit the Persian did, and others far more wonderful. These must be admitted as facts, because the proof is too strong to allow of rejecting them; and if they really do occur, they are unquestionably regulated by established laws of the universe, which seem to us miraculous, simply because we do not understand them, and are unaccustomed to such manifestations of them.

The action of souls upon each other, both while clothed in the flesh, and *not* so clothed, is a great mystery, lying much nearer the foundations of our life, than we imagine. We see one man place another in magnetic sleep, and simply *will* that he shall drink vinegar, or touch fire, and straightway the countenance and the muscles give indignation of the sour taste and the scorching sensation; he simply *wills* that a cow shall be lifted, and excessive fatigue follows, as if a cow had been really lifted. Here is certainly a most marvellous power of one soul over another; and thousands of intelligent persons have proved it, both as witnesses, and as subjects of the experiment. Did George Fox, and Madame Guyon, and Madame St. Amour,[4] perform their wonderful cures of diseases by means of this concentrated will? Does the concentrated will, the intense desire of disembodied spirits, have a similar effect on our souls, producing presentiments, and dreams of startling significance? Has this power anything to do with the simultaneous invention of the same thing, in widely distant parts of the world? These are but passing thoughts, not deliberate conclusions. They were suggested to my mind by the following stories; the first of which I read in some Cyclopedia, years ago. As I remember it, it was thus: A man had puzzled himself to invent a machine to make shot. Time after time he tried, and repeatedly came very *near* accomplishing his object; but he was continually defeated by the impossibility of obtaining a perfect equilibrium of pressure. The shot would be oval, or elongated, or three-sided. His mind grew more and more intent upon the object. In this state he fell asleep, and dreamed that he was walking in the open fields. Suddenly a quantity of black hail fell around him. He took up a handful, and lo, it was round, just like shot. He looked upward to see whence it came, and saw that it fell from a high tower. A man seemed to be throwing it down. "What are you doing there?" inquired the dreamer. "I am making shot," replied the unknown. "What are you pouring it down in that way for?" "Don't you perceive that nothing gives a perfectly equal pressure on all sides, except the air?" was the answer. The dreamer awoke, and invented the shot-tower. Had the intense abstraction of his spirit put him into magnetic connection with some other spirit, who understood mechanics better than he?

The other story, I have often heard repeated, but cannot vouch for its correctness. Mr. Slater,[5] the famous manufacturer at Pawtucket, Rhode Island, was in his youth a common workman in an English manufactory. That was before the manufacture of cotton was introduced into the United States; and Great Britain had adopted a very jealous policy, in order to monopolize the manufacture herself. Whoever attempted to export any machinery, or plans of machinery, rendered himself liable to very heavy penalties. Mr. Slater was soon observed for his mechanical skill. Whenever any of the machinery was out of order, *he* was always called upon to repair, or reconstruct it. An accidental conversation one day turned his thoughts toward America, as a country of great manufacturing capabilities; and created in him an intense desire to emigrate. With this idea in his head, he noticed with particular care every part and portion of the machinery. He was afraid to make drawings, lest attention should be attracted toward him. When he thought he could carry the whole in his brain, he left the manufactory, saying that he preferred to devote himself to agriculture. His employer, though sorry to part with so skillful a hand, gave him letters of recommendation. He went into a distant part of the country, and let himself to a farmer. Here he made drawings in secret, and matured his favorite project. After the lapse of several months, he told his employer that he wished to emigrate to the United States, and would thank him for letters recommending him to the employ of some farmer.

He came here, and met with many discouragements; to establish manufactories, required capital; and capitalists were not much disposed to listen to the schemes of a nameless adventurer. At last, it happened that some wealthy gentleman in Pawtucket wanted a job done, which required great mechanical nicety; and some one said there was a young Englishman, by the name of Slater, at work in the neighborhood, who could do it, if anybody could. The job was finished to their great satisfaction, and let to further acquaintance. He talked of his favorite scheme, and of the wonderful capabilities of Pawtucket for manufacturing. By degrees, they imbibed a degree of his enthusiasm, and at last a company was formed for the purpose he desired. As they observed his progress in the machinery, from day to day, they had more confidence in his knowledge and skill. At last, it was all completed, and a day appointed to set it in motion. The day came, and not a wheel would move. The machinist was vexed, and mortified. He said he must have overlooked something, and would give them information as soon as he discovered the obstruction. All that night, he spent anxiously examining the long-projected machine; all the next day, and all the next night. Surely it was in perfect order; what *could* be the reason it would not move? The third night found him still watching over cogs and springs. At last, completely exhausted in mind and body, he lay down and wept. He fell asleep, and dreamed that he was still bending gloomily over the unlucky machine, when some one slapped him on the shoulder, and said with friendly heartiness, "Why, Slater! don't you know what is the matter? Friction is all it wants. Chalk the strap, man! chalk the strap!"

He sprang up, followed his directions, and in a few hours all was in successful motion. He died a few years ago, a wealthy manufacturer.

Did the weakness of his body, and the intense abstraction of his mind, put him in a state to be peculiarly sensitive to magnetic influence from some other mind? For all things that take place, there is doubtless a rational cause, if we did but know it. In that other world, we shall see with a larger vision.—L.M.C.

Letter 47
January 19, 1843

A friend, whose mind is ever open to light from above, writes thus: "Your editorial on 'Means and Ends,'[1] suggested one illustration, which you have not mentioned; and I would ask if it seems to you a legitimate one? With what view, and in what spirit, are the sympathy, approbation, and love of others sought for and desired? Is it as a *means* of spiritual growth, as an aid to the development of those infinite powers and affections, which are the essence of our being, and the harmonious exercise of which is its highest purpose? Seldom, I fear, is it thus. The attainment of those rich blessings is made an *end,* instead of a *means.* We too often value them as a treasure laid up on earth; and thus regarded, we seek a satisfaction in their possession, which the immutable laws of spirit suffer them not to give. They are infinite treasures held in earthen vessels, but we bestow on the vessels and its adornings that reverence and love, which are due to its contents alone. We strive to convert a means into an end, and the consequence is defeat and disappointment."

The chief reason of the common disappointments in love and friendship is recorded in those few wise words. Selfishness is finite in all its perceptions; it mistakes the means for the end, and trusts in the temporary, as if it were permanent; its gospel is expedience, its deity is Self. Love looks beyond the means to the end, and values them only as steps in the ladder that ascends to Heaven; its gospel is faith, and its deity the Universal Father.

In forming a matrimonial alliance, how few think whether they shall promote each other's spiritual progress. The question is not, "Shall I thus learn to overcome my selfishness?" It is rather, "Will my selfishness be ministered unto?" Seldom is it the aim to help each other cure pride, vanity, or faults of temper; it is rather to find more convenient indulgence for these evils. The same mistake makes the generality of friendships so shallow and unproductive. Men are prone to love those friends who make them pleased with themselves; who exaggerate their merits, and gloss over their faults. That which was given as a means to help us onward, is converted into an end in which we rest. There are few, indeed, strong enough to covet a real friend; one who is so unselfish that he will even sacrifice the luxury of pleasing, for the sake of doing us good; yet who would fain give *us* pleasure, rather than receive it *himself*.

"May my friend," says Emerson, "never express, even by a glance, more interest in me than he really feels. Still worse would it be, if, from a mistaken spirit of kindness, he should forbear to dissent from my opinions, or practice. God forbid that when I looked to friendship as a firm rock, to sustain me in any given emergency, I should find it nothing but a mush of concession. Better be a nettle in the side of my friend, than to be merely his echo."

The same reflected selfishness which unhallows marriage, and perverts friendship, is shown in the education of children. The *means* which are given us to make them angels, are made *ends;* and thereby they become barred gates to close their communication with the angels. We seek for them worldly indulgence, ease, and respectability, without asking to what spiritual end will these administer? I shall never forget words which I once heard, on this subject, from the same eloquent tongue already quoted. It was a beautiful sketch of a family of poor but intelligent boys, compelled to perform the laborious duties of life, yet struggling after infinite perceptions with inexpressible longing. Reciting scraps of orations and poetry in the woodshed, and working diligently at their chores, so as to commit the required lesson, and yet gain time to peep at the last new book. Eager to have more money, that they might ride abroad amid beautiful scenery, and see famous pictures, and graceful statuary, and hear eloquent lectures, as richer boys could do. "Alas for them," said he, "if their wishes were crowned! Through privation and earnest humility must they learn to reverence the good, the true, and the beautiful. Ministering angels are weaving spiritual laurels for their young brows; and those angels are Toil, and Want, and Truth, and Mutual Faith."

It is well for us that overruling Providence so often makes the means, in which we would rest, subservient to a higher end than we either perceive or love. In looking back upon my pilgrimage, how many points do I see in the distance, by which I have risen, one after another, to the place where I now stand and overlook them all; yet each one seemed to me the end, where I would fain have stopped, had not the pressure of circumstances ever pushed me onward. It is thus that we attain to those "heights of virtue, which overlook the plain of innocence." Thus rushing, leaping, and struggling, the fountain, after its long winding passage, springs upward to its level.

Yet in this retrospect of old landmarks, there mixes with the consciousness of spiritual progress, that deep sadness which belongs to the words, "They return no more!" To my *eye*, they stand like Dido, on the lone sea-shore, "waving her love from Carthage."[2] To my *ear*, they float in that mournfullest of all sweet tunes, "The light of other days." The path by which we have climbed the mountain, we can tread no more; on the points where we *have* rested, we can never rest again. Moore, in his Epicurean,[3] represents the noviciate seeking after spiritual truth, as compelled to pass through fire, and flood, and then ascend, he knew not whither, by a ladder, swinging to and fro in the gusty wind, over a deep and dark abyss. But *he knew not, till he had nearly reached the top, that every step broke under him, as he left it*. Who, that has tried to live a true and earnest life, does not see here the record of his progress?

There are times, when I long inexpressibly to return to that period in my religious experience, when "the morning stars sang together for joy;" but the same stars would not sing to me so gloriously now; for I now comprehend that they were but one part of the great chorus of the universe; whereas they then seemed to me *all*. "That which we can see, and not see over, stands to us in place of the infinite," says Carlyle.[4]

When I look back upon the enthusiasm and mutual joy of early friendships, I covet their renewal; but should I meet the selfsame individuals, we could be friends no longer; we should not even understand each other's language. I remember one, who, in my youthful days, was the very Magnus Apollo of my imagination. I listened to him in reverence, and took truth (or fancied I took it) upon his authority; for it seemed to me that he knew all, and that I could never hope to be half as wise as he. We met ten years after, and I knew not what to say to him! We walked in the summer woods, and it reminded him of Thompson's Seasons,[5] which he recited, as of old. But I, in the meantime, had become intimate with Wordsworth, and dwelt in friendly companionship with Herder, Schiller, and Jean Paul.[6] Strangely, like some meagre, foreign tongue, his words fell upon my ear. Yet he, and Thompson too, had once rendered me most pleasant and effectual service. I remembered it with gratitude; but could enjoy it no more. The step by which I had risen, had broken behind me, and fallen into the measureless abyss of the past. Our disappointment arose from trying to meet at the point from where we *had* met; forgetful that the pleasant communion we then enjoyed was but a *means*, not an *end*; that the law of perpetual progress had separated us widely, to meet no more. My friend had not remained stationary, but had moved in another direction. He had become an acute lawyer, and could have opened Blackstone[7] to me, with marvellous learning, had such knowledge been an appropriate means to the end whither I was wending. But I had gone from Thompson, to Byron,[8] and dwelt awhile with him, as in a magician's hall, through which came aeolian complaints, and wild, grand crashes of the organ, from the dim vastness of an unseen world. With increase of knowledge, I saw that the pictures and statues in the hall were living demons; and I felt the breath of evil spirits crowding around me. But they had done me no harm, for I knew not of their presence, while I listened entranced to that wild rush of music from the invisible. When I saw them, I turned shuddering away, and they could not follow me; for from them, I went lovingly to the serene beauty of Wordsworth, reflecting the heavens like a clear, deep lake, in its mountain stillness. I loved him the better, because I had gone awhile with Byron, on his tempestuous path. Passing upward, I met Herder, who "dwelt with the great of all ages, yet with a divine Spinozism[9] of the *heart*, loved the humblest reptile, the meanest insect, and every blossom of the woods."

From these have I learned, (and God forever bless them for the lesson,) that

> "The poet dwells in a golden world,
> With golden stars above;
> Born in the hate of hate, the scorn of scorn,
> The love of love."

> L.M.C.

Letter 55
March 30, 1843

Passing up the Bowery, the other day, I saw two ingenious little toys of slight construction, representing men sawing planks; one of them rapidly, the other more slowly. The moving power was ascending current of warm air from the blaze of two astral lamps. My thoughts are set in motion by even a slighter impetus than are these toys. Once in motion, they go circling round, Past, Present, and Future; and where they may light, it is hard to tell. That Bowery window carried me back to the walking statues of Doedalus, and the flying dove of Archytas;[1] showing how very ancient was the instinct in man to imitate all animated forms. Then I thought how every tool was but a portion of some form of perfect life. The ichneumon[2] had a patent borer before ever gimblet or augur was invented; the bee knew how to take up the least possible room in the construction of her cells, long before mathematicians discovered that she had worked out the problem perfectly; the beetle had an excellent pair of forceps, before the steel instrument was dreamed of; and I doubt not the fish had the best of submarine reflectors, before the Brooklyn lady invented hers. Then recurred an idea which has for years been familiar to my mind; that every conceivable thing that has been, or will be invented, already exists in nature, in some form or other. I tried to recall, but could not, the name of the ancient philosopher, who spent his days in watching insects and other animals, that he might gather hints to fashion tools. I saw clearly why it was that man alone could reproduce all things in creation, and apply them to new uses; because he alone contains the *Whole* in himself, and all things bear relation to him, as to the common centre. Higher ideas I had also; but they were floating clouds; though some of them had a wondrous golden edge. Mixed with these were some odd notions about machinery; as how men sought to pray by machinery, and convert the world by machinery, and advance temperance and anti-slavery by machinery; and teach grammar by a machine, in which the active verb is a little hammer, pounding on the objective case. I smiled to think how the subtle, all-pervading power, which instils religion, and changes public sentiment, and clothes thought in language, slips away from all such efforts, like quicksilver, that runs to meet its kindred drop, and will not be fashioned in any mould.

With such cogitations, I pursued my walk, till the homeward path brought me again before the busy toymen. The sight of them awakened recollections of the water clock presented to Charlemagne by Haroun-al-Raschid. Each hour was a little door, out of which issued an armed knight on horseback, and rode round the dial-plate, till noon, when all went in, and shut their respective doors behind them;—of Bonaparte's vase, which being touched, exhibited a palm-tree, under which a shepherdess was spinning;—of Maelzel's chessplayer, and Maillardet's musician, which sat at a piano and played eighteen tunes, while the bosom heaved, the eyes moved, and the motions of the fingers were strangely like life.[3]

These brought up reminiscences of that pleasant book, Miss Edgeworth's Rosamond,[4] and of the account it gives of M. Bautte,[5] the wonderful watchmaker of Geneva, whose fame drew half of travelling Europe into his little dark shop, up seven flight of stairs. I never saw one of his famous mice, with jewelled eyes, which run about the room, nibble crumbs, prick up their ears, and imitate all the motions of a living mouse, so perfectly that even cats are deceived by them; nor the fuzzy caterpillars, which, being wound up, crawl over leaves, and writhe, and wriggle, when touched by a pin. But I have seen one of his music-boxes, from which rises a most perfect and brilliant little bird, no bigger than a humming bee, and pours forth a gush of melody, like a nightingale. Every little glossy feather is perfect, and the motions are wonderfully bird-like, especially when it droops its pretty head under its wings, and seems to fall asleep.

I have heard that this remarkable mechanician had a daughter, to whom he was so strongly attached, that he could not bear to have her out of his sight. He loved to have her sit in a corner of his workshop, where the light fell on her beautiful countenance, as she diligently spun flax on her little foot-wheel. The angels came for this beloved young creature, and took her away. The bereaved father tried to beguile his sorrow by making a perfect image of her, seated in the accustomed corner. The face was done in enamel, and the resemblance was striking. When wound up, like a watch, this image spun her thread, moving eye, foot, and hand, as if alive. The busy hum of the wheel was to the fond father's ear a remembered joy; and the happy countenance, shaded by the very cap his daughter used to wear, was like a dream of sunshine. But even of this imperfect consolation he was soon deprived. The maiden had been beloved by two of his apprentices, one of whom ran away in despair, when he suspected that the other was preferred. Afterward he heard of her intended marriage, and stung with jealousy, resolved to murder her, rather than suffer her to be the wife of his hated rival. He came back to Geneva, ignorant of her death, rushed into the workshop, and deceived by the perfect resemblance of the machine, discharged his pistol, and cracked the fair image into fragments.

In this figure, there was no attempt to imitate the voice; but it is said that M. Glantz,[6] a celebrated mechanic in Vienna, has succeeded in making an instrument which very perfectly imitates the human voice. By pressing a spring, it executes different melodies in a tenor voice, a barytone, or deep bass. The instrument is to be introduced into the head of an automaton, to be exhibited as a public singer.

It is a pity that some skillful machinist does not make a set of automata, to do the business of this nation in Congress. It would be a great saving of traveling expenses, and board; they would be in no danger of attacking each other with bowie-knives and pistols, though the southern members might be so constructed as to *talk* about it, if deemed necessary to keep up their reputation; and by means of electro-magnetic mediums, they might be guided by political wire-pullers at home, as well as they now are.—L.M.C.

Notes

Letter I

1. Letter I is a revision of "Letters from New-York.—No. 1.," *NASS* 19 August 1841, vol. 2, no. 11: 43. The changes were minor and could be partly attributed to compositors of the text: punctuation (deletion or addition of commas, dashes omitted or replaced by semi-colons) and spelling changes or corrections ("muscal" to "musical," "splendor" to "splen-dour," "Wall Street" to "Wall-street"). The most significant revision from the newspaper copy is Child's deletion of sentences describing the derivation of the name "Bowery" noted below.

2. While the "you" that recurs throughout *Letters from New-York* can be read as an in-timate acknowledgment of individual readers, Child initially conceived of her letters as addressed to Boston lawyer and abolitionist, Ellis Gray Loring, with whom she maintained a close friendship until his death in 1858. In January 1842, Child admitted to Loring, "I *thought* I addressed [the letters] to an abstraction; but I find you are *always* in my mind as the person addressed" (*CC* 13/326).

3. Known for its theaters, music halls, and opera houses, Broadway evolved from a nat-ural ridge used as a trail by Native Americans into an important trade route to upstate New York. Beginning at the southern tip of Manhattan and running through Manhattan and the Bronx, Child saw this thriving avenue as an emblem of the urban flux quickly transform-ing the sensibilities of many citizens.

4. Extending for less than a mile between Broadway and the East River in lower Man-hattan, Wall Street became the home of the New York Stock Exchange beginning in 1817. By the 1840s and 50s, many writers, including Child, represented the materialistic focus of the financial district as a threat to spiritual well-being. For a revealing tale using Wall Street as a backdrop, see Herman Melville's "Bartleby, the Scrivener: A Story of Wall-Street" (1853).

5. Within *Letters from New-York,* Child laces the sounds of the city. Walking the streets, New Yorkers would have been accosted with cries of vendors marketing meats and veg-etables, cider, brooms, newspapers, and the services of chimney sweeps, knife sharpeners, and bootblacks. In *The Cries of New York* (1812), sand vendors are said to utter a cry simi-

lar to the one for corn: "Here's white sand; choice sand: here's your lily white s-a-n-d" (cited in Jackson, *The Encyclopedia of New York,* 1129).

6. Having lived in the Boston area for most of her life and, at least in part, imagining an audience of friends such as Ellis Gray Loring and fellow New England writers and abolitionists, Child naturally compares Boston's well-known commons with New York's famous public park. Located at the southern end of Manhattan and thus at the access point to both the Hudson River and the harbor, Battery Park derived its name from the gun batteries formerly positioned there.

7. The *NASS* version of this second line of the couplet was "The ever bright, the ever free!" Loring made this correction in the manuscript.

8. Alphonse de Lamartine (1790–1869) was a French poet and politician whose *Meditations poetiques* (1820) led to his reputation as a leading figure in French romanticism.

9. Frequently mentioned in the Old Testament, Chaldea refers to the land in southern Babylonia (modern-day southern Iraq).

10. Formerly Castle Clinton, a fort not far offshore from the western edge of Battery Park that was ceded to New York in 1823, Castle Garden was a leading entertainment hall until the mid-1850s.

11. In Greek religion, the Nereids are any of the numerous daughters of the sea god Nereus. The Esterhazys were a noble family of Hungary distinguished for their wealth.

12. By the early 1840s, Bowery Street had become known as more than the main route to Boston. As the city grew, the street evolved into a broad and refined thoroughfare housing wealthy New Yorkers as well as points of entertainment, including the Great Bowery Theater. After the Civil War, the Bowery lost the clientel that contributed to its earlier reputation and became more associated with cheap entertainment, homelessness, and brothels. During Child's time, Bloomingdale (from the Dutch word meaning "vale of flowers") was the name used for the Upper West Side. In the newspaper version of the letter, Child also included the etymology of "Bowery" after the current sentence noting the flowery sounds of the street names: "The first derives its name from the fact, that, in primitive days, the rear of the town was composed of *farms,* called *Bouwerys,* by the Dutch; the German word *Bauer,* you know, means peasant, from which our Boor is probably derived."

13. The *Standard* version of this line did not include "within me." Interestingly, Ellis Gray Loring suggested this change.

Letter II

1. Apparently at the guidance of Ellis Gray Loring, this second letter combines "Letters from New-York.—No. 2.," *NASS* 26 August 1841, vol. 2, no. 12: 47, and "Letters from New-York.—No. 22.," *NASS* 21 April 1842, vol. 2, no. 46: 183. In the scrapbook margins next to Loring's copy of letter no. 2 at Radcliffe College's Schlesinger Library, he has written out the changes that make up the final form of the letter. The April letter described a Washingtonian Temperance Society procession and thus becomes a natural addition to the August letter which had made reference to these leaders within antebellum temperance reform. Substantive revisions, including the deletion of the final paragraphs of no. 22 are noted below.

2. A comic character in Sir Walter Scott's *Rob Roy* (1818).

3. In this reply to remarks occasioned by her first letter praising the Battery, Child names three additional Manhattan parks that, in the early 1840s, were surrounded by fash-

ionable neighborhoods, theaters, or concert halls. Washington Parade Park, or Washington Square, had been developed on land purchased by the city in 1827. Near the intersection of Bowery and Bloomingdale, Union Square opened in 1831. Modeled after residential parks of London, St. John's Park was known as a fashionable neighborhood until its decline during the later 1840s.

4. Child had concluded the 26 August 1841 *Standard* version of this sentence differently. The Society, she wrote, "has been organized, on the sure basis of the Law of Love." While not specifically linking the "Law of Love" to the Washington Temperance Society, Child does go on to attribute the divine principle to temperance reform societies in general. Again, Loring apparently suggested the current version of these remarks. The purifying and unifying "Law" is also underscored at critical points elsewhere in the volume. See her reflections on race and the "Law of Love" in Letter XXXVI. Following this statement, Child accepts Loring's advice and completes the paragraph with all but the first sentence of the introductory paragraph to her 21 April 1842 letter on the Washington Temperance Society.

5. While occasional attempts were made in the seventeenth century to limit the use of alcohol, it was not until Billy J. Clark's efforts in 1808 at Moreau, New York, that the first temperance society was formed. Inspired by Benjamin Rush's *An Inquiry Into the Effects of Spiritous Liquors on the Human Mind and Body* (1784), Clark and the soon-to-be Calvinist minister Lyman Beecher—father of Catherine Beecher, Harriet Beecher Stowe, and Henry Ward Beecher—actively sought to curb the sale and use of liquor in the first two decades of the nineteenth century. Beginning in the spring of 1841, the Washingtonian Temperance Society initiated a resurgence of the movement through meetings not unlike evangelical revivals. Inspired by the sensational presentations of lecturers, listeners by the thousands answered the call to sign the temperence pledge. The "fifteen-gallon law" of Massachusetts (1838) represented an attempt to limit alcohol consumption by forbidding the sale of less than fifteen gallons of liquor, thus preventing easy access and consumption.

6. According to New Testament gospels (Matthew 3.1–12, Mark 1.1–8, Luke 3.1–18, and John 1.6–8, 19–28) and Christian tradition, John the Baptist resembled Old Testament prophets and, through his preaching and baptism of Christ, prepared the way for Jesus.

7. The three previous paragraphs describing the Washingtonian procession were part of the 21 April 1842 *Standard* letter (no. 22). One revision in these three paragraphs is substantive; after a recognition of the men "who first started a Temperance Society on the Washingtonian Plan," the letter had previously included "and who were going about delivering addresses in various parts of the country." Cited below are also the two closing paragraphs of no. 22 that were deleted in the composing of Letter II for *Letters:*

> Thus far have I wandered, led on unconsciously by the music; and so have forgotten to tell you that in Philadelphia, too, the Washingtonians have lately had a procession of some twelve or fifteen thousands, with music, banners, and the badges of various trades. A correspondent of the Journal of Commerce says:
> "As a mere display of tastefully-decorated and chastely-mottoed banners, interspersed at intervals through a long line of men, thickly studded with bands and martial music, the sight was imposing and exhilarating—but when viewed in a moral sense, and the present feeling on temperance compared with five and ten years ago, when a groggery stared you in the face at almost every other door, and when drunkenness was looked upon as no crime, and hardly esteemed a fault, the procession of to-day presents an aspect truly sublime. In the line of the procession, I saw several so-

cieties of reformed drunkards—young men and old—and as they passed, their wives and families raised from want and misery to competence and comfort, rose to my mind, and in their joyous faces and happy homes, I saw the full reward of those whose exertions have been devoted to the cause for the past, and ample remuneration for them to proceed in the good work, until drunkenness shall not find a foot-hold in the land."

When, oh when, shall anti-slavery march forward her thousands, her course cheered on by the multitude, her banners inscribed "LIBERTY TO ALL THE IN-HABITANTS!" If I can but live to hear of that day, methinks I could say, cheerfully, "Now let me depart in peace." But what matters it, whether I live till the Jubilee, or depart weary and wayworn in the midst of the struggle? The clear note of victory will ring through the world, and I shall hear it, there beyond.

8. Located at Broadway and Fulton Streets, St. Paul's Church (1766) was a well-known historical site to New Yorkers, being the place of the thanksgiving service after George Washington's inauguration. In the first-edition description of St. Paul's, Child added the line voicing the critique that the church had a "gingerbread" appearance.

9. Completed in 1836 by the millionare fur trader John Jacob Astor (1763–1848), the five-story Astor House on the west side of Broadway was the first luxury hotel in New York. Even before the Croton waterworks opened in 1842, an event that Child celebrates in Letter XXX, the hotel had water pumped to its upper stories.

10. The period during the French Revolution (1789–1799) marked by mass executions. The Reign of Terror began in the spring of 1793 and ended with the fall of Robespierre on 27 July 1794. Child had originally ended this paragraph with the statement, "In Philadelphia, the dogs are killed privately."

Letter III

1. Letter III is a slight revision of "Letters from New-York.—No. 3.," *NASS* 2 September 1841, vol. 2, no. 13: 51. The substantive changes are noted below.

2. Child's reference to the "God within" signals her own familiarity with and, to an extent, acceptance of a Transcendentalist sensibility. In a column entitled "Transcendentalism," first printed in the 25 November 1841 *Standard* and later revised as Letter XIII in *Letters from New York, Second Series* (1845), Child links the "God within" to the philosophical roots of Transcendentalism:

The German school of metaphysics, with the celebrated Kant at its head, rejects this proposition [that all knowledge is received into the soul through the senses] as false; it denies that all knowledge is received through the senses; and maintains that the highest, and therefore most universal, truths are revealed within the soul, to a faculty *transcending* the understanding. This faculty they call pure Reason; it being peculiar to them to use that word in contradistinction to the Understanding. To this pure Reason, which some of their writers call "The God within," they believe that all perceptions of the True, the Good, and the Beautiful, are revealed, in its unconscious quietude; and that the province of the Understanding, with its five handmaids, the Senses, is confined merely to external things, such as facts, scientific laws, &c.

For many Transcendentalists, the "God within" was synonymous with Intuition.

3. Child added this sentence in the first edition.

4. Between "could not" and "transmit," the *NASS* version of this sentence had included the clause "by reason of necessity and their own souls."

5. Child follows Loring's advice, changing the newspaper version of the couplet that had read "From the same grim tower, / The *music* and the *shadow* fell."

6. According to Greek mythology, the Hamadryads (or Dryads) were among the class of nymphs (lesser female divinities) who presided over forests and trees.

7. In ancient geography, the Ilissus was the river in Attica, Greece, that flowed just south of Athens. In Greek myth, the Ilissus River was the site where Boreas carried away Orithyia to become his consort.

8. Five Points was the intersection point of five Manhattan streets: Mulberry, Anthony (now Worth), Cross (now Park), Orange (now Baxter), and Little Water (now defunct). While the site had become a well-kept neighborhood after the filling of a nearby pond in 1808, it soon sank—as did the land—in reputation around 1820. A well-known brewery was subdivided in the 1830s, and parts were called "murderer's alley" and "den of thieves." While some of the residents included freed African Americans, the area primarily was the home of poor Irish immigrants. By the 1840s, the reputation of the neighborhood drew the eye of prominent writers, politicians, and reformers. Perhaps one of the best-known descriptions of Five Points came in *American Notes* (1842) by Charles Dickens. His rendering of the filth and wandering pigs echoes Child's own heartfelt lament of some of the worst urban conditions in the country.

9. William Hogarth (1697–1764), an English painter and engraver. *Gin Lane,* one of Hogarth's series of engravings on moral subjects, charted the destructive effects of drinking.

10. In Greek legend, Myrmidons were any of the inhabitants of Phthiotis in Thessaly. Most relevant to the allusion, as devoted followers of Achilles, their name came to be associated with subordinates who carry out orders without question.

11. For a fuller description of the Croton waterworks, see Letter XXX.

12. In the January 1845 issue of the *American Review,* Donald G. Mitchell's review of *Letters from New York* ridicules Child's recurring assertion that social conditions often foster crime, suggesting that some acts signal a "nature" in need of choking rather than choked-up nature. Mitchell's critique marked the ongoing debate—sparked by the writings and activities of Child, Charles Dickens, Dorothea Dix, and others—over the conditions of prison facilities and the assumptions guiding their management. The Hall of Justice, known by the 1840s as the "Egyptian Tombs," was constructed in 1838. According to Greek mythology, Sisyphus was the king of Corinth eternally forced to enact the seemingly fruitless labor of pushing a huge stone up a hill only to have it roll down just as he had reached the top.

Letter IV

1. Letter IV represents substantially the same text as "Letters from New-York.—No. 4.," *NASS* 9 September 1841, vol. 2, no. 14: 55. With the exception of correcting "great fire of 1837" to "great fire of 1835" (Loring's emendation) and changing references that wrongly refer to the Hudson as the sea, the revisions were minor punctuation and spelling alterations.

2. Staten Island, Jersey, Hoboken, Brooklyn, and Fort Lee form areas surrounding Manhattan. Staten Island lies at the meeting point between lower and upper New York Bay, a region south and slightly east of Manhattan; Jersey (or Jersey City) is located to the west

across the Hudson; Hoboken and Fort Lee also border the west bank of the Hudson, north and slightly east of Jersey; and Brooklyn is located just across the East River, to the south and east. During the 1830s and 1840s, these communities were still relatively small in population. When Brooklyn was chartered as a city in 1834, for instance, it had less than sixteen thousand people; during the same time, Staten Island had just over ten thousand residents. For Child, then, short excursions from Manhattan represented an escape to a more picturesque natural setting away from frenetic realities of urban life.

3. Child is referring to Lake Winnipesaukee in central New Hampshire.

4. Settled in the 1630s and incorporated as a town in 1705, Brookline was bordered by Boston and known for its scenic beauty.

5. In classical mythology, Elysium (also called the Elysium Fields) was the home of the blessed after death. As many of Child's readers would also know, the French "Avenue of the Elysian Fields" (Avenue des Champs-Élysées) was one of world's most famous streets, stretching from the Arc de Triomphe to the Place de la Concorde.

6. In the summer of 1815, thirteen-year-old Lydia Maria Child (then Lydia Francis) was sent to Norridgewock, Maine, to live with her sister Mary Francis Preston and her brother-in-law Warren Preston. During the nearly five years at Norridgewock, Child met members of the Penobscot tribe. The Penobscots were formerly part of the Abenaki, a confederacy of Algonquian-speaking peoples who lived in Maine and also included the Malecite, Norridgewock, and Passamaquoddy tribes. The memories of her encounters with the Penobscot inform a range of her early writings, including *Hobomok* (1824), "The Lone Indian" (1828), "Chocorua's Curse" (1830), and numerous pieces for the *Juvenile Miscellany*.

7. Born near Springfield, Pennsylvania, Benjamin West (1738–1830) became a celebrated painter in both the United States and England where he lived from 1763 until his death. According to accounts of his life, Native Americans gave West red and yellow soil with which to attempt his first color paintings. Found in the sixteenth century on the coast south of Rome and owned by the Vatican, the Apollo Belvedere is a statue that, during Child's time, would have been thought to represent the perfect masculine form.

8. Weehawken (or Weehauken), New Jersey, was the site of one of the best-known duels in United States history. Both combatants were distinguished politicians in the early years of the republic: Alexander Hamilton (1755–1804) was an advocate of a strong federal government and the first secretary of the treasury, and Aaron Burr (1756–1836) was a prominent New York politician and former U.S. senator. Their political differences developed into a bitter rivalry, fed to a large degree by Hamilton's successful opposition to Burr's bid for the presidency in 1800 and for the New York governorship in 1804. The duel occurred 11 July 1804, ending Hamilton's life and Burr's political career.

9. As an abolitionist, Child would quite naturally have been familiar with the works of John Pierpont (1785–1866). In 1840, James Munroe and Company of Boston had published Pierpont's *Airs of Palestine, and Other Poems,* a collection that included a number of poems written on the subject of slavery. In 1843, abolitionist publisher Oliver Johnson released *The Anti-Slavery Poems of John Pierpont.*

10. A British-born sculptor, Ball Hughes (1806–1868) gained acclaim in the United States after moving to New York in 1829. William Pitt (1759–1806) was a British statesman known for his brilliant oratory and opposition to the Revolutionary War.

11. One of the most disastrous occurrences in New York history, the "Great Fire" of 16–17 December 1835 destroyed more than twenty square blocks of the city and caused an

estimated twenty to forty million dollars in damages. The fire was contained in the area bounded by Wall and Broad Streets, Coenties Slip, and the East River.

12. Mary Rogers, a clerk at a tobacco store frequented by James Fenimore Cooper, Washington Irving, and Edgar Allan Poe, was murdered in July 1841. Her body was discovered in the Hudson River near Hoboken, and her killer was never found. Poe made the case famous in his story "The Mystery of Marie Roget" (1843).

In a letter to Ellis Gray Loring dated 23 November 1842, Child related a possible scenario, described by a woman under hypnosis (or magnetic sleep), concerning the death of Mary Rogers:

You remember, perhaps, that it was generally supposed that four or five rowdies were concerned in the murder of Mary Rogers; and that the testimony of the doctors was strong to that effect? Well—now for animal magnetism. Some time last Spring, *five or six months ago,* Mr. Page told me that the blind girl, who has been magnetized here, was casually inquired of by some of the family where she staid, "Who murdered Mary Rogers?" In her magnetic sleep she answered, "It was not several men, as folks say. Only one . . . had anything to do with the murder." When asked if no one else knew anything about it, she replied, "There is a young man over at Hoboken, who helped about the body." She described the complexion and appearance of the murderer, and said he had now gone a great way off. I repeated this to different members of the family, at the time; but thought no more of it, until ten days ago, an old woman died at Hoboken; and on her death-bed confessed that a young physician brought Mary Rogers to her house, to procure premature delivery; that she died under the process; that he was terrified, and pledged her to secresy, and persuaded her son to help him carry the body to the river. The clothes were afterward scattered in the thicket, as a decoy.

This came out, you will observe, *months after* the girl in magnetic sleep gave her answers.

Verily, this being of ours is a mysterious thing. (*Selected Letters* 181–82)

The historical record of the murder does not provide evidence to confirm this version of events.

Letter V

1. Letter V is a revised version of "Letters from New-York.—No. 5.," *NASS* 16 September 1841, vol. 2, no. 15: 58. In the newspaper column, Child opened with this paragraph:

I trust you do not keep the rapid sketches I send you, for materials to compose some future Gazeteer; if so, I must be more heedful how I guide my pen. "A Reader of the Standard" takes me to task for including the *sea* in the description of Weehawken; and asks if it were "an effort to reach the sublime." You know I never make an *effort* to attain either the sublime or the beautiful; well knowing it is the very process to destroy them both. In good truth, the inaccuracy arose from simple forgetfulness; as the broad and billowy Hudson presented itself to my recollection, I forgot, for the moment, that it was *not* the sea.

In Letter II of *Letters from New-York,* Child did correct these "inaccuracies" of the initial column. Except for this deletion and Ellis Gray Loring's suggested addition of the second to last paragraph which includes the verse from Pierpont, the revisions were minor.

2. In part because of England's lifting of their ban on the emigration of craftsmen in 1825, New York experienced an influx of skilled Scottish workers during the fourth and fifth decades of the nineteenth century. One of the best-known Scots of the period, James Gordon Bennett Sr. (1795–1872), began the *New York Herald,* a financially successful "penny paper," in 1835. The popularity of the *Herald,* the increasingly noticeable presence of Scottish immigrants, and the emergence of groups celebrating Highland heritage no doubt led to Child's journalistic interest in the events at Hoboken.

3. Torquil of the Oak is a huge, grizzled woodsman in Sir Walter Scott's *The Fair Maid of Perth, or St. Valentine's Day,* in *Chronicles of the Canongate: Second Series* (1828). The young Scotsman's physique and athletic skills reminded Child of characters presented in the other "age" and "clime" of classic literature. In Greek legend, Hector was the eldest son of the Trojan king Priam and queen Hecuba and the chief leader of the Trojan army. In Homer's *Iliad,* Achilles killed Hector to avenge the Trojan warrior's slaying of his friend Patroclus.

4. The Cairngorm Mountains are the highest mountain massif in the British Isles; St. Andrew is the patron saint of Scotland. According to Scottish lore, the thistle became the national emblem after a Danish invader yelled after stepping on one and thus provided a warning to the Scots at the battle of Luncarty.

Letter VI

1. In revising "Letters from New-York.—No. 6.," *NASS* 23 September 1841, vol. 2, no. 16: 63, Child accepted the guidance of Loring and made some substantive additions: two paragraphs describing events surrounding the anniversary meeting of the New York Hebrew Benevolent Society and, near the end, two briefer paragraphs noting Rev. Solomon Michael Alexander and Reformed Jews. It appears as if Loring composed these paragraphs himself. These additions are identified in the notes below.

2. As editor of the *National Anti-Slavery Standard,* Child used her newspaper—and her popular columns—to report on the unique sites, peoples, and events of the city. Since by 1850 nearly a third of the country's fifty thousand Jews lived in New York, it is not surprising that she would devote one of her longest letters to her visit to the synagogue on Crosby Street (which was built in 1834). The congregation, dating back to the twenty-three Sephardic refugees from Brazil who arrived in 1654 and were the first Jews in the city, had constructed its first synagogue on Mill Street in 1730. The first month of the Hebrew calendar usually falls in either September or October.

3. Child would later write a three volume comparative study of religions, *The Progress of Religious Ideas, through Successive Ages* (1855), a book known for its ecumenical spirit.

4. The Koran (Qur'an) is the sacred scripture of Islam, considered by Muslims to contain the word of Allah as revealed to the prophet Muhammad.

5. In antebellum America, phrenology—the study of the conformation of the skull as indicative of mental faculties and character traits—became popular. Veneration, ideality, and conscientiousness were just three faculties among the thirty-five to forty-three "organs" of the skull. According to phrenological taxonomy, veneration produced the sentiment of respect, ideality evoked the desire for what embodies beauty and perfection, and conscientiousness invoked the feeling of obligation or of right and wrong. This pseudo-science was popularized in New York by Orson Fowler (1809–87) and Lorenzo Fowler

(1811–1896), who set up shop in 1835 at 135 Nassau Street. Orson Fowler gave a reading of Child's head during a visit to his office. He later printed a copy of the examination in the *American Phrenological Journal* (September 1841). Supposedly, her identity was unknown to Fowler, who characterized her strongest moral trait as love of justice. His remarks struck Child as surprisingly accurate: "She would rather avoid opposition and difficulty, if possible; but fearlessly defends what she thinks true, regardless of consequences. . . . She is radical in her notions; does not go by old landmarks; is not satisfied with the world as it is, and has more than an ordinary degree of ambition to turn over a new leaf, and bring about moral, social, and intellectual reforms."

6. Within Jewish history, the Ark (or Ark of the Covenant) was the chest of acacia wood that occupied the most sacred place in the sanctuary. According to tradition, the Ark held the two tables of stone containing the Ten Commandments.

7. This phrase most likely arises from the fact that, in the early part of the nineteenth century, Shrewsbury, Massachusetts, was known as a major producer of clocks.

8. In both Judaism and Christianity, the Pentateuch refers to the first five books of the Old Testament. In all Jewish synagogues, the written Torah contains the Pentateuch which is preserved on handwritten parchment scrolls that lay inside the Ark of the Law. Reading from the Torah forms an important part of liturgical services.

9. As Child suggests, a significant number of Jews immigrated to the United States during this period, many arriving from Germany and other countries of central Europe. According to *The Encyclopedia of New York City*, by 1850, fifteen synagogues representing different groups existed in the city; by 1859, the number had grown to twenty-seven (620).

10. Child refers here to Shearith Israel, the oldest congregation in the country. The Mill Street Synagogue (1730) was built just south of Wall Street.

11. Aaron, the brother of Moses, is considered the traditional founder and head of the Jewish priesthood. Moses and Aaron led the Israelites in their exodus from Egypt. See *The Book of Exodus* in the *Old Testament.*

12. The Vistula, Danube, and Dnieper are rivers that take in a great deal of eastern Europe and the south and western region of the former republic of Russia. Specifically, the Vistula flows through Poland into the Gulf of Danzig, the Danube through southeast Europe into the Black Sea, and the Dnieper through the Ukraine to the Black Sea. Significantly, Child's depiction of the Benevolent Society meeting resonates with the broader cultural mythology of the nation as a multitude of peoples drawn together and transformed by democratic principles.

13. Titus Flavius Sabinus Vespasianus (c. 40–81), Roman emperor from 79–81.

14. First published by *Fraser's Magazine* from November 1833 to August 1834, *Sartor Resartus,* literally meaning the "tailor retailored," is Thomas Carlyle's best expression of Transcendentalist beliefs. Through the guise of Professor Diogenes Teufelsdroockh (literally "God-begotten Devil's-dung"), Carlyle (1795–1881) explores his philosophy of clothes. The book traces the way all external forms can be seen as the visible clothing of some greater transcendent truths.

15. The two preceding paragraphs on the Hebrew Benevolent Society and the "vending of 'old clo'" were added to *Letters.*

16. The opening sentence of the paragraph includes some noteworthy revisions. The *NASS* version read as follows: "Not all the proverbial worldliness of the Jews, their modern costume, or mechanical mode of perpetuating ancient forms, can altogether divest

them of a sacred and even romantic interest." These changes were apparently composed by Loring.

17. Beginning with a Frankfurt banking house, Mayer Amschel Rothschild (1744–1812) and his sons became international bankers. By the 1820s, they had established banks in London, Paris, Vienna, and Naples.

18. The controversy between European nations and the East likely refers to the Damascus blood libel affair. In February 1840, an Italian Capuchin friar and his Muslim servant disappeared. While evidence suggests that the friar had been involved with corrupt business dealings and might have been murdered as a result, the Capuchins spread the rumor that Jews had killed both men in order to obtain blood for Passover. In aligning himself with the accusers, the French consul fueled anti-Semitic feelings. In the ensuing weeks, a number of Jews were arrested and, when tortured, compelled to offer "confessions." Eventually, after efforts by various parties—including regional and European governments as well as Western European Jews—those individuals accused who had not died under torture were released in August 1840. The controversy involved a number of European figures, including Prince Metternich (1773–1859), the Austrian minister of foreign affairs who had been a supporter of Jewish rights in the German confederation and had ordered his diplomatic agents to reveal France's involvement in the Damascus affair. By the 1840s, however, Metternich had actually begun to lose the influence that had helped restore Austria as a leading European power, and he became a symbol of repression. He was forced to resign in the revolution of 1848.

At the end of the paragraph, Child also notes a more historically distant anti-Semitic overture. In 1817, Alexander I (1777–1825) of Russia founded the Society of Israelitic Christians in order to promote the conversion of Jews to Christianity. Few converted, and the Society disbanded in 1833.

19. Child refers to Michael Solomon Alexander (1799–1845). Alexander was raised an Orthodox Jew in Germany and moved to England where he eventually converted to Christianity in 1825. Sent by the London Society for the Promotion of Christianity among the Jews, Alexander spent some time as a missionary to Danzig in the late 1820s. During the Damascus blood libel affair of the early 1840s, he joined other Jewish converts to Christianity in signing a protest. In 1841, he was appointed the first Anglican bishop to Jerusalem.

20. Unlike Orthodox Judaism—which asserts that the laws of the Torah and Talmud (a collection of legal, ritual, and ethical writings, as well as Jewish history and folklore) were direct revelations from God—Reformed Jews, whose beginnings can be traced to the early 1800s, consider such laws as created by humans, not God.

21. This paragraph on Reformed Jews and the preceding one on Rev. Solomon Michael Alexander were added to the *Letters* version of the essay.

Letter VII

1. Letter VII includes relatively few changes from "Letters from New-York.—No. 7.," *NASS* 30 September 1841, vol. 2, no. 17: 66–67. The only change of relative interest occurred in the concluding paragraph and is noted below.

2. During the Revolutionary War, Brooklyn was the site of the Battle of Long Island

(August 1776), the first major battle of the war. After defeating the Continental Army, the British controlled the area for the next seven years, retaining thousands of prisoners in ships in Wallabout Bay. According to historical accounts, more than eleven thousand soldiers died because of the horrible conditions of the prison ships.

3. Born in England, John Summerfield (1798–1825) was a Methodist clergyman whose eloquent preaching in Ireland, England, and the United States gained him immense audiences. Shortly before his death, he helped found the American Tract Society.

4. First settled by the Dutch around 1640, Gowanus in northwestern Brooklyn grew significantly after the construction of the Gowanus Canal in the 1840s.

5. During the antebellum period, the picturesque and beautifully situated "rural" or "garden" cemeteries, such as Greenwood (Brooklyn) and Mount Auburn (Boston), represented attitudes toward death and burial that contrasted sharply with the melancholy and grimness of previous periods. It was not uncommon for residents to spend an afternoon walking or riding in Greenwood or Mount Auburn.

6. The end of this sentence marks the sole substantive revision of the letter. In the newspaper version, Child had written "between the living and the dead." Apparently, Loring suggested this current version.

Letter VIII

1. Letter VIII is a revision of "Letters from New-York.—No. 8.," *NASS* 7 October 1841, vol. 2, no. 18: 71. Except for the deletion of a brief paragraph on the steamboat *Rainbow* and the last line of the original (both noted below), the changes were minor and almost entirely spelling and punctuation alterations.

2. After a brief depression in the industry around the time of the War of 1812 (caused by the British blockade), shipbuilding and repair grew dramatically, and, by the end of the Civil War, more than thirty shipyards extended along the East River. The growth in New York's shipbuilding trade was a natural outcome of their thriving port. From 1830 (until 1960), the city was the busiest port in the world.

3. Child intends her audience to read "'Change" as a reference both to economic exchange on Wall Street and to the dramatic "changes" altering the social, economic, and political structures of antebellum America.

4. First developed by Chesapeake Bay shipbuilders in the 1700s, the Baltimore clipper was a small sailing ship whose speed led to its use in the clandestine slave trade of the nineteenth century. While the domestic slave trade dramatically increased in the first half of the century, the importation of slaves from Africa had been made illegal beginning in 1807. As Child indicates, the *Catharine* had evidently been one of the numerous clippers involved in importing slaves.

In the newspaper version of the letter, the following paragraph had been included after the one on the *Catharine:*

> In excursions to Hoboken, my attention has often been attracted by an extremely pretty little steamboat, called the Rainbow; which is indeed fleet enough to be named for Iris, the winged messenger of the gods. It was built by Stevens, the famous engineer, and is expected to move at the rate of thirty miles an hour.

Loring had crossed out this paragraph in his copy of the letter, indicating that he had suggested this omission.

5. George Mifflin Dallas (1792–1864) was appointed the minister to Russia in 1837 by Pres. Martin Van Buren, a position that he occupied for just two years. He later served as vice president of the United States during the James Polk administration (1845–49).

6. Cronstadt, or Kronstadt, a city on an island in the Gulf of Finland, west of St. Petersburg.

7. Emperor Nicholas I (1796–1855), czar of Russia from 1825–55.

8. Frances Trollope (1780–1863) wrote the first of her forty books after her fiftieth birthday. *Domestic Manners of the Americans* (1832) was the author's biting impressions of American life arising from her travels in the States during the early 1830s.

9. In 1812, the Russian army, retreating from the advance of Napoleon's forces, set fire to parts of Moscow.

10. Louis Phillippe (1773–1850), king of France (1830–48).

11. Madame de Mirbel (1796–1849), French miniaturist.

12. The letter had originally ended with "God strengthen us all to labor for him!" Loring had struck out the line in his copyediting of the manuscript.

Letter IX

1. Letter IX is a version of "Letters from New-York.—No. 9.," *NASS* 14 October 1841, vol. 2, no. 19: 75. The significant revisions are noted below, the most substantive being the omission of two paragraphs describing an exchange with Grant Thorburn. In making these changes, Child accepts Loring's suggestions for the letter.

2. Grant Thorburn (1773–1863) arrived in the city in 1794 and became well known for his gardening and landscaping (having published *The Gentleman and Gardener's Kalendar for the Middle States of North America* in 1812). Hell Gate is a narrow strait between Astoria and Ward's Island (just east of the Upper East Side and south of the Bronx) that connects the East River to Long Island Sound. Still a difficult passage to navigate, the name comes from the Dutch Hellegat, or "hell channel."

As Child later confirms, Ravenswood—the name given the shore of Long Island City in Queens along the East River—comes from Sir Walter Scott's *The Bride of Lammermoor* (1819). During the nineteenth century, the historical novels of Scott (1771–1832) were widely read. In the preface to her first novel *Hobomok,* Child herself—through the persona of the author's friend—utters a common assessment: "Scott wanders over every land with the same proud, elastic tread—free as the mountain breeze, and majestic as the bird that bathes in the sunbeams. He must always stand alone—a high and solitary shrine, before which minds of humbler mould are compelled to bow down and worship."

3. Washington Irving (1783–1859), one of the first American authors of the nineteenth century to gain an international reputation as a writer. He is most famous for *The Sketch Book of Geoffrey Crayon, Gent.* (1820), a collection of sketches and tales that includes "Rip Van Winkle" and "The Legend of Sleepy Hollow."

4. In the *NASS* letter, Child had included the following after the reference to Pluto: "an agency peculiarly desirable to all who would enter New-York."

5. The dahlias are named for historical and literary figures: Lord Wellington (1769–1852), or Arthur Wellesley, First Duke of Wellington; Kate Nickleby, sister of Nicholas Nickleby in Charles Dickens's novel *Nicholas Nickleby* (1839); Grace Darling (1815–1842),

a celebrated British heroine who, in 1838, had assisted her father in rescuing individuals shipwrecked near her home.

6. John Galt (1779–1839), a Scottish novelist, whose three-volume *Lawrie Todd or The Settlers in the Woods* was based upon Grant Thorburn's memoirs and published in 1830.

7. St. Leonard's Crags, Jeannie Dean's cottage, and the Porteous mob allude to people, places, and events in Scottish history that Sir Walter Scott immortalized in *The Heart of Mid-Lothian* (1818). Dandie Dinmont is a character in Scott's *Guy Mannering* (1815). Child had given more life to Grant Thorburn in the original letter, including the following two paragraphs after this allusion to Dandie Dinmont:

> From some remarks in the old gentleman's autobiography, I misdoubted that he might be gifted in polemical skill. I forbore to waken his Presbyterian zeal, as you may well suppose; for you know that a blister of Spanish flies is at any time more agreeable to me, than a dose of doctrine, or a whiff of theological controversy, of any sort. But I was pleased to hear him talk of Dr. Mason, "that vehement dresser of the Lord's vineyard, in Cedar street," New-York; under whose poweful preaching, Rebecca, the sainted love of his early youth, was first gathered into the fold of Christ. On this subject, he told a "merry toy," as Jeremy Taylor would call it. It was quite characteristic; for Grant Thorburn constantly reminds one of what Baillie Waft said to Lawrie; "Ye will hae your jokes, come what may. Ye're a funny man—oh, but ye're very funny, Mr. Todd."
>
> "The minister and I had been indulging in some jocularity together," said he; "and as I came across him with a home-thrust, he looked down upon me, and said, in his pleasant way, 'Be done, you little mortal! if you don't, I'll take you up and put you in my pocket.' 'An if ye do,' said I, 'ye'll hae mair sound sense in your pocket, than ever ye had in your big head.'"

Again, evidence from Loring's working copy of the letter indicates that he suggested this omission.

8. As defined in the *Oxford English Dictionary,* "pawkrie" in this context appears to mean trickery or cunning.

9. Thomas Moore (1779–1852), Irish poet, known especially for his romance *Lalla Rookh* (1817).

10. As Child had noted in the deleted portion of the original letter, Rebecca was "the sainted love of [Grant Thorburn's] early youth." See note 7 above.

11. Mrs. Leo Hunter, a character in Charles Dickens's *Pickwick Papers* (1836) known, as the name implies, for her desire to make the acquaintance of all the "lions" (or famous people) of the day.

12. During the time of Child's writing, the latest (eighth) Duke of Devonshire was Spencer Compton Cavendish (1833–1908). More generally, of course, the reference contrasts the rich gallery of Child's imagination with the famed wealth of English dukes.

13. Currently known as Roosevelt Island, located in the East River off the shore of the Upper East Side in Manhattan, Blackwell's Island became the site of a "Lunatic Asylum" in 1839. It became known as the location for numerous city institutions, including a prison completed just three years earlier. See also Child's "Letters from New-York.—No. 44." in the Appendix for a further description of Blackwell's Island.

14. For information on phrenology, see Letter VI, note 5.

15. In the early part of the century, almshouses in New York accommodated prostitutes, paupers, and homeless immigrants. Long Island Farms, which started taking "foundlings and orphans" in 1832, was one of the first homes strictly designated to house children.

Letter X

1. Letter X is a revision of "Letters from New-York.—No. 10.," *NASS* 21 October 1841, vol. 2, no. 20:183. Except for a handful of spelling and punctuation changes, the letter is as it appeared in the *Standard*.

2. According to Mormon tradition, the founder of the Mormon faith, Joseph Smith, was directed to a set of golden records buried in a hill near his parents' farm. Smith translated the records and published them as the Book of Mormon—also known as the Golden Book—in 1830.

3. Flibbertigibbet is the name of a fiend mentioned in *King Lear;* it is also a name given to Dickon Sludge in Sir Walter Scott's *Kenilworth* (1821). The term has come generally to mean a gossiper or chatterer or is used to describe one who is giddy or frivolous.

4. Sawney is another word to designate a Scotsman.

5. This reference alludes to the differing reputations of William Wordsworth (1770–1850), British writer whose poetry and theories profoundly shaped the romantic movement in Europe and the United States, and Molière, pseudonym for Jean Baptiste Poquelin (1622–1673), a French dramatist known especially for his biting satires. Wordsworth was often praised for his keen eye for nature. Through his satires of French society, Molière frequently offended his audience by allowing his characters to "mouth" sentiments considered impious and vulgar.

6. Claude Lorrain (1600–1682), a French painter.

7. Sixteenth-century explorers believed that El Dorado, a city of immense riches, existed somewhere in the Americas. In the nineteenth century, the term came to signify the hope of finding the mythic (and metaphoric) "city of gold" in the uncharted territory of the West.

Letter XI

1. Letter XI is a version of "Letters from New-York.—No. 13.," *NASS* 9 December 1841, vol. 2, no. 27: 107. Child had originally opened the letter with the following paragraph:
> In my last, I promised to give you an account of another colored heroine. You will probably think my description is colored, and highly, too; knowing as you do, how largely nature has endowed me with imagination. All I can say in answer to this charge is, Go and hear Julia Pell for yourself; and you will then acknowledge that language has no power to describe her as she is.

Child accepts Ellis Gray Loring's suggestion to omit this opening. Other important changes are cited in the ensuing notes.

As in part implied by the earlier introduction, this letter describing the "eloquent coloured preacher" Julia Pell was originally part of a sequence of letters narrating the lives of "remarkable" Africans and African Americans: no. 12 (2 December 1841), focusing on Cinquez and the other Africans who had taken over the slave ship *Amistad* in 1839; this letter, no. 13, relating the preaching of Julia Pell; and no. 14 (16 December 1841), noting the "religious experience of a poor, uneducated woman, once a slave." The omitted letters (nos. 12 and 14) are included in the Appendix.

2. Child was witness to a rich segment of African American culture in New York. Within this culture, the Methodist church played a vital role. As early as 1796, racial tensions led Peter Williams, James Varick, Christopher Rush, and other black members of Wesley Chapel (which came to be known as the John Street Methodist Church in the early nineteenth century) to conduct separate services. The church constructed its own building in 1800 and became known as Zion Church, considered to be the first African American congregation in New York. Led by William Stillwell, they eventually formed the African Methodist Episcopal Zion Church in 1821 after failing to achieve separate status within the white church. From the 1820s through the 1840s, numerous African American churches affiliated with this original congregation were formed.

While New York was more active than many northern cities in seeking to end slavery, ultimately granting all slaves freedom as of 4 July 1827, its history of tensions connected to the continually changing racial and ethnic mix formed the necessity for such supportive African American institutions. While Africans or those of African heritage (almost entirely enslaved) accounted for 20 percent of New York's eleven thousand people in 1741, for instance, they formed just under 5¼ percent of the total population in 1840 — and, because of the immigration increase in the decade of Child's stay in the city, only 2.68 percent of more than five hundred thousand by 1850. (According to the 1860 census, 47 percent of the population of New York was foreign born.) These statistics signal an urban area undergoing dramatic transformations. Not surprisingly, violence directed against Blacks — as well as ongoing discriminatory practices — were frequent. As recently as 1834, antiabolitionist mobs assaulted a black minister, leading to two days of attacks directed at individual African Americans and black and white abolitionist churches.

3. In the newspaper column, Child had noted that Julia Pell was "of Philadelphia, lately married to a Mr. White, but seldom called her new name." Records of Ellis Gray Loring's copyediting marks reveal his hand in this revision.

4. Throughout her stay in New York, Lydia Maria Child lived at the home of Isaac T. Hopper (1771–1852). Hopper was a Quaker reformer disowned by the Society of Friends for his abolitionist views.

5. George Whitfield (1714–1770), a British Methodist preacher.

6. Hannah More (1745–1833), an esteemed member of the Blue Stocking Circle in England, established her literary success with the tragedy *Percy,* produced by David Garrick in 1777. Not long after this play, she devoted her writing to various treatises and tracts that urged conservative social practices and Christian piety. No doubt these writings and ensuing help from politicians and clergy who supported her admonishments against growing democratic sentiments led to Child's suggestion that she sacrificed her own views to accommodate those of church and state.

7. David Garrick (1717–1779) was one of the most renowned actors of the British stage. Various sources detailing Garrick's career do not mention any play entitled "Mad Tom." While the phrasing of the reference seems to suggest a play, not a character, one wonders whether Child does not have in mind Poor Tom — the disguised figure of Lear's loyal Earl — in Shakespeare's tragedy *King Lear.*

8. The preceding sentence, beginning with "Go search among the angels . . . ," was added to the *Standard* version of the letter.

9. Child refers to *Village Hymns for Social Worship* (1828), edited by Asahel Nettleton (1783–1844), a Congregational evangelist. This paragraph, including the verse, represents Loring's addition to the original version of the letter.

10. Sarah Siddons (1755–1831), considered one of the greatest English tragic actresses.

11. Throughout *Letters from New-York*, Child describes the African or "Ethiopian" race as embodying the more intuitive powers linked to the heart and, as witnessed in the emotional preaching of Julia Pell, leading listeners to an understanding of central truths through engagement of the affections. Interestingly, at the end of Letter XXXIII, she writes that, like Ireland, "Africa furnishes another class, in whom the heart ever takes guidance of the head; and all over the world the way is opening for them among nations." For the period, this connecting of the Irish and African—two groups whose disenfranchised social and economic status within New York eventually led to some of the city's worst interracial violence—marks a remarkable effort to imagine new and constructive affinities. More-over, in her letter describing a visit to Barnum's American Museum (see Letter XXXVI), Child suggests that environmental factors shaped racial features, noting that the races are undoubtedly different, "spiritually as well as physically." Explaining physical differences, she argues: "The facial angle and shape of the head, is various in races and nations; but these are the *effects* of spiritual influences, long operating on character, and in their turn becoming *causes;* thus intertwining, as Past and Future ever do." Like the beliefs of many fellow abolitionists, such views still diminished the status of African Americans and of non-Western cultures, setting up "whiteness" and European intellectual history as supe-rior or as the norm with which to judge all ideas and values.

As demonstrated in her abolitionist work *An Appeal in Favor of That Class of Americans Called Africans* (1833), Child's conception of that "class of Americans called Africans" and her characterization of their moral and intellectual strengths were more complex. Still, seeing African Americans as guided by the affections rather than the intellect, as more do-mestic in character and tone, and, thus, as offering America a voice that could counteract the materialist tendencies of the culture, she betrays the racialist thinking shaped by her own individual needs, a way of thinking that, while more inclusive than that of her con-temporaries, could and did limit the real and imagined roles of blacks.

For additional reflections on the religious sentiment of the African race, see Letter No. 12 in the Appendix.

12. In the *NASS* version of the letter, Child had been even more glowing in her praise of Matthews, writing that he is "a most excellent, and religious-minded man. . . ."

13. Adam Clarke (c. 1760–1832), writer and Methodist minister.

14. In the earlier version of the letter, Child had noted that the comments had been made at an abolitionist meeting. ("The first comparison I heard most wittily replied to, in an anti-slavery meeting, by a colored woman who had once been a slave.") The current version of the letter indicates that she had accepted Loring's omission of the phrase "in an anti-slavery meeting." More than likely, she has Sojourner Truth in mind here. On a docu-ment contained in a "Scrap Book" dated 1876 and housed at Cornell University's library, Child writes of an abolitionist meeting where an Orthodox minister, irritated by criticisms of the clergy, said, "I have heard much of the eloquence of your *free* meetings; but I never desire again to enter one of these meetings where women, and jackasses are allowed to speak." According to Child's record of the event, Sojourner Truth rose and replied: "The

gentleman is a clergyman, and I presume he is acquainted with Scripture, but he seems to forget that the *Ass* saw the angel, and Balaam *didn't.*"

The paragraph below had originally followed this anecdote and was deleted at the suggestion of Loring:

Julia told me that she had had, "a very troubled dispensation" with regard to this prejudice [against women's preaching]. Father Matthews was the only one that would allow her to enter his pulpit; though there are in this city four Methodist churches for colored people. This change in Methodist discipline, it seems, was first urged by a colored minister, who was a member of the former committee of the American Anti-Slavery Society. He was probably affected by Presbyterian influence, without being conscious of it. How oddly are truths, and their antagonist falsehoods, linked together in the circumstances of this strange world.

The "colored" minister may have been Theodore Sedgwick Wright. For information on Wright, see Appendix, "Letters from New-York.—No. 12.," note 10.

Letter XII

1. Letter XII represents a slight revision of "Letters from New-York.—No. 15.," *NASS* 6 January 1842, vol. 2, no. 31: 123. In its republication, the letter was dated January 1, 1842. The one revision of importance, which appears in the conclusion, is noted below. Starting with this letter, Ellis Gray Loring's copies of the *Standard* epistles contain no copyediting suggestions.

2. In her reflections on the past and future, Child asserts that the reader (and America itself) represents the culmination of changes initiated by central figures in the religious, philosophical, and political history of the West. According to the Old Testament, Moses was saved from death by the daughter of the Pharaoh (Exodus 2.1–10). In the story of Christ's birth, angels visited Judean shepherds in their fields to direct them to the newborn savior (Luke 2.8–20). One of the greatest rulers of the Middle Ages, William the Norman (c. 1028–1087), or William the Conqueror, was king of England from 1066 to 1087. The writings of Martin Luther (1483–1546) helped initiate the Reformation. The actions of Bishop Laud (1573–1645), English prelate and Archbishop of Canterbury from 1633 to 1645, led to the immigration of Puritans to New England. William Penn (1644–1718) was the founder of Pennsylvania who shaped the frame of government to secure the principle of religious tolerance during the proprietorship of the Duke of York (1633–1701). The Duke of York, whose title provided New York with its name, would rule England as James II from 1685 to 1688.

3. Caryatids are draped female figures that, in the place of a column or pilaster, support upper sections of walls. Herculaneum is an ancient Roman city buried during the eruption of Mt. Vesuvius in 79 A.D.

4. Johann Wolfgang von Goethe (1749–1832), a writer whose novels, poems, and plays exemplified German romanticism. In nineteenth-century America, Goethe was especially known for *The Sorrows of Young Werther* (1774), *Wilhelm Meister's Apprenticeship* (1795–96), which was translated into English by Carlyle in 1824, and *Faust* (First Part, 1808; Second Part, 1832).

5. An Irish voice.

6. Madame Roland (1754–1793), or Marie Jeanne Roland de la Platiere, was guillotined during the French Revolution. Child wrote of Roland in *The Biographies of Madame de Staël, and Madame Roland,* vol. 1 of *Ladies' Family Library* (1832).

7. In this version of the letter, Child added all but the closing sentence of the final paragraph. The *Standard* letter concluded in the following manner: "But I will not moralize. Let us all have virtue, and then there will be no further need to talk of it, as the German wisely said. Only this one scrap of morals I leave you, with my heart's blessing. May you treat every human being as you would treat him, and speak of every one as you would speak, if sure that death would part you before next New-Year's Day." It is unclear who "the German" might be here.

Letter XIII

1. Letter XIII is a revision of "Letters from New-York.—No. 16.," *NASS* 20 January 1842, vol. 2, no. 33: 130–31. Again, as in a number of other letters, the revisions were minor. The one noteworthy change is Child's attribution of closing reflections on friendship to Emerson. See note below.

2. Louis-Jacques-Mandé Daguerre (1787–1851), along with Joseph Nicéphore Niepce, produced the first photograph through the use of what became known as the "daguerreotype" machine. Unlike later technology that enabled the production of an image on specially treated paper, the daguerreotype produced an image on a silver plate. The invention was announced in 1839.

3. Plynlimon is the gritstone plateau of central Wales known for its mist and boggy surface.

4. An allusion to Queen Victoria's son, Albert Edward, born 9 November 1841, just over two months before this letter. By pairing the "eternal" possibilities of a child of Five Points with those of the son of Victoria, whose royal lineage offered the promise of meeting any material want, Child invites readers to emphasize spiritual not worldly realities.

5. In the original letter, Child had not included "says Emerson."

6. The *Standard* letter did not put these reflections in quotation marks.

Letter XIV

1. Letter XIV is a version of "Letters from New-York.—No. 17.," *NASS* 17 February 1842, vol. 2, no. 37: 147. The only substantive change is the revision of the opening paragraph. The following served as the original introduction to the letter:

Weeks have passed since I wrote you; not from want of inclination, but because the wrangling at Washington leaves no room for gentle thoughts and poetic fancies. I know not whether you long as earnestly as I do to have Congress stop its discord, and the birds begin their harmony. I was always impatient for the spring-time, but never so much as now; compelled as I am to watch the vile game of venality and passion, which men dignify with the name of government. Patience yet a few months longer, and Congress will *disband;* I do not think it will ever *rise,* until slavery is abolished; unless, indeed a portion of them "rise," in the *southern* sense of the phrase, to cut up facts with bowie-knives, and exterminate truth with rifle-balls.

2. The sight and sound of newsboys would have been commonplace by the early 1840s.

As a result of the growth of the penny press in the previous decade, children were needed to distribute an ever-increasing number of newspapers. Often, these children were orphans or sons of immigrants. To draw the interest of customers and manage the harsh realities of the streets, they naturally had to become loud and tough. The working conditions of the newsboys inevitably led reformers, including the Children's Aid Society in 1854, to open a number of Newsboy Lodging Houses.

Letter XV

1. Letter XV is a minor revision of "Letters from New-York.—No. 19.," *NASS* 17 March 1842, vol. 2, no. 41: 163. The most significant change—additional examples of Clarke's "fanciful metaphors"—is noted below.

2. Macdonald Clarke (1798–1842), known as the "Mad Poet," became a well-known figure in New York. According to accounts of his life, Clarke experienced an unhappy childhood; the death of his mother when he was twelve left him alone and without financial resources. A short-lived marriage to actress Mary Brundage added to his tragic history and apparently contributed to his deteriorating mental health. Striking in physical appearance, he made a lasting impression through his volatile temperament and impatience with social injustice. Clarke grew increasingly insane and died on 5 March 1842 in the asylum on Blackwell's Island.

3. Written by Catharine Maria Sedgwick (1789–1867), a popular novelist and short fiction writer, *Hope Leslie* (1827) was one of the first novels, along with Child's *Hobomok* (1824) and James Fenimore Cooper's *The Pioneers* (1823) and *The Last of the Mohicans* (1826), to answer the call for an American literature by making use of the nation's landscape and history.

4. Charles Calistus Burleigh (1810–1880), an abolitionist known for editing the antislavery newspaper *The Unionist* and for being one of the early advocates of women's rights.

5. Mary Anne Brundage first appeared on stage at the Park Theater in April 1815. She married Clarke on 16 July 1820. That Brundage appeared at the Park suggests her status as a first-rate actress. The Park was built in 1798 and soon became one of the city's leading theaters. First producing farces, musical plays, and melodramas, the theater began staging operas in the 1820s. The musician Child came to revere and befriend, Norwegian violinist Ole Bull, also debuted at Park Theater in 1843.

Nineteenth-century readers would have understood the significance of Brundage's role as Ophelia. In Shakespeare's *Hamlet,* Ophelia loses her sanity under the duress of Hamlet's antics. As Elaine Showalter notes in *The Female Malady: Women, Madness, and English Culture, 1830–1980* (1985), "[t]he Romantics . . . were captivated by the spectacle of Ophelia's sexuality and emotionality" (11). The mad Ophelia became a popular image in the period's lithographs.

6. In architecture and decorative art, grotesques are figures of mixed animal, human, and plant forms; arabesque is an ornamental style that most often employs flowers, foliage, and fruit and figural outlines to create an intricate pattern of interwoven lines.

7. In the *Standard* version of the letter, this line formed the paragraph's original conclusion. The examples of Clarke's fanciful metaphors currently ending the section were added to the first edition.

8. Mirabeau Buonaparte Lamar (1798–1859) held the position of president of Texas

from 1838 to 1841. It is somewhat surprising that Child would quote from Lamar's poem. She had vehemently opposed the Texas War, seeing it as another manifestation of efforts to expand slavery. By the early 1840s, William Page (1811–1885) had begun to establish his reputation as an artist, a reputation that would eventually lead to his selection as president of the National Academy from 1871 to 1873. Page was one of the many young artists and musicians that Child befriended and supported during their time in New York. In a letter to her friend Frances Shaw dated 12 October 1841, she writes that she had "been to see Page's poor little children, and shall do so often if he remains in New York this winter. I have likewise given him a ticket of admittance to my own private room, throughout the season" (*SL* 150).

9. In the nineteenth century, "Zip Coon" stands as one of the many racist characterizations of African Americans. In the era's sketches, fiction, and, most notably, in the performances of white actors dressed in "black face," the foolish and "comic" Zip Coon stood as an emblem of racial inferiority.

10. According to the Genesis story (Genesis 4.21), Jubal is a descendant of Cain and considered the father of those who play the harp and organ.

11. The vagueness of the reference prevents any certain idea as to the identity of the "philosopher of the East."

12. As related in Genesis 11.1–9, the Babylonians sought to gain a worldly reputation by building a tower that reached to the heavens. According to the Genesis story, however, the Tower of Babel was never completed because God disrupted the work by confusing the language of the builders.

13. It is possible that Child alludes to Walt Whitman (known as Walter Whitman during his newspaper days of the 1840s) who began editing the *New York Aurora* (1842–44) some time in 1842.

14. Fitz-Greene Halleck (1790–1867), a leading member of the Knickerbocker Group of New York and a well-known poet of the period.

Letter XVI

1. Dated August 7, 1842, Letter XVI actually represents a combination and revision of two essays written earlier in the year: "Letters from New-York.—No. 20.," *NASS* 7 April 1842, vol. 2, no. 44: 175, and "Letters from New-York.—No. 23.," *NASS* 5 May 1842, vol. 2, no. 48: 190–91. Both letters—in whole (no. 20) or in part (no. 23)—had offered reflections upon a fire in Child's neighborhood. In no. 23, Child had begun by responding to a reader's being "shocked" by her seeming greater sympathy for the loss of Jane Plato's garden than for the destruction of houses. The part of no. 23 not included in this letter— the description of the experiences of a "Non-Resisting Colony" out West—became Letter XXII in *Letters*. Significant revisions within the specific letters are noted below.

2. Shadrach, Meshach, and Abednego were three Hebrew youths who came forth unharmed from the fiery furnace into which they were thrown by Nebuchadnezzar (Daniel 3).

3. The phrase "one hundred houses were burned, and not less than two thousand persons deprived of shelter for the night" had been italicized in the 7 April 1842 letter. In eliminating the italics, Child enacts a common type of revision. With such minor changes, she creates a less sensational tone.

4. The excerpt from the 5 May 1842 *Standard* letter begins with this paragraph and runs through the paragraph beginning with the sentence, "And all the highest *truths*, as well as the genuine good, are universal." This beginning of this excerpt represents a revision of the earlier text. In "Letters from New-York.—No. 23.," Child had opened with the following response: "You tell me some minds were shocked that, in my letter describing the great fire, I seemed to sympathize more with Jane Plato for the destruction of her little garden-patch, than I did with others for the loss of houses and furniture. The fact is, the idea in my own mind was so familiar to me, that I uttered it too briefly, and without explanation. I simply meant that *money* does not in any case, constitute *wealth*."

5. This line had originally read: "I have said this much, not for the paltry purpose of vindicating myself, but to prove that money is not wealth, and that *God's* gifts are equal."

6. While the event is termed a "great fire" by Child, it should not be mistaken for the "Great Fire of 1835" to which she alludes in Letter IV.

7. John Martin (1789–1854), an English historical and landscape painter.

8. In the 7 April 1842 *Standard* letter, these remarks followed this sentence: "In Boston, the two lower stories would certainly have been saved. Common rumor, says no effort was made to extinguish it, because its owner is 'a hard man, who grinds the face of his poor tenants.' I trust, for the credit of the firemen, that this is not true; for be the landlord what he may, there would be deep wickedness in such frightful retaliation. When I began to watch it, the fire had apparently not descended below the third story; but I did not perceive a single hose directed toward it."

9. Abolitionists saw ex-president John Quincy Adams (1767–1848) and Joshua Reed Giddings (1795–1864) as champions of the cause of freedom. While representing Massachusetts in Congress, Adams vehemently attacked the "gag-rule" of 1836, a rule that prevented the discussion of slavery and the acting upon any resolution submitted in relation to it. Like Adams, Giddings stood against the "gag-rule" and, in February 1841, argued that the war with Native Americans in Florida was waged solely in the interest of slavery, noting that the South sought to enslave the Maroons of the state who were affiliated with the Seminoles and destroy the asylum for escaped slaves. In this and subsequent editions, Child drew attention to their role in the antislavery cause by adding the phrase "against Southern aggression."

10. This concluding paragraph replaces two lengthy paragraphs in the original. In closing with a description of her and her neighbors' responses to the devastation of the fire, the 7 April 1842 letter ended much differently than the current one. The version of the *Standard* letter is included at length below:

You must not imagine that I stood amidst the uproar amusing myself with sparkling wreaths and fiery fountains. You would think far otherwise, if you had met me, pushing through the crowd, with bags, baskets, and heavy bundles; my bonnet knocked into a cocked hat, and my hair drenched by the engines. I never before had an opportunity of testing my presence of mind in such an emergency; and I was pleased to find that it did not fail me. When, after three or four successive efforts, the progress of the flames made it absolutely impossible to return to the house, I paused, to think over what I had saved. All the Dagons of my *heart* had been remembered, even to Anna's profile; the items necessary for the next week's paper were not forgotten; and I could very seriously regret nothing I had left behind, except two books of extracts from volumes I never expect to own. Jean Paul [Richter], and Schiller, and

Herder, how could I lose the echo of their friendly earnest tones, that ever spake to me like a voice from the gods?

But I did not lose them; for by the blessing of heaven on the energy and presence of mind of those who came to our help, our walls stand unscathed, and nothing was destroyed in the tumult. All around us comes a voice of wailing from the houseless and the impoverished. One poor woman, who lived in a little room in the second story, was ignorant of her danger until the flames burst through the wall. In the confusion of the moment, half suffocated by the smoke, she either left or lost three little children; and it is supposed they perished in the flames. The wind was so strong, that the fire came like a whirlwind, and left small chance to save household goods. A large proportion of those who suffered by it were poor people; three or four families living in one house. The firemen worked like giants; but to increase the calamity, their attention was distracted by two other fires raging frightfully in other parts of the city. The loss by the one near us is estimated at about $120,000. Measures are being taken for the relief of the poor sufferers, and I trust they will be prompt and effectual. I. W. Hardenbrook, a respected citizen, aged about 80, was so much excited by the sight of his blazing property, that he fell down and died of apoplexy.

Anna refers to Anna Loring, the daughter of Ellis Gray Loring. See Letter I, note 2.

Letter XVII

1. Letter XVII is a revision of "Letters from New-York.—No. 21.," *NASS* 14 April 1842, vol. 2, no. 45: 179. Substantive changes are noted below.

2. No doubt Child has in mind *The Correspondence and Diary of Philip Doddridge. D.D., Illustrative of Many of His Contemporaries* . . . (1829–31). In the 14 April 1842 *Standard* letter, Child introduced Doddridge's story differently: "The pleasant, buoyant sensation, recalled to my mind Doddridge's dream, which made so strong an impression when I told it, that you have asked me to put it down in writing. I will endeavor to do so. It is many years since I read it, in Doddridge's Life and Correspondence; and I will not vouch for it, that my copy is a perfect likeness of the original." More than likely, the "you" here is Ellis Gray Loring.

3. The verse and paragraph closing this letter was not a part of the *Standard* column.

Letter XVIII

1. Letter XVIII combines two *Standard* letters: "Letters from New-York.—No. 25.," *NASS* 26 May 1842, vol. 2, no. 51: 203 and "Letters from New-York.—No. 29.," *NASS* 23 June 1842, vol. 3, no. 3: 11. Changes of note are identified below.

2. In the first two decades of her writing career, Child wrote a number of stories integrating Native American history and myth. Like many of her contemporaries, she often plotted tales that imagined the "solitary Indian" either living in a majestic wilderness before European settlement or not long after initial intrusions by colonists. See Letter IV, note 6.

3. Henry Hudson (d. 1611), English navigator and explorer.

4. While some have traced the name "Manhattan" to the Munsee word "manahacta-

nienk" ("place of general inebriation"), others suggest that the term comes from "mana-hatouh" ("place where timber is procured for bows and arrows") or "menatay" ("island").

5. Evidently, "swine" as well as residents shared the space of Pearl Street. During the early 1840s, pigs were not an uncommon sight on some New York City streets—a fact to which Child alludes in her opening letter of the volume.

6. Petrus (or Peter) Stuyvesant actually lived from 1592 to 1672. St. Mark's Church in the Bowery still stands at East 10th Street and 2nd Avenue in the East Village.

7. Bowling Green was a public park established in 1733; George II (1683–1760) was King of England from 1727 to 1760.

8. Child omits one sentence from the original. In this paragraph, the one that con-cluded the 26 May 1842 letter, she had closed with the following: "I have no more leisure now; but at some future time, perhaps you and I will look through parting clouds for an-other peep at the olden time." The next paragraph begins the 23 June 1842 letter. The orig-inal introduction—"I promised again to take a glimpse of the *antiquities* of New York; but, alas, in this new country the very word is calculated to arouse ridiculous associa-tions"—has been revised slightly in this version.

9. Though not necessarily confining their remarks to New York, writers of the pe-riod—including such well-known figures as James Fenimore Cooper and Nathaniel Hawthorne—lamented the fact of the country's youth. The sparseness of antiquities and shared myths, then, was seen as a disadvantage to writers seeking a shared past and com-mon traditions in attempts to forge a national literature.

10. George Combe (1788–1858), a Scottish phrenologist whose works included *The Constitution of Man* (1828) and *Moral Philosophy* (1840). From 1838 to 1840, Combe lec-tured on phrenology and the treatment of criminals in the United States, later publishing *Notes on the United States of North America* (1842).

11. Under the pen name Poor Richard, Benjamin Franklin created the persona of an un-schooled, sometimes dull countryman who had a propensity for speaking in aphorisms. As Child suggests, Franklin's homespun wisdom contained in his widely popular *Poor Richard's Almanac* (which he edited from 1732 to 1757) contrasts sharply with the elevated rhetoric of learned discourse. No wonder Franklin's humor is considered typically "Ameri-can" and seen as a precursor to the writings of ensuing figures, such as Davy Crockett and Will Rogers.

12. The Parthenon is a celebrated Doric temple of Athena built on the acropolis at Athens in the 5th century B.C. Alhambra is the palace of the Moorish kings at Granada, Spain. Near Melrose, a small burgh in Scotland, are the ruins of a monastery, dating back to the Middle Ages. Sir Walter Scott supervised the repair of the ruins in 1822.

Letter XIX

1. Letter XIX is a revision of "Letters from New-York.—No.26.," *NASS* 2 June 1842, vol. 2, no. 52: 207. See note below for the one substantive revision.

2. From the 1830s into the 1840s, "animal magnetism" captured the imagination of the public and seemed to promise the possibility of understanding and thus affecting the link between material and spiritual worlds. Now considered synonymous with hypnotism, the "science" of animal magnetism emerged from the work of Austrian physician Franz

Anton Mesmer (1734–1815). Mesmer noted the presence of dynamic forces that, when controlled, might lead to dramatic cures. Animal magnetism is the term Mesmer used to describe this invisible force or fluid connecting all aspects of the natural world. French physician Armand-Marie-Jacques de Chastenet, Marquis de Puysegur (1751–1825), became Mesmer's most influential disciple and, in turn, mentored Charles Poyen (birth and death dates unknown) who, in a series of lectures in 1836, most directly and dramatically brought the science of animal magnetism to the United States. Poyen's *Progress of Animal Magnetism in New England* (1837) became a source book for those interested in the new science.

3. Peter Parley was the pseudonym for Samuel Griswold Goodrich (1793–1860). In 1827, Goodrich began writing under the name Peter Parley in books designed to educate young readers on geography, biography, and history.

4. Following this sentence in the original letter, Child had included these remarks: "Poor devil! Doth not thy cow calve? Doth not thy bull gender?"

5. Persian magician.

6. Thomas Taylor (1758–1835) published popular translations of Plato in the late eighteenth and early nineteenth centuries. The figure mentioned in Taylor's book is most likely Clearchus of Soli who combined Plato's and Aristotle's views on the human soul.

7. Mesmeric or hypnotic trances.

8. Many women writers of the period grew fascinated with what Child terms "spiritual philosophy." Both in the expectation that they take primary responsibility for nurturing proper moral and religious sentiments (especially in the private sphere) and in the professed belief that, as women, they were predisposed to spiritual influences and insights, the culture established a powerful link between the feminine and the spiritual. In this context, Child can be grouped with many other women writers of the period who explored the "spiritual" in their lives and writings, including Louisa May Alcott (1832–1888), Rose Terry Cooke (1827–1892), Margaret Fuller (1810–1850), Elizabeth Stuart Phelps (1815–1852), and Harriet Beecher Stowe (1811–1896).

Letter XX

1. Letter XX represents only a minor revision of "Letters from New-York.—No. 27.," *NASS* 9 June 1842, vol. 3, no. 1: 3. The one substantive change is noted below.

2. A German refugee to the United States, Dr. Charles Follen (1796–1840) began a promising career as first professor of German literature at Harvard. However, Follen's antislavery convictions, made known as early as his "Lectures on Moral Philosophy" in Boston in 1830, eventually led to Harvard's failure to renew his position in 1835. Continuing as an active abolitionist, Follen died with other passengers when the steamer he was aboard caught fire off Long Island Sound.

3. That in walking down Mulberry Street Child could not have been far from the devastated neighborhood Five Points gives greater meaning to this description of the beauty of the birds' flight. Clearly, as in other sections of the book, Child seeks to foster a perspective that invites a constructive orientation toward the world around her—even while acknowledging harsh urban realities in other letters.

4. Alexandre Pétion (1770–1818), first president of the Republic of Haiti, had helped defeat the French and establish an independent nation. He was known for his liberal rule.

5. Witch's Hill was the name given the site in Salem, Massachusetts, where those suspected of being witches were executed during the infamous trials of 1692.

6. Child added the emphasis in this letter. The *Standard* version of the letter did not include any italics.

7. For Child's reflections on her day's discussion of the "woman question," see Letter XXXIV.

Letter XXI

1. Letter XXI is a version of "Letters from New-York.—No. 28.," *NASS* 16 June 1842, vol. 3, no. 2: 7. Aside from the omission of a description of the Sailor's Home on Cherry Street and a reference to an astronomical theory (see below), the changes were minor.

2. To Staten Islanders, the quarantine hospital and burying ground was a less desirable part of the area. While forming a natural entrance point to monitor immigrants and sailors who carried such feared diseases as cholera and yellow fever, the island also saw a dramatic increase in population from the 1830s to the 1850s (10,960 to 25,492) and thus a growing concern about the enforcement of quarantine laws. In 1857–58, residents burned the quarantine station to the ground.

3. As with Randalls Island and Blackwell's Island, Staten Island became the site of many philanthropic and health-care institutions. Besides Sailor's Snug Harbor (built between 1831 and 1833), the island housed the Seamen's Retreat (1834–37) and, not long after Child's publication of *Letters,* the Society for Seamen's Children (1849).

4. It is likely that Child alludes to individuals associated with an institution now obscured by history. Greenwich Village, to which Child no doubt refers, is a neighborhood in lower Manhattan. Enclosing such sites as the potter's field (which was closed in 1826), public gallows, and Newgate Prison (1797–1829) through the first third of the nineteenth century, the area soon drew more respectable residents and business as it quadrupled in size from the 1820s to the 1840s. By the time of Child's editorial work in New York, Greenwich was being compared to the fashionable neighborhoods of London.

5. Instead of this brief paragraph, the *Standard* letter had included a more detailed description of the Sailor's Home, noted in full below:

Within the limits of the city, in Cherry street, is a fine establishment, on strict temperance principles, called the Sailor's Home. Spacious, well-ventilated, supplied at every turn with abundance of pure water, and from garret to cellar as neat as a Quaker parlor. The chamber windows open upon verandas supplied with seats; there is the beginning of a fine museum; a large, convenient reading-room, supplied with books, papers, and pamphlets; a pleasant bowling-alley, the top of which forms a promenade as extensive as the deck of a merchant-ship; and all this for the same price that is paid at the lowest and dirtiest boarding-houses. Capt. Richardson, who has charge of this admirable establishment, has been a sea-captain himself; and in that capacity was remarkable for religious principle, a conscientious discharge of duty, and kind, judicious treatment of his sailors. He is the very man to superintend such a place; and he gives himself to the task, with his whole heart.

6. In the *NASS* letter, the following remarks had originally concluded this paragraph: One class of astronomers bring forth ingenious theories to prove that the poles of the earth, through a series of spiral movements, will at last be brought into harmonious

relation with the poles of the heavens, and so perpetual spring over-shine the entire globe. This *outward* result cannot take place, till in man's *inner* world the polls of earth and heaven are brought into harmonious relation. Through ascending spiral series, I think I see the human soul slowly approaching to this glorious state.
See the third paragraph of Letter XXVI for mention of this astronomical theory.

Letter XXII

1. Letter XXII is a revision of "Letters from New-York.—No. 23.," *NASS* 5 May 1842, vol. 2, no. 48: 190–91. Revisions worth noting are included in the ensuing annotation.

2. In the *Standard* letter, Child had concluded the sentence differently, writing that, within this reform community, there was no need of any agency "to discover their duties to the enslaved."

3. The first half of the nineteenth century saw the beginning of a number of peace societies, that is, organizations striving to end violence and war as a means of resolving conflict. In August 1815, David Low Dodge began one of the first of the societies. In the same year, Reverends Noah Worcester and William Ellery Channing organized the Massachusetts Peace Society. Founder of the American Peace Society (1828), William Ladd promoted legislative action in the 1830s to encourage the formation of a congress of nations. For information on Channing, see Letter XXXII, note 4.

4. Child replaced "God-culture" with "spiritual culture" in *Letters.*

Letter XXIII

1. Letter XXIII represents a significant revision of "Letters from New-York.—No. 30.," *NASS* 7 July 1842, vol. 3, no. 5: 19. While the original letter is intact, revealing for the most part only unimportant spelling or punctuation changes, Child did add the five closing paragraphs reflecting upon the need for a "fixed point of view."

2. While attributing this pamphlet to Z. Kinsley later in the letter, Child actually had in mind Zephaniah Kingsley (1765–1843) whose "A Treatise on the Patriarchal, or Co-operative, System of Society as It Exists in some Governments, and Colonies in America and in the United States, under the Name of Slavery with its Necessity and Advantages" was first published in 1828. The treatise went through at least four editions between 1828 and 1834.

3. The *Standard* letter did not include "softer skins."

4. Child attributes a closing disclaimer to Kingsley in the earlier letter: "If my own were to run away, I wouldn't go after 'em, I think."

5. The clause "where he says he has planned some of his best bargains" was not in the original letter.

6. George Thompson (1804–1878) was a widely known British abolitionist. Coming to the United States in 1834, he joined Garrison, Child, and others in urging abolition. After a speech in 1835, Child and a number of women abolitionists had to help Thompson escape angry mobs. See "Letters from New-York.—No. 33." in the Appendix for a description of Thompson and this event.

7. During this time, the Malay, African, North American Indian, and European (or

Caucasian) were seen as the four races of man. Advertisements for such magazines as the *American Phrenological Journal* often included images of each race along with busts of individuals representing definitive phrenological types. In noting that he has traveled widely enough to see such different peoples, then, Kingsley means to give authority to his understanding of the world. Unlike many of his readers, he asserts a firsthand knowledge of what distinguishes different races.

8. Before he became an evangelical minister, John Newton (1725–1807) worked in the slave trade. In *An Authentic Narrative* (1764), Newton describes his experiences and the immorality of the slave trade.

9. Thomas Clarkson (1760–1846), British abolitionist. His pamphlet "A Summary View of the Slave Trade and the Probable Consequences of Its Abolition" (1787) provided documentation for William Wilberforce, British philanthropist, in his arguments before the Parliament to end slavery. Abolitionists in the United States held up Clarkson as a saint of the antislavery cause.

10. This sentence represents a small but noteworthy change from the *Standard* version. In the *NASS* letter, the point read as follows: "He was accused of plotting treason and insurrection, with as much bitterness as abolitionists now are. Plots were laid against his life; and the difficulty of combating his obviously just principles, led to the same misrepresentations and false assumptions which we now have to encounter."

11. At twenty-three, James Boswell (1740–1795) befriended Dr. Samuel Johnson (1709–1784). His *Life of Samuel Johnson* (1791) is a record of literary England during the last half of the eighteenth century as well as an account of Johnson.

12. This paragraph marked the original conclusion to the piece. In *Letters,* Child added the five ensuing paragraphs.

13. Samuel Taylor Coleridge (1772–1834) was an English poet and critic. He is best known for *Lyrical Ballads* (1798), co-written with William Wordsworth, and *Biographia Literaria* (1817), two works that heralded the English Romantic movement.

Letter XXIV

1. Letter XXIV is a revision of "Letters from New-York.—No. 31.," *NASS* 28 July 1842, vol. 3, no. 8: 31. Important changes are cited below.

2. The following remark had originally followed this sentence: "I might have applied to the city authorities to abate the nuisance; but luckily my aversion to such authorities was even greater than to red roofs, under a July sun."

3. Fata Morgana was a mirage that occasionally appeared in the Strait of Messina between Italy and Sicily and was named after Morgan le Fay, fairy enchantress of Arthurian legend.

4. Veracruz, or Veracruz Llave, a city and port on the Gulf of Mexico.

5. Bettina von Armin (1785–1859), also known as Bettine, was a German Romantic writer who wrote an epistolary novel *Die Gunderode* (1840) celebrating her friendship with Caroline von Gunderode (1780–1806). Gunderode was a German poet whose despair over gender restrictions and a failed love affair led her to commit suicide. Child is more than likely quoting from Margaret Fuller's *Gunderode* (1842), a partial translation of Bettina's novel.

The 28 July 1842 *Standard* letter had not included this paragraph, but instead had ended with the following verse:

> Oh, how my heart ran o'er with joy!
> I saw that all was good;
> And how we might glean up delight
> All round us, if we *would!*

Letter XXV

1. Letter XXV is a version of "Letters from New-York.—No. 32.," *NASS* 4 August 1842, vol. 3, no. 9: 34–35.

2. The events near Tarrytown involving British officer John André (1751–1780) and the infamous traitor Benedict Arnold (1741–1801) were quite familiar to readers well-versed in the history and lore of the Revolutionary War. Growing increasingly dissatisfied with his position in the colonial army, Arnold, then commander of West Point, had met with André and agreed to surrender the post for twenty-thousand pounds. Caught within the American lines with Arnold's papers, André was eventually found guilty of being a spy and hanged. Once discovered, Arnold joined the British. Loathed by Loyalists for his culpability in André's death and equally hated by Americans, especially after leading a raid on his former neighbors in September 1781, Arnold remained an outcast in England where he lived from the end of 1781 until his death in 1801.

3. Child had been more emphatic in her earlier letter, writing "would" instead of "might" in this and the next two clauses.

4. This comment on Washington's actions was added to *Letters.*

5. *On Christian Doctrine,* written around 1658–60 but only first printed in 1825, is considered most important for its delineation of the theological framework of *Paradise Lost.*

6. King George III (1738–1820) ruled England from 1760–1820 and thus became infamous for his role in the Revolutionary War and the War of 1812. Queen of Great Britain from 1837 until her death, Alexandrina Victoria (1819–1901) gave the Victorian Age (1832–1901) its name.

7. Novalis, the pseudonym for Friedrich Leopold, Baron von Hardenberg (1772–1801), was a German Romantic poet and theorist whose works were popular among the Transcendentalists. Two writings were especially influential: *Hymns to the Night* (1800), which depicts night (death) as a passage to a higher life, and the mythical romance *Heinrich von Ofterdingen* (1802), which presents the mystical pilgrimage of a young poet.

8. For many rural communities in the nineteenth century, the introduction of the railroad represented the symbolic—and, in some cases, the literal—end of a pastoral life and the traditions accompanying it. Entering areas whose social and economic rituals revolved around agrarian cycles, the railroad dramatically changed the pace of country life. The New York and Erie Railroad Company was one of the earliest railroads in the state. It was incorporated in 1832 to set up a line from Piermont, New York, on the west bank of the Hudson, to Dunkirk on Lake Erie. In *Walden* (1854), Henry David Thoreau describes the passage of a train near Walden Pond and, in doing so, captures some of the period's equivocal attitudes toward this intrusion of industrialization.

9. In the *Standard* letter, "the image of Stephen S. Foster" stood in place of the current "the image of our modern disturbers." Like William Lloyd Garrison, Stephen Symonds

Foster (1809–1881) was an uncompromising abolitionist whose lectures often drew the ire of audiences. His denunciatory rhetoric as well as such works as *The Brotherhood of Thieves; or a True Picture of the American Church and Clergy* (1843), one of the era's most scathing indictments of the church, earned Foster the reputation of a "modern disturber."

10. Child omitted the following remarks originally included after this sentence:
I am afraid I did not view the subject with anything like the solemnity that would be required of me, by Beriah Green on the one hand, or N. P. Rogers on the other; for never was mad-cap boy more amused with the idea of aiming a rocket into Quaker meeting, than I was, to think of Stephen S. Foster uprising among those imperturbable Dutchmen. If Abigail Folsom, "that flea of conventions," should be added, I verily believe they would acknowledge that railroad was a blessing in comparison.

11. Married in 1773, Honora Sneyd (died 1780) and Richard Lovell Edgeworth (1744–1817) wrote the children's book, *Harry and Lucy* (1778). Honora Edgeworth's register of her observations concerning children guided Maria Edgeworth in her own works, especially *The Parent's Assistant* (1796) and *Practical Education* (1798). Maria Edgeworth was known for both her children's books and such novels as *Castle Rackrent* (1800). Her children's works influenced Child's own writing for children during the 1820s.

12. Written by William Austin (1778–1841), "Peter Rugg, the Missing Man" depicts the exploits of Rugg, a man whose ride to Boston turns into an endless and timeless journey. The story was originally published in Henry St. Clair's *Tales of Terror; or, The Mysteries of Magic* (1833).

Letter XXVI

1. Letter XXVI is a revision of "Letters from New-York.—No. 34.," *NASS* 1 September 1842 vol. 3, no. 13: 51. Except for the omission of poetry originally concluding No. 34, the letter underwent only minor changes.

2. The following verse marked the end to the *Standard* version of this letter:
> Flowers are around me bright of hue,
> The quaint, old favorites, and the new,
> In form and color infinite,
> Each one a creature of delight.
> But with this fair array is brought
> Full many a deep and holy thought;
> And for me garden-beds and bowers,
> Like the old pictures of the flowers,
> Within their bloomy depths enshrine
> Ever some sentiment divine.

Letter XXVII

1. Letter XXVII is a revision of "Letters from New-York.—No. 35.," *NASS* 8 September 1842, vol. 3, no. 14: 55. The one minor change worthy of note relates to Child's reference to Polish musician and composer Michal Jozef Guzikov and is cited below.

2. It is likely that Child refers here to the title character of *Festus* (1839). Written by Philip James Bailey (1816–1902), the work was an immensely popular retelling of the Faust

legend. After this first edition, Bailey published a longer version in 1845 and a final edition in 1889 that incorporated poetry written after the second.

3. An ordained Unitarian minister who served as pastor of the Unitarian church in Northampton, Massachusetts, John S. Dwight (1813–1893) eventually left the ministry and became best known as a music critic, contributing to numerous Transcendentalist journals until forming *Dwight's Journal of Music* in 1852. Child befriended Dwight when both were in Northampton in the early 1840s.

4. Michal Jozef Guzikov (1806–1837), musician and composer, became famous for his virtuosity on the xylophone and his celebrated arrangements of well-known works. In the *Standard,* Child had written: "Guzikow, or Guzikoff, (one never knows how to spell those outlandish names,) was a Polish Jew."

5. Italian Niccolo Paganini (1782–1840), a virtuoso who revolutionized violin technique, embodied the Byronesque qualities of the Romantic period. His gambling and numerous love affairs coupled with his musical genius led to stories that he was in league with the devil.

6. Given her tendency to discern those aspects of experience (and of New York life) that manifested a connectedness between the material and spiritual, the Finite and the Infinite, it is not surprising that Child would be drawn to the mystical dimensions of astronomical theory. An idea embraced during the Romantic Period, the music of the spheres was thought by Pythagoreans to be created by the vibration of the celestial spheres. Joannes Kepler (1571–1630), a German astronomer, was one of the early defenders of the Copernican system and famous for his own observations of planetary motion. In his *Harmonice mundi,* Kepler elaborated upon Pythagorean theory, finding celestial music in the movements of the planets. During the 1670s, Sir Isaac Newton (1642–1727) would find the work of Kepler vital to his own discoveries.

7. Friedrich M. Retszch (1779–1857), German miniaturist, captured in painting one of Schiller's most famous lyrics, "Lied von der Glocke" or "The Song of the Bell," written along with a number of ballads in 1797. A German poet, dramatist, and literary theorist, Johann Christoph Friedrich von Schiller (1759–1805) was greatly influenced—as were the American Transcendentalists—by the philosophy of Immanual Kant. His study of Kant led to his own artistic formulation of philosophical idealism and, as a consequence, to his popularity with such writers as Emerson, Child, and others.

8. The Aeolian harp (from the Greek Aeolus, god of the winds) was a stringed instrument played by the wind and was especially popular during the Romantic period.

9. The Pascagoula Indians lived in the region surrounding the Pascagoula and Mississippi Rivers in Louisiana. While the Pascagoula population approached one thousand near the end of the seventeenth century, estimates in the 1820s put the figure at between one to two hundred.

Letter XXVIII

1. Letter XXVIII represents a modest revision of "Letters from New-York.—No. 37.," *NASS* 29 September 1842, vol. 3, no. 17: 67. In this volume's version of the letter, Child added the anecdote of the woman singer bringing fellow worshipers to harmony. The story had long been a favorite of Child's. In a private journal entry (1827?), she relates the

anecdote, attributed to a "Mr. Graeter," in a lengthy description of a conversation that included Convers Francis and other Boston acquaintances. A German-born artist who had lived with the Childs in Boston in the early 1830s, Francis Graeter had also "made engravings and translated stories for [Lydia Maria Child's] *Juvenile Miscellany* in 1831–32" and "taught drawing at Bronson Alcott's Temple School in 1835" (*SL* 186). The journal is included among Child's private writings housed in the Department of Rare Books, Cornell University Library, Ithaca, New York.

2. Emanuel Swedenborg (1688–1772) was a powerful influence on Romantic writers, including such figures as William Blake, Ralph Waldo Emerson, and Child herself, who, in 1822, had joined a Swedenborgian church in Boston. Spending the early part of his career absorbed in the study of natural philosophy and chemistry, Swedenborg eventually directed his efforts to theological matters. This latter interest, sparked by what he considered a divine call, resulted in thirty volumes of writings, including perhaps his best-known work, *On Heaven and Its Wonders and on Hell* (1758). His theory of "correspondences," which Child knew well, asserted that the universe had a spiritual structure and that everything in the natural world corresponded to a spiritual reality.

3. This statement marks the original ending to the *Standard* version of the letter. The remaining sentences of the paragraph and the ensuing anecdote of the one voice that brought others into harmony has been added to Letter XXVIII.

Letter XXIX

1. Letter XXIX combines "Letters from New-York.—No. 38.," *NASS* 6 October 1842, vol. 3, no. 18: 71, and "Letters from New-York.—No. 39.," *NASS* 13 October 1842, vol. 3, no. 19: 74–75. Significant changes are noted below.

2. Sources listing New York newspapers within the time of the visit to Blackwell's Island do not include the *Flash,* the *Libertine,* or the *Weekly Rake*—though such publications as the *Evening Tattler,* printed in the early 1840s, echo such titles. Child intends these apparently fictitious names to refer to the "penny papers" that had begun in the 1830s and numbered thirty-five during the decade. Before 1830, conventional newspapers carried a pricy annual subscription rate and catered to an elite readership. Selling for a penny, the sensationalized reporting of such papers as James Gordon Bennett Sr.'s *New York Herald* was meant to appeal to a broader audience. Horace Greeley's *New York Tribune,* begun in 1841, represented a more restrained "penny paper" and included on its staff Margaret Fuller.

3. Inevitably, the influx of young women from rural areas of Europe, the combination of few and low-paying jobs for women, and the double standard that permitted male extramarital sexual activity resulted in the proliferation of prostitution beginning in the 1820s. Between 1820 and 1850, the areas of Five Points and Water, Church, and Chapel Streets contained the most active prostitution "trade." In the period from the early 1830s to the 1840s, antiprostitution movements began in earnest. John R. McDowall, Presbyterian missionary working for the American Tract Society in Five Points, formed the New-York Magdalen Society, which opened a refuge house in 1831. In 1834, a number of women's groups affiliated with various churches formed the New York Female Moral Reform Society. While not involved in any specific organization, Child's public and private writings reflected concern over the conditions that led women into prostitution. Her story

"Rosenglory"—published in the October 1846 issue of the *Columbian Lady's and Gentle-man's Magazine*—traced the tragic fall of a woman into prostitution and prison (on Black-well's Island).

4. Child's description of this "fitting candidate for the presidency" bears a striking re-semblance to Andrew Jackson (1767–1845) who served as president from 1829 to 1837. Dur-ing Jackson's military service, he oversaw the massacre of Native American villages and ordered the execution of numerous Indian leaders.

5. Sing Sing was a state prison in Ossining, New York. With construction beginning in 1825, it originally had a building to house women prisoners and, in part for this reason, re-ceived attention from Child and other reformers during the period.

6. This sentence marked the original end to the 6 October 1842 *Standard* letter. The re-mainder of the current paragraph and the whole of the following one were added. The 13 October 1842 *Standard* letter begins after this addition.

7. An Italian writer, Silvio Pellico (1789–1854) was imprisoned by the Austrians in 1820 for his political views and writings. In 1832, two years after his release, Pellico published *Le mie Prigioni* (*My Prisons*), a moving and widely translated account of his sufferings as a political prisoner.

8. In *Letters,* Child omitted a lengthy excerpt from Pellico's book. The deleted section— which had followed this paragraph in the original letter—is included at length below:

Sylvio Pellico relates the following incident, which shows, in a remarkable manner, that the divine spark within the human soul is never quite extinct, though it be en-crusted with stone, and rubbish piled over it:

"My new prison was very dismal. It was a miserable chamber, dark and gloomy, with paper instead of glass in the window, and the walls polluted with vile-colored daubings, I dare not say of what. In the places which were not painted, were inscrip-tions. Many simply told the name of the country of some unhappy man, with the date of the sad day of his arrest. Others added exclamations against false friends, against a mistress, against a judge, &c. In one place was written, 'I bless the prison, since it has made me know the ingratitude of men, my own misery, and the goodness of God.'

"By the side of these humble words, were the most violent and haughty impreca-tions, by one who called himself an atheist, and who vented his passion against God, as if he had forgotten that he had said there was no God. After a column of such blas-phemies, followed another, reviling those mean spirits (so he called them) whom the misfortune of imprisonment made religious.

"I showed this wickedness to one of the keepers, and asked him who had written it. 'I am glad to have found that writing,' said he; 'there are so many of them, and I have so little time to look for them.' And without saying more, he began to erase it with a knife. 'Why do you do that?' said I. 'Because the poor devil who wrote it, be-ing condemned to die for premeditated murder, repented, and sent to beg me to do him this kindness.' 'God pardon him!' exclaimed I. 'What was the murder?' 'Not be-ing able to kill his enemy, he avenged himself by killing his son, the most beautiful boy in the world.'

"I shuddered. Could ferocity go so far? To kill an innocent being—a child!"

Yet this same murderer,—made ferocious by the "code of honor," which early taught him that society deemed it contemptible to forgive an injury,—this same murderer begged the jailer to erase the wicked words he had written! He could not leave the world, with a consciousness of being the means of hardening others, as he had himself been hardened. Here, in the midst of recklessness, revenge, and despair, was a glimmering evidence that the divine spark was not quite extinguished, even in him. Who can tell into what a holy flame of benevolence and self-sacrifice it might have been kindled, had he been surrounded from his cradle by an atmosphere of love? Would that we could learn to be kind—always and everywhere kind! Every jealous thought I cherish, every angry word I utter, every repulsive tone, is helping to build penitentiaries and prisons, and to fill them with those who merely carry the same passions and feelings farther than I do. It is an awful thought; and the more I realize it, the more earnestly do I pray to live in a state of perpetual benediction.

"Love hath a longing and a power to save the gathered world,
And rescue universal man from the hunting hellhounds of his doings."

9. For the public good.

10. Shakers were a religious sect known for their ascetic communal life. Their name is derived from the shaking movements that made up the dance performed as part of their worship.

11. Quakers were also known as the Society of Friends.

Letter XXX

1. Letter XXX, dated 13 November 1842, actually represents the combination of a brief excerpt from "The Croton Celebration," *NASS* 20 October 1842, vol. 3, no. 20: 79, and, with minor revisions, the whole of "Letters from New-York.—No. 41.," *NASS* 17 November 1842, vol. 3, no. 24: 95. In the initial article, Child described the 14 October "welcome" of the Croton water, a city-wide celebration that included a large parade. She only includes around two paragraphs of the lengthy piece. As noted below, the excerpt forms part of the new opening to the letter. Substantive revisions to "Letters from New-York.—No. 41" are also noted in ensuing annotation. In the Croton Aqueduct, Child saw an emblem of hope. For a detailed description of the engineering features of the aqueduct, see also "Croton Water Works," *NASS* 30 June 1842, vol. 3, no. 4: 15.

2. The Croton Aqueduct, first approved in April 1835 and completed in 1842, represented a major engineering achievement. Prior to the project, New York did not have a dependable water supply, and the impact of the aqueduct can be understood in the awe with which Child describes the fountains. The water itself came from the Croton Dam in upstate New York and covered a distance of forty-one miles in its trek from the dam to the receiving reservoir between 79th and 86th streets. The aqueduct officially opened on the Fourth of July 1842 though celebrations continued throughout the year.

This opening paragraph has been added to *Letters;* it occurred in neither "The Croton Celebration" nor the *Standard* version of the letter.

3. In "The Croton Celebration," this line read as follows: "I am a novice, and easily made wild with beauty."

4. Undine is a water nymph adopted by a humble fisherman. After marrying the knight Huldbrand, Undine receives a human soul. Later, tormented by Huldbrand while on the Danube, Undine is snatched back to the water. She returns to kill her husband when he is

about to marry another woman. Friedrich, baron de la Motte Fouqué (1777–1843), wrote of the myth in his fairy romance *Undine* (1811). E. T. A. Hoffman (1776–1822), German composer and writer, also used the story as a libretto in 1816.

"The Croton Celebration" offered a slightly different opening to the paragraph: "The Fountain in Union Park is smaller, but scarcely less beautiful—a weeping-willow of crystal drops—now sporting as gracefully as Undine in her wildest moods, and then sinking into the vase under a veil of woven pearl."

5. Harlaem is the old Dutch spelling for Harlem, the neighborhood in Manhattan that has become best known in literary history as the cultural center that produced the Harlem Renaissance. While more recently an African American neighborhood, during the 1840s and 1850s the area was largely unproductive farmland taken over by Irish squatters. At the end of the nineteenth century, German immigrants settled the area, then into the first part of the twentieth century eastern European Jews, and eventually, in the second and third decades of the century, African Americans.

This opening paragraph noting the trip to Harlem marks the introduction to the *Standard* letter of 17 November 1842. Child does omit a sentence that had originally concluded the paragraph: "Yet over the pearly drops, the rainbow smiles with heavenly promise."

6. Child possibly refers to Robert Blair, whose *Scientific Aphorisms, Being the Outline of an Attempt to Establish Fixed Principles of Science* . . . was published in 1827. Following the reference to Blair in the *Standard* letter, Child had written "never to illustrate the spiritual by the natural" rather than the current "never to liken the natural to the spiritual."

7. In the 17 November 1842 letter, after these brief reflections on conscience and "Freewill," Child had included the following paragraph and the first statement of the ensuing one:

I meant to alight on some branch or twig of the actual; but I find myself in the air again. Nothing short of infinite space seems to give my soul elbow room this morning. But now I *will* come down to earth, and stay there, through the rest of the letter.

I have said that I would not, if I could, free myself from the necessity imposed by conscience; but there is a *false* necessity . . .

8. It is possible that Child is referring to Oliver Wendell Holmes (1809–1894), physician and author, though no clear evidence confirms this possibility.

9. A street in Boston known for its wealthy residents.

10. Child makes a small, though revealing omission from the *Standard* letter. The earlier version read "You little black rascal."

Letter XXXI

1. Letter XXXI represents significant revision of two previous letters: "Letters from New-York.—No. 42.," *NASS* 24 November 1842, vol. 3, no. 25: 99, and "Letters from New-York.—No. 48.," *NASS* 2 February 1843, vol. 3, no. 35: 139. Child begins with no. 42 (on murderer John C. Colt) and then adds no. 48 (on capital punishment), having deleted lengthy sections from both. From the 24 November 1842 letter, she excised certain sensational descriptions of the circumstances of the crime and six final paragraphs speaking of convicted murderer John C. Colt's more sympathetic qualities. From the 2 February 1843 letter, she removed the opening two paragraphs, sections noting a debate on the question

of capital punishment. These omissions and other important changes within each letter have been cited in the annotation below.

2. John C. Colt (1810–1842) was convicted of murdering New York printer Samuel Adams whose body had been found in 1841 packed in salt and awaiting delivery to New Orleans. Not long after the writing of her 24 November 1842 letter on the Colt affair, Samuel Colt, John's brother, sought Child's aid in finding a home for a woman named Caroline Henshaw. While Henshaw had apparently married John Colt on the day of his execution, she was actually wed to Samuel Colt. It is unlikely that Child knew of these circumstances when solicited for help. In her letter to John S. Dwight inquiring of the possibility of relocating Henshaw to the reform community of Brook Farm, she describes the young woman as an "ignorant, worthy, affectionate German girl, apprentice to a corsetmaker in Philadelphia" who was misled by strong affections for John Colt. She presents Samuel Colt as a concerned brother who "says he feels it a duty to do more for [Henshaw] than feed and clothe her; that he ought, as far as possible, to throw a protecting influence around her and the child, . . . whom he shall in all respects treat as if he were his own son" (*Selected Letters* 183–84). For more on these events, see *SL,* 182–85.

In the *Standard,* the final three sentences here (suggesting that specimens of the invitations to the execution be preserved in museums) had originally formed a separate paragraph and followed the next section describing the day of execution.

3. Uncharacteristically mirroring the language of the more sensationalized "penny papers" of the day, the *Standard* letter included a more graphic description of the murder and the crowd's disappointment on hearing of Colt's suicide: ". . . he was found with a dagger thrust in his heart up to the hilt, and turned round, to make immediate death more certain. The tidings were received without doors, with fierce mutterings of disappointed rage. Those assembled as performers and spectators growled like a hungry bull-dog when a bloody bone is plucked from him."

The circumstances surrounding Colt's death are suspicious. After a visit from Caroline Henshaw, a fire broke out in his cell. Afterward, he was found with a number of stab wounds, suggesting that the death could not have been self-inflicted.

4. After this sentence, the 24 November 1842 *Standard* letter had included the following: . . . *they* made cool, deliberate preparations to take life, and with inventive cruelty sought to add every bitter drop that *could* be added to the dreadful cup of vengeance. Knowing him to be a proud man, they imported from Jersey the gallows and rope on which Robinson was hung for the murder of Suydam. They had a gallows of their own, in the prison yard; but as the memory of Robinson was execrated more than other criminals, they sent for *his* gallows, to add to the degradation. I will not enter into an examination of the comparative merits of the two cases; though I shall always believe that the murder committed by John C. Colt, awful as it was, was not premeditated, but done under the sudden excitement of violent rage. The question is not as to the degree of his sin, but the nature of that spirit, which led to the importation of Robinson's gallows to give an additional pang to a dying fellow mortal. If it came not straight from the infernal pit, then Satan never tempted the soul of man. Here Child refers to Peter Robinson's murder of banker Abraham Suydam. First holding him for a number of days in his cellar, Robinson killed Suydam after forcing him to watch the digging of his own grave. Robinson was hanged for the murder in 1841. (For discus-

sion of the impact of such sensational crimes upon the antebellum imagination, see part 2 of David S. Reynolds's *Beneath the American Renaissance: The Subversive Imagination in the Age of Emerson and Melville.*) The current ending to the paragraph and the ensuing paragraph were added to the first and subsequent editions of *Letters.*

5. Child added this final question and response inviting a maternal identification with Colt.

6. William Ladd (1778–1841) founded the American Peace Society in 1828.

7. The following paragraph had originally followed this section:

It is said that Mr. Hart, the sheriff, manifested the greatest repugnance to the painful and disgraceful task assigned him by law. Though he hired a subordinate to perform the legal murder, and was merely obliged to superintend ceremonies, he could ill conceal his relief when news came that the preparations were useless. He is said to have treated the prisoner with all the humanity the nature of his office permitted. They would have chained his hands as well as his feet; but to this Mr. Hart objected, as unnecessary cruelty: a manifestation of kind-heartedness for which he was vociferously blamed by those who were enraged at the suicide [of Colt], because it deprived them of a feast of vengeance.

8. Antoine Quentin Fouquier-Tinville (1746–1795) was the public prosecutor during the French Revolution who himself was executed in 1795. Callot is a misspelling of Jean Marie Collot d'Herbois (1750–1796), member of the Committee of Public Safety in Paris whose actions were responsible for numerous executions during the Reign of Terror.

9. Following this question in the *NASS* letter, Child had inserted, "The slave trade was once honorable business, in the eyes of that large proportion of mankind who have merely legal consciences."

10. Thomas McKean (1734–1817), Chief Justice of Pennsylvania from 1777 to 1799 and governor from 1800 to 1808.

11. This sentence had originally been italicized.

12. After this paragraph, Child includes the excerpt from the 2 February 1843 letter. This excerpt, however, begins the third rather than the first paragraph of the *Standard* epistle. Cited at length below are the original introductory paragraphs:

They are holding a series of discussions now at Broadway Tabernacle, on a variety of topics interesting to the community. This is certainly a troublesome age for one who loves quiet. It is not sufficient that one is willing to sit in his own old arm-chair, out of everybody's way. Committees *will* wait upon him, to convince him that his old chair is not of the best construction, or that it is a duty to split it up for firewood, for benefit of the public. However, I trust that many do not "run to and fro" in vain; but that knowledge is really increased.

Of all the subjects proposed for discussion none have interested my mind so much as that of Capital Punishment; it seems to me so shockingly at variance with the civilization of the age, and the benign character of our religion. It was singular enough that on the first evening of discussion the speaker in favor of abolishing this inhuman custom, was Major Davezac, an old *military* hero, one of General Jackson's aids; and the one in favor of it was the Rev. Dr. Cox, a "minister of the *gospel!*" This would be more surprising, had we not become accustomed to see theology stretching its shield over slavery and war. Yet it is strange that every man, whatever may be his creed, does not perceive and acknowledge that the laws given to the Jews could not possibly be

adopted into the code of any civilized nation. It is our blessed privilege to live under
a clearer dispensation of heavenly light. "It was said by them of *old* time, an eye for
an eye, and a tooth for a tooth; but *I* say unto you resist not evil."

13. While Child may have in mind Peter Robinson (see note 4 above), she may also be
referring to another case involving a man named Richard P. Robinson, which had been
sensationalized by the penny press. Richard Robinson had allegedly killed Helen Jewett
(1813–1836), a New York prostitute, in April 1836. While evidence pointed to Robinson's
guilt, he was slow to be arrested and, after a five-day trial, eventually acquitted. In the eyes
of many New Yorkers, the affair dramatically demonstrated the injustice of the court system and the false morality governing American society. Before the trial, many begged sympathy for Robinson, some asserting that the young man should not suffer the rest of his
life for the murder of a prostitute. The case also further fired reformers' efforts to address
the larger moral and social concerns that led to prostitution.

The White case may be a reference to Capt. Joseph White who had been murdered in
the early 1830s in an attempt to destroy his will. According to David S. Reynolds, this killing drew the attention of Nathaniel Hawthorne and may have influenced his portrayal of
Clifford Pyncheon in *The House of the Seven Gables* (1851) (*Beneath the American Renaissance*, 176).

It is unclear who Child may have in mind with her allusion to Jewell, though it is possible that she has misnamed Helen Jewett.

14. John Anthon (1784–1863) began his law practice in New York around 1807 and later
helped found the New York Law Institute (1830). He was considered one of the best and
most tireless practitioners in the city.

15. Child had originally written that he "left her with a tarnished reputation, and under
circumstances which indicated the most consummate baseness on his part."

16. This paragraph ends the 2 February 1843 letter. The penultimate paragraph of Letter XXXI again comes from the 24 November 1842 *Standard;* the final paragraph is new to
this volume. Included at length below is the original culmination of the November letter
on Colt that had followed the next to last paragraph:

   . . . If our "eyes were lifted up," we should see, not Moses and Elias, but *Jesus only.*

   The tone of some of the papers with regard to the infant son of John C. Colt, seems
totally unworthy of a Christian age, and a republican country. They talk of "his inheritance of infamy." Because the father has left us an awful record of the danger and
the guilt of ungoverned passions, is the innocent babe to blame? In countries which
still cling to a hereditary rank, such remarks would be in better keeping. The idea
they express is a vestige of old, aristocratic times, when men, having divided the hon-
ors and possessions of the world, by physical force, had a keen desire to hand down
to their posterity, with all their rank and wealth, all the hatred and revenge they cherished toward their enemies. It is a sentiment every way unworthy of the 19th century.
Such a child has *peculiar* claims on human sympathy; he should be guarded with a
more earnest love, for the sake of his misfortune.

   I mean no extenuation of the awful crime of John C. Colt, when I say, that through
the whole course of this terrible tragedy, he has shown the self-same qualities which
men admire under the name of military greatness. The stern silence with which he
shut up in his own breast his secrets and his plans; his cool self-possession, under circumstances that would have crazed a common brain; his bold defiance of the law,

which he regarded as a powerful enemy; the strong pride which bore him up under a long imprisonment, and prompted him to suicide; all these indicate such elements of character as military heroes are made of; and both with regard to him and them, they would be *really* great, if applied to good purposes; when applied to the perpetration of crime, they only render it more appalling.

But the sternest human heart has somewhere in its corners, a nest for love. When the wretched victim of his own violent passions thought of the girl with whom he had lived as his wife, and of the infant son she had borne him, his proud heart melted to womanly softness. He spoke of her with strong affection, and whenever mention was made of the babe born since his imprisonment, he wept the bitterest tears. Carlyle, in his French Revolution, speaking of one of the three bloodiest judges of the Reign of Terror, says: "Marat too, had a brother, and natural affections; and was wrapt once in swaddling clothes, and slept safe in a cradle, like the rest of us." We are too apt to forget these gentle considerations when talking of public criminals.

The deep shadow that rests on the memory of this unfortunate man, is lightened by one bright gem. He wished to make all the atonement he could for the wrong he had done Caroline Henshaw. They were married a few hours before his death, in that gloomy cell, with the grim spectre of the gallows before them. Ah, what a bridal was that! How fearfully must have echoed the words, "What God had joined together, let not man put asunder!" They took their last farewell, with an intensity of anguish and despair, heart-rending to witness. His last words were an entreaty that she would love his child, and rear him virtuously. May God help her to keep the promise she made under circumstances of such awful solemnity!

The prisoner maintained to the last that he did not *intend* to kill Adams; and said he was willing to carry this assertion to the bar of God, whether man ever believed it or not. He wrote a long letter to his son, which he left with his poor heart-broken wife, with instructions that it should not be opened till the boy was old enough to understand it.

Another ray gilds this mournful tragedy. The brothers of John C. Colt, all of them respectable men, in the genteel walks of life, never forsook their disgraced and suffering brother; but sustained him throughout by their presence and sympathy; and made almost superhuman efforts to save him from his untimely end. A few hours before his death, one of them gave him $500, as a present for his wife and child. Let us be thankful for these gleams through the darkness. Are we not all children of the same father? And shall we not pity those who, among pit-falls, lose their way home? These questions concluding no. 42 in the *Standard* are inserted at the end of Letter XXXII. For additional information regarding Caroline Henshaw, see note 2 above.

Letter XXXII

1. Letter XXXII is a revision of "Letters from New-York.—No. 43.," *NASS* 1 December 1842, vol. 3, no. 26: 103. Substantive changes are cited in the annotation.

2. Child is referring to lawyer John Anthon who had assisted in defending John Colt. See Letter XXXI, note 14.

3. Published in three volumes, Thomas Carlyle's *The French Revolution* (1837) offered an assessment of the Revolution in the context of Western history, examining as well the role of the divine in human affairs. Jean-Paul Marat (1743–1793), politician, journalist, and

physician, led the radical Montagnard faction during the French Revolution. As editor of *L'Ami du Peuple* ("The Friend of the People"), he suggested that millions of brothers would lose their lives for the failure to cut off the heads of a few hundred royalists and aristocrats. This paragraph was originally part of the section from "Letters from New-York.— No. 42" that was omitted from Letter XXXI. See Letter XXXI, note 16.

4. Like Lydia Maria Child, Elizabeth Gurney Fry (1780–1845), a British prison reformer, believed that social conditions contributed significantly to crime and that punishment was not necessarily an effective means to alter criminal behavior. Fry attacked the conditions at Newgate Prison in London and assisted prisoners and their families by finding work and developing schools. William Ellery Channing (1780–1842), the period's leading Unitarian minister, was active in numerous reform efforts. Channing and Child knew each other well, having met to discuss concerns over the slavery question in the mid-1830s. Reportedly, Child's *An Appeal in Favor of That Class of Americans Called Africans* (1833) influenced Channing to begin speaking out against slavery.

5. This final question and the preceding sentence were not in the *Standard* version of the letter.

6. In her revision of the letter, Child added this couplet and the paragraph preceding it.

7. In Greek myth, Hylas was taken away by the naiads (water nymphs) who were said to drown those that they loved.

8. This sentence marked the original conclusion to the paragraph. What follows has been added to *Letters*.

9. See Letter XXX.

10. To conclude her letter, Child refers to a number of writers, artists, ministers, and musicians known for their role in reforms or for the way their art embodied spiritual concerns: Mary Howitt (1799–1888), a British writer of biographies, histories, novels, and children's tales; Charles Dickens (1812–1870), British novelist; Francois de Salignac de la Mothe Fénelon (1651–1715), French theologian and educator; Thomas à Kempis (1379/80–1471), Augustinian monk and writer of Christian mystical works; John Woolman (1720–1772), Quaker writer best known for his posthumously published *Journal* (1774) and his early antislavery work; William Ellery Channing (1780–1842), Unitarian minister; John Keble (1792–1866), British clergyman and poet; Raphael (1483–1520), Italian painter known for his depictions of the Madonna; and George Frederick Handel (1685–1759), German-born composer.

In the original conclusion of the letter, Child had written

> . . . or it may be sweet Mary Howitt, who always "turns the *sunny* side of things to human eyes;" or the serene and gentle Fenelon; or the devout Thomas à Kempis, or the meek-spirited John Woolman, or the heavenly Doddridge, or the saintly beauty of Raphael, or the clear melody of Handel, or the eloquent hopefulness of Channing, or the cathedral tones of Keble, or a laughing child; but whoever it may be, when they find me waiting, they all welcome me into their hearts, and "make me a nice little bed there."

Letter XXXIII

1. Letter XXXIII represents a significant revision from earlier letters, primarily in Child's effort to combine reflections on Catholicism and Puseyism scattered in three distinct issues of the *NASS*. The sources for this letter are the following: "Letters from New-

York.—No. 11.," *NASS* 25 November 1841, vol. 2, no. 25: 99; "Puseyism," *NASS* 14 July 1842, vol. 3, no. 6: 22–23; and "Letters from New-York.—No. 46.," *NASS* 5 January 1843, vol. 3, no. 31: 123. In this compilation, the letter begins with no. 11 (lines 1–77), includes an excerpt from no. 46 (lines 71–95), returns to a brief portion of no. 11 (lines 78–80 and 92–96), incorporates reflections on "Puseyism" (lines 41–67 and 203–28), and then closes with the last part of no. 11 (lines 82–91, 108–97).

The first letter on Child's visit to the Catholic church and her reflections upon Catholicism came after a month-long break in her editorial duties in New York. During this time, she had visited her husband in Northampton, Massachusetts. The first part of the initial introduction to the letter informs her readers of this short sabbatical:

After a month's absence in the woods, here I am again, in the editorial tread-mill. One of the first places of interest which I visited after my return, was the Catholic Cathedral, a fine-looking Gothic edifice of grey stone. The interior is in a rough state, undergoing the process of enlargement, to accommodate the numerous congregation. St. Peter's is the aristocratic church; this is the church of the poor. The temporary rough boards behind the altar were adorned with no paintings or images, and the music was inferior to what I have been accustomed to hear in Catholic churches; yet was I sensible of that feeling of reverence, that bowing down of the spirit, always inspired by a venerable relic of the Past.

Child's patching together of the various texts—and the important revisions reflected in the process—are noted below. The deletions from nos. 11 and 46 are also cited.

2. Written between 1390 and 1440 and first translated into English in the middle of the fifteenth century, *De Imitatione Christi* (*The Imitation of Christ*) traces in four books the progression of the soul to union with God.

3. Child inserted from "with the tiara . . ." through "This is all natural;" in this edition. This addition came from "Letters from New-York.—No. 46." See note 7 below for how it originally appeared in no. 46.

4. Protestant reformers associated with the Reformation.

5. Johann Lorenz von Mosheim (1694–1755), Lutheran theologian. It is possible that Child had read a recent translation of Mosheim's work entitled *Institutes of Ecclesiastical History, Ancient and Modern* (1841).

6. Constantine I (c. 280–337), Roman emperor from 306–37.

7. This paragraph is taken from the fifth paragraph of "Letters from New-York.—No. 46" and represents the sole excerpt from this letter. The sections from no. 46 originally surrounding this letter are included below:

I went last week to look on the earthly remains of the late Bishop Dubois, the third Catholic Bishop of New-York. He was a French gentleman, of great refinement and cultivation, who emigrated to this country during the terrible struggles of the revolution, in 1791. He came warmly recommended by Lafayette, and was cordially received by Washington, Patrick Henry, Judge Marshall, &c. For some time, he supported himself by giving French lessons in the distinguished families of Virginia. He afterward returned to the priesthood, and founded St. Mary's College, and an establishment of that valuable order called Sisters of Charity. His blameless and exemplary life inspired universal respect. The crowds that flocked to his funeral testified the strong veneration of the Catholics for his memory. Masses for deceased relations and friends are now redoubled; with the hope that the good old bishop will help them in purgatory, as he was ever ready to help them in this life. This gives rise to some jests among the unbelieving; but I despise no thought that is born of the affections. Let poor, bereaved human love construct such bridges as she can, between this land of illusions and yon bright region of realities. We Protestants are too prone to pull up our flowers, to see whether they have any roots.

Bishop Dubois lived fifty-five years in the priesthood; and the advancement of the Catholic church was the central object of his existence. The angels know better than I do how much the errors of his faith weighed against the purity and benevolence of his life.

He was buried from St. Patrick's cathedral. A few years ago, he was seen on the roof of this building, watching the flames of a neighboring conflagration. As the danger increased, he knelt across the roof, his venerable white hairs streaming in the wind, and prayed fervently for the preservation of the church. It is said that the irreverent firemen directed their hose toward his head, and compelled him to retreat; if so, there certainly were no sons of Erin among them; or if there were, their relations would never hope to pray them out of purgatory.

A multitude of thoughts crowded into my mind, as I looked on the aged form, lying in all the splendor of Episcopal robes, with the mitre on his head, the crucifix in his hand, and at his feet vessels of silver and gold, containing consecrated water and oil for anointing. What a painted shadow of that priestly power which once governed the kings of the earth! I thought of the fishermen of Galilee, with scrip and staff, and of their successors reading the proscribed gospels in dens and caves. I saw how the oriental glitter of Judaism, and the tasteful pageantry of Pagan Rome, had mixed with the religion of Him, who preached to the people on the hill-sides of Judea. I thought of the eloquent boast of Tertullian, that the influence of Christianity was purely spiritual; that it aimed at no temporal power, and coveted no worldly wealth. Then I saw splendid domes, costly statues, and altars covered with gems. Instead of the seamless garment, and the hair simply parted, after the manner of the Nazarines, there was the tiara of the Persian priest, the crosier of the Roman augur, and the embroidered mantle of the Jewish rabbi. All religions had brought of their cumbrous ornaments, and well nigh buried the vestal under their gorgeous weight. Alas, thought I, were it the outward *form* only that had been adulterated by these foreign mixtures; but the true and false in *principle* have intertwined; and who can foreshow the end thereof?

I thought of the period so falsely called the "triumph of Christianity," when the religion of the poor ascended the throne of the Caesars. Wo for the hour, when moral truth became wedded to politics, and religion was made to subserve purposes of the state! . . . They *through* whom it acts, constitute the real church of the world, by whatsoever name they are called.

The Catholic church, with all its errors and its vices, (and they are many,) has furnished its quota of brave, self-denying, holy men. There is little of Christian kindness, or sound philosophy, in reiterating the evil doings of that church in the corrupting plenitude of its power, while all its good deeds are buried in oblivion. Among those old abbots, whom Luther fought like a son of thunder, were many men as good as he, though they could not as easily let go their hold upon the Past. To them, the faith of their fathers was the Ark of Safety, and they had not courage to lay rude hands upon it. It requires little bravery to do it in this age, when papal pollutions are every schoolboy's theme. But how are we with regard to the superstitions and selfishness in which *we* have been educated? "He alone deserves to have weight or influence with posterity, who has shown himself superior to the particular and predominant error of his *own* times; who, like the Peak of Teneriffe, has hailed the intellectual sun, before its beams have reached the horizon of common minds; who, standing like Socrates, on the apex of wisdom, has removed from his eyes all film of earthly dross, and has foreseen a purer law, a nobler system, and a brighter order of things; in short, a *promised land!* which, like Moses, on the top of Pisgah, he is permitted to survey and anticipate for others, without being himself allowed either to enter, or enjoy."

It is midnight; and this noisy population have begun popping out the old year, and popping in the new, with gunpowder. A savage, and most inappropriate salutation, to the circling group of Hours and Seasons. The old Greeks would have pelted them with garlands; but we are not Grecians, nor have we attained to the truer gracefulness of Christianity.

This midnight hour, though but ideally a passing place for the heavily-laden trains of Past and Future, (any more than *every* hour is so,) yet makes me sad. Another large fragment of the brief space allotted me for usefulness, is gone! How much have *I* done to correct "the dominant errors of my *own* times?" How much have I done to fix the eye of faith on "a purer law, a brighter order of things, a *promised land?*" Alas, how little have I attempted; and of that little, how much has been defeated!

A cheerful voice shouts over that desponding tone, "No, not defeated! Scattered truth is *never* wasted!" Accept the prophecy, kind reader; and God grant thee a Happy Year, with frequent glimpses of the *promised* land, and will and power to help thy doubting fellow-travellers up to that Hill of sunlit vision.

"Thro' strife to peace!—And tho' with bristling font,
A thousand frightful deaths encompass thee,
Good cheer! good cheer! Brave thou the battle's brunt,
For the peace march and song of victory."

8. In the *Standard* letter (no. 11), Child followed this sentence with this observation: "Yet I am scrupulous for perfect freedom to this form of opinion, as for all others."

9. The beginning of this paragraph does not appear in the *Standard* pieces. The remainder of this paragraph and the next two represent the portion of Letter XXXIII that has been excerpted from "Puseyism."

10. Child refers to sites included in Sir Walter Scott's *Kenilworth* (1821), an historical novel set in Elizabethan England.

11. This sentence originally read: "Such souls walk in a golden atmosphere of mysticism, like Coleridge and Wordsworth; and as years revolve, this tendency leads them back from their youthful wanderings in the fields of free inquiry, to the established laws of the realm, and the ancient usages of the Church."

12. The Oxford or Tractarian Movement—more commonly known as Puseyism in the United States—began in 1833 in the Church of England and underscored Catholic heritage in doctrine and worship practices. The term Puseyism is derived from Edward B. Pusey (1800–1882), canon of the Church of Christ at Oxford.

13. In "Puseyism," Child had written: "Episcopacy may rebuke, and Dissenters may argue; but Puseyism spreads, because it ministers to the sentiment of reverence; a sentiment

never quite extinguished in any human soul, and of overpowering strength in all poetic temperaments."

14. These first two sentences forming the transition from the "Puseyism" excerpt were added. The rest of the paragraph originally appeared earlier in no. 11 (lines 82–91).

15. This beginning reflects a minor revision. The original read "Another reason why I cannot laugh at the ceremonial of the Catholic church, is the sincere devotion of its ignorant devotees." In no. 11, the following paragraph had also preceded this section:

What can be more beautifully significant of a great and glorious idea than the custom observed at Easter? On that day, all distinction of ranks is laid aside. A beggar may kiss the king, unreproved; saying as he salutes the monarch, "Christ is risen!" The answer, returned with a kiss, is "He is risen indeed!" What though the ignorant multitude perform this as a traditionary rite, and know not that because Christ has risen, the human race are indeed all brethren? To the reflecting mind the form is still beautiful with the spiritual light that shines through it.

Letter XXXIV

1. Letter XXXIV represents a compilation of two letters on "Women's Rights" that Child had first thought of omitting from the collected volume: "Letters from New-York.— No. 50.," *NASS* 16 February 1843, vol. 3, no. 37: 147, and "Letters from New-York.—No. 51.," *NASS* 23 February 1843, vol. 3, no. 38: 151. Given that the original essays were related, the revisions largely attempt to provide a coherent joining of sections that had not first been connected. Interestingly, Child begins the revised letter with the first three paragraphs of the second epistle (no. 51), changing the beginning from "I had not room, in my last, to say all that I wished, on the subject of Women's Rights." Substantive changes to both nos. 50 and 51 are noted below.

2. The phrase "Women's Rights" (or Woman's Rights) had fully entered the culture by the early 1840s. While antebellum society urged separate spheres for men and women, women's participation in reform endeavors, including antislavery and temperance societies, led to an increasing involvement in public forums and thus to a growing dissatisfaction with laws and social customs limiting full participation in the public sphere. In the 1830s and 1840s, the period most often considered the era of the first women's movement in the United States, numerous works were published exploring the status of women nationally and internationally—some of the most prominent being Child's *The History of the Condition of Women, in Various Ages and Nations* (1835), Sarah Grimké's *Letters on the Equality of the Sexes and the Condition of Women* (1837), and Margaret Fuller's *Woman in the Nineteenth Century* (1845). More organized efforts to secure women's rights emerged from the well-known Seneca Falls Convention in 1848, a gathering that produced the *Declaration of Sentiments and Resolutions* authored by Elizabeth Cady Stanton, Lucretia Mott, and others.

3. A devout Unitarian as a youth, Harriet Martineau (1802–1876) published her first work, *Devotional Exercises,* at just twenty-one. In 1834, Martineau traveled to the United States, in part to provide support for the country's abolitionists. Her book *Society in America* (1837) and *The Hour and the Man* (1840), a biography of Toussaint L'Ouverture, were widely read in the States and solidified her popularity among antislavery advocates. In

"The Martyr Age of the United States" published in the December 1838 issue of the *Westminster Review*, Martineau "mentions the public censure of the Childs after they gave legal counsel to a black family in Boston" (*SL* 106).

For information on Edgeworth, see Letter XXV, note 11.

4. Jesus's sermon on moral behavior recorded in the Gospel of Matthew, chaps. 5–7.

5. The Tartars (or Tatars) are a Turkic-speaking people of Europe and Asia.

6. William Hazlitt (1778–1830), British essayist and satirist, was known for his critical and personal essays on English writers, including Coleridge and Wordsworth. It is not clear who Child has in mind when alluding to Stephen's remark.

7. This paragraph forms what was originally the fourth paragraph of "Letters from New-York.—No. 50." In joining the two letters from the *Standard,* Child omitted the opening three paragraphs cited below:

I have of late received two or three epistles, expressing a strong wish that I would "come out concerning the Rights of Women;" giving, as a reason therefor, that "it is a legitimate branch of the anti-slavery enterprise."

Every subject, bearing any relation to the contending influences of moral attraction and physical force, is a *branch* of anti-slavery, or, more properly speaking, a branch *with* anti-slavery. All truths flow from One, and tend to one; and whosoever has a mind sufficiently comprehensive to follow out one great principle, reaches another in the process. I do not perceive, however, that the doctrine of Women's Rights, as it is called, has a more immediate connection with anti-slavery, than several other subjects, which bring in question the law of physical force.

I have no objection to ["]coming out;" though, it seems to me of very little consequence to others what my opinion is, and I am conscious of being in that state of mind, which is unlikely to satisfy either party. I am not ultra enough to suit the reformer, and too reforming to please the conservative.

8. William Pitt. See Letter IV, note 10. For information on Hannah More, see Letter XI, note 6.

9. Emerson first delivered the lecture "Being and Seeming" in Boston on 10 January 1838 and repeated the performance on 15 March in Cambridge. The lecture was also delivered in a Framingham series on 12 March and, perhaps, under the title "Intellectual Integrity" on 16 May in Concord. For a copy of the address, see *The Early Lectures of Ralph Waldo Emerson,* vol. 2, ed. Stephen Whicher, Robert E. Spiller, and Wallace E. Williams (Cambridge: Belknap P of Harvard UP, 1964), 295–309.

10. One of Child's earliest surviving letters, written when she was just fourteen, also questions Milton's depiction of women. "I perceive," she writes brother Convers Francis in September 1817, "that I never shall convert you to my opinions concerning Milton's treatment to our sex" (*SL* 2).

11. In "Letters from New-York.—No. 50.," Child had followed this sentence with further reflections on the differences between men and women. These remarks, noted below, concluded this paragraph and began a new one:

I believe that the natures of men and women are spiritually different, yet the same. Two flutes on the same key do not produce harmony; but on different keys they do. There is no inferiority or superiority. The same tune is played, and with the same skill; but it is played on different keys, and the unity of variety is harmony.

I do not think the paths of man and woman are identical; but in a true order of society they must ever run side by side, start from the same point, run the same length,
and reach the same end. Kinmont, in his admirable book, called the Natural History
of Man, expresses my views more completely than I can myself.

For a fictional representation of this idea, see Child's "Thot and Freia," *Columbian Lady's
and Gentleman's Magazine* 3 (January 1845): 1–7.

12. *Twelve Lectures on the Natural History of Man, and the Rise and Progress of Philosophy,* by Alexander Kinmont (1799–1838), was published in 1839.

13. This paragraph concludes the portion of the letter taken from "Letters from New-
York.—No. 50." The next paragraph returns to no. 51.

14. An influential French philosopher, novelist, dramatist, and art critic, Denis Diderot's (1713–1784) enlightenment ideals—his scientific approach to philosophy and the
passion with which he popularized scientific knowledge—proved antagonistic to the Romantic sensibilities of Carlyle.

In the second letter from the *Standard* addressing "Women's Rights," Child originally
included the following paragraph after this one:

Hence it is, that the question of "Women's Rights" has become so generally associated, in the popular mind, with infidelity; and the same thing may be truly said of
other struggles of the human soul for *freedom.* But, after all, these errors, broached in
extreme re-action to other errors, are but perverted truths. They utter yearnings and
prophesies of the soul, though vaguely and imperfectly.

Letter XXXV

1. Dated February, 1843, Letter XXXV actually joins two letters originally published
before and after this time: "Letters from New-York.—No. 36.," *NASS* 22 September 1842,
vol. 3, no. 16: 63, and "Letters from New-York.—No. 53.," *NASS* 16 March 1843, vol. 3,
no. 43: 163. Child begins with no. 53 (on electricity) and then adds no. 36 (on the effects of
climate); both address her fascination with forces associated with animal magnetism. Substantive revisions are cited in the annotation.

2. *The Westover Manuscripts: Containing the History of the Dividing Line betwixt Virginia
and North Carolina; A Journey to the Land of Eden, A.D. 1733; and A Progress to the Mines.
Written from 1728 to 1736, and Now First Published* (1841) by William Byrd (1674–1744).

3. In the popular mind during the antebellum period, "electricity" became increasingly
associated with animal magnetism. Writing to the *American Phrenological Journal* in 1849,
one reader asks, "Is Electricity, under God, to be looked upon in the light of a common
father? Look at electric action from the equator to the poles, as connected with vegetation, with animal life, with phrenological and physiological development, with temperaments, habits, dispositions." For a more "feminist" application of the meaning of the
"electric," see Margaret Fuller's description of the Seerest of Prevorst in "Wisconsin" in
Summer on the Lakes (1843) and her notions of the especial genius of women toward the
end of *Woman in the Nineteenth Century* (1845).

4. Child may have in mind Pierre Thouvenel (1745–1815), a Paris physician who wrote
several professional works.

5. In the *Standard* letter (no. 53), this assertion was fleshed out with the following ex-

ample: ". . . and it was but lately that the French chemists told us of trying experiments with a dead cat, whose brains being taken out, and the place filled with galvanic fluid, she arose and staggered about the room, for a few minutes."

6. In no. 53, Child had inserted "which flow into his being as a common centre" after "being."

7. Following "*colour,*" the following had been included in the original letter:

Man *can* invent things, because they already *are,* and because he stands in intimate relation to all; but he might do it by intuition; instead of groping for it by study.

There is a spiritual medium, too, which brings us into harmonious relation with all things of spirit, as well as matter; but we attain to this only by reverent obedience to the inward voice.

In this current version of the letter, Child added the remainder of this paragraph (on the bee and Mrs. Mather), the ensuing section, and, finally, the opening three questions of the paragraph that begins, "Of what spiritual thing is electricity the type?"

8. Sarah Mather (birth and death dates unknown) invented a submarine telescope and lamp, for both of which she was awarded a patent in 1845.

9. Quakers.

10. This paragraph ends the portion from no. 53. Child then continues with the fourth paragraph of no. 36. The following was omitted from the *National Anti-Slavery Standard* letter:

You say, "give us letters from New-York oftener." I am as much astounded at your requiring impudence, as were the almshouse-keepers, when "Oliver Twist asked for *more!*" I had supposed that I gave too much of what a gifted young friend calls the "painted oriels of my editorial life." I have expected reproof from wholesale reformers, for so often stepping off the railroad track, to gather butter-cups in the meadows, or weave moss-garlands on the sea-shore. I have even looked for epistles of tender expostulation from some "weighty Friends," saying, "Maria, I have testimony to bear against thy paper. It is thy pleasure to deck it in too many colors." But instead of that, to hear a call for "more," quite surprises me. Your request puts me in mind of the theological student, who inquired of Dr. Mayhew, "why the Song of Solomon was put into the Bible, and the Wisdom of Solomon left out." "I don't know, indeed," exclaimed the doctor, "except that mankind are always prone to prefer songs to wisdom."

Since you like my wayward warblings better than more solid wisdom, I would fain gratify you; but truth to tell, I am this week like the ministers, who when Saturday night comes, often have a sermon to write, and not a word to say. But as *they* can preach an hour and a half and—"make *nothing* of it," (as Dr. Kirkland used facetiously to remark,) why should not I?—Luckily, this sort of material, like blond lace, needs the smallest conceivable quantity of *material;* all the value lies in the weaving.

Yet after all, my difficulty does not so much consist in *want* of thought, as in the *character* of my thoughts. They are all tinged with sadness, like the falling leaves of autumn; and I will not throw my shadow across another's sunshine, unless I can make it play gracefully there, like the shadow of grape-vines in the breeze. Wise advice is that of Stirling:

"In silence mend what *ills* deform thy mind,
But all thy *good* impart to all mankind."

Even Autumn, which grows more and more ghostly as our own autumn advances, speaks hopefully to the wise in *heart*. "The year is dying away, like the sound of bells," says Goethe: "The wind passes over the stubble, and finds nothing to move. Only the red berries of that slender tree seem as if they would fain remind us of something cheerful; and the measured beat of the thresher's flail calls up the thought, that *in the dry and fallen ear lies so much of nourishment and life.*"
Child also revised the opening of the fourth paragraph that begins the section from no. 36. The beginning of the paragraph had originally read: "Thus cheerfully can I usually look on the fading season, even when it reminds me too powerfully of my own autumn; for I resolutely turn away my eye from the lone stubble, waving in the wintry wind, and think only of the ripe, golden seed, which the sower will go forth to sow."

11. While Benjamin Franklin (1706–1790) may be best known for his public role in events leading to and following the Revolutionary War and his *Autobiography,* he first gained an international reputation in the eighteenth century for his scientific experiments, especially those experiments begun in 1747 concerning electricity. While in France in 1784, Franklin had also been involved, though not extensively, with the controversy surrounding the practice of Anton Mesmer. He was listed as one of the members of a panel appointed to assess the scientific validity of Mesmer's findings regarding animal magnetism and its curative properties.

12. Interestingly, Child omitted a paragraph on the effect of climate on complexion. The section cited below had followed this paragraph in no. 36:

The effect of climate on complexion is so obvious, that some philosophers have naturally enough concluded that climate is the *only* cause of difference in complexion. That it is the heat of the sun, acting on successive generations, through the lapse of centuries, that chars the skin and crisps the hair in Africa, there can be little doubt. South America lies in the same latitude, but the effect is produced to a less degree, because that continent abounds in mountains, while a large portion of Africa stretches out in deserts of arid sand, over which no mountain breezes blow. All mountainous countries are inhabited by fair complexions. The Scotch, the Swiss, and the Hungarians, are blue-eyed and fair-haired. The Italian, Spaniard, and Maltese, are black haired, and swarthy. But the Jews afford the best test we have, with regard to the effect of climate on complexion. As they never intermarry with foreigners, there is of course among them no admixture of the blood of different races; yet the Hungarian Jew has blue eyes and fair complexion, while the Maltese Jew is dusky, and a Hindoo, of the same tribe, is nearly black.

13. Sappho (fl. c. 610–c. 580 B.C.) was a Greek lyric poet whose passionate expressions of love for women has led to her reputation as a lesbian writer.

14. "Letter from New-York.—No. 36" ended as follows:
The safe rule is to condemn no sin faintly in ourselves; and of our brother to remember ever, that

"He who *made* the heart, alone
Decidedly can try us;
He knows each chord, its various tone,
Each note, its proper bias.
Then at the balance let's be mute—
We never can adjust it;

What's *done,* we partly may compute,
But know not what's *resisted.*"

Letter XXXVI

1. Letter XXXVI emerges from some extensive and revealing revisions. Specifically, it pulls together three columns in the *National Anti-Slavery Standard:* the whole of "Letters from New-York.—No. 52.," *NASS* 2 March 1843, vol. 3, no. 39: 155, and parts of "Letters from New-York.—No. 54.," *NASS* 23 March 1843, vol. 3, no. 42: 167, and "The Different Races of Men," *NASS* 5 January 1843, vol. 3, no. 31: 122–23. The current letter begins with no. 52 (lines 1–34), moves to excerpts from "The Different Races," returns to no. 52 (lines 35–183), and then closes with the postscript from no. 54 (lines 185–227). The important addition comes from "The Different Races of Men." In this article, Child responded to "scientific" facts concerning facial angle and brain mass that were used to support the period's racial prejudices. Thus, in the final compilation, Letter XXXVI takes on a more philosophical tone as Child attempts to accommodate "material" measurements with "spiritual" truths. Significant revisions are noted below.

2. P. T. (Phineas Taylor) Barnum (1810–1891) established the American Museum at the intersection of Broadway and Ann Streets in 1841. Having purchased the museum from John Scudder, he soon transformed the building from a five-story exhibit of stuffed animals and waxworks to the home of live "freaks," dramatic performances, and other sensational events. At the time of Child's visit, the museum was just beginning to become a central tourist attraction for both New Yorkers and foreign visitors.

3. It was not uncommon for Barnum to bring people representing "exotic" cultures to his establishment. Members of the Sac (or Sauk) and Fox tribes were a popular "exhibit." Both tribes, originally located in the Michigan and Wisconsin Great Lakes region, joined forces in the early seventeenth century to prevent their annihilation. Both tribes were removed to Iowa in 1804. The Iowa lived in the northwest and southeast regions of the state bearing their name. For the most part, the three tribes currently reside in Oklahoma and Kansas.

4. Black Hawk (or Ma-Ka-Tai-Me-She-Kia-Kiak, 1767–1838) was a leader of a faction of the Sauk and Fox who, during the early 1830s, fought Illinois militias and U.S. troops in an attempt to prevent white settlers from further encroachments upon Native American land. By the 1840s, Black Hawk had come to represent the emblematic "Indian," striking in his carriage and courage but prone to violence. The leading phrenologists of the period, Orson and Lorenzo Fowler, published a phrenological reading of Black Hawk in the November 1838 issue of the *American Phrenological Journal,* noting his unusually pronounced organ of destructiveness—the same organ that Child observes in the features of Nan-Nouce-Fush-E-To.

5. This couplet was added to *Letters.*

6. This paragraph on facial angle begins the excerpts from "The Different Races of Men." Developed by Petrus Camper (1722–1789) as a means to assess why Grecian statuary seemed especially beautiful, craniometry, or the study of facial angle, evolved into a means of justifying certain racial hierarchies. According to Camper, a higher facial angle marked a greater beauty. By the 1830s, scientists were asserting that cranial shape provided clear evidence of Caucasian moral and intellectual superiority.

The section from Child's column began differently: "The *facial angle* is measured to account for the supposed impossibility of attaining a certain degree of cultivation. We are told that this angle. . . ."

7. After the U.S. government passed the Indian Removal Act (1830), both the Choctaws and Cherokees were forced to move from their homelands to what is now Oklahoma. Resulting in thousands of deaths, the journey westward became known as the Trail of Tears. Child and her husband had been involved in supporting the Cherokees' right to remain in their ancestral homeland in the southern Appalachian region.

This paragraph marks the end to the excerpts from "The Different Races of Men." The following paragraph to the closing postscript is taken from "Letters from New-York.— No. 52."

8. John Knox (1505–1572) led the Protestant Reformation in Scotland and helped establish the Presbyterian church as the national church in the 1560s.

9. Johann Gottfried von Herder (1744–1803), German philosopher known for his part in the *Sturm und Drang* (Storm and Stress) movement of the 1770s.

10. Jean Paul Richter, a pseudonym for Johann Paul Friedrich Richter (1763–1825), German romantic novelist whose mysticism appealed to English and American romantic writers.

11. The last two sentences of this conclusion had originally been preceded by the following remarks and formed the final paragraph of no. 54: "I find it hard to forgive the insatiable avarice which hurried these noble children of the forest from one scene of exhibition to another, till it pushed them into the grave. If they themselves were tempted by money to prolong their stay, oh how the bleeding heart of that young chieftain will hate the yellow dust for which he sold a life so precious!" Except for this change and some reordering of portions of the postscript, this version of Child's closing reflections remain substantially the same of those written in the *Standard*.

Letter XXXVII

1. Letter XXXVII appeared first as "Letters from New-York.—No. 49.," *NASS* 9 February 1843, vol. 3, no. 36: 143. There were no significant revisions to the original.

2. Pegasus was the winged horse of Greek myth that sprang from the blood of the Gorgon Medusa when she was beheaded. According to myth, Pegasus caused the stream Hippocrene to spring from Mount Helicon with the striking of its hoof. In the romantic period and modern times, the mythic creature has come to symbolize poetic inspiration.

3. In Greek legend, Tithonus is the son of Laomedon (king of Troy) and Strymo (daughter of the river Scamander). According to myth, it was Tithonus's wife Eos (Aurora) who asked Zeus to grant her husband eternal life. Eos, however, forgot to request eternal youth as well. When Tithonus grew old, he was transformed into a cicada.

4. Child's allusion might reflect a translation or continuation of the Roman designation *Arabia felix,* or happy Arabia. The particular reasons for this happiness are not clear.

5. François Marie Charles Fourier (1772–1837) was a French socialist and reformer who believed that society would improve without the ownership of private property. His ideas regarding ways to form self-sufficient farm communities influenced American reformers and shaped the social and economic structure of such utopian communities as Brook Farm. The aurora borealis, or northern lights, became a popular symbol of the period. Not

unlike the music of the spheres, the luminous phenomenon, believed to be electrical in origin, seemed to manifest the beauty of a divine and unifying hand in natural creations.

Letter XXXVIII

1. Letter XXXVIII is a slight revision of "Letters from New-York.—No. 54.," *NASS* 23 March 1843, vol. 3, no. 42: 167. One change of minor importance is noted below.

2. In 1820, while teaching school in Gardiner, Maine, Child did not live far from the Kennebec River.

3. Bettina von Arnim (1785–1859). See Letter XXIV, note 5.

4. In this version, Child's comments reflect more humility. In the *Standard* letter, she had followed this remark about her worship of beauty with "and to none have I been disloyal." For a Transcendentalist reflection on the nature of beauty, see Child's "What Is Beauty?" in the April 1843 issue of the *Dial*, a journal edited by Margaret Fuller and George Ripley (1840–42) and Ralph Waldo Emerson (1842–44).

Letter XXXIX

1. This letter represents the joining of two letters published consecutively in the *Standard*: "Letters from New-York.—No. 56.," *NASS* 20 April 1843, vol. 3, no. 46: 183, and "Letters from New-York.—No. 57.," *NASS* 27 April 1843, vol. 3, no. 47: 187. The substantive revisions emerge in relation to omissions from no. 57. In fact, only approximately seventeen lines of the original was kept. Letter XXXIX begins with no. 56 (lines 1–29), inserts a revised excerpt from no. 57 (lines 12–40), and returns to no. 56 (lines 29–113). The 27 April 1843 *Standard* letter is cited at length in the notes below.

2. Jean Paul Richter. See Letter XXXVI, note 10.

3. In ending the remarks on misfortune here, Child interrupts the third paragraph of no. 56; the closing lines of the paragraph (beginning with "Blessed indeed are the ministrations of sorrow!") have become the seventh paragraph of Letter XXXIX. The three paragraphs that follow this one represent a revision of the second and third paragraphs of no. 57. The whole of the *Standard* letter no. 57 is cited at length below:

I spoke, in my last letter, of the blessed ministrations of sorrow. On reading it over, I am reminded of a remark made by a friend, years ago, the truth of which is confirmed by my own observation: "It may all be very true," said he, "what the preachers say about people's being made better by affliction; but among all my acquaintance, I have not found one who was improved by trouble. It seems to render them either indifferent, or bitter toward the world. I believe prosperity is good for people; it makes them more sunny in their tempers, and more genial in their sympathies."

There is great truth in this remark; but I apprehend it is applicable mainly to *pecuniary* trouble. I have known many a temper spoiled, many a kind heart chilled, and many a domestic paradise blighted, by trials of this kind. "Pecuniary difficulties, in all their wretched and entangling minutiae, like the diminutive cords by which Gulliver was bound, tame the strongest mind, and quell the most buoyant spirit."

But *these* trials man has brought upon himself; they are owing to a false state of society. The sorrow which comes from the hand of God has in it something ennobling and purifying. It raises us from the material into the spiritual, and brings us into close relation with the unseen world. To part from those we love—to hear no more the one dear voice, whose tones are *all* remembered—to miss the thousand little daily acts of kindness—to have none left to look *into* our eyes, as the loved one—this is agony. Oh, God! how terrible is the agony! But this is part of the plan of our being. Our Father, seeing that this wo was necessary, has made it holy, and elevating. In the shadow of the Cross stands ever the sepulchre with the stone rolled away, and angels declare to the mourner, "He is not here; he is risen. Why seek ye the living among the dead?" And a voice higher than the angels, proclaims, "Because I live, ye shall live also."

"There *is* no Death to those who know of life;
No Time to those who see Eternity."

On the hearth-stone of human sorrow rises the religious altar; and men become angels by meekly laying thereon the sacrifice of broken and contrite hearts. Pecuniary entanglements *may* produce this result, but they rarely do. It is not their natural and appropriate office. Within human *love* there is ever somewhat divine; and this rises from the tomb into heaven. But it is not so with the accumulation of wealth. From the sepulchre of *such* hopes, no angels watch to roll away the stone.

Such anxieties are heart-rending, and such disappointments dreadful, even to a degree that unsettles reason, and makes existence an insupportable burden. Yet the whole structure of society tends to stimulate these false hopes, and increase the anguish of defeat. We send our sons out into the world to pass through a fire worse than that of Moloch; and where one escapes, a thousand fall. Urged on by a false education, and false surrounding influences, young men rush after the Jack-o'-Lantern of wealth, believing that thus only can they light the taper of a pleasant *home*, which seems to shine on them from afar, as they struggle along through the wilderness of care. The boundaries of right and wrong are so indistinctly marked—there is so much *legal* which is not *moral*, and so much *moral* which is not *legal*, that it seems a mere chance whether the wayfarer keeps within safe limits. One man goes out deliberately to shoot his enemy, and all the nation honor him, and name him for the highest office in their gift; another man kills his enemy in the sudden heat of passion, and is hung. One man swindles, as banker or merchant, and lives rich and respected; another, who swindles as forger or thief, is imprisoned for years, and branded as an outcast. In this whirl of falsity and corruption, thousands go down to ruin and despair; victims of a grief which has in it nothing divine, and brings no healing on its wings; and therefore more to be compassionated than that sorrow which raises and consecrates the soul.

The newspapers abound with such items as the following:

Last moments of Col. Shelton.—In noticing the death of Colonel Shelton, by suicide, the Vicksburg Sentinel says he was a kind and affectionate father, and was humane in all the relations of life. He left some memoranda behind him, in which the horrors of his mind, during the period which immediately preceded his death, are forcibly depicted. No one can read these hasty notes, with other feelings than sympathy for the fate of the wretched man:

20th.—I fear my fate is fixed. Graves will do nothing to-day, and Crane is uneasy—so are others, who have entrusted me with their funds. If I am deceived, I cannot survive it. My fortune is gone—my credit also. If I am deceived, I cannot meet my friends who have relied on me. How am I to meet my God! Must my destroyer live, and I die? Oh, God, how awful! Yet it is better to die by my own hands, than to live in agony; or meet my God with my own, than the blood of another on my hands. It must be, if I am deceived—Monday. Tuesday, 10 o'-clock.—No better. What is to be done? Night, 11 o'clock.—I have received nothing but promises, depending upon government. The truth is, my warrants have been used to fill up examination. As far as gone, the specie is in amount full. If the investigation was over, or excitement at an end, I would receive all in gold, or as much as I need at present, to satisfy all who have entrusted me.

22nd.—The question now is, Will those persons continue to delay longer? I am sure myself that all is safe; if they do not, I die today by my own hands. Oh, God, forgive me! Oh, God, take care of my wife and little ones!

The following is a copy of a note left upon the bank of the river, and supposed to have been written just before his death:

Before I take this dreadful leap, I swear, before the living God, that Graves has all the funds I could get. It was invested in State warrants, left him under the promise that gold should be paid at par as soon as the investigation was over. All is gone.

The only warrants which I can describe, I have no doubt are in the treasury: An old warrant, $1,226; Tracy warrant, $736, belonging to T. P. Ware; $875, wrapped in Tracy's account, left as collateral security, belonging to W. R. Crane.

I further swear, I have not a dollar—my family has. Mr. Graves has $7,283, and about $4,000 besides. Not one cent have I received, unless it be $300, borrowed of Mr. Thomas, and $291 of E. Graves; so help me God! W. H. SHELTON.

March 30, 1843.

The wife of this wretched man died of grief at his untimely end, and his children are left to poverty. He had loaned money to R. S. Graves, State treasurer of Mississippi, and a brother politician, in order to screen him from shame, when his accounts were undergoing scrutiny; and Graves did not return the money, as promised.

Who can say that this Colonel Shelton might not have been a Fenelon, a Howard, or a William Penn, if he had lived under healthy social influences? Who but the All-seeing can decide how far he was an innocent victim to a false structure of society? He is but one of thousands. The streets of New-York are full of anxious, care-worn faces, on which I see written discouragement, desperation, crime, and suicide. Never did I witness such universal marks of internal restlessness and wretchedness, as this spring. *Is* there no help for this state of things? The tinkering and soldering of governments, with their banks and anti-banks, their tariffs and anti-tariffs, evidently make "confusion worse confounded." If there *be* no way to stop this great game of venality and corruption—to take away the stimulus which now goads nine-tenths of the civilized human family into vice and crime—no means of substituting therefor healthy incitements to real happiness and genuine progress—why, then, Heaven send that Miller's theory prove correct! It is better to blow up this miserable world, and begin anew.

But there *is* a path out of all this confusion; and the earnest "pathfinders," who are abroad seeking for it, *will* find it. Anxiety, embarrassment, dishonesty, and despair, are *not* man's natural destiny. Look at the cantons of Switzerland, where, if neighbors differ in opinion about the boundaries of their land, one sends the other before the judge, to tell *both* sides of the story; saying, "Thou wilt tell the truth, I know, and that is all they need, to help them decide aright." Our defaulters, repudiators, forgers, treaty-breakers, and swindlers in general, have precisely the same human nature, as those honest Swiss peasants. It is obvious that *social influences* are at fault. The hu-

NOTES   259

man soul *cannot* grow and prosper under them. In England, France, and all the civilized world, the same proofs, under various modifications, stand visibly forth to challenge the observation of all thinking men. Some lay the fault on *commerce*, and say the Swiss peasant would become corrupt if he traded. But surely, in the nature of commerce, rightly considered, there is nothing bad. For nations to interchange goods with each other, for the happiness and benefit of all, has in it something noble. It is love to the neighbor in a universal form; and can be made bad in its effects, only by being made to minister to a love of self. If trade were on a right foundation, the merchant would rank next to the true priest in the social scale. That he is now content to "turn a penny" on war, pestilence, and famine, is one of many proofs that the world is an inverted pyramid.

If the clue has not already been given to lead man out of this labyrinth of care and crime, it surely will be given. Hope on, and hope ever.

4. Edward George Earle Lytton Bulwer-Lytton (1803–1873), British author, known especially for his historical novels. His works include *Pelham* (1828), *Paul Clifford* (1830), a novel attacking capital punishment, and the drama *Money* (1840). While Edward's older brother Henry Lytton Bulwer (1801–1872), who would eventually become ambassador to the United States from 1849 to 1852, might also have been the source of the remarks, it is more likely that Child is drawing from the novelist's writings.

5. Gulliver is the journeying protagonist in Jonathan Swift's *Gulliver's Travels* (1726). His first voyage takes him to the land of Lilliput where he is tied down by the six-inch-tall Lilliputians.

6. Child probably has in mind Bridget Richardson Fletcher (1726–1770), writer of the popular *Hymns and Spiritual Songs* (1773).

Letter XL

1. Letter XL is a slight revision of "Letters from New-York.—No. 58.," *NASS* 4 May 1843, vol. 3, no. 48: 191. None of the revisions—largely minor spelling, punctuation, or typesetting changes—are substantive.

2. John Bunyan (1628–1688), English preacher and writer, best known for *Pilgrim's Progress* (1678). Narrating the journey of Christian to the Heavenly City, this allegorical tale is considered one of the best expressions of Puritan belief.

3. In connecting reflections upon May Day celebrations with moving, Child accurately captures the New York translation of ancient practices. In short, the custom of arranging first of May leases provided city dwellers with their own ritual of new beginnings, a ritual that resonated with old world May Day practices celebrating spring. Because of housing shortages and high rents, many New Yorkers sought to improve their housing arrangements through relocating. Business ceased for the day because the streets were packed with people transferring belongings from home to home, apartment to apartment. Thus, as implied in this concluding letter, "Moving Day" in New York became a kind of urban ritual of new beginnings.

4. Orestes Augustus Brownson (1803–1876) is most often associated with the Transcendentalists. During the 1830s and 1840s, he had the reputation as a radical reformer and, having been both a Universalist and Unitarian minister, as one who often switched worldly and religious allegiances. In 1844, he converted to Catholicism.

5. The "City Directory" was a valuable resource for New Yorkers, serving a function

comparable to the twentieth-century telephone book. It contained an alphabetical listing of the "heads of households," "homemakers," business partnerships, judges, politicians, ministers, and fraternal organizations. The collection and cataloging necessary for the publication of the directory began on Moving Day (May 1) of each year.

6. Elias Hicks (1748–1830), devout Quaker minister, was a profoundly influential force in the Society of Friends, traveling widely within the United States during his lifetime. His dissatisfaction with theological interpretations on the life of Christ resulted in a division among the Quakers. Members of the society that adhered to Hicks's teachings became known as Hicksites.

7. Jean Paul Richter.

8. Gunnhild of Denmark (c. 1020s–1038), also known as Kunigunde of England, became the German empress or queen after her marriage to Henry III of Germany.

9. Carlyle published a translation of Goethe's *Wilhelm Meister's Apprenticeship* in 1824. His *Sartor Resartus* also manifests the profound influence of German philosophy and literature. See also Letter VI, note 14. Mary Howitt translated the work of Frederika Bremer (1801–1865), Swedish author, reformer, and supporter of women's rights, in the 1840s. Known internationally for her novels and travel narratives, Bremer shared Child's antislavery sentiment. During the Swedish author's visit to the United States in 1849, travels that led to her book *The Homes of the New World* (1853), Child visited Bremer at the Astor House in New York and, not long after this visit, at a friend's home.

APPENDIX

Letter 12

1. Printed in the 2 December 1841 issue of the *National Anti-Slavery Standard,* Child's twelfth letter describes a gathering that included Cinquez (or Cinque) and fellow Africans who, for the most part, were from the Mende region of West Africa. Kidnapped from their homeland in 1839, the Africans gained national and international renown for their mutiny aboard the *Amistad.* After commandeering the Spanish slave ship, Cinque ordered the sailors to take the vessel back to Africa. Instead, the Spaniards steered near the coast of the United States until the ship was eventually boarded by the navy off Long Island, New York. Having killed the captain and cook, the Africans were charged with both murder and mutiny. The case, however, drew the indignation of numerous supporters, including Lewis Tappan. John Quincy Adams represented the Africans before the Supreme Court when an earlier court victory was appealed. The Mendians left the United States on 4 December 1841.

2. Lewis Tappan (1788–1873), merchant and abolitionist, was nationally known before the *Amistad* affair for his antislavery views. At odds with William Lloyd Garrison's belief that most moral reforms centered in the abolitionist cause, Tappan nonetheless was tirelessly devoted to antislavery work. It was Tappan who played a major role in mobilizing widespread financial and legal support for the Africans aboard the *Amistad.*

3. African Methodist Episcopal Zion Church. See Letter XI, note 2.

4. A. T. Williams was a teacher from the Yale Divinity School hired by Tappan to instruct the Africans.

5. Plutarch (c. 46–c. 120), Greek biographer and moralist whose works strongly influenced the form of the essay and biography into the nineteenth century.

6. George Washington (1732–1799), of course, was the commander of the Revolutionary forces and first president of the United States. Tadeusz (Thaddeus) Kosciuszko (1746–1817) was a Polish patriot who fought for the United States during the Revolutionary War; he returned to Poland in 1784 to fight against its partition. While there is no historical evidence of the actual existence of William Tell, he lives in memory as the legendary Swiss hero who was forced to shoot an apple off his son's head and who fought for Swiss independence from Austria. German dramatist and poet Johann Friedrich Schiller made the story of Tell famous in his play *Wilhelm Tell* (1804).

7. José Ruiz, a slave speculator from Porto Principe. It was Ruiz who had purchased the Africans after they arrived in Havana and who was among those held by Cinque during the "mutiny."

8. Serving on a British African patrol vessel, James Covey came from a region in West Africa that shared the same language as those captured and transported on the *Amistad* and, as Child relates, took on the role of translator.

9. Richard Lemon Lander (1804–1834), British explorer of West Africa.

10. Theodore Sedgwick Wright (1797–1847) was a prominent clergyman and abolitionist. Educated at the African Free School in New York, he became the first African American graduate from an American theological seminary (Princeton Theological Seminary) and eventually the pastor at New York's First Colored Presbyterian Church, also known as Shiloh Presbyterian Church. He helped found the American Anti-Slavery Society in 1833, only later to withdraw after disagreements with those devoted to combating slavery solely through moral suasion.

11. See Letter XXVIII, note 2.

12. For a brief discussion of Child's views on the African race, see Letter XI, note 11.

13. See Letter XXXIV, note 12.

14. William Ellery Channing. See Letter XXXII, note 4.

15. For abolitionists in the United States, the British emancipation of the West Indies in 1833 served to inspire the cause because it demonstrated the possibility of a peaceful end to slavery. Channing's optimistic reporting of the changes in the British West Indies, however, fails to account for enduring inequities attributable to white racism and the economic and social effects of the plantation system. While in theory free to move, sell their labor, and purchase land, the freed slaves often found their options to be limited. Many continued to labor as plantation workers.

Letter 14

1. Major Alexander Gordon Laing (1794–1826) wrote *Travels in the Timannee, Kooranko, and Soolima Countries in Western Africa* (1825).

2. Child's reference may be inaccurate. No record of *Memoirs of Harlan Page* exists in listings of publications for the period.

Letter 18

1. No doubt Child omitted this letter from *Letters from New-York* because she had already included a lengthy essay on the Washington Temperance Society. See Letter II.

2. Jersey City is located to the west of the southern tip of Manhattan Island on the peninsula between the Hudson and Hackensack rivers. Delevan Institute, more than

likely, was situated near the current streets of Danforth Avenue and Old Bergen Road in southwestern Jersey City.

3. See Letter III, note 8.

4. See Letter XXXVII, note 5.

Letter 24

1. A revised version of no. 24 was included as Letter XXVI in *Letters from New York, Second Series* (1845).

2. William Miller (1782–1849), farmer and leader of the Adventists or Millerites. Miller gained a large following in the early 1840s preaching that Christ's second coming would occur in 1843 or 1844.

3. The Book of Daniel describes the life and visions of a Jewish hero who lived in Babylon in 600 to 500 B.C. Chaps. 7–12 is the section that contains the prophetic visions of Daniel.

4. Child alludes to James Fenimore Cooper (1789–1851), best known for his historical novels of the United States, including *The Last of the Mohicans* (1826).

5. In this section, Child refers to Sir Henry Cary, first Viscount of Falkland (died 1633), and his wife, Elizabeth Cary (1585–1639), who was the first woman dramatist in England to be published). Given that Henry and Elizabeth Cary did not live during the period described in the anecdote, it is apparent that Child has wrongly attributed the history and tradition associated with the old house to the Carys.

Letter 33

1. Child refers to George Thompson as well in her letter describing an interview with Z. Kingsley. See Letter XXIII, note 2.

2. Abolitionists.

3. See Appendix, Letter 12, note 2.

4. Not an actual figure in New York at the time, Judge Lynch signals the mob's intention to "lynch" Thompson should they catch him.

5. See Appendix, Letter 12, note 15.

6. Samuel Joseph May (1797–1871), Unitarian minister and abolitionist. Child dedicated *An Appeal to That Class of Americans Called Africans* (1833) to May.

7. Child uses the name M. Guillotine to signify "executioner," that is, the man in league with Stetson to attack Thompson.

8. Quakers were known for their pacifist beliefs. As described, the term "Quaker militia" humorously refers to the women's nonviolent strategy of surrounding abolitionist speakers to protect them from assault.

9. For an interview with Kingsley (whom Child had misnamed Z. Kinsley), see Letter XXIII. She notes Kingsley's admiration for Thompson in this letter as well.

10. Ralph Randolph Gurley (1797–1872), philanthropist, devoted himself to the American Colonization Society and was considered an expert on African colonization.

11. The British Corn Laws regulated trade in wheat and other grains and were designed to create a sufficient supply of grain to meet England's domestic needs while maintaining prices at profitable levels. The duties on imported and exported grain, however, tended to

serve the interests of landlords who sold the grain rather than the working classes who purchased the product at a higher price.

Letter 40

1. An expanded version of no. 40 was included as Letter XXIV in *Letters from New York, Second Series*.

2. "Catochus: A Thrilling Sketch" (*NASS* 3 November 1842, vol. 3, no. 22: 88) is a short tale that Child lifted from the *Boston Miscellany*. It is the first-person narration of a man who, after suffering a severe head pain upon going to bed, awakes in a cataleptic state. Mistakenly assumed to be dead, he is revived just before being buried alive after small drops of perspiration are noticed on his forehead.

3. Asphyxia refers to a condition that occurs when breathing stops. Such a condition leads to unconsciousness and death. The fear of asphyxia—and thus being wrongly diagnosed as dead and prematurely buried—was prevalent in the nineteenth century. Some coffins were especially designed to allow air into the compartment and provided with a mechanism to enable the "deceased" to ring a bell if regaining consciousness. Poe employed the period's obsession with this condition (and thus in being buried alive) in such stories as "The Fall of the House of Usher" (1839) and "The Premature Burial" (1844).

4. Henry Grafton Chapman (1804–1842) was a wealthy Boston merchant who contributed significant financial support to the abolitionist movement. His wife, Maria Chapman (1806–1885), was a prominent Garrisonian abolitionist.

5. Antonio Canova (1757–1822), famous Italian sculptor whose work was strongly influenced by Greek and Roman sculptures.

Letter 44

1. See also Letter XXIX for another description of this visit to Blackwell's Island.

2. East Indian sailor.

3. For a brief description of phrenology, see Letter VI, note 5.

Letter 45

1. Child alludes to Plato's allegory of the cave. In the allegory, Plato (c. 427–347 B.C.) sets up the cave as a representation of the world experienced by the senses. Locked within the cavern, the dwellers only see shadows and unreal objects and images cast upon the walls. Only by rejecting this deceptive sensual world can the cave dwellers achieve a higher knowledge of a more permanent reality. In the allegory, this knowledge is symbolized by the sun, the object that casts the shadows.

2. Persian magician.

3. See Letter XIX, note 2.

4. George Fox (1624–1691) was an English religious leader who founded the Quakers, or Society of Friends; Madame Guyon (1648–1717) was a French mystic and writer. The reference to Madame St. Amour is not as clear. As named, the figure does not appear in a wide range of reference sources.

5. As Child relates, Samuel Slater (1768–1835) founded the textile industry in the

United States, arriving in the country in 1789 and building the spinning machine from memory in 1790.

Letter 47

1. Child's editorial "Means and Ends" was part of the 1 December 1842 issue of the *National Anti-Slavery Standard*. Child wrote that our "proneness to have faith in man, rather than God, is exemplified in the universal tendency to convert means into an end. Means belong to the finite, and are therefore temporary; the end exists in the infinite, and is eternal." It is unclear who wrote the letter that Child cites.

2. Dido, also known as Elissa, was the legendary founder and leader of Carthage. One of the greatest cities of ancient times, Carthage stood near the present city of Tunis, Tunisia, in North Africa.

3. *The Epicurean. A Tale* by Thomas Moore (1779–1852).

4. Thomas Carlyle (1795–1881), British romantic writer. For additional information on Carlyle, see Letter VI, note 14.

5. Child has in mind James Thomson (1700–1748), a Scottish poet whose *The Seasons* (first published in 1730) was immensely popular.

6. Child names a number of English and German Romantic writers who influenced her work: William Wordsworth, Johann Gottfried von Herder, Johann Christoph Friedrich von Schiller, and Jean Paul Richter. For brief information on the individual writers in the order they are named, see Letter X, note 5, Letter XXXVI, note 9, Letter XXVII, note 7, and Letter XXXVI, note 10.

7. Sir William Blackstone (1723–1780) was a British jurist and legal scholar. His four-volume *Commentaries on the Laws of England* (published from 1765 to 1769) served as the foundation for legal studies in Great Britain and the United States.

8. Byron, or Lord Byron (1788–1824), one of the most widely known of the English romantic poets.

9. Baruch Spinoza (1632–1777), Dutch philosopher.

Letter 55

1. Child is probably referring to Daedalus, mythic craftsman, known for his building of the labyrinth; Archytas (fl. 400–350 B.C.) was a Greek philosopher and Pythagorean mathematician.

2. Among the several thousand species of parasitic insects commonly known as ichneumon, a number of the species have a long egg-laying organ that can pierce the earth or wood.

3. In this paragraph, Child refers to a number of historical figures and craftsmen, some of whom can be identified. Harun ar-Rashid (766–809), not Haroun-al-Raschid, was the fifth caliph of the Abbasid dynasty of Baghdad. The water clock is one of the gifts reportedly exchanged with Charlemagne (742–814), Frankish king from 768 to 814. Harun ar-Rashid is best known as the caliph whose court is described in *Arabian Nights*. Bonaparte refers to Napoleon Bonaparte (1769–1821) who ruled France from 1804 to 1815. The particular importance of the vase is not clear. The chess player was evidently a creation of Johann Nepomuk Maelzel (1772–1838), a German mechanician. It is possible that Child

wrongly names Maillardet, for no craftsman with that appellation (or one that approximates it) occurs in reference sources. Child's fascination with such mechanisms served as background to her story "The Rival Mechanicians" first published in the January 1847 issue of the *Columbian Lady's and Gentleman's Magazine.* For a comparable tale, see also Nathaniel Hawthorne's "The Artist of the Beautiful."

4. *Rosamond. A Sequel to Early Lessons* (1821) by Maria Edgeworth (1767–1849).

5. Evidently Child alludes to the cofounder of the firm of Bautte and Bouline, which in 1791 began a factory to manufacture watches.

6. It is possible that the Vienna mechanic has been misnamed, for no information under this appellation exists in relevant reference works.

Selected Bibliography

For those interested in further exploring the works of Lydia Maria Child, the brief bibliography below offers a selective list of her extensive writings. (For an exhaustive list of Child's publications, see "Works of Lydia Maria Child" in Carolyn L. Karcher's *The First Woman of the Republic: A Cultural Biography of Lydia Maria Child*.) Included below are also those secondary materials that provide additional background into Child's life and writings and, more generally, her literary and cultural milieu.

Selected Works by Lydia Maria Child

An Appeal for the Indians. New York: Wm. P. Tomlinson, 1868.

An Appeal in Favor of That Class of Americans Called Africans. Boston: Allen and Ticknor, 1833. Reprint, with an introduction by Carolyn L. Karcher. Amherst: U of Massachusetts P, 1996.

Autumnal Leaves: Tales and Sketches in Prose and Rhyme. New York: C. S. Francis, 1857.

Fact and Fiction: A Collection of Stories. New York: C. S. Francis/Boston: J. H. Francis, 1846.

The Frugal Housewife. Boston: Marsh & Capen and Carter & Hendee, 1829. 2d ed., *The American Frugal Housewife*. Boston: Carter & Hendee, 1832. Boston: Applewood Books, 1985.

The History of the Condition of Women, in Various Ages and Nations. Vols. 4 and 5 of *Ladies' Family Library*. Boston: John Allen, 1835.

Hobomok, A Tale of Early Times. Boston: Cummings, Hilliard, 1824.

Hobomok and Other Writings on Indians. Ed. Carolyn L. Karcher. New Brunswick, NJ: Rutgers UP, 1986.

Letters from New York. Second Series. New York: C. S. Francis/Boston: J. H. Francis, 1845.

The Mother's Book. Boston: Carter, Hendee & Babcock/Baltimore: Charles Carter, 1831.

Philothea. A Romance. Boston: Otis, Broaders/New York: George Dearborn, 1836.

The Rebels, or Boston before the Revolution. Boston: Cummings, Hilliard, 1825.

A Romance of the Republic. Boston: Ticknor and Fields, 1867.

Biography and Criticism

Baer, Helene G. *The Heart Is Like Heaven: The Life of Lydia Maria Child.* Philadelphia: U of Pennsylvania P, 1964.

Clifford, Deborah Pickman. *Crusader for Freedom: A Life of Lydia Maria Child.* Boston: Beacon, 1992.

Conrad, Susan Phinney. *Perish the Thought: Intellectual Women in Romantic America, 1830–1860.* New York: Oxford UP, 1976.

Hersh, Blanche Glassman. *The Slavery of Sex: Feminist Abolitionists in America.* Urbana: U of Illinois P, 1978.

Holland, Patricia G. "Lydia Maria Child as a Nineteenth-Century Professional Author." In *Studies in American Renaissance 1981.* Ed. Joel Myerson. Boston: Twayne, 1981.

Karcher, Carolyn L. *The First Woman of the Republic: A Cultural Biography of Lydia Maria Child.* Durham: Duke UP, 1994.

Meltzer, Milton. *Tongue of Flame: The Life of Lydia Maria Child.* New York: Crowell, 1965.

Mills, Bruce. *Cultural Reformations: Lydia Maria Child and the Literature of Reform.* Athens: U of Georgia P, 1994.

Osborne, William S. *Lydia Maria Child.* Boston: Twayne, 1980.

Yellin, Jean Fagan. *Women and Sisters: The Antislavery Feminists in American Culture.* New Haven, CT: Yale UP, 1989.

General Studies

Baym, Nina. *Woman's Fiction: A Guide to Novels by and about Women in America, 1820–1870.* Ithaca, NY: Cornell UP, 1984.

Buell, Lawrence. *New England Literary Culture: From Revolution through Renaissance.* Cambridge, ENG: Cambridge UP, 1986.

Douglas, Ann. *The Feminization of American Culture.* 1977; rpt., New York: Anchor, 1988.

Harris, Susan K. *Nineteenth-Century American Women's Novels: Interpretive Strategies.* New York: Cambridge UP, 1990.

Kelley, Mary. *Private Woman, Public Stage: Literary Domesticity in Nineteenth-Century America.* New York: Oxford UP, 1984.

Reynolds, David S. *Beneath the American Renaissance: The Subversive Imagination in the Age of Melville and Emerson.* New York: Knopf, 1988.

Tompkins, Jane. *Sensational Designs: The Cultural Work of American Fiction, 1790–1860.* New York: Oxford UP, 1985.